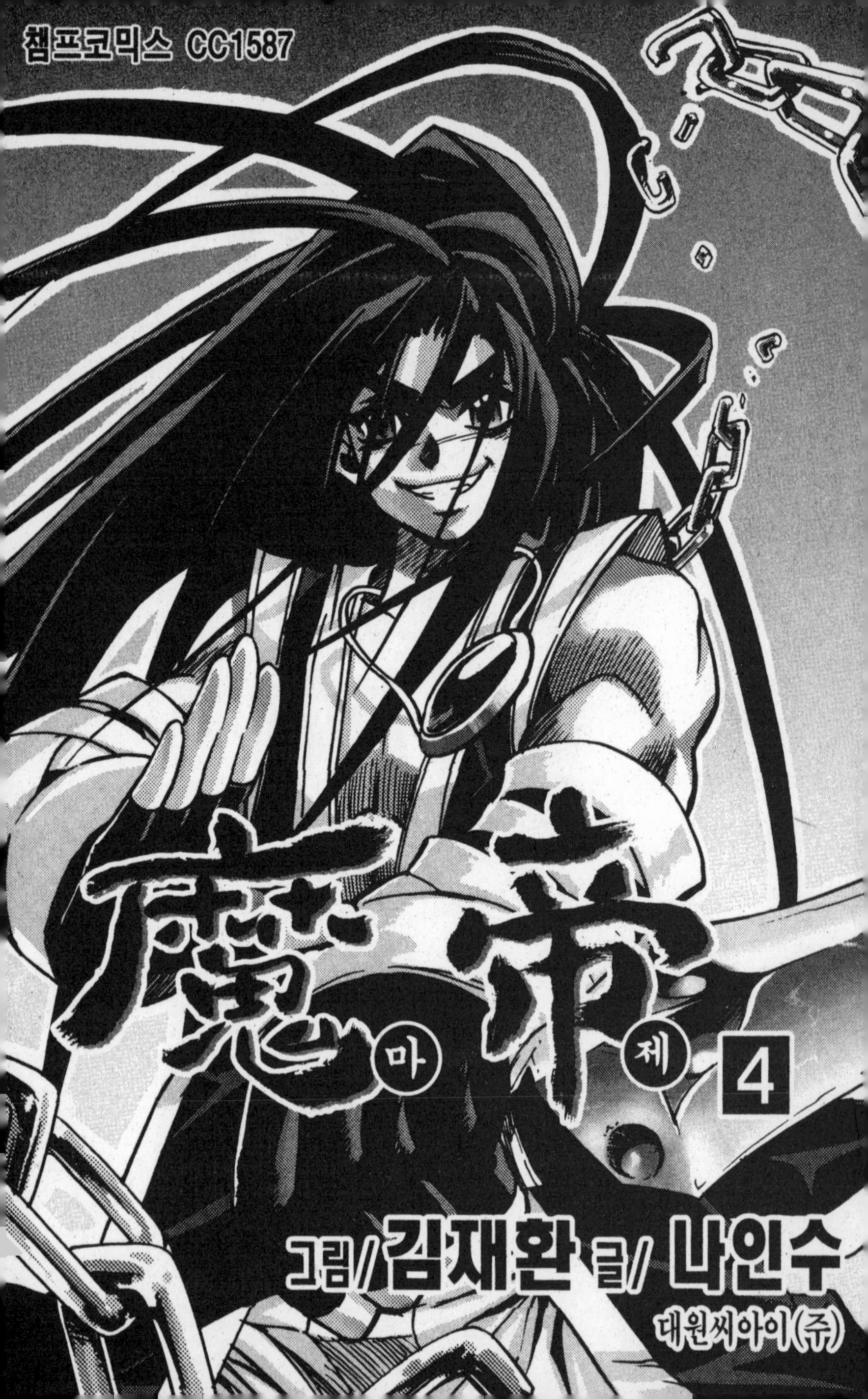
챔프코믹스 CC1587
魔帝
마 제
4
그림/ 김재환 글/ 나인수
대원씨아이(주)

# KING OF HELL

Translator - Lauren Na
English Adaptation - R.A. Jones
Associate Editor - Bryce P. Coleman
Retouch and Lettering - Tom Misuraca
Cover Layout - Patrick Hook
Graphic Designer - James Lee

Editor - Rob Tokar
Managing Editor - Jill Freshney
Production Coordinator - Antonio DePietro
Production Managers - Jennifer Miller & Mutsumi Miyazaki
Art Director - Matt Alford
Editorial Director - Jeremy Ross
VP of Production - Ron Klamert
President & C.O.O. - John Parker
Publisher & C.E.O. - Stuart Levy

Email: editor@TOKYOPOP.com
Come visit us online at www.TOKYOPOP.com

A  Manga

TOKYOPOP Inc.
5900 Wilshire Blvd. Suite 2000
Los Angeles, CA 90036

*King of Hell Vol. 4*

ISBN:1-59182-482-6

First TOKYOPOP printing: January 2004

10 9 8 7 6 5 4 3

Printed in the USA

# KING OF HELL

## VOLUME 4

### BY
### RA IN-SOO
### &
### KIM JAE-HWAN

LOS ANGELES • TOKYO • LONDON

# King of Hell

# Who the Hell...?

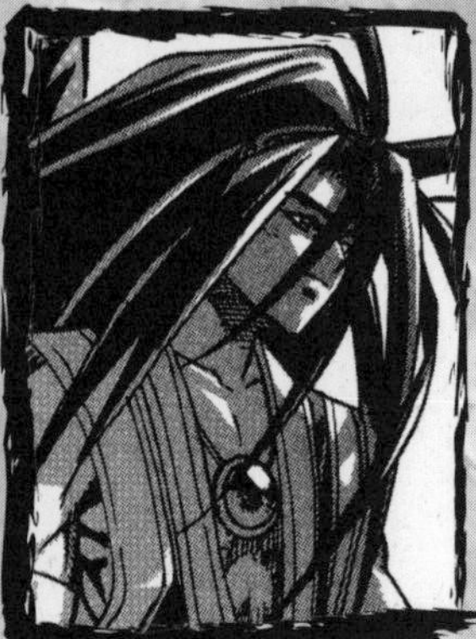

**MAJEH:**
A feared warrior in life, now a collector of souls for the King of Hell. Majeh has recently been returned to his human form in order to carry out the mission of destroying escaped evil spirits upon the earth. There are two catches, however:
1. Majeh's full powers are restrained by a mystical seal.
2. His physical form is that of a teenage boy.

**CHUNG POONG NAMGOONG:**
A coward from a once-respected family, Chung Poong left home hoping to prove himself at the Martial Arts Tournament in Nakyang. Broke and desperate, Chung Poong tried to rob Majeh. In a very rare moment of pity, Majeh allowed Chung Poong to live...and to tag along with him to the tournament.

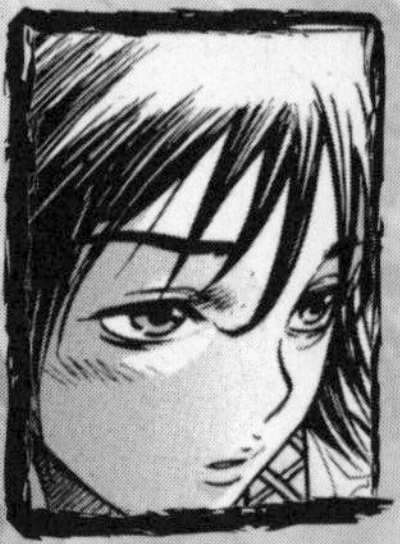

## THE MARTIAL ARTS CHILD PRODIGIES

**"BABY":**
A mysterious, shy, 15-year-old from the infamous Blood Sect, his weapon is the deadly "snake hand" technique. Much to the relief of his fellow contestants, this fearsome ability hasn't yet reached full maturity...or has it?

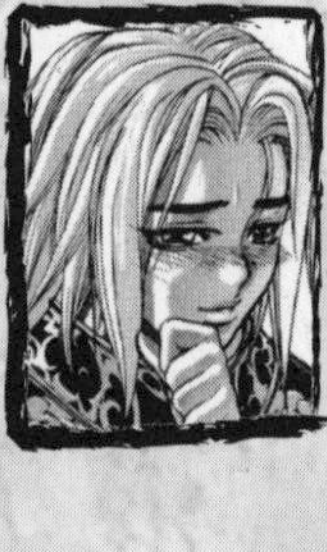

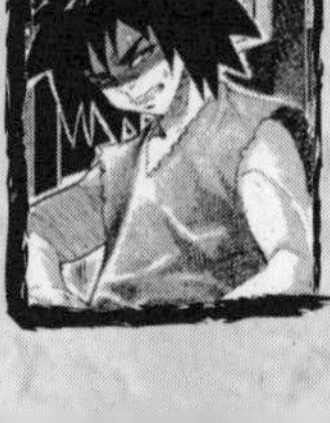

**CRAZY DOG:**
A 6-year-old hellion who is partial to using a club, this wild child hails from a remote village.

**SAMHUK:**
Originally sent by the King of Hell to spy on the unpredictable Majeh, Samhuk was quickly discovered and now--much to his dismay--acts as the warrior's ghostly manservant.

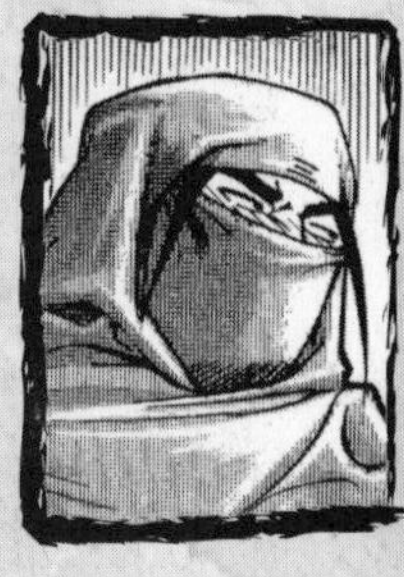

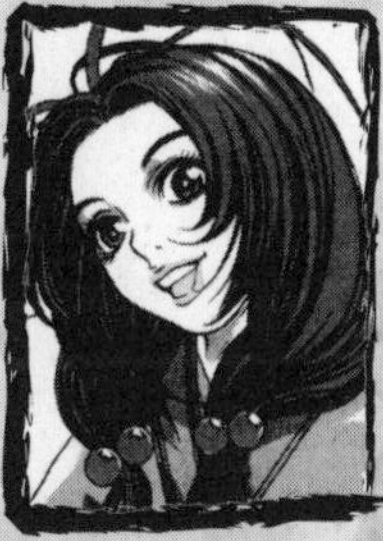

**DOHWA BAIK:**
A vivacious vixen whose weapons of choice are poisoned needles. She joined Majeh and Chung Poong on the way to the tournament.

**KING OF HELL:**
You were expecting horns and a pitchfork? This benevolent, otherworldly ruler reigns over the souls of the dead like a shepherd tending his flock.

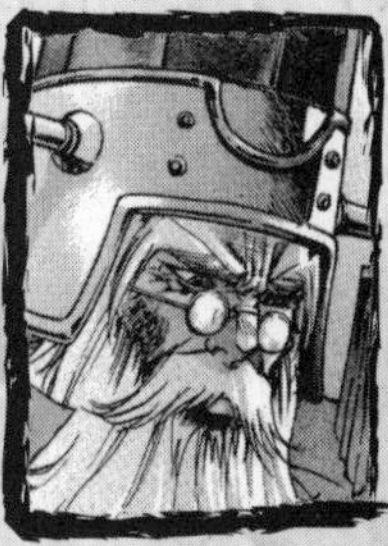

**DOHAK:**
A 15-year-old monk and a master at fighting with a rod, he is affiliated with the Sorim Temple in the Soong mountains.

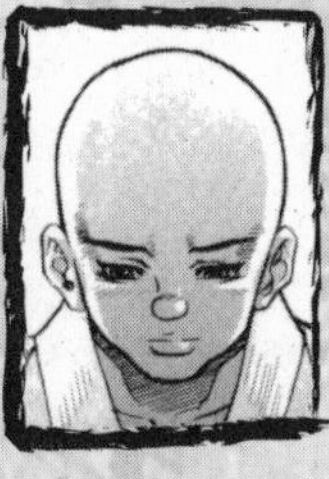

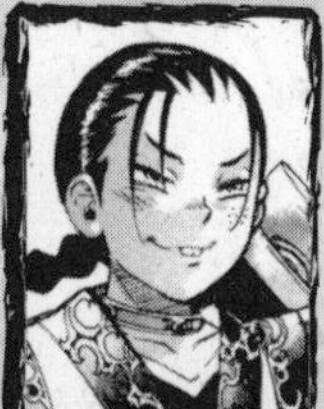

**POONG CHUN:**
A 12-year-old expert with the broad-sword, he is affiliated with the Shaman Sect.

**YOUNG:**
A 15-year-old sword-master, possessing incredible speed, he is affiliated with Mooyoung Moon-- a clan of assassins, 500 strong.

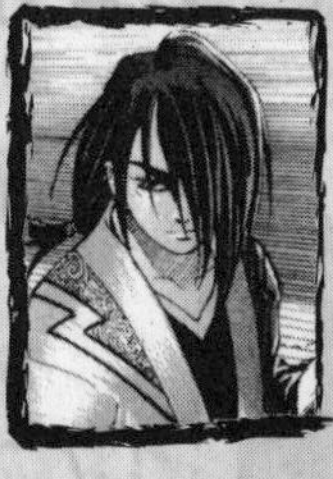

Hell's worst inmates have escaped and fled to Earth. Seeking recently-deceased bodies to host their bitter souls, these malevolent master fighters are part of an evil scheme that could have dire consequences for both This World and the Next World. It is believed that the escaped fiends are hunting for bodies of martial arts experts, as only bodies trained in martial arts would be capable of properly employing their incredible skills.

To make matters even more difficult, the otherworldly energy emitted by the fugitives will dissipate within one month's time...after which, they will be indistinguishable from normal humans and undetectable to those from the Next World. The King of Hell has assigned Majeh to hunt down Hell's Most Wanted and return them to the Next World...but Majeh doesn't always do exactly what he's told.

Majeh was a master swordsman in life and, in death, he serves as an envoy for the King of Hell, escorting souls of the dead to the Next World. Majeh caught Samhuk--a servant for the King of Hell--spying on him and, after making the appropriate threats, now uses Samhuk as his own servant as well.

The King of Hell has reunited Majeh's spirit with his physical body, which was perfectly preserved for 300 years. Due to the influence of a Superhuman Strength Sealing Symbol (designed to keep the rebellious and powerful Majeh in check), Majeh's physical form has reverted to a teenaged state. Even with the seal in place, however, Majeh is still extremely formidable.

Along with the young, wannabe-warrior called Chung-Poong Namgoong and a beautiful femme fatale named Dohwa Baik, Majeh has made his way to the heralded Martial Arts Tournament at Nakyang--the most likely place for the warrior demons to make their appearance.

But more questions remain: Who is sending assassins to kill Majeh? What is the evil scheme being plotted by a trio of mysterious, cloaked figures? And could Baby--a shy, unimposing tournament entrant--be a cold-blooded killer?

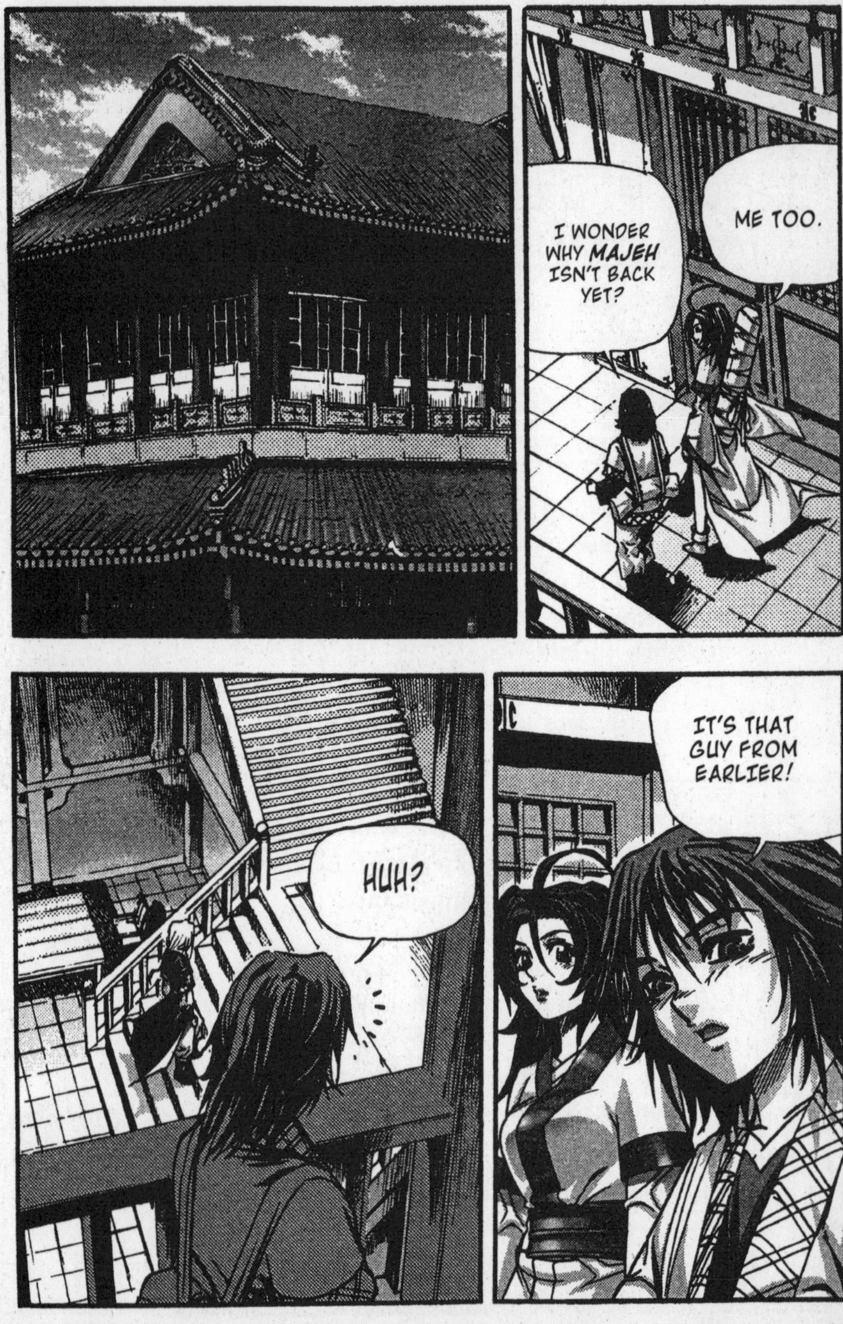
I WONDER WHY MAJEH ISN'T BACK YET?
ME TOO.
HUH?
IT'S THAT GUY FROM EARLIER!

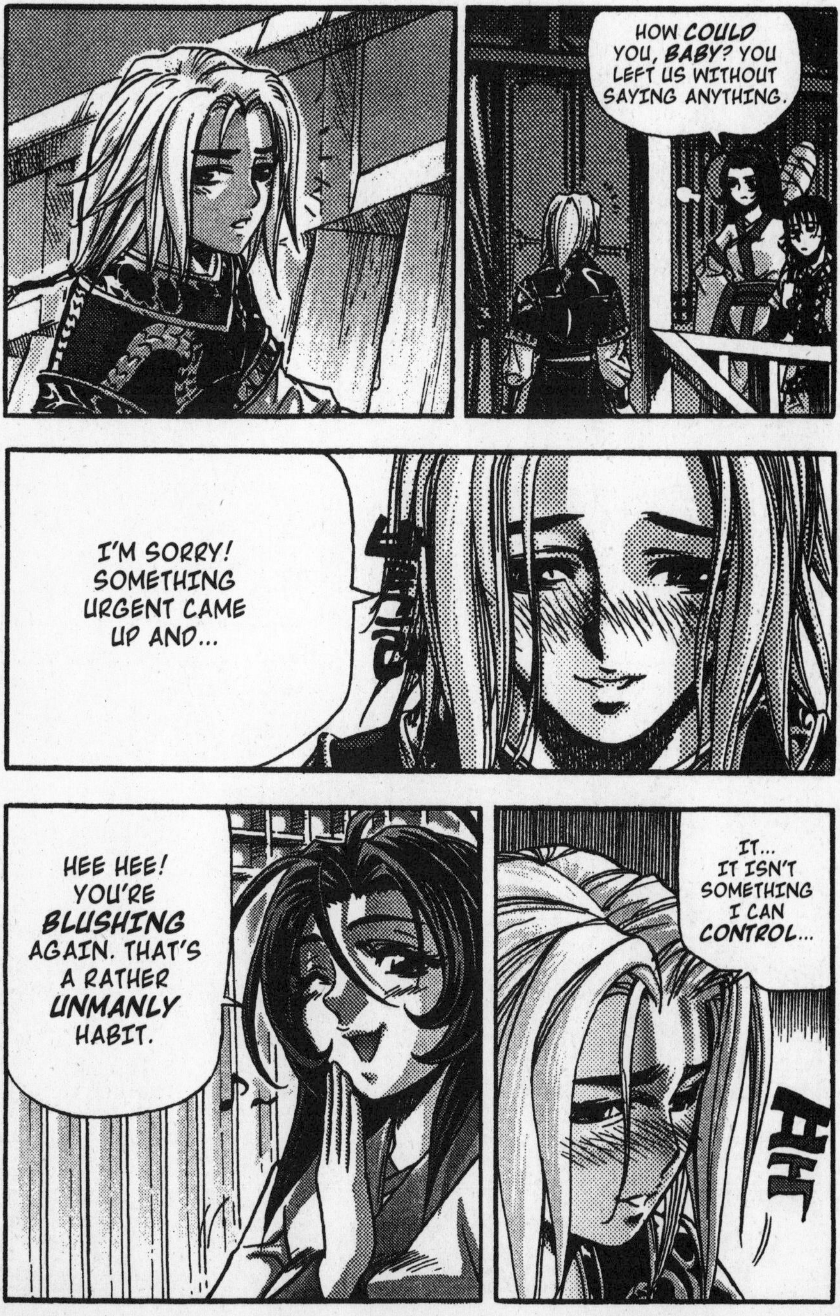
HOW COULD YOU, BABY? YOU LEFT US WITHOUT SAYING ANYTHING.
I'M SORRY! SOMETHING URGENT CAME UP AND...
HEE HEE! YOU'RE BLUSHING AGAIN. THAT'S A RATHER UNMANLY HABIT.
IT... IT ISN'T SOMETHING I CAN CONTROL...

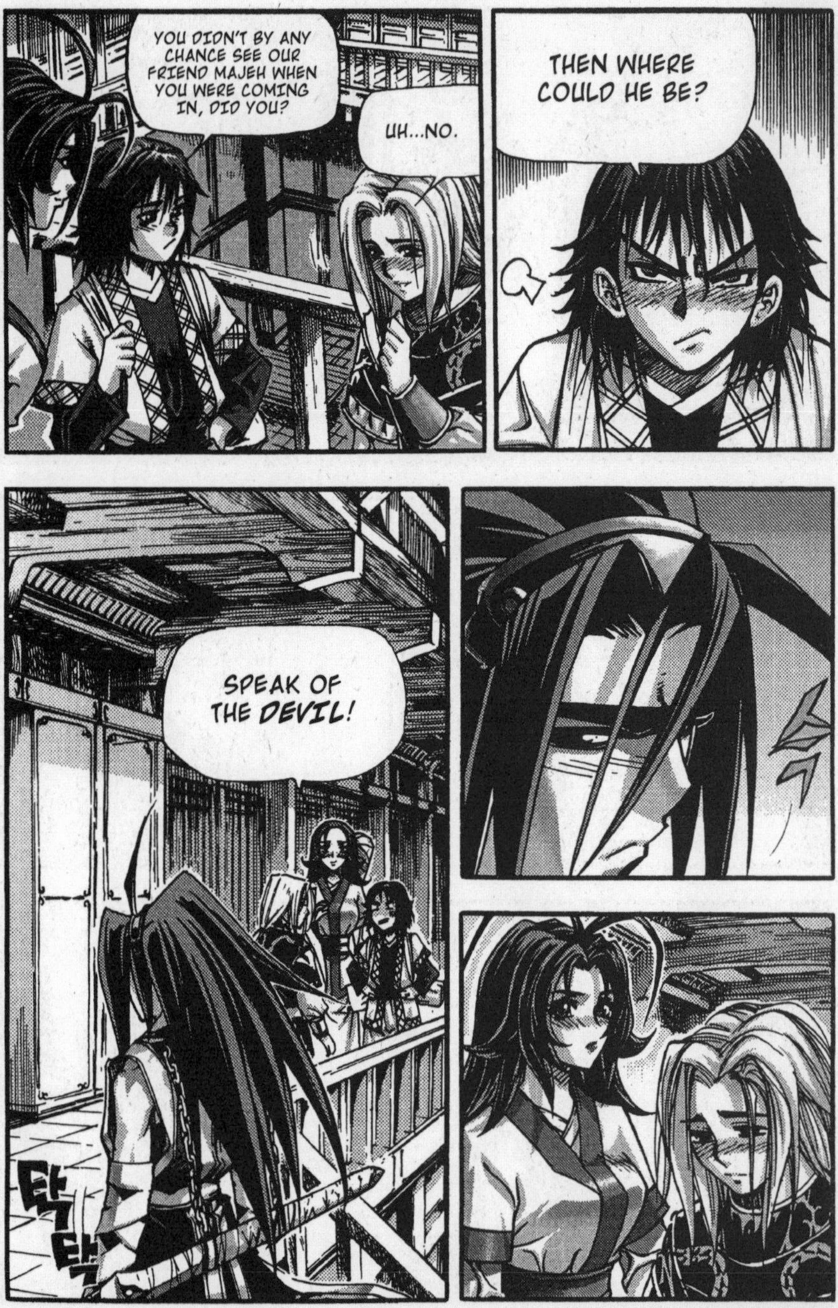
YOU DIDN'T BY ANY CHANCE SEE OUR FRIEND MAJEH WHEN YOU WERE COMING IN, DID YOU?
UH...NO.
THEN WHERE COULD HE BE?
SPEAK OF THE *DEVIL*!

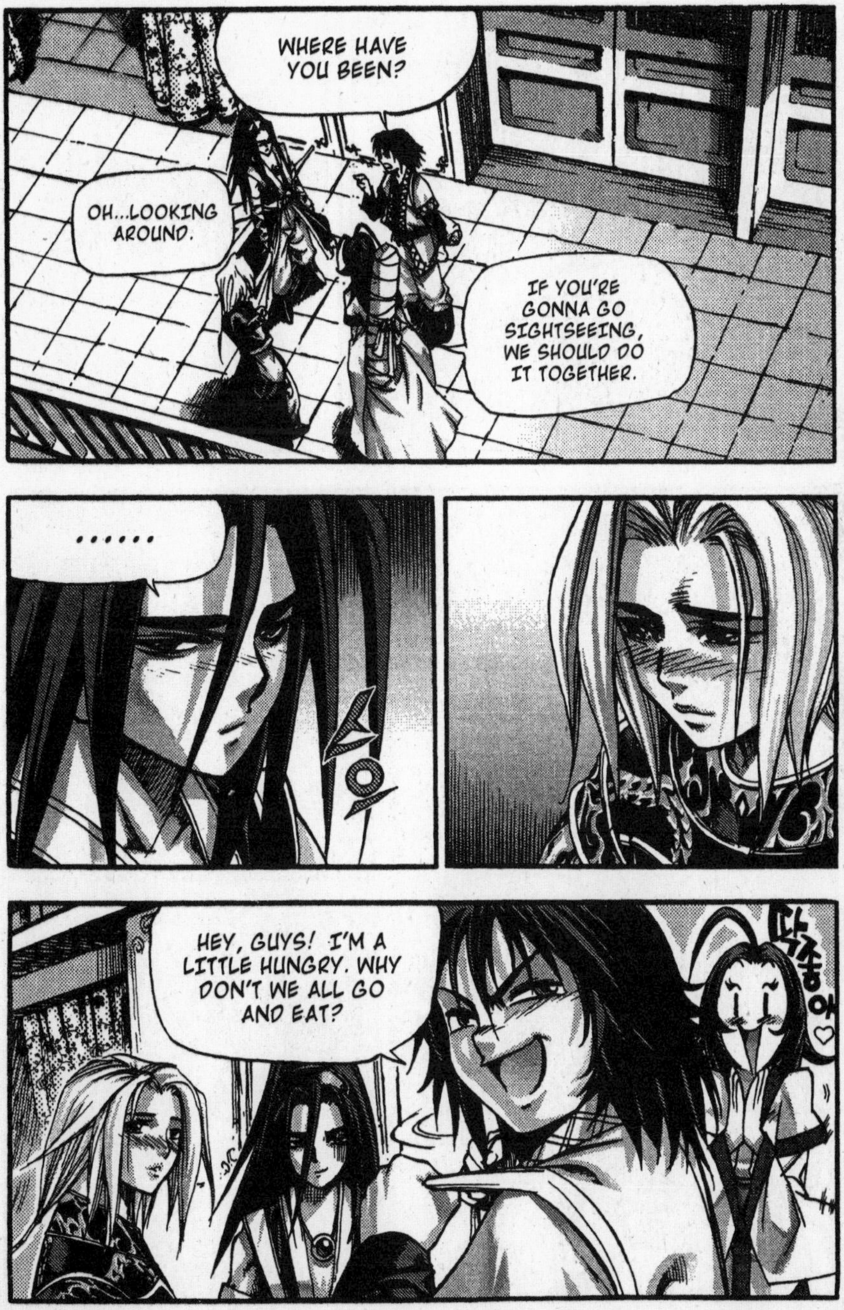
WHERE HAVE YOU BEEN?
OH...LOOKING AROUND.
IF YOU'RE GONNA GO SIGHTSEEING, WE SHOULD DO IT TOGETHER.
......
HEY, GUYS! I'M A LITTLE HUNGRY. WHY DON'T WE ALL GO AND EAT?
딱좋아♡

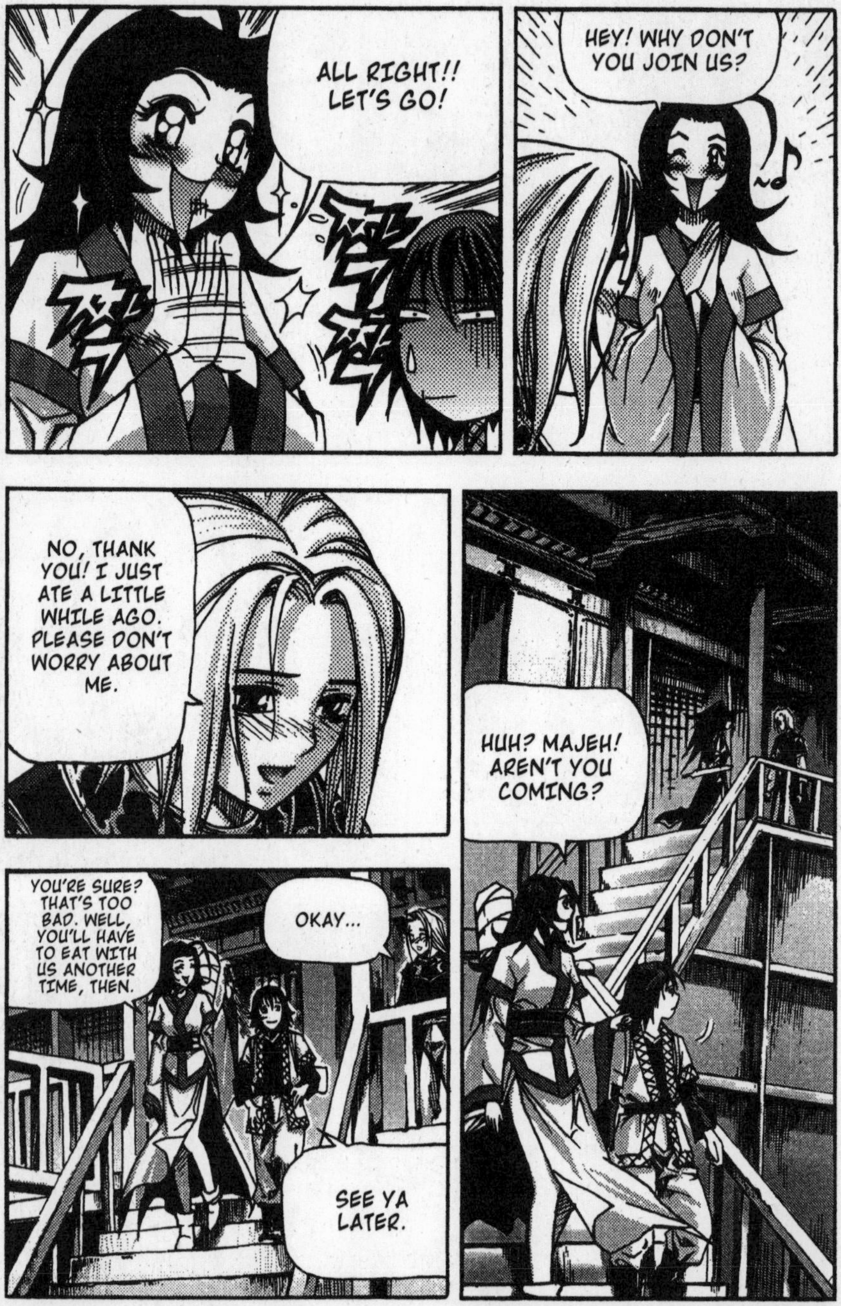
ALL RIGHT!! LET'S GO!
HEY! WHY DON'T YOU JOIN US?
NO, THANK YOU! I JUST ATE A LITTLE WHILE AGO. PLEASE DON'T WORRY ABOUT ME.
YOU'RE SURE? THAT'S TOO BAD. WELL, YOU'LL HAVE TO EAT WITH US ANOTHER TIME, THEN.
OKAY...
SEE YA LATER.
HUH? MAJEH! AREN'T YOU COMING?

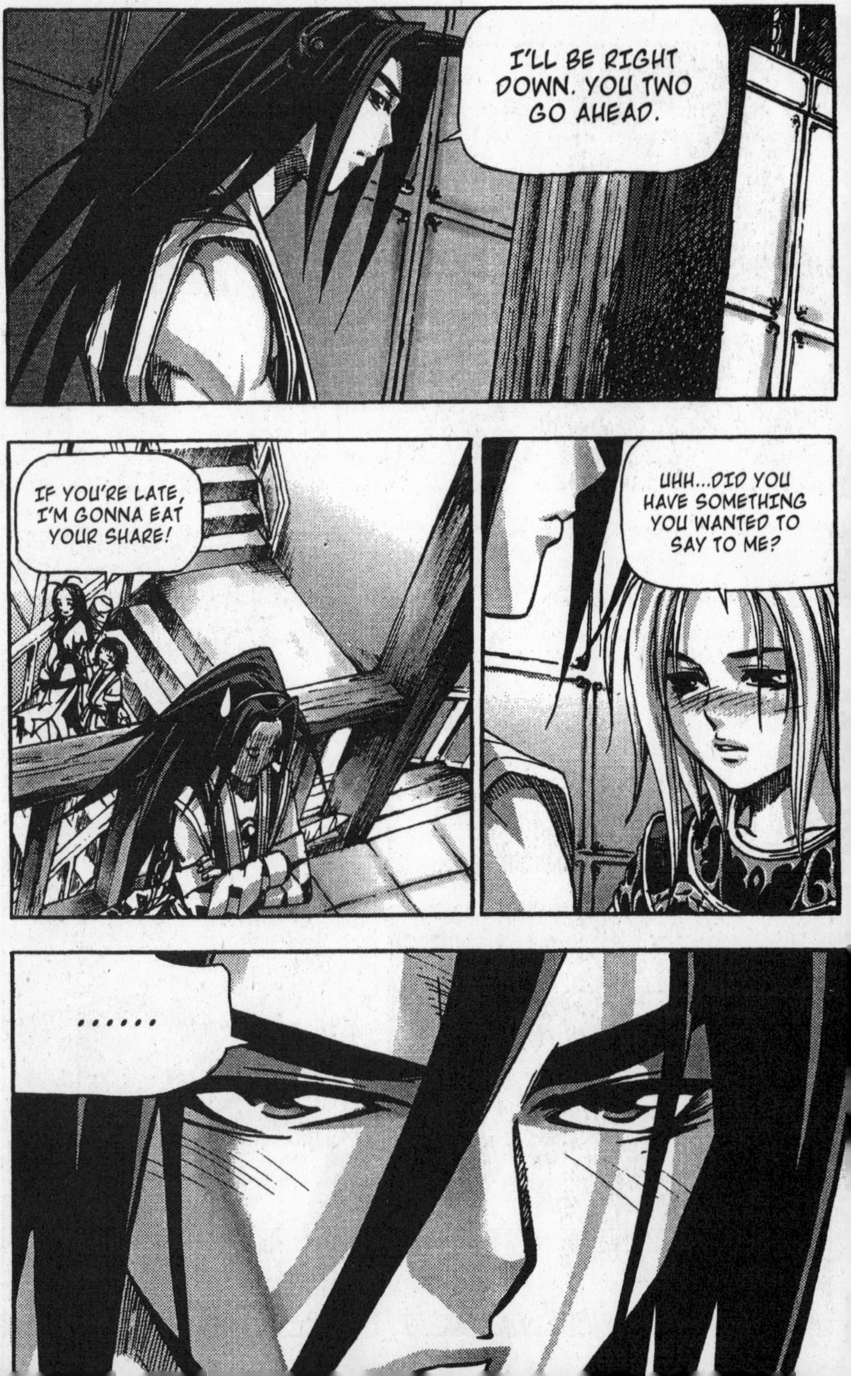
I'LL BE RIGHT DOWN. YOU TWO GO AHEAD.
IF YOU'RE LATE, I'M GONNA EAT YOUR SHARE!
UHH...DID YOU HAVE SOMETHING YOU WANTED TO SAY TO ME?
......

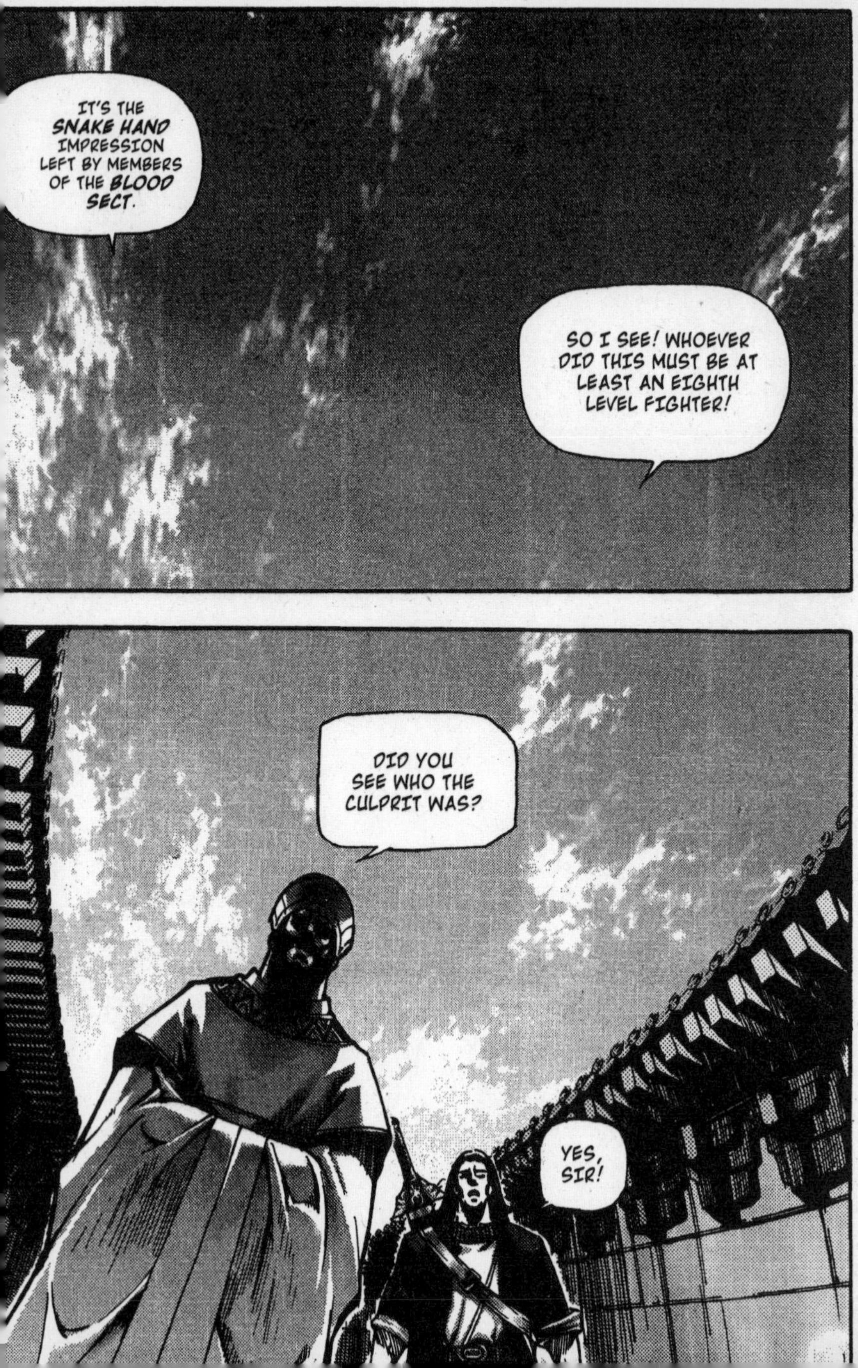

IT'S THE SNAKE HAND IMPRESSION LEFT BY MEMBERS OF THE BLOOD SECT.
SO I SEE! WHOEVER DID THIS MUST BE AT LEAST AN EIGHTH LEVEL FIGHTER!
DID YOU SEE WHO THE CULPRIT WAS?
YES, SIR!

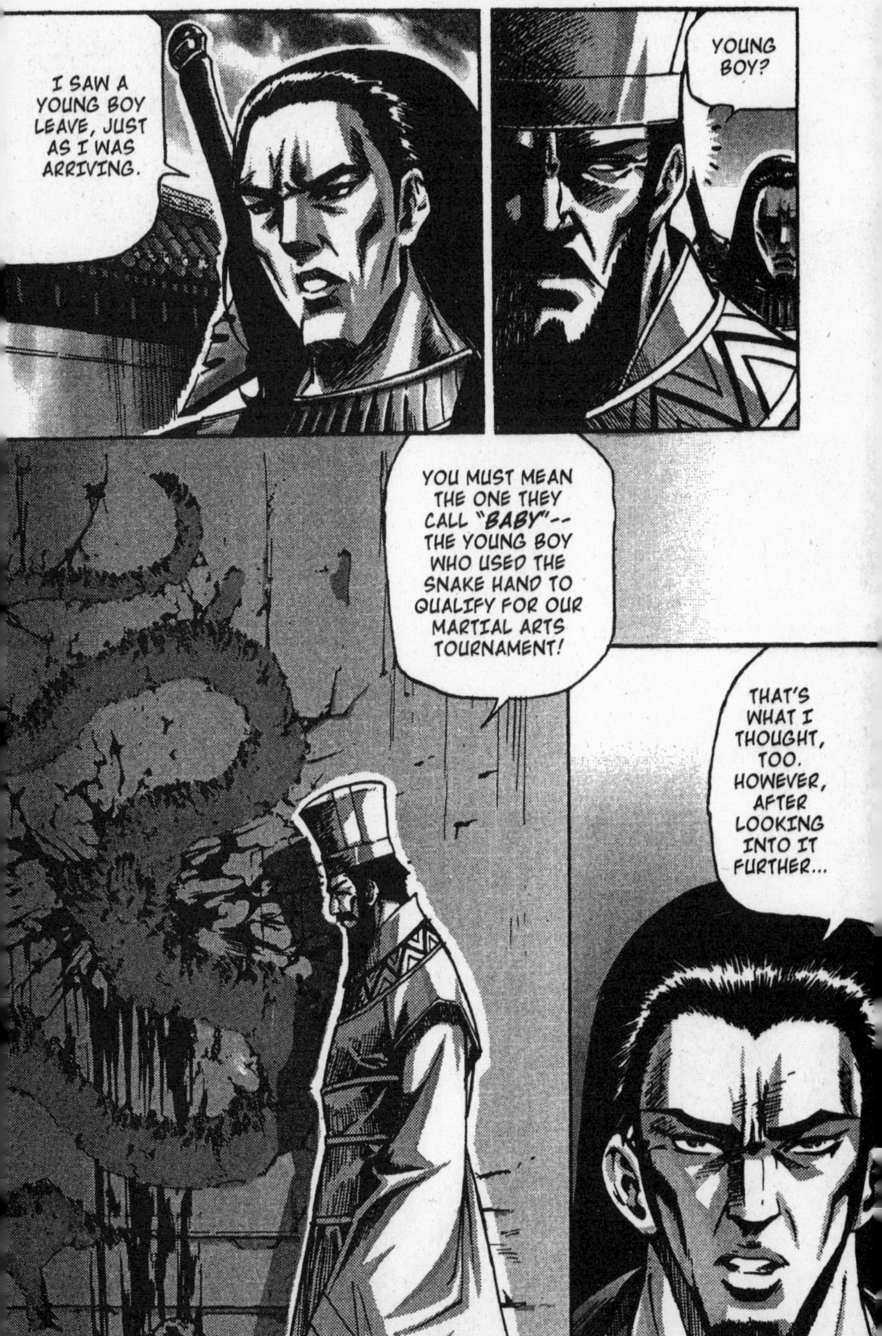
I SAW A YOUNG BOY LEAVE, JUST AS I WAS ARRIVING.
YOUNG BOY?
YOU MUST MEAN THE ONE THEY CALL "BABY"-- THE YOUNG BOY WHO USED THE SNAKE HAND TO QUALIFY FOR OUR MARTIAL ARTS TOURNAMENT!
THAT'S WHAT I THOUGHT, TOO. HOWEVER, AFTER LOOKING INTO IT FURTHER...

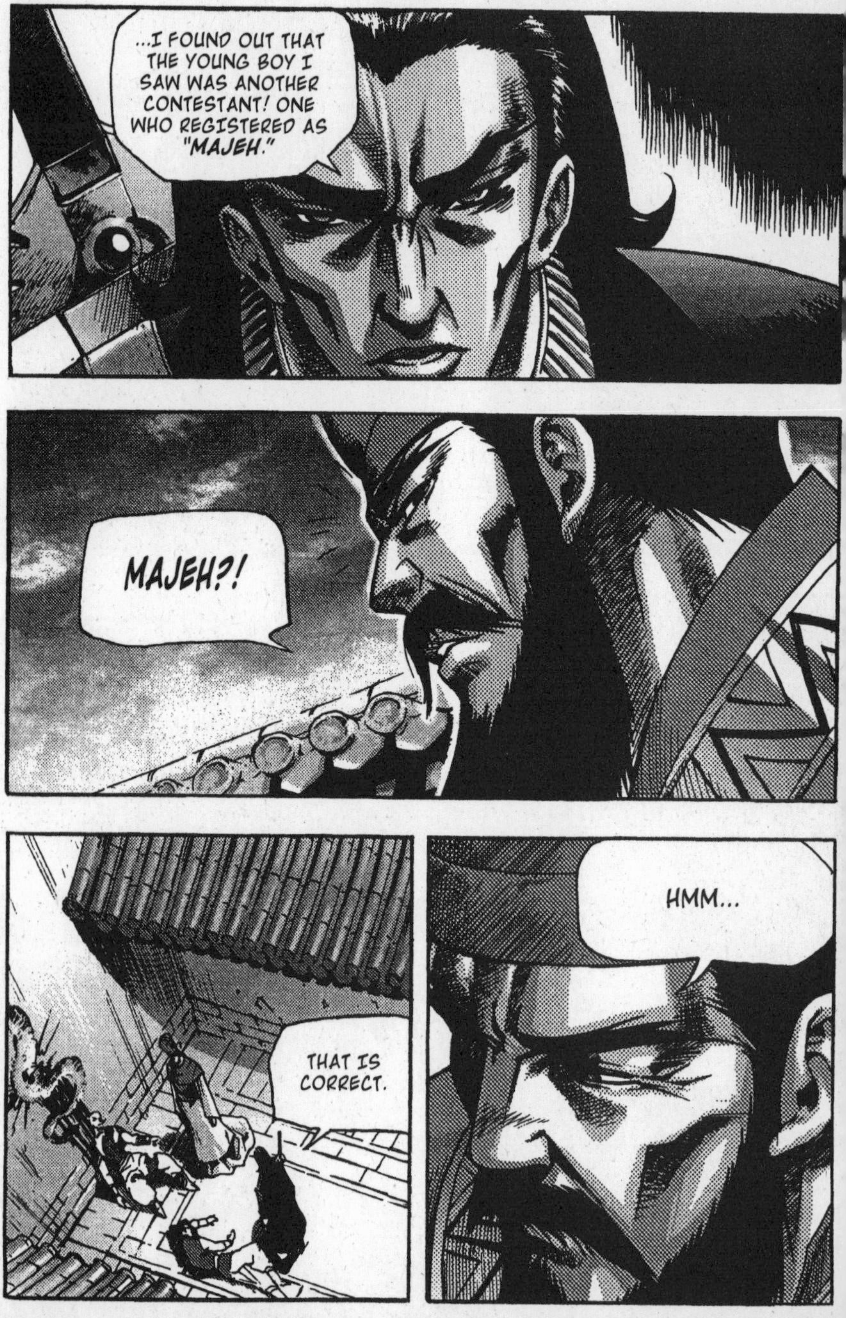
...I FOUND OUT THAT THE YOUNG BOY I SAW WAS ANOTHER CONTESTANT! ONE WHO REGISTERED AS "MAJEH."
MAJEH?!
THAT IS CORRECT.
HMM...

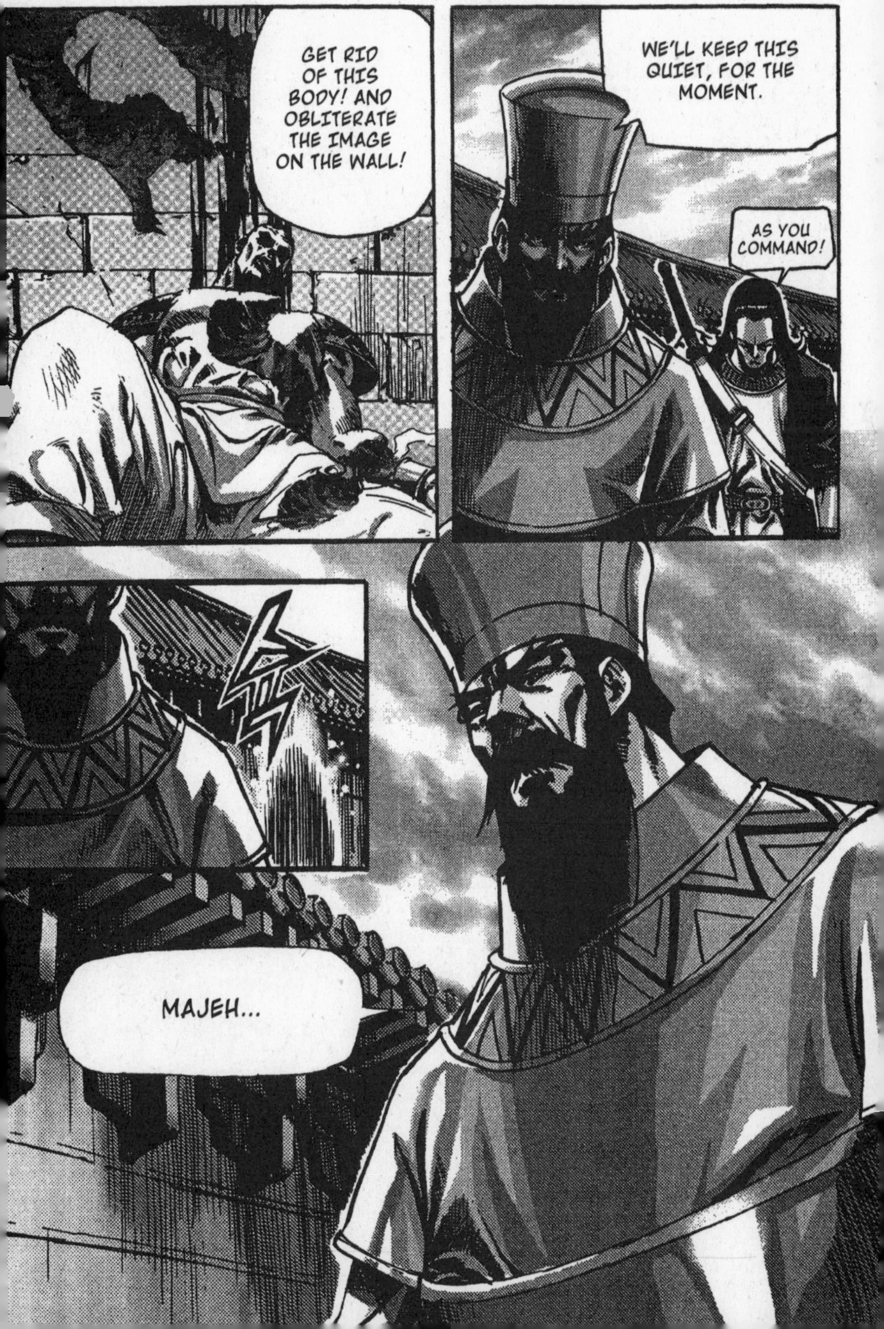
GET RID OF THIS BODY! AND OBLITERATE THE IMAGE ON THE WALL!
WE'LL KEEP THIS QUIET, FOR THE MOMENT.
AS YOU COMMAND!
MAJEH...

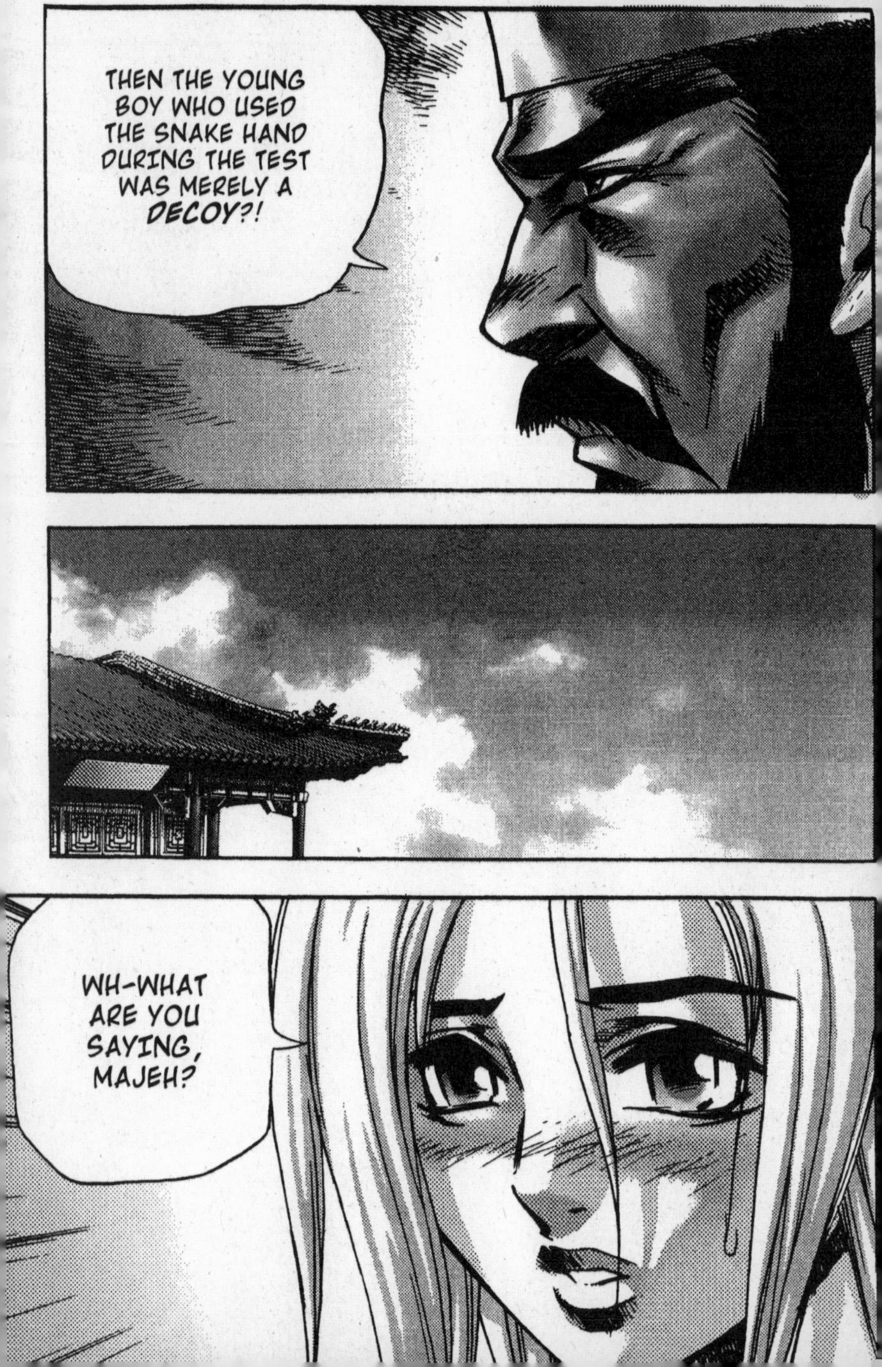
THEN THE YOUNG BOY WHO USED THE SNAKE HAND DURING THE TEST WAS MERELY A DECOY?!
WH-WHAT ARE YOU SAYING, MAJEH?

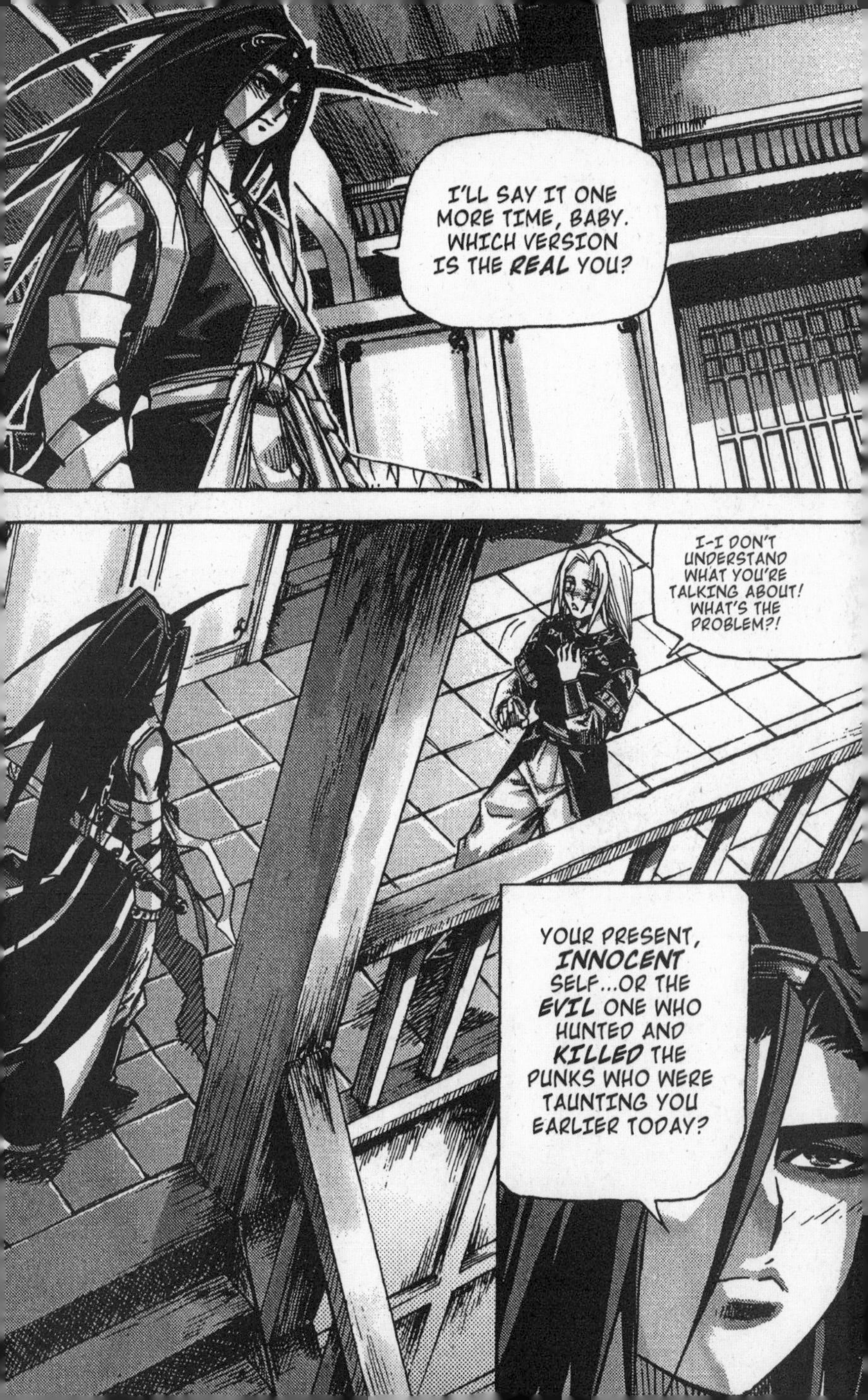
I'LL SAY IT ONE MORE TIME, BABY. WHICH VERSION IS THE REAL YOU?
I-I DON'T UNDERSTAND WHAT YOU'RE TALKING ABOUT! WHAT'S THE PROBLEM?!
YOUR PRESENT, INNOCENT SELF...OR THE EVIL ONE WHO HUNTED AND KILLED THE PUNKS WHO WERE TAUNTING YOU EARLIER TODAY?

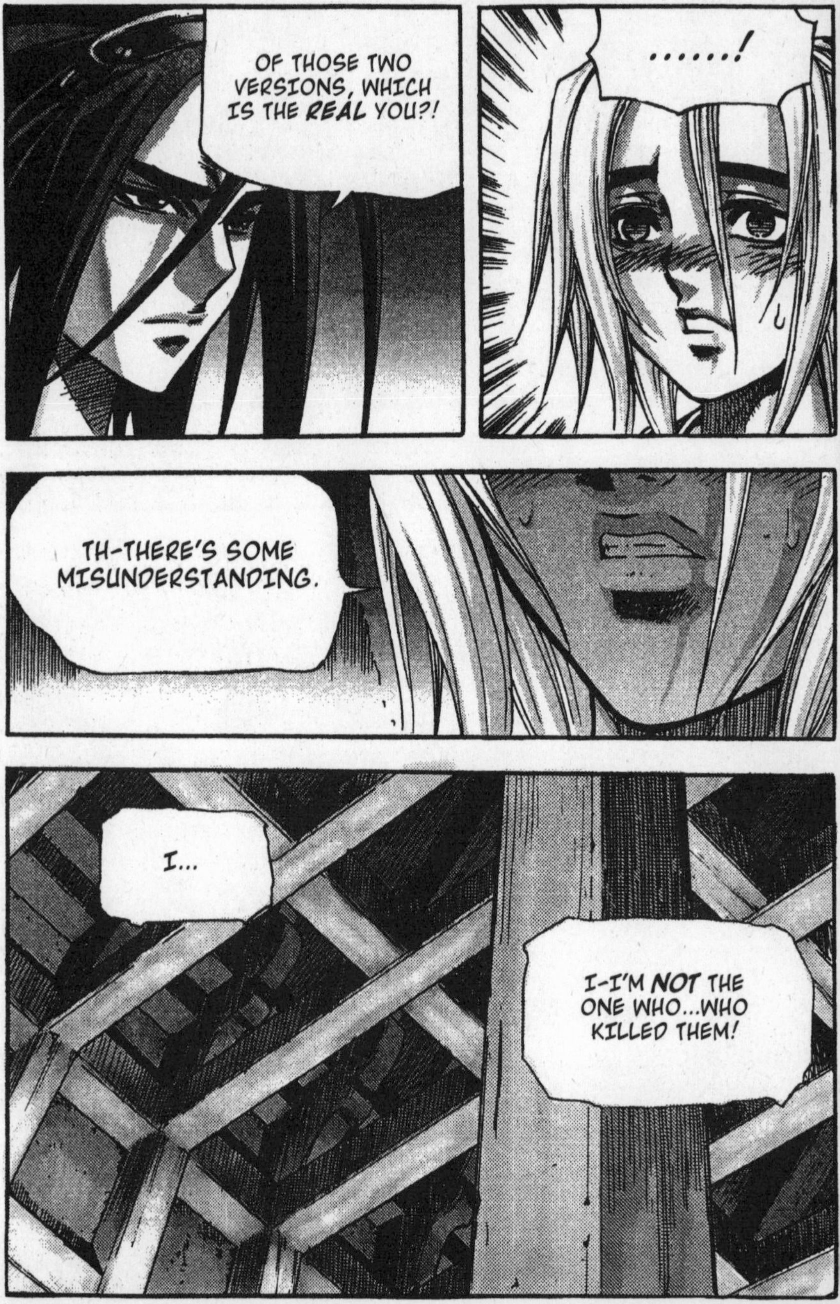
OF THOSE TWO VERSIONS, WHICH IS THE REAL YOU?!
......!
TH-THERE'S SOME MISUNDERSTANDING.
I...
I-I'M NOT THE ONE WHO...WHO KILLED THEM!

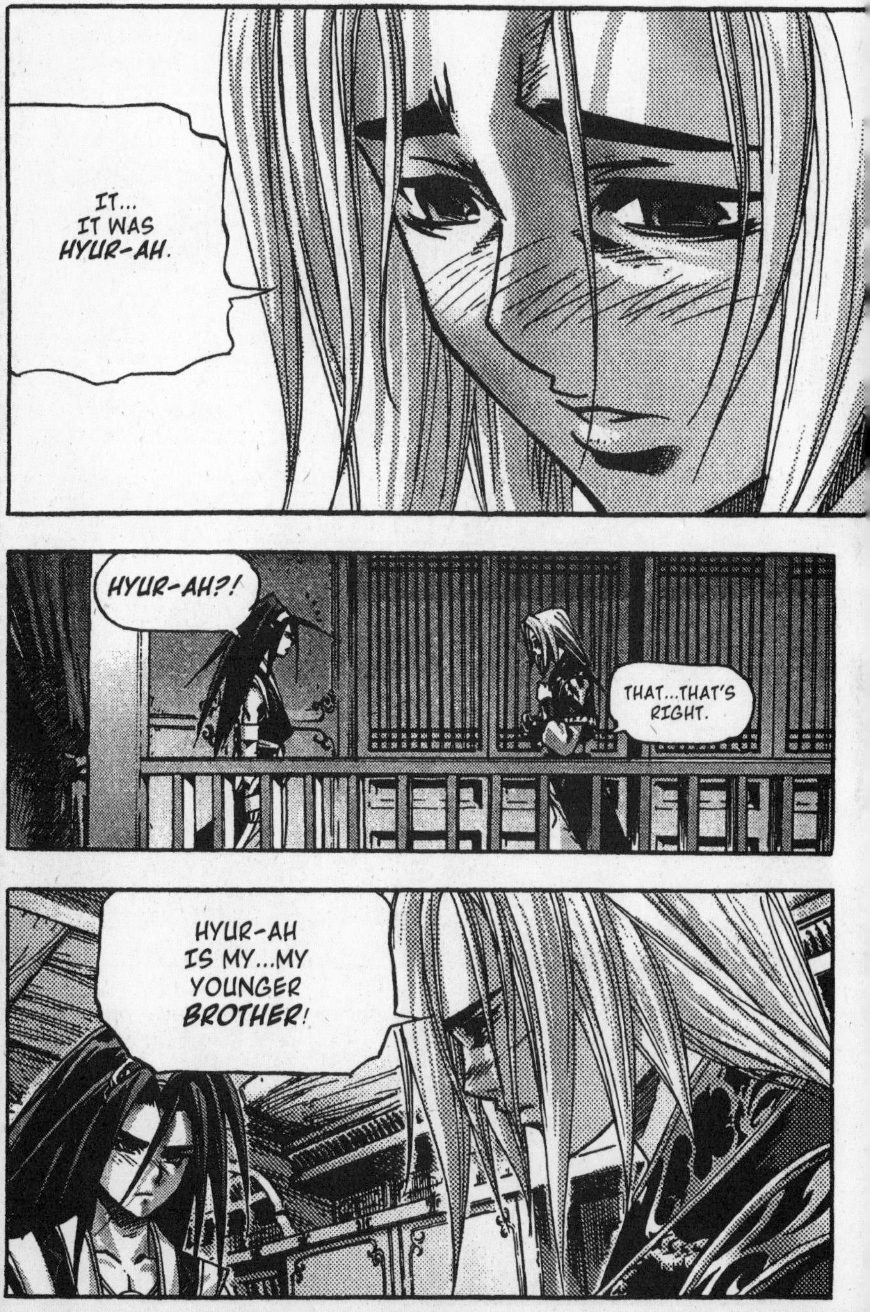
IT... IT WAS HYUR-AH.
HYUR-AH?!
THAT...THAT'S RIGHT.
HYUR-AH IS MY...MY YOUNGER BROTHER!

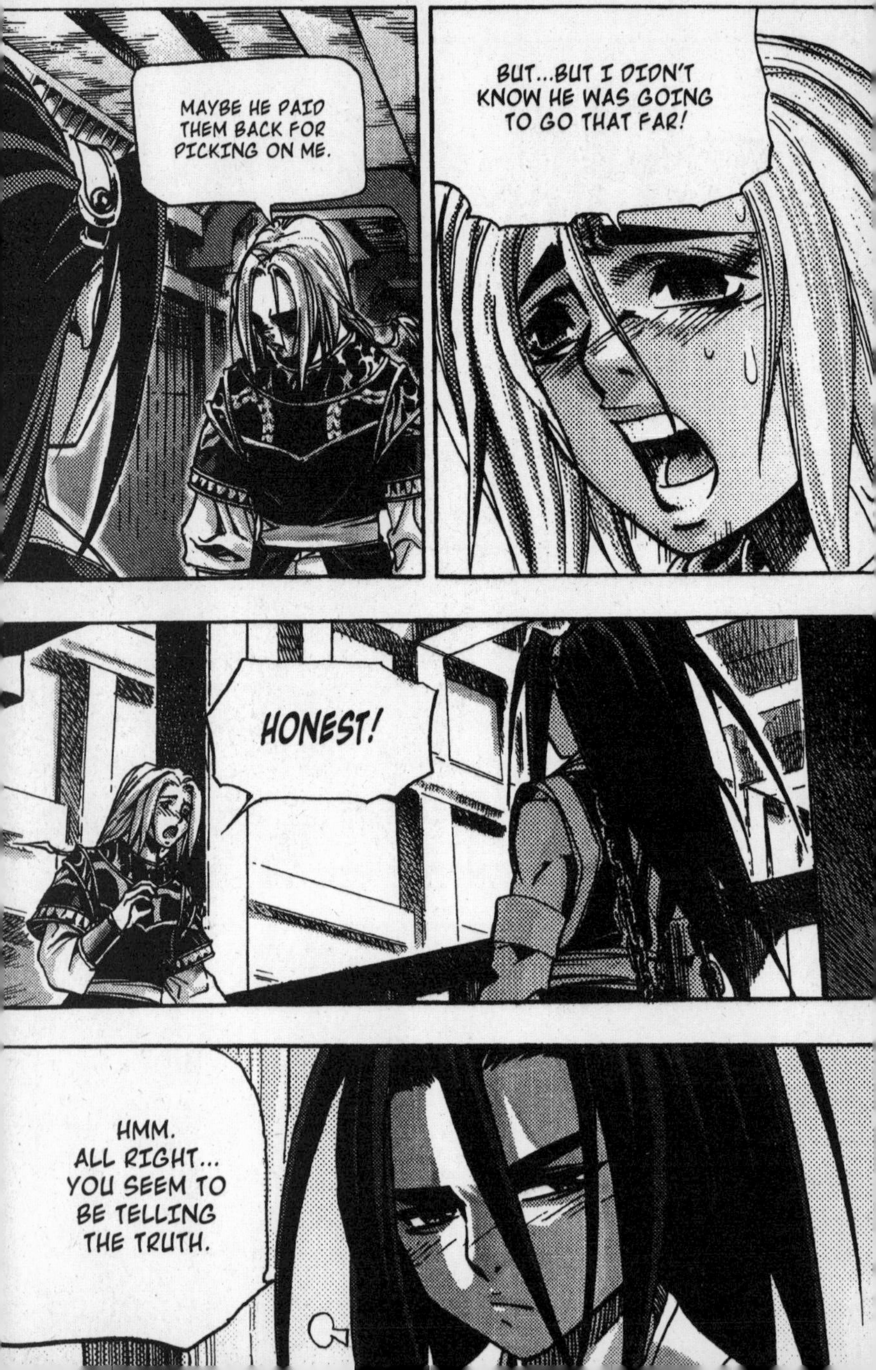
MAYBE HE PAID THEM BACK FOR PICKING ON ME.
BUT...BUT I DIDN'T KNOW HE WAS GOING TO GO THAT FAR!
HONEST!
HMM. ALL RIGHT... YOU SEEM TO BE TELLING THE TRUTH.

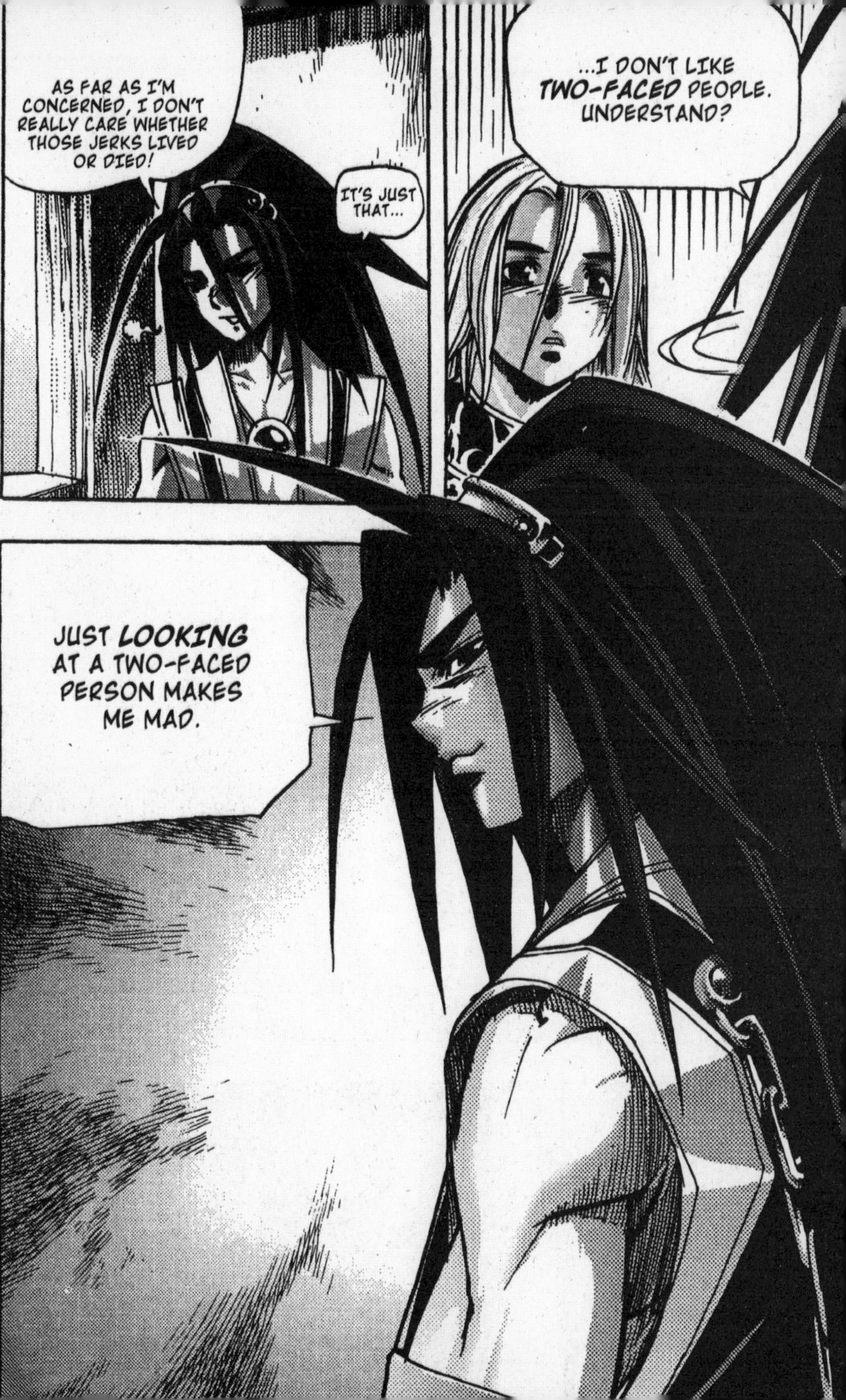
AS FAR AS I'M CONCERNED, I DON'T REALLY CARE WHETHER THOSE JERKS LIVED OR DIED!
IT'S JUST THAT...
...I DON'T LIKE TWO-FACED PEOPLE. UNDERSTAND?
JUST LOOKING AT A TWO-FACED PERSON MAKES ME MAD.

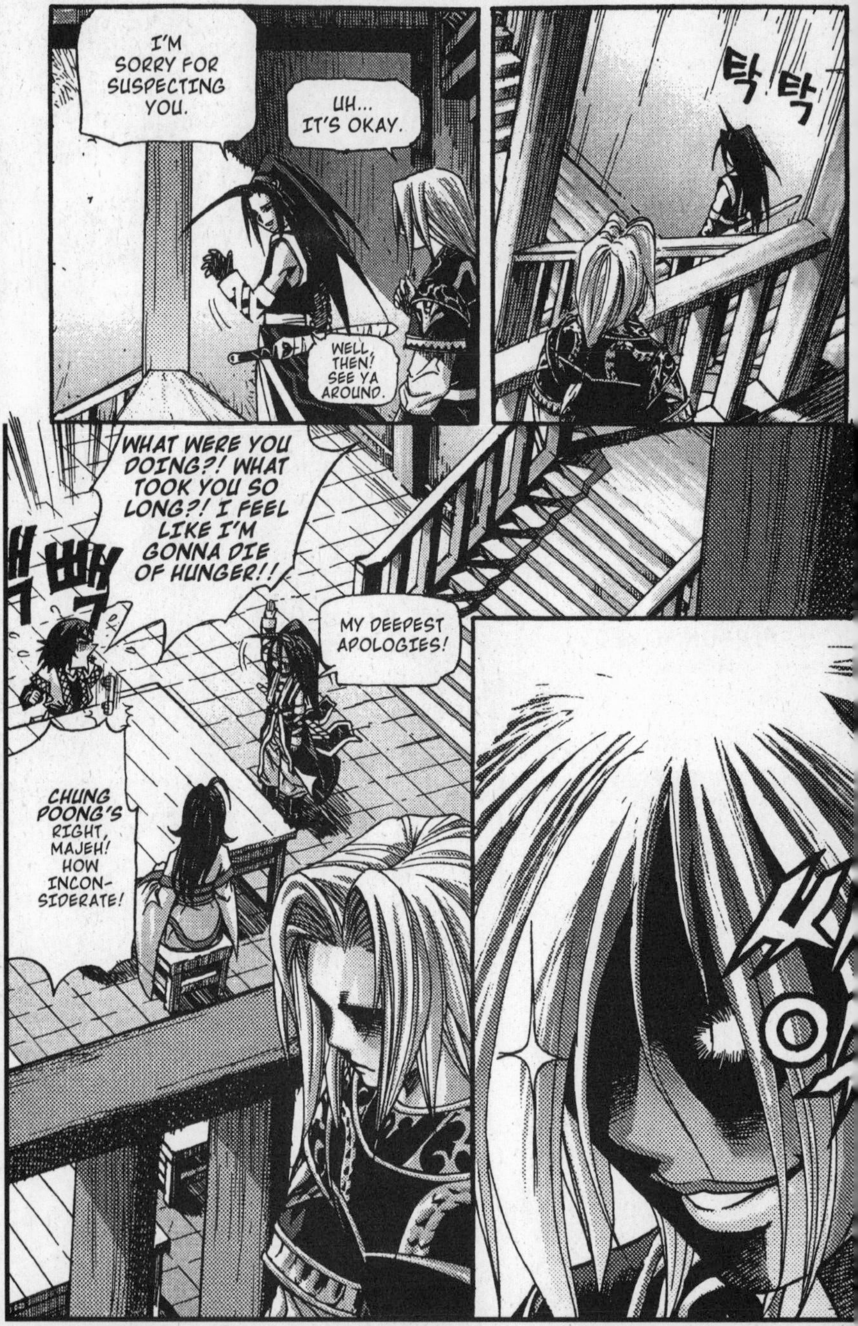
I'M SORRY FOR SUSPECTING YOU.
UH... IT'S OKAY.
WELL THEN! SEE YA AROUND.
탁 탁
WHAT WERE YOU DOING?! WHAT TOOK YOU SO LONG?! I FEEL LIKE I'M GONNA DIE OF HUNGER!!
빽 빽
MY DEEPEST APOLOGIES!
CHUNG POONG'S RIGHT, MAJEH! HOW INCON-SIDERATE!

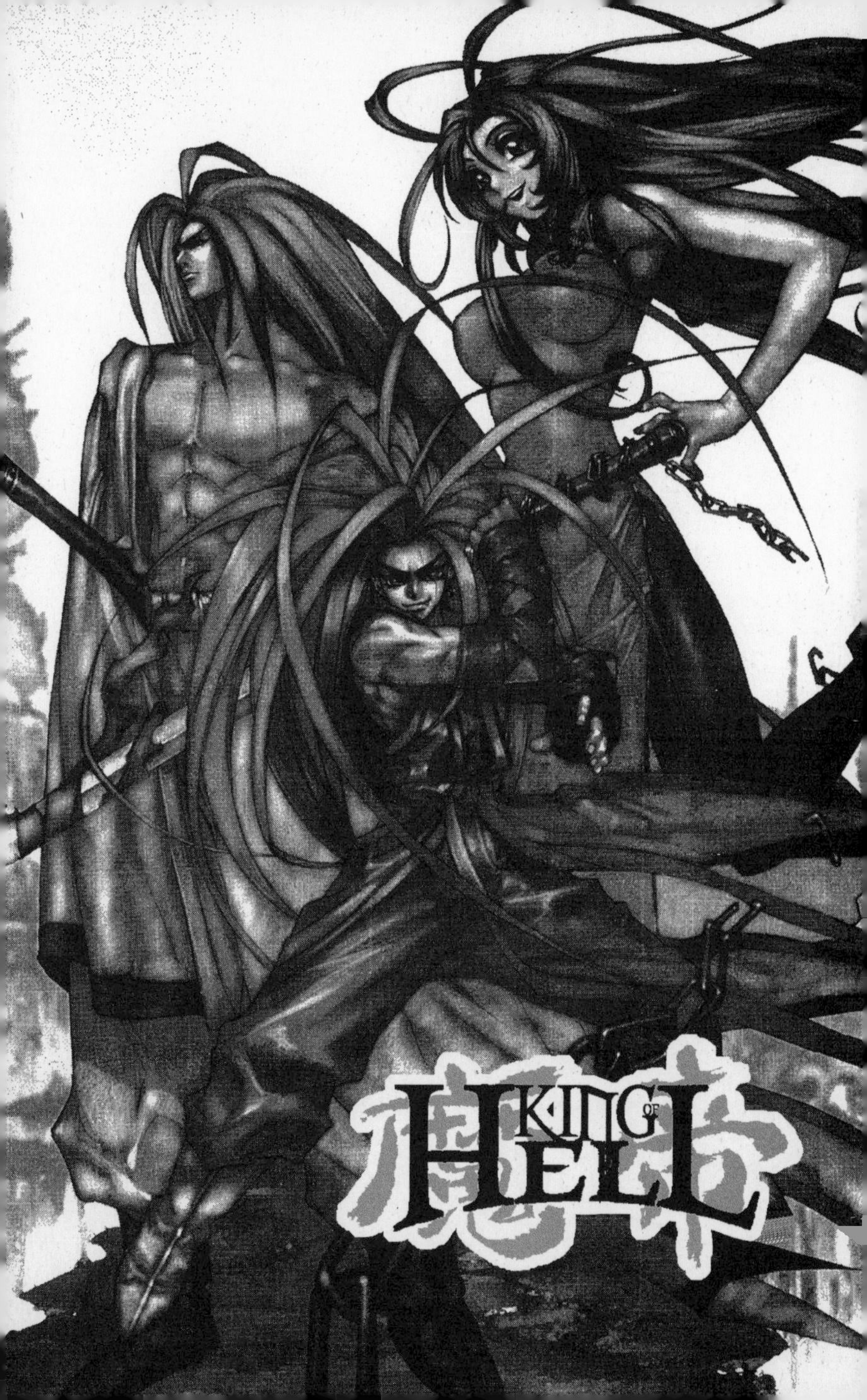
KING OF HELL

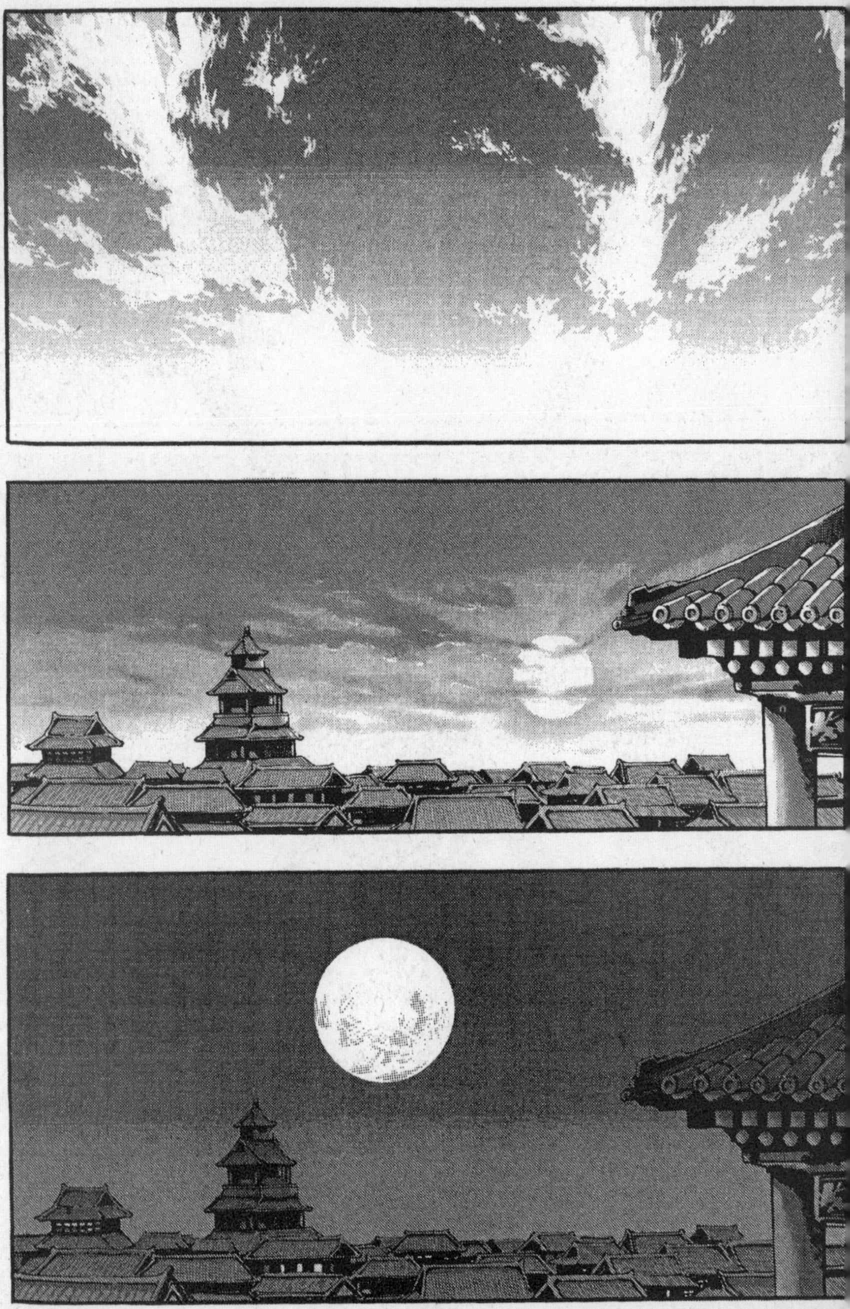

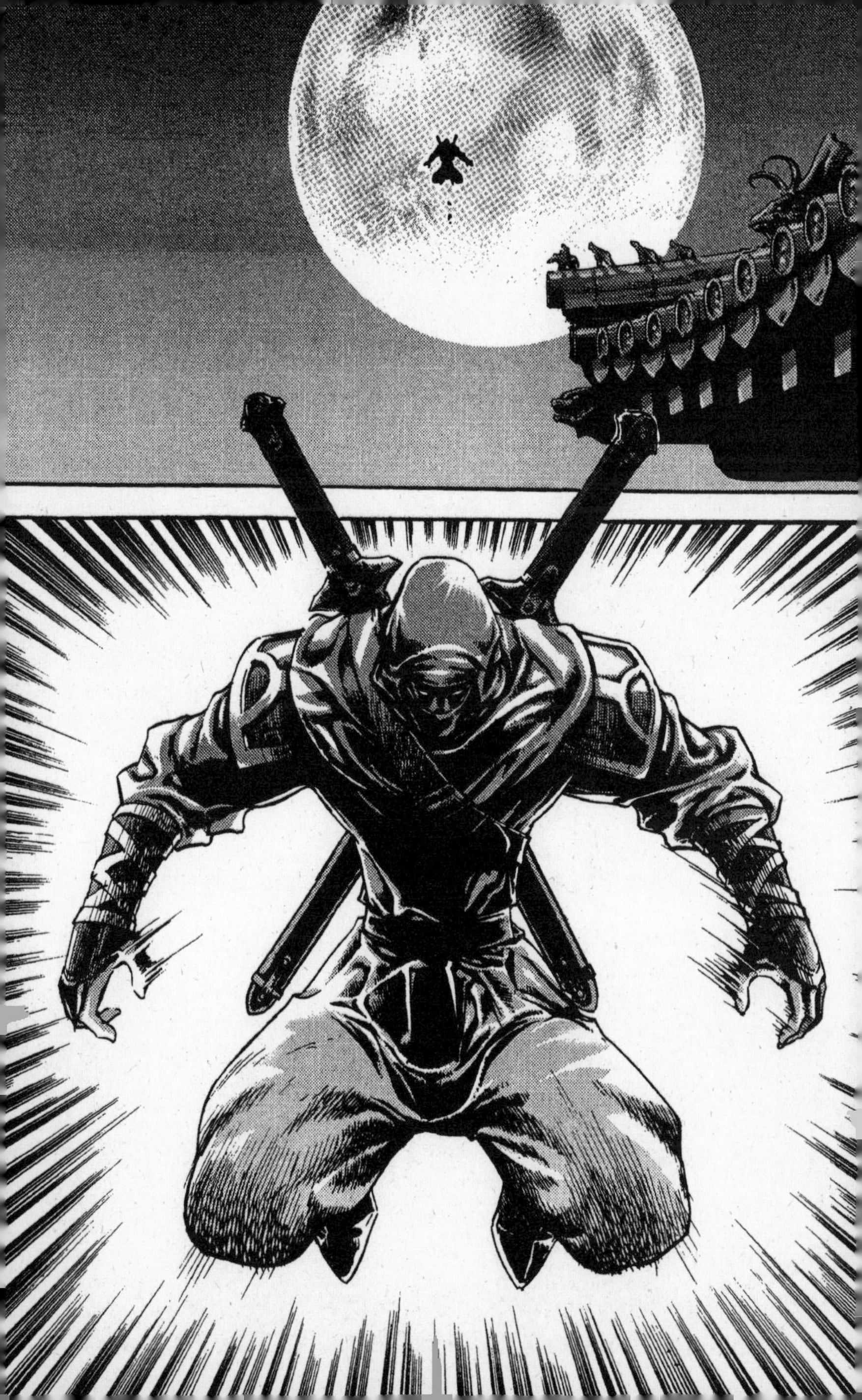

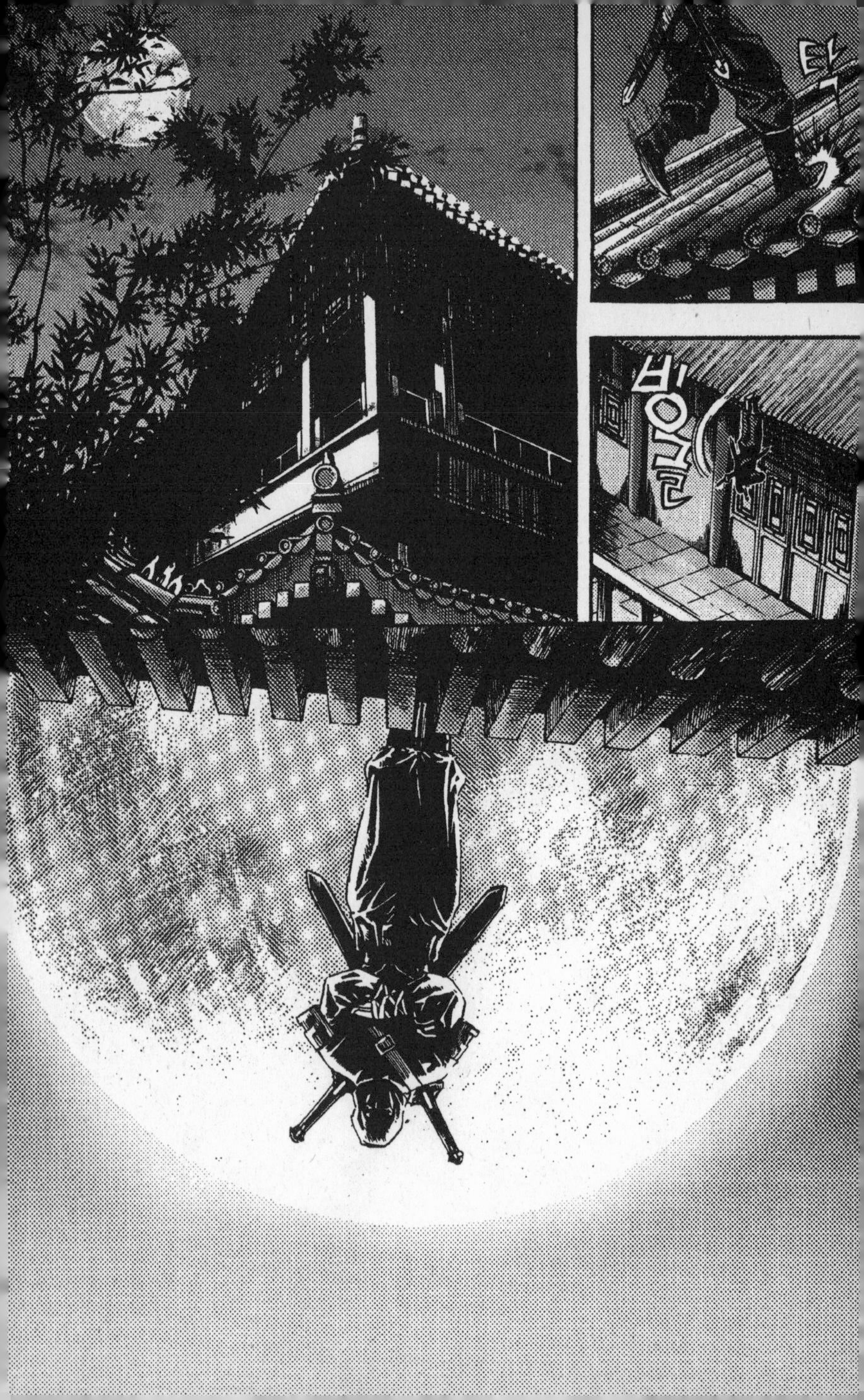
탁
빙그르

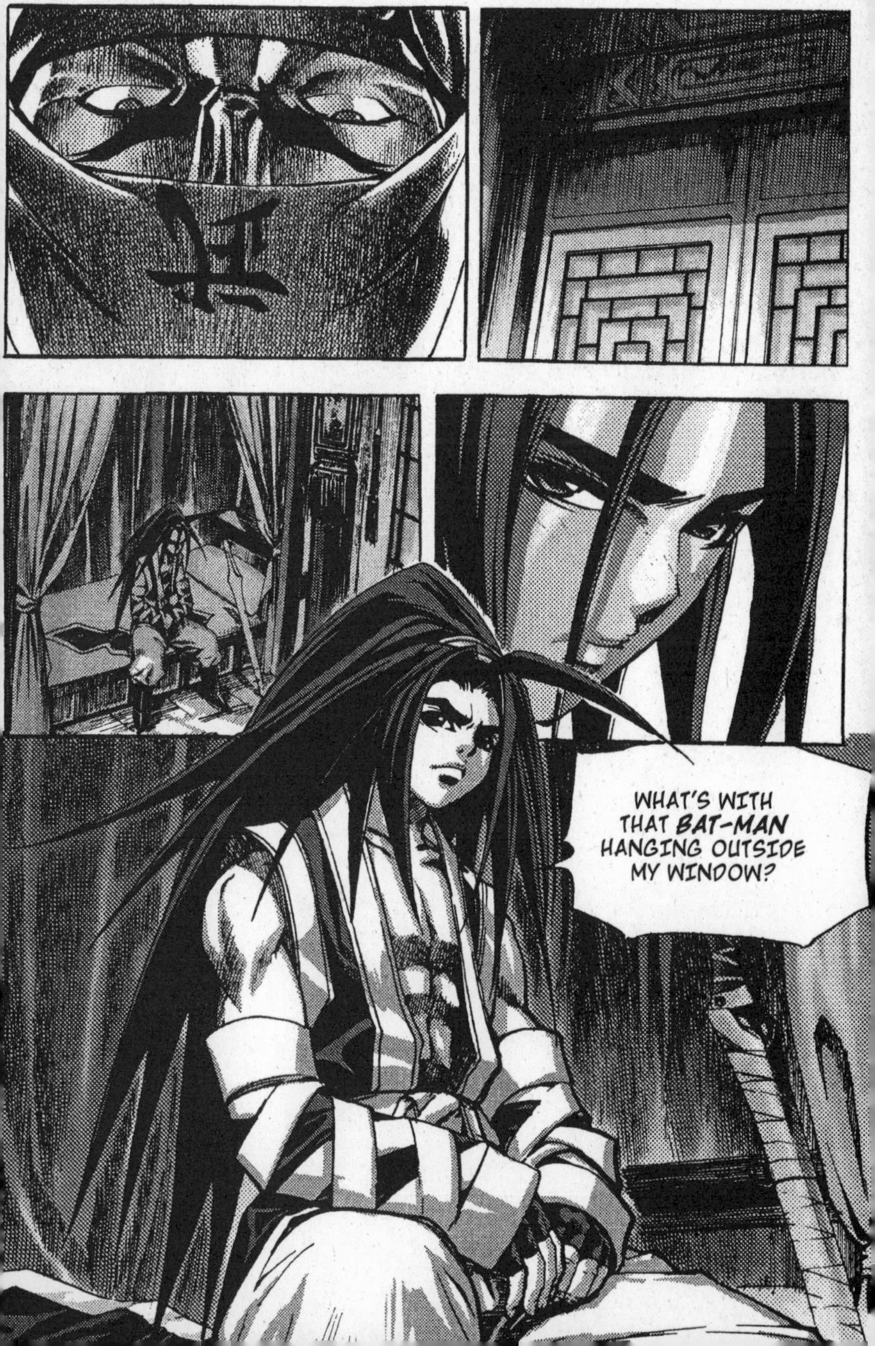
WHAT'S WITH THAT BAT-MAN HANGING OUTSIDE MY WINDOW?

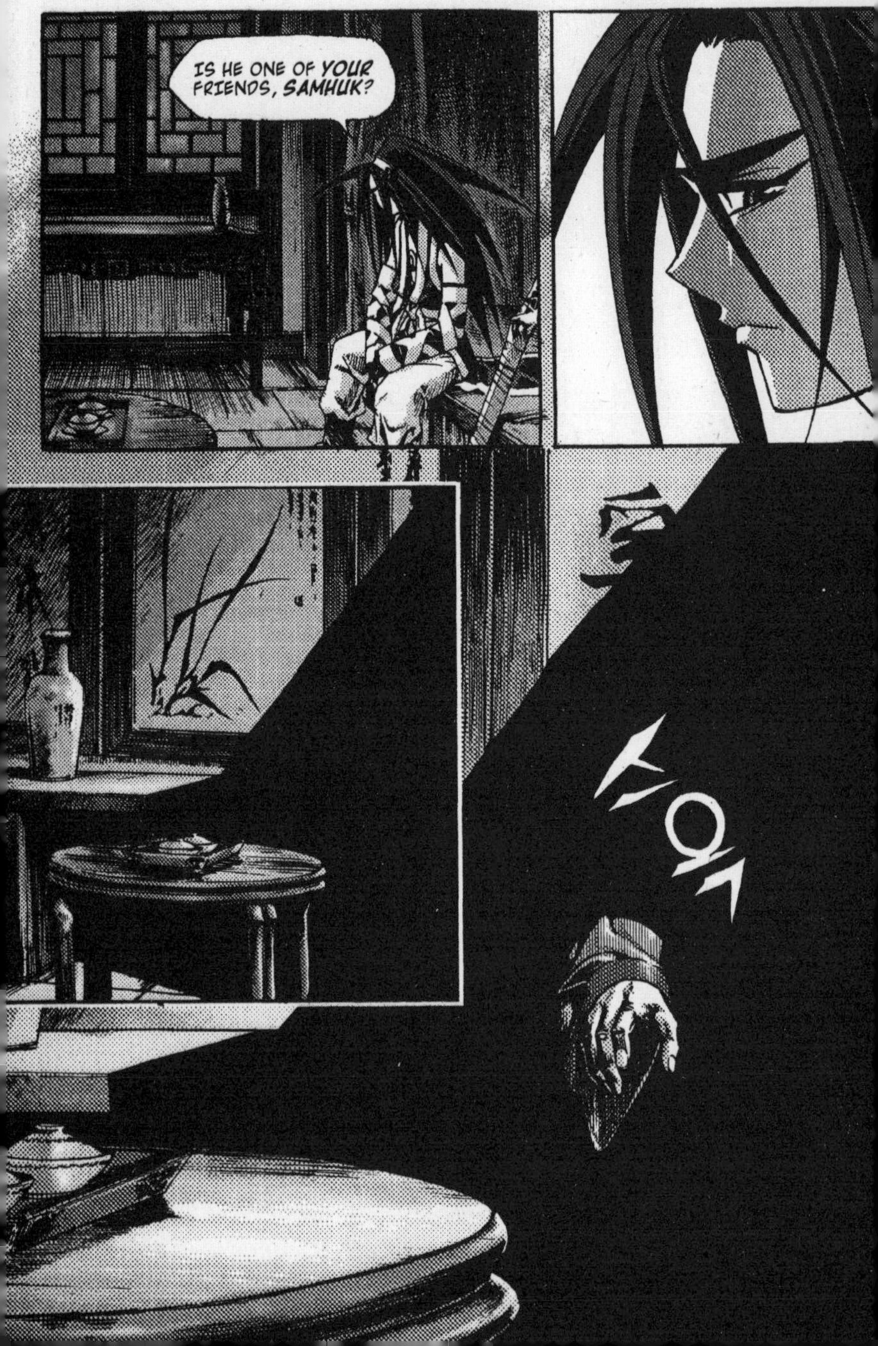
IS HE ONE OF YOUR FRIENDS, SAMHUK?

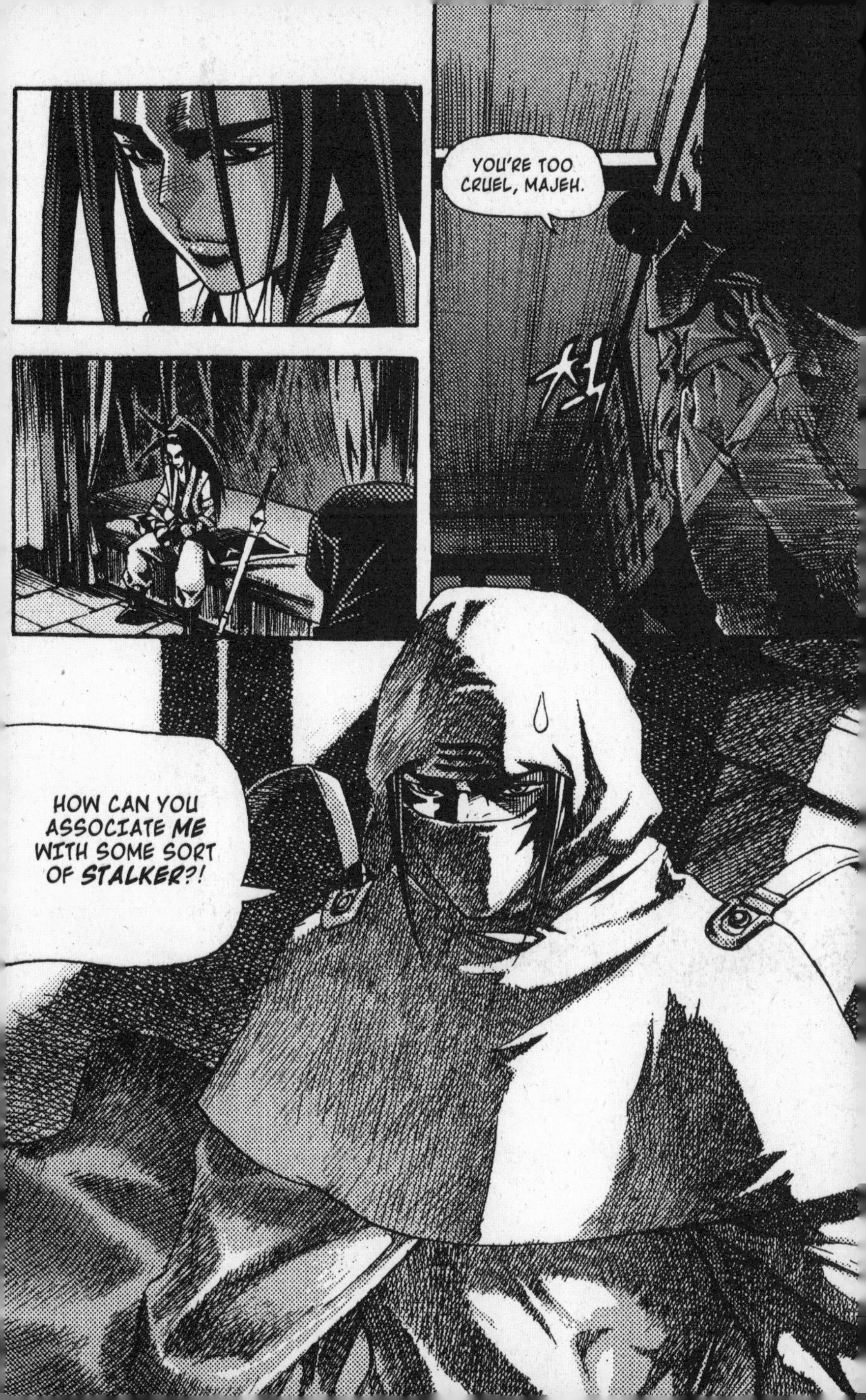
YOU'RE TOO CRUEL, MAJEH.
HOW CAN YOU ASSOCIATE ME WITH SOME SORT OF STALKER?!

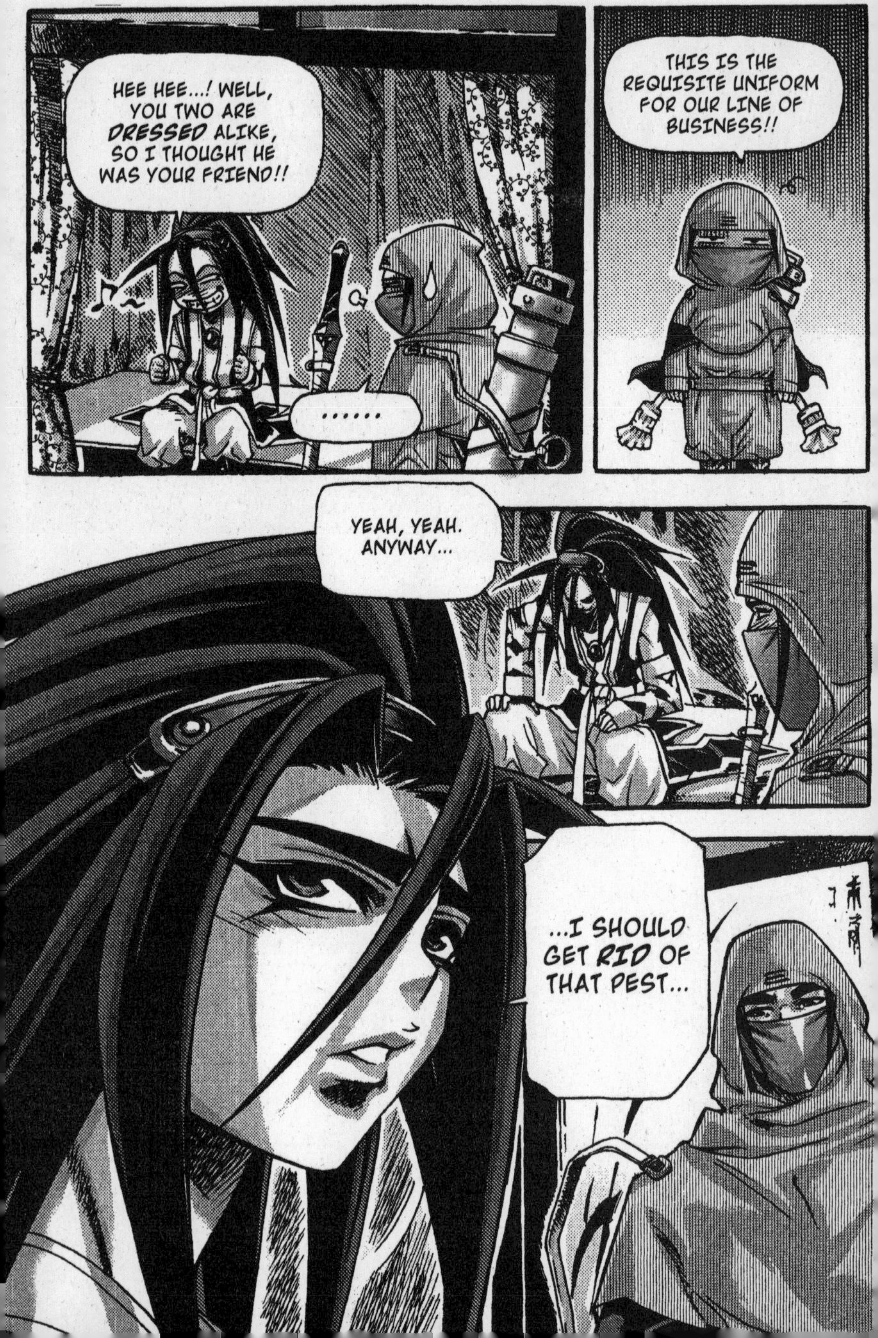
HEE HEE...! WELL, YOU TWO ARE DRESSED ALIKE, SO I THOUGHT HE WAS YOUR FRIEND!!
......
THIS IS THE REQUISITE UNIFORM FOR OUR LINE OF BUSINESS!!
YEAH, YEAH. ANYWAY...
...I SHOULD GET RID OF THAT PEST...

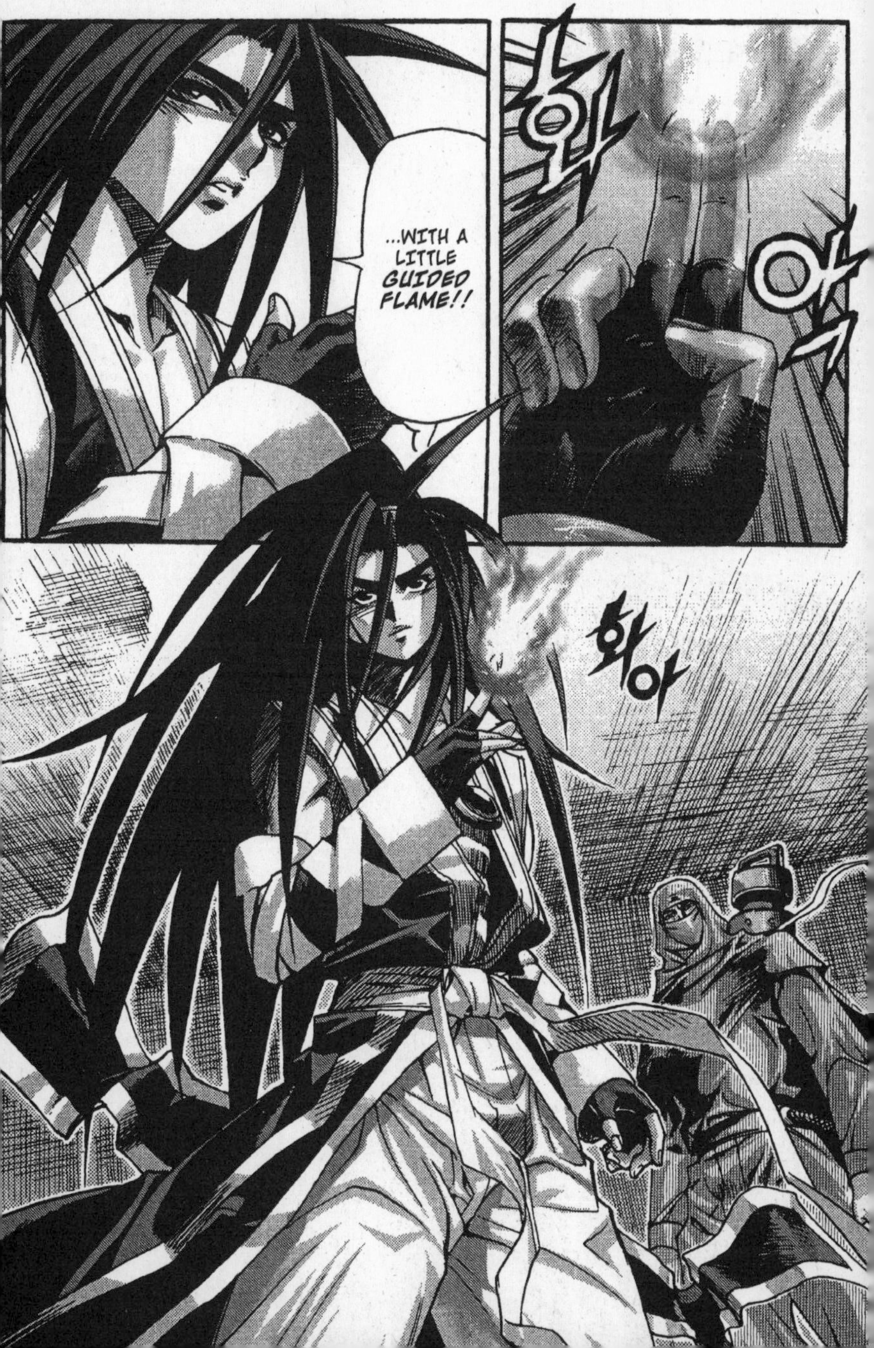
...WITH A LITTLE GUIDED FLAME!!
화아

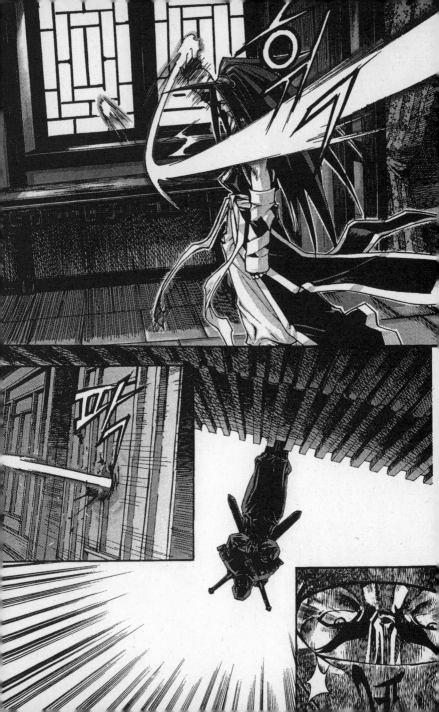

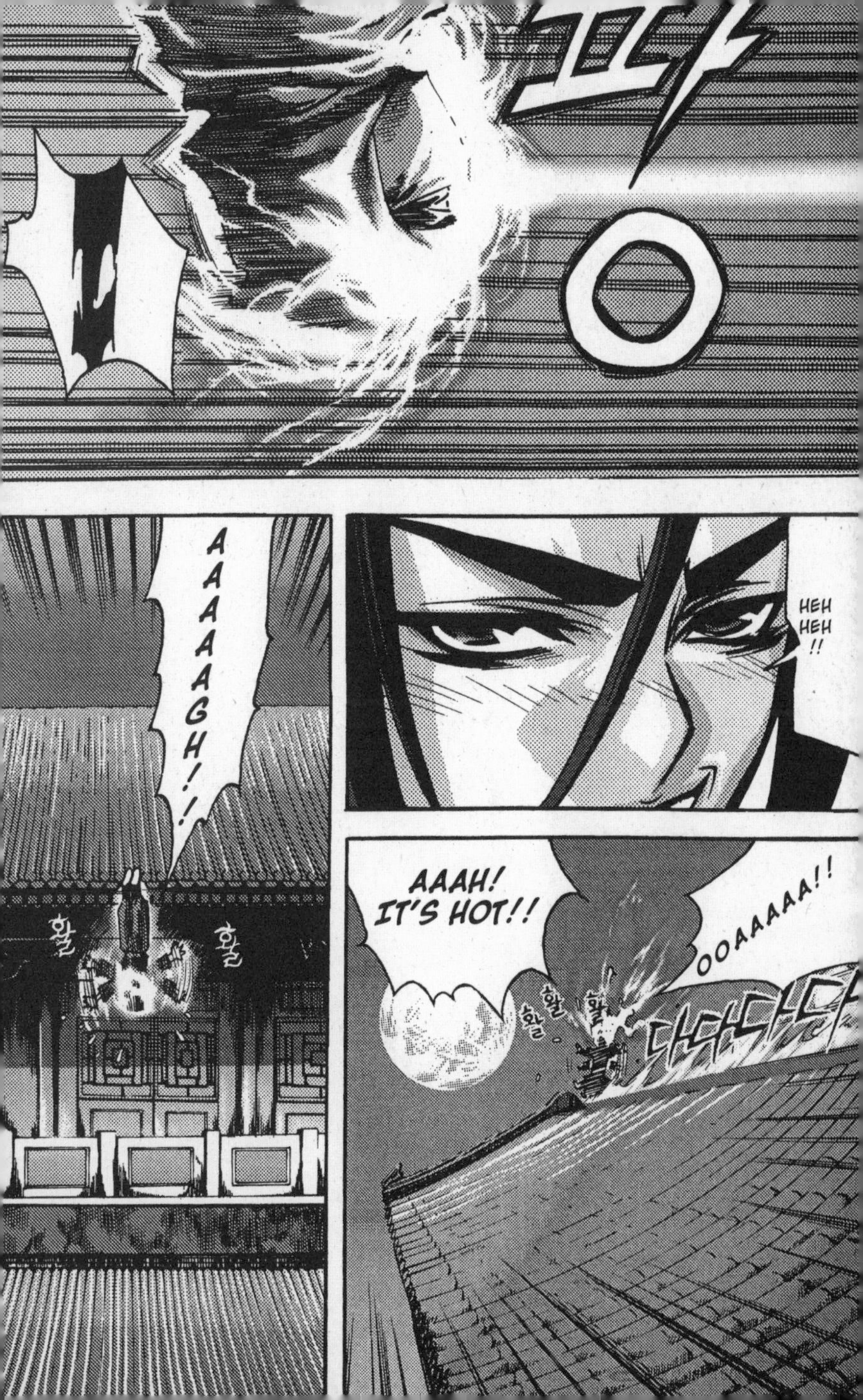
AAAAAGH!!
활
활
HEH HEH!!
AAAH! IT'S HOT!!
OOAAAAAA!!
활
활
다다다다다

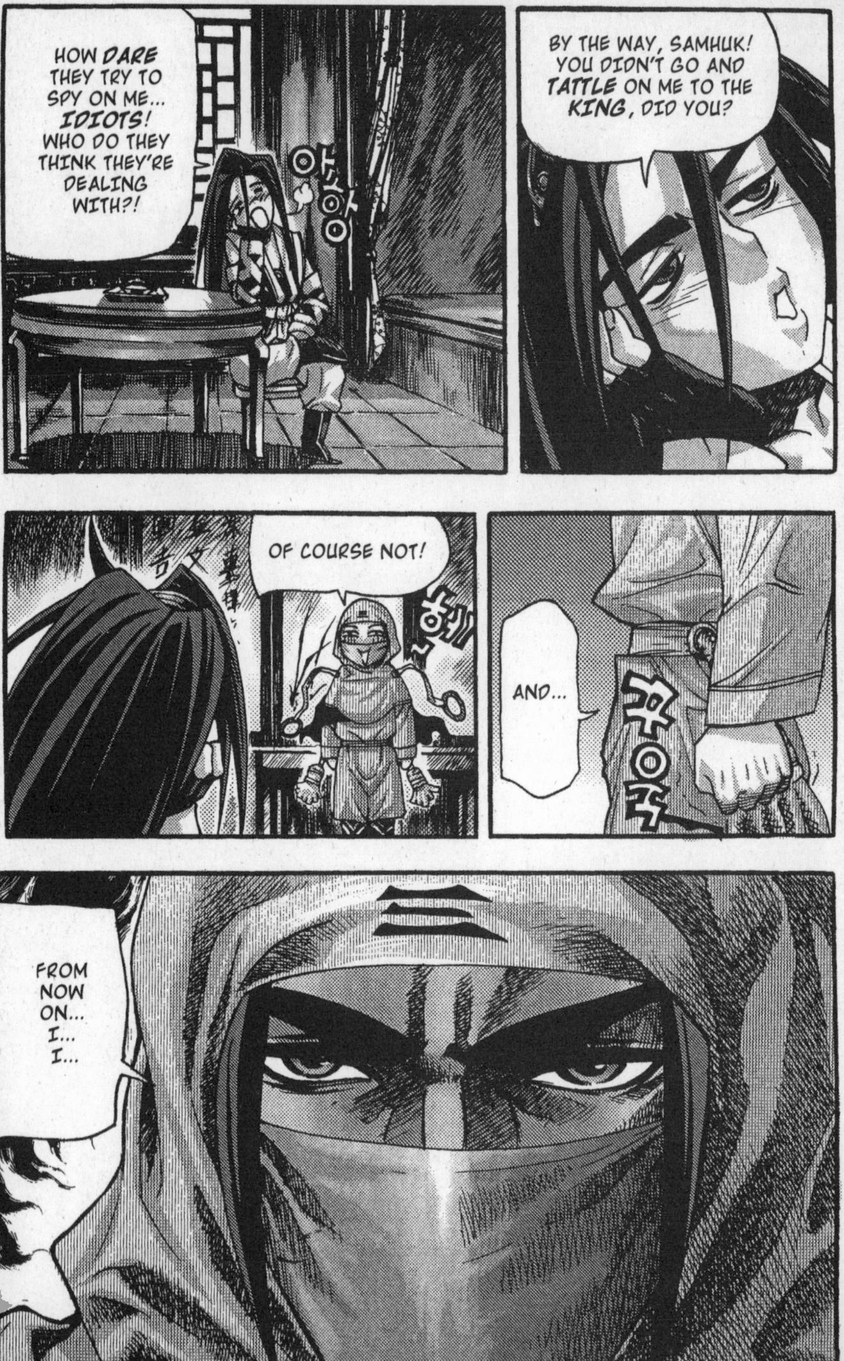
HOW DARE THEY TRY TO SPY ON ME... IDIOTS! WHO DO THEY THINK THEY'RE DEALING WITH?!
BY THE WAY, SAMHUK! YOU DIDN'T GO AND TATTLE ON ME TO THE KING, DID YOU?
OF COURSE NOT!
AND...
FROM NOW ON... I... I...

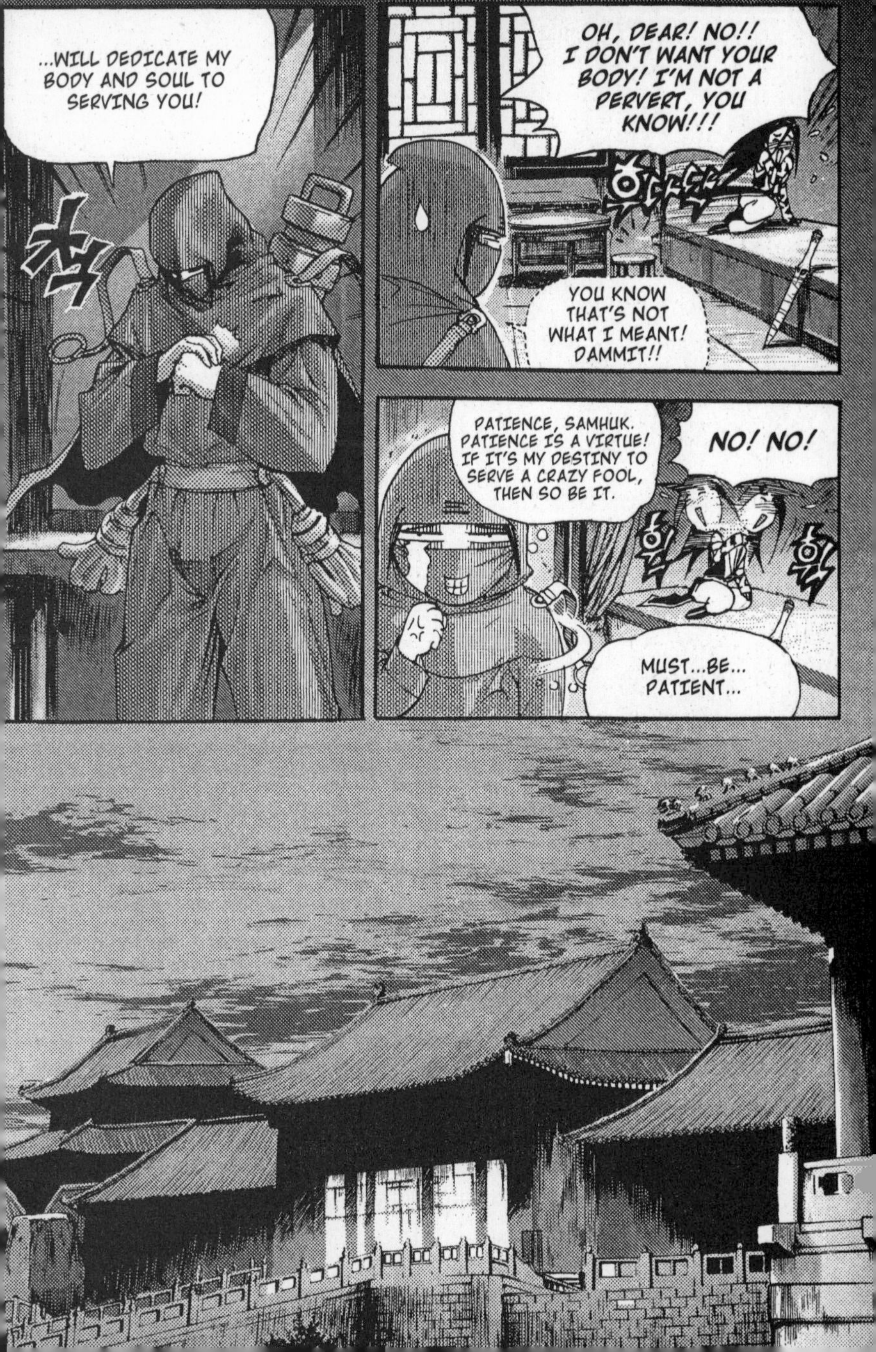
...WILL DEDICATE MY BODY AND SOUL TO SERVING YOU!
OH, DEAR! NO!! I DON'T WANT YOUR BODY! I'M NOT A PERVERT, YOU KNOW!!!
YOU KNOW THAT'S NOT WHAT I MEANT! DAMMIT!!
PATIENCE, SAMHUK. PATIENCE IS A VIRTUE! IF IT'S MY DESTINY TO SERVE A CRAZY FOOL, THEN SO BE IT.
NO! NO!
MUST...BE... PATIENT...

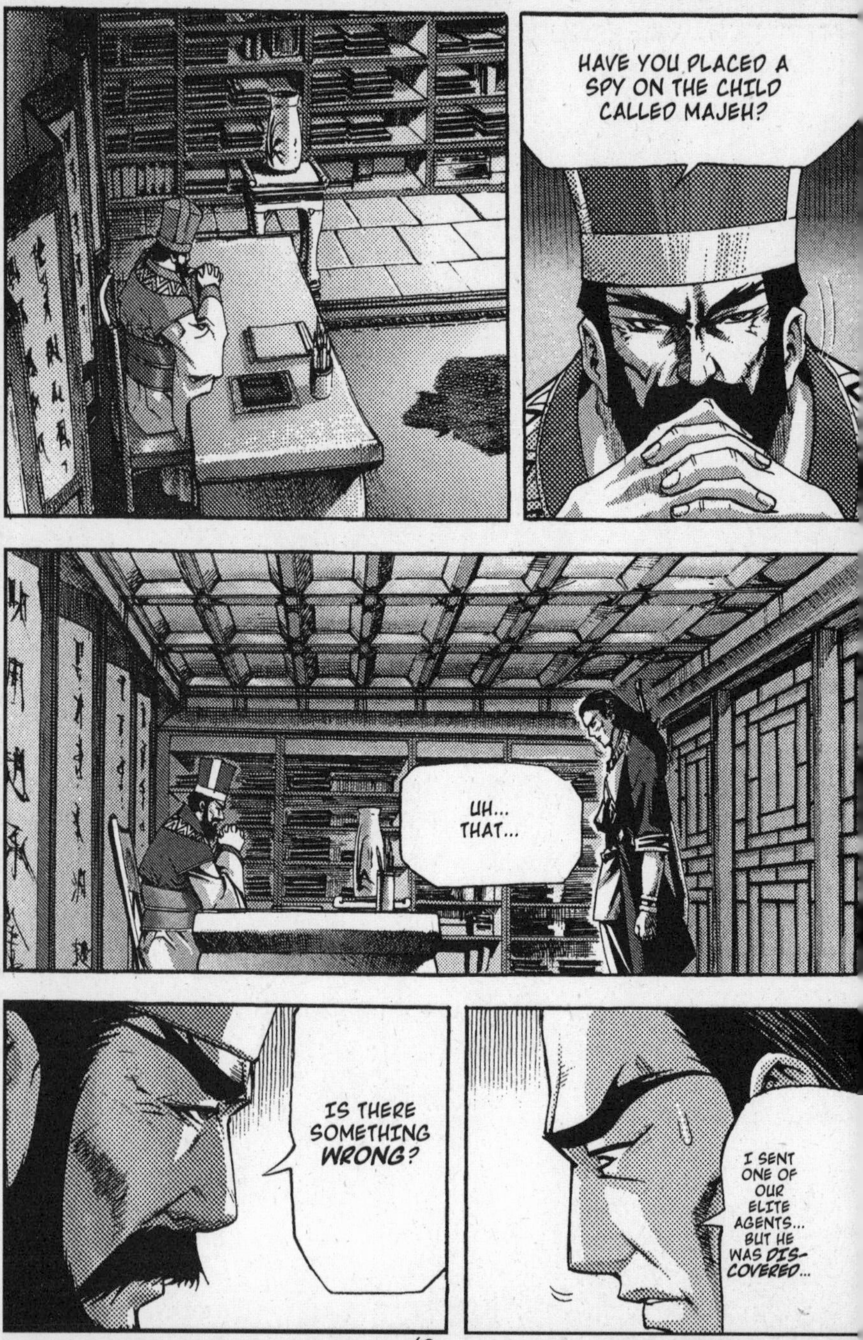
HAVE YOU PLACED A SPY ON THE CHILD CALLED MAJEH?
UH... THAT...
IS THERE SOMETHING WRONG?
I SENT ONE OF OUR ELITE AGENTS... BUT HE WAS DIS-COVERED...

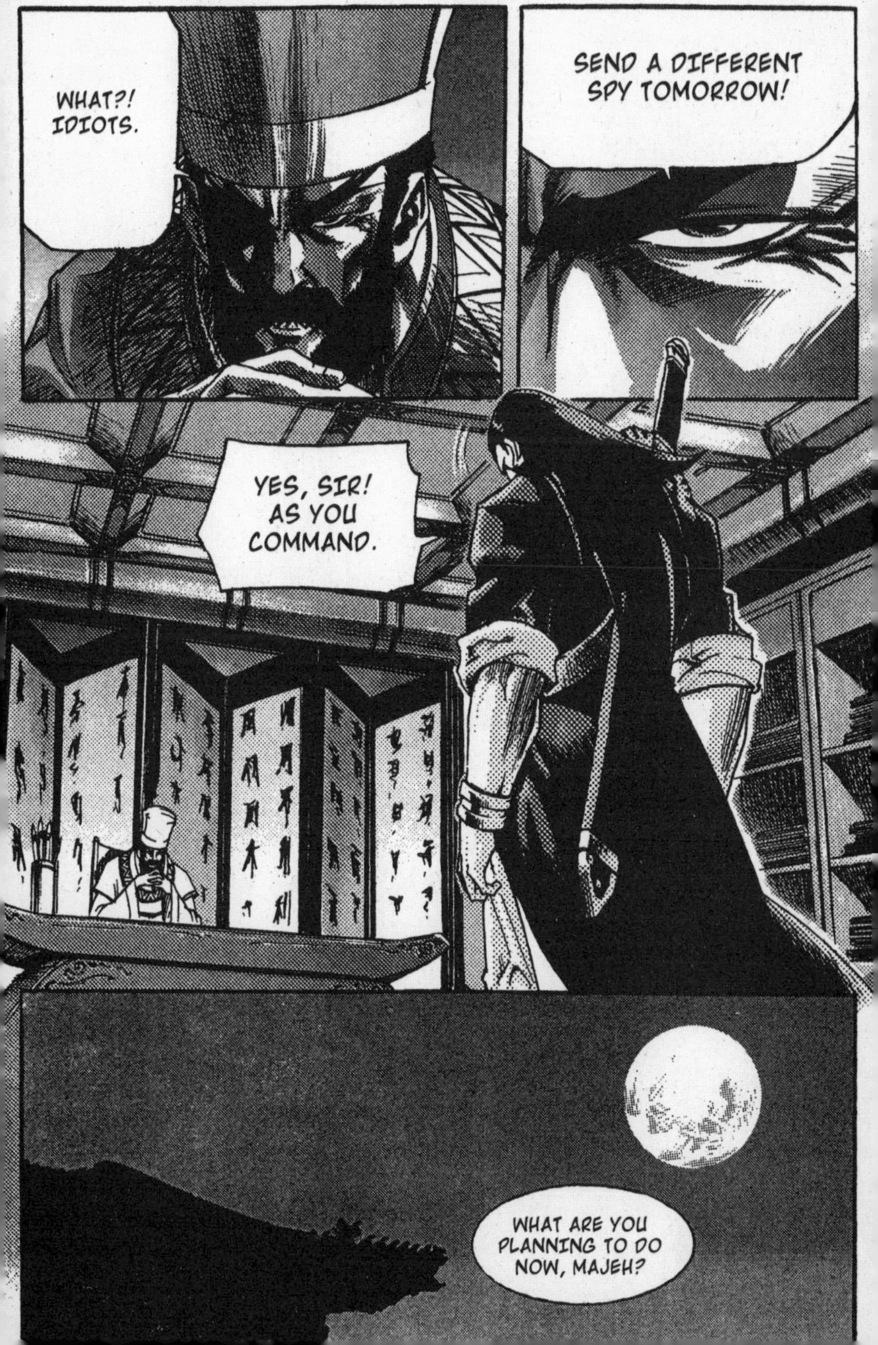
WHAT?! IDIOTS.
SEND A DIFFERENT SPY TOMORROW!
YES, SIR! AS YOU COMMAND.
WHAT ARE YOU PLANNING TO DO NOW, MAJEH?

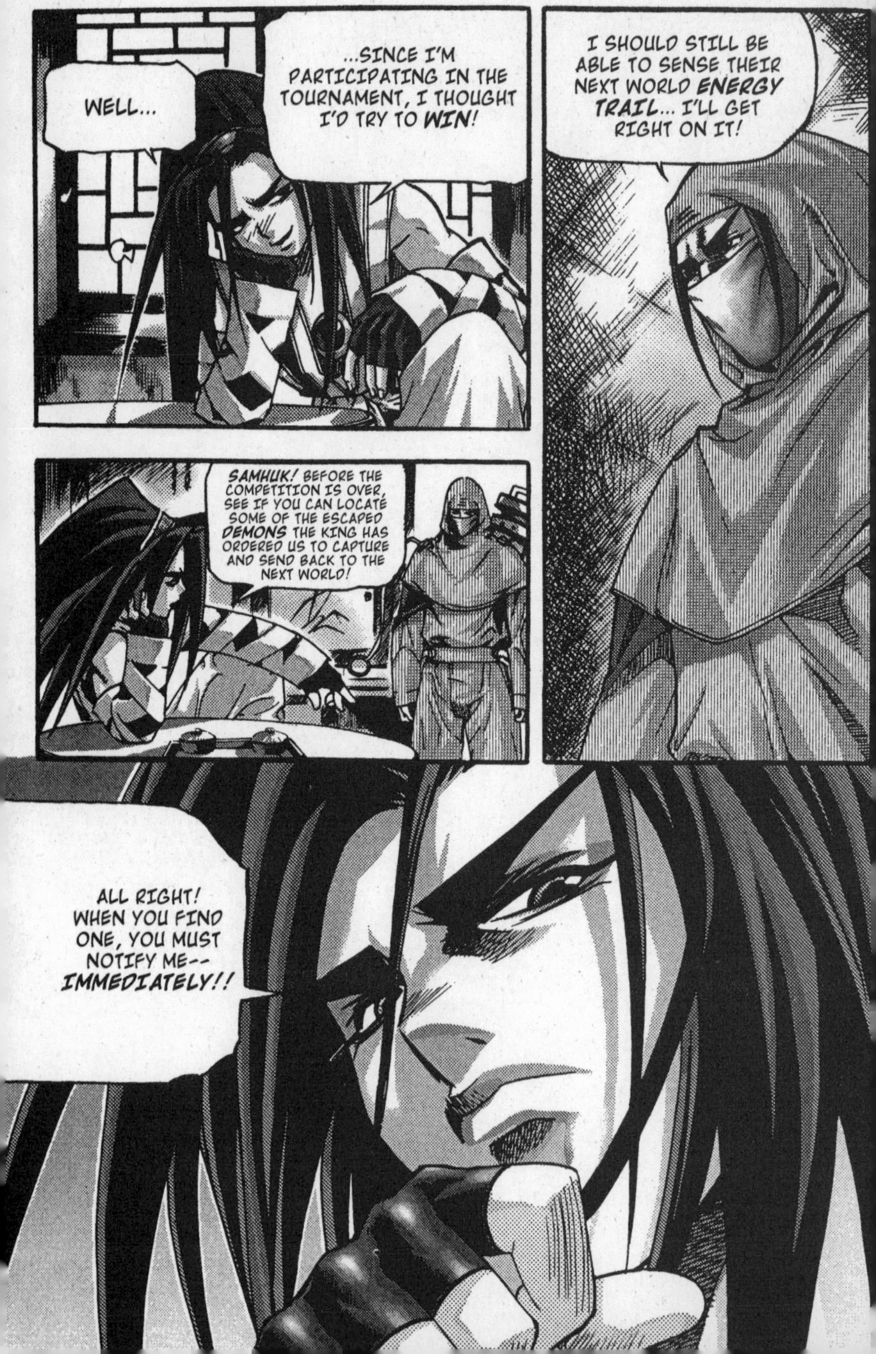
WELL...
...SINCE I'M PARTICIPATING IN THE TOURNAMENT, I THOUGHT I'D TRY TO WIN!
I SHOULD STILL BE ABLE TO SENSE THEIR NEXT WORLD ENERGY TRAIL... I'LL GET RIGHT ON IT!
SAMHUK! BEFORE THE COMPETITION IS OVER, SEE IF YOU CAN LOCATE SOME OF THE ESCAPED DEMONS THE KING HAS ORDERED US TO CAPTURE AND SEND BACK TO THE NEXT WORLD!
ALL RIGHT! WHEN YOU FIND ONE, YOU MUST NOTIFY ME-- IMMEDIATELY!!

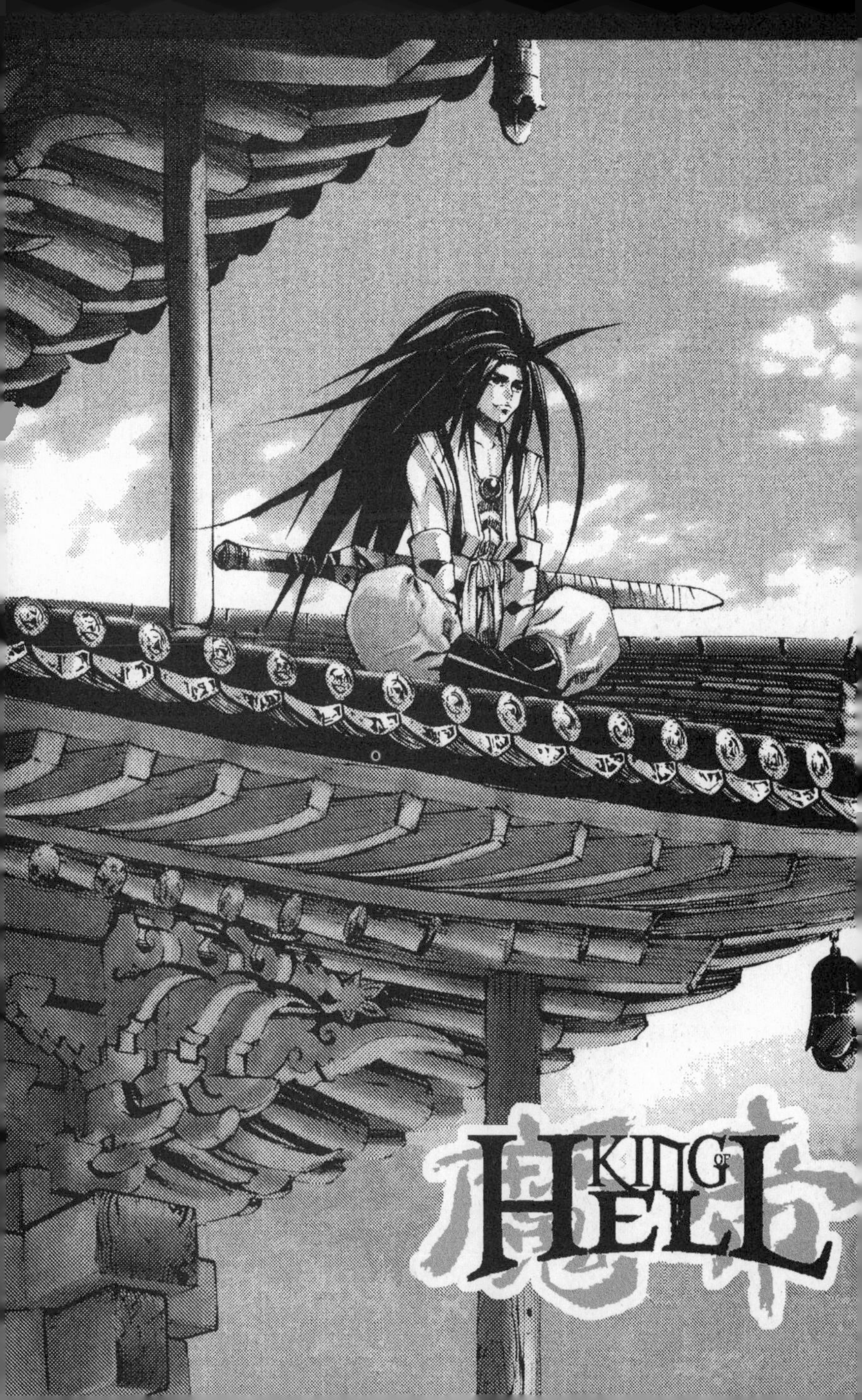
KING OF HELL

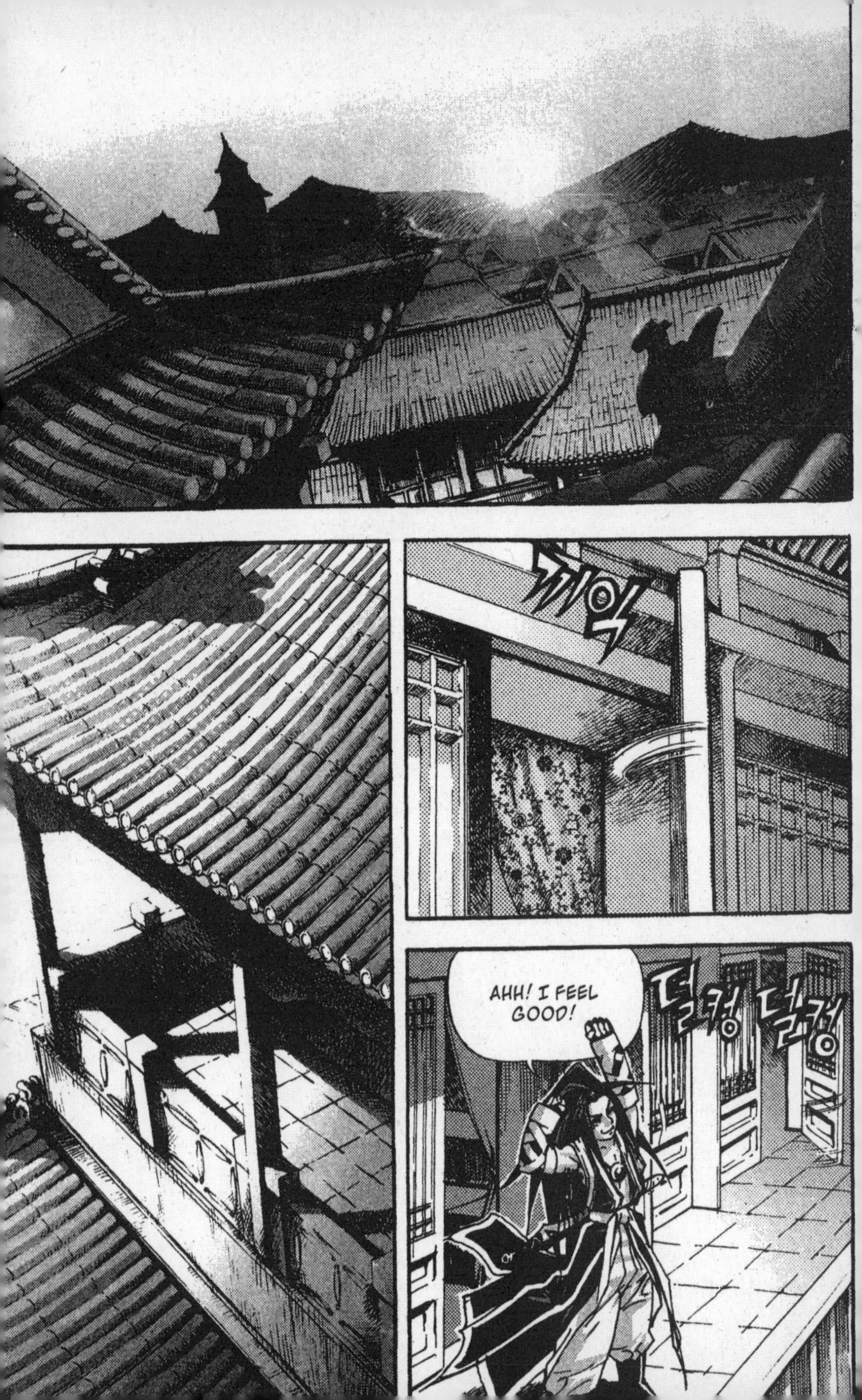
끼익
AHH! I FEEL GOOD!
덜컹 덜컹

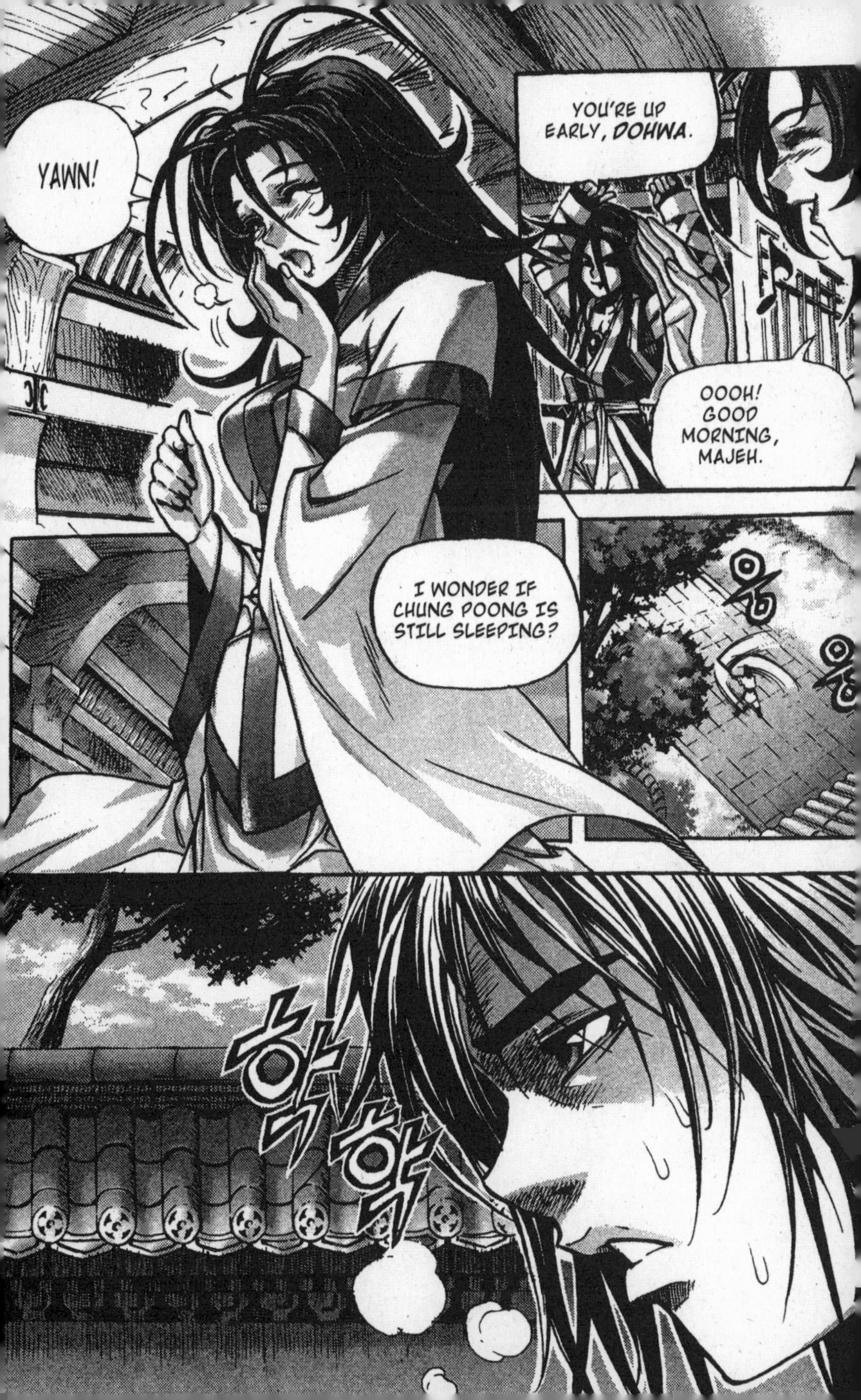
YAWN!
YOU'RE UP EARLY, DOHWA.
OOOH! GOOD MORNING, MAJEH.
I WONDER IF CHUNG POONG IS STILL SLEEPING?

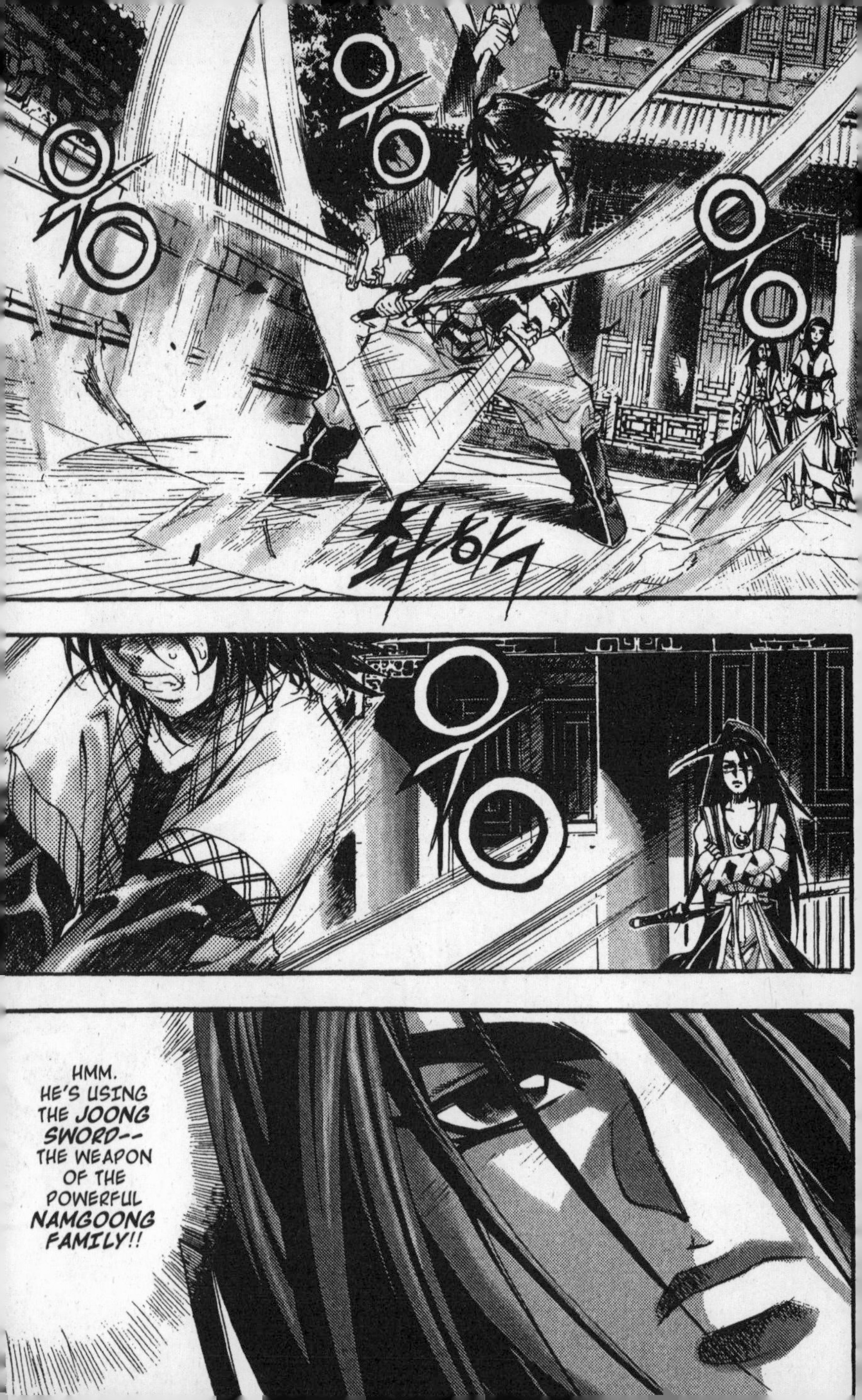
HMM.
HE'S USING THE JOONG SWORD--
THE WEAPON OF THE POWERFUL NAMGOONG FAMILY!!

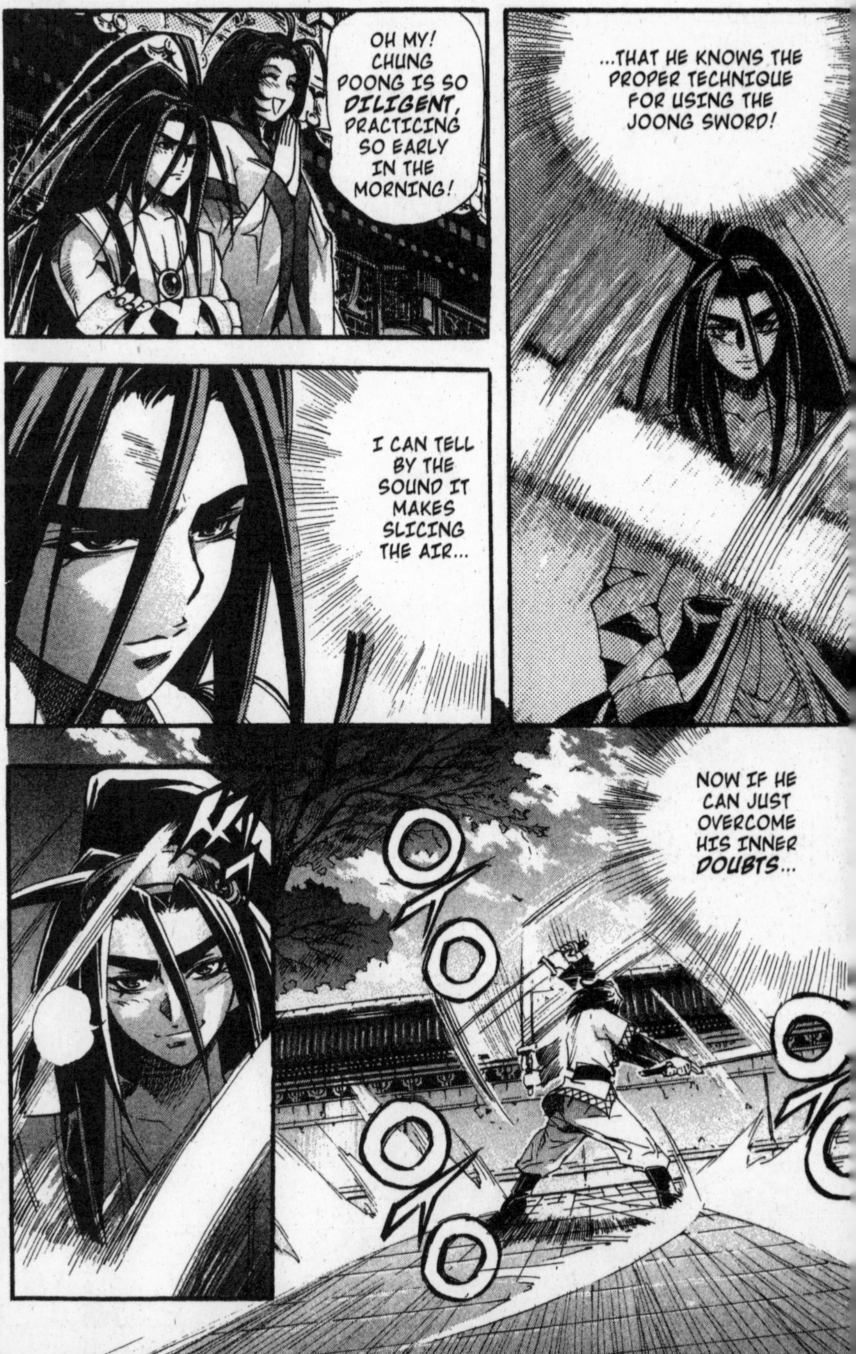
OH MY! CHUNG POONG IS SO DILIGENT, PRACTICING SO EARLY IN THE MORNING!
I CAN TELL BY THE SOUND IT MAKES SLICING THE AIR...
...THAT HE KNOWS THE PROPER TECHNIQUE FOR USING THE JOONG SWORD!
NOW IF HE CAN JUST OVERCOME HIS INNER DOUBTS...

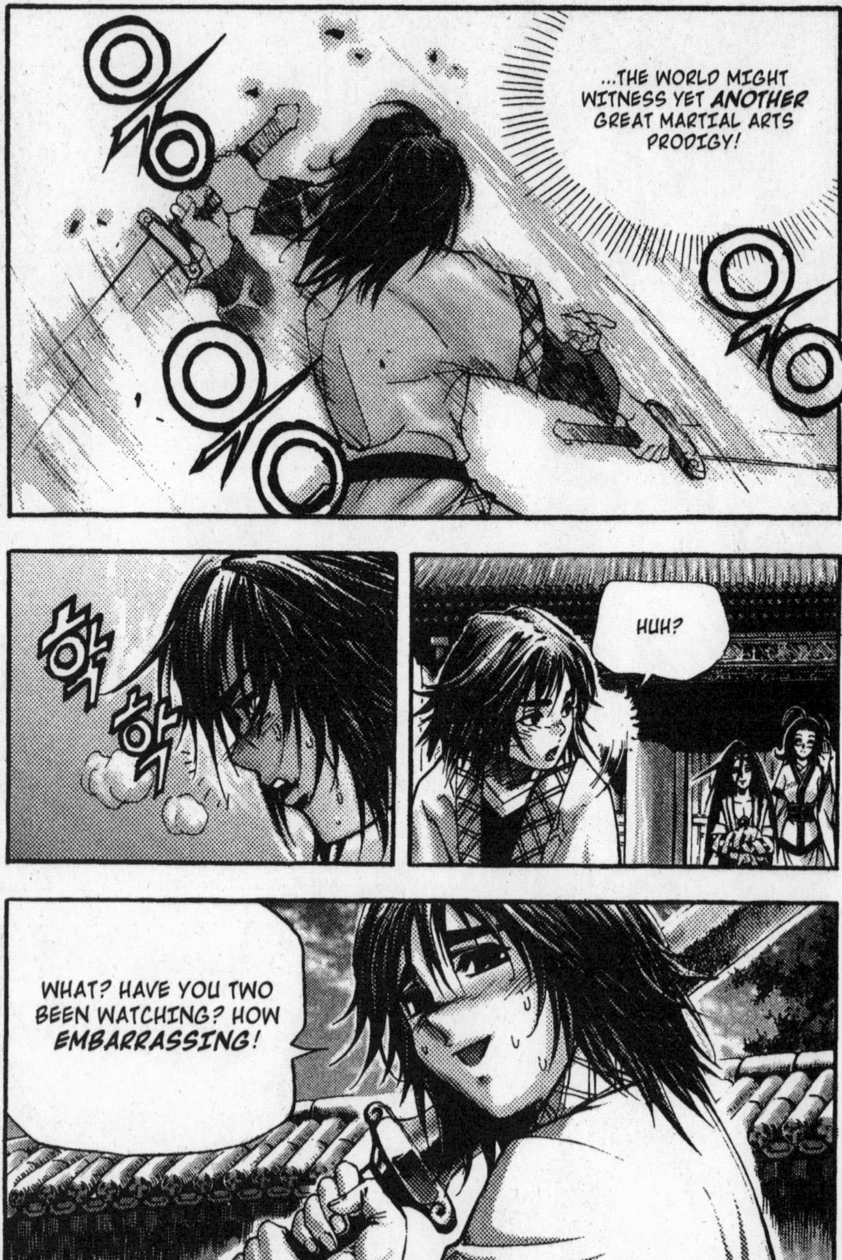
...THE WORLD MIGHT WITNESS YET ANOTHER GREAT MARTIAL ARTS PRODIGY!
헉
헉
HUH?
WHAT? HAVE YOU TWO BEEN WATCHING? HOW EMBARRASSING!

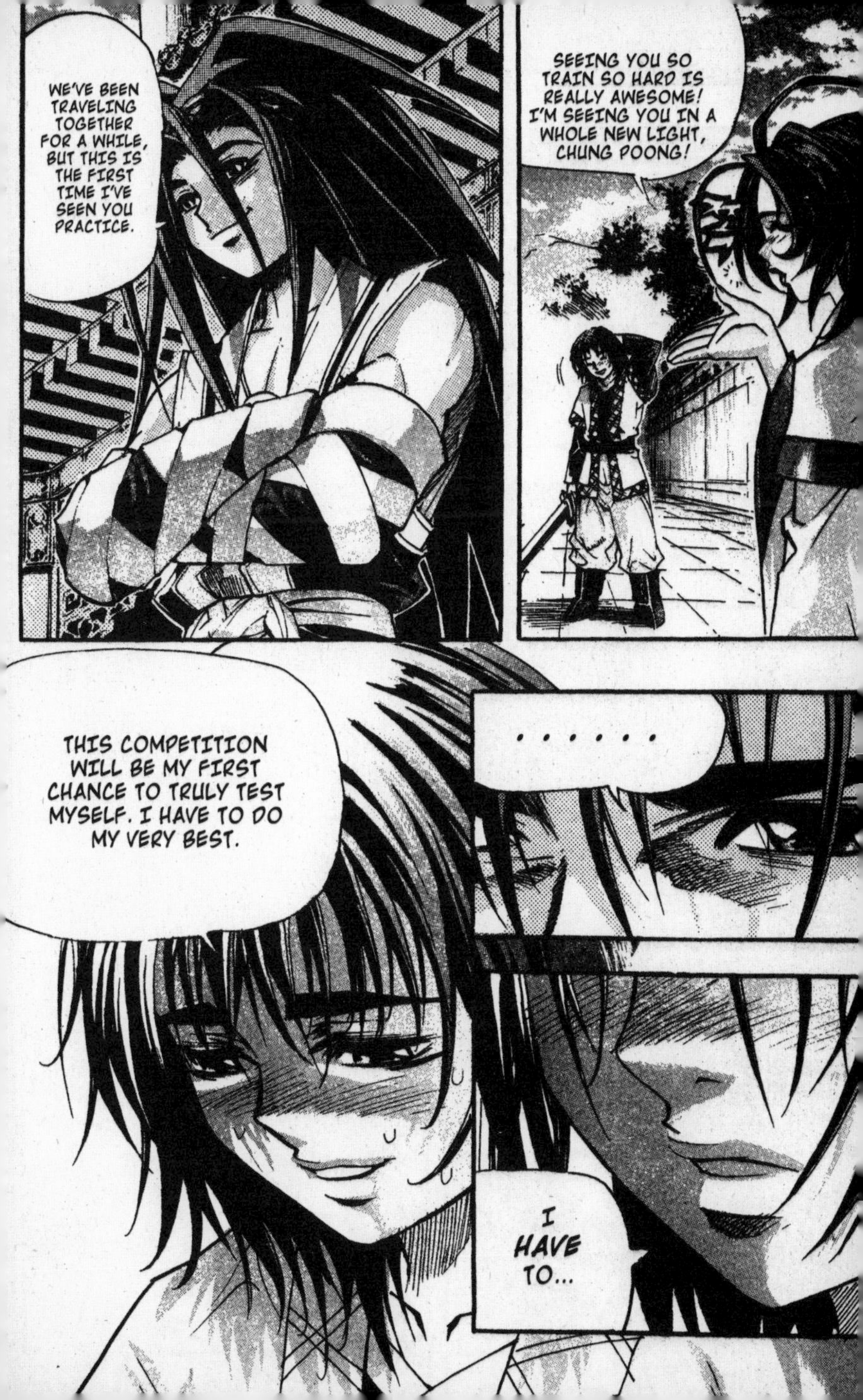

WE'VE BEEN TRAVELING TOGETHER FOR A WHILE, BUT THIS IS THE FIRST TIME I'VE SEEN YOU PRACTICE.
SEEING YOU SO TRAIN SO HARD IS REALLY AWESOME! I'M SEEING YOU IN A WHOLE NEW LIGHT, CHUNG POONG!
THIS COMPETITION WILL BE MY FIRST CHANCE TO TRULY TEST MYSELF. I HAVE TO DO MY VERY BEST.
......
I HAVE TO...

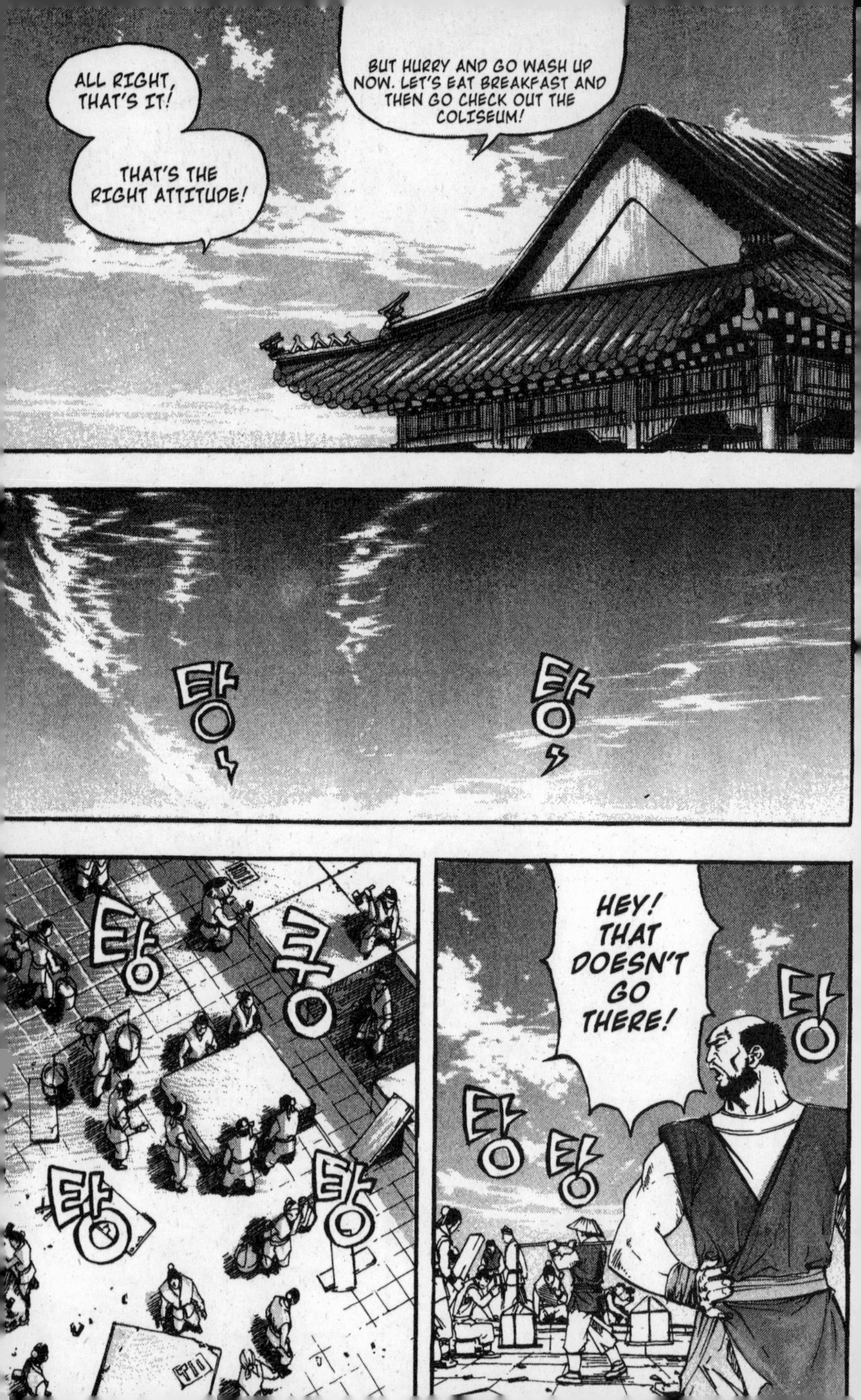
ALL RIGHT, THAT'S IT!
THAT'S THE RIGHT ATTITUDE!
BUT HURRY AND GO WASH UP NOW. LET'S EAT BREAKFAST AND THEN GO CHECK OUT THE COLISEUM!
탕
탕
탕
쿵
탕
탕
HEY! THAT DOESN'T GO THERE!
탕
탕
탕

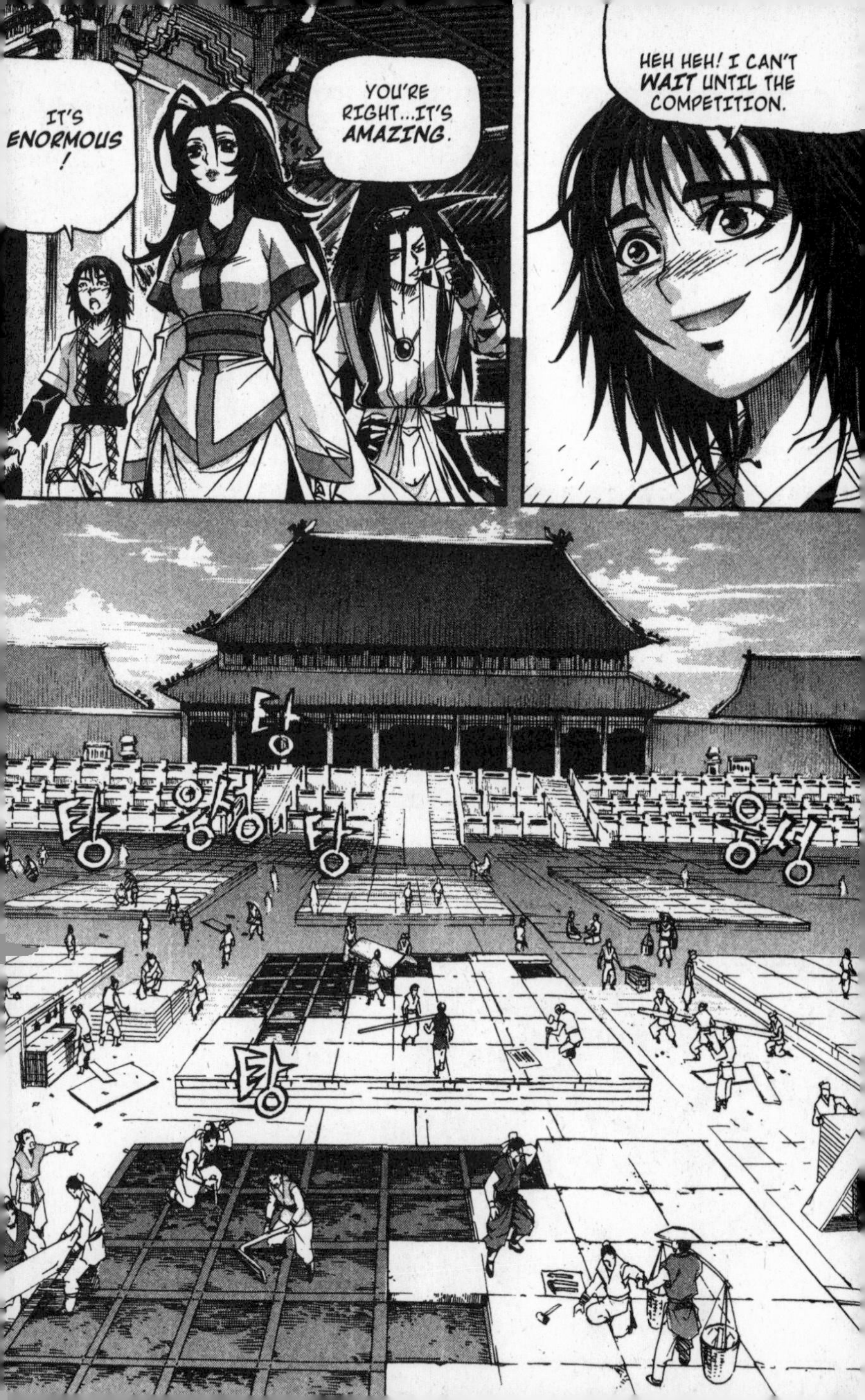
IT'S ENORMOUS!
YOU'RE RIGHT...IT'S AMAZING.
HEH HEH! I CAN'T WAIT UNTIL THE COMPETITION.
탕
탕
웅성
탕
웅성
탕

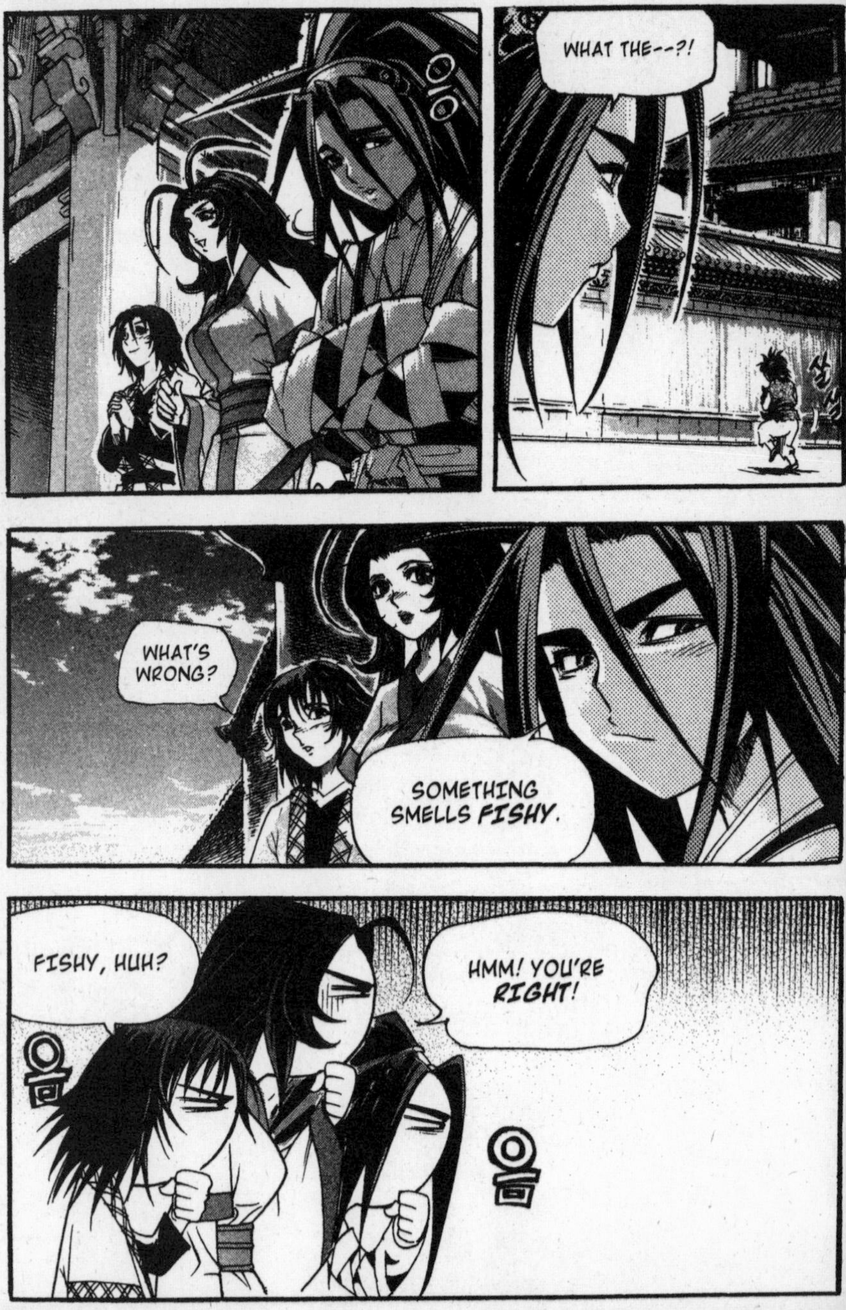
WHAT THE--?!
WHAT'S WRONG?
SOMETHING SMELLS FISHY.
FISHY, HUH?
HMM! YOU'RE RIGHT!

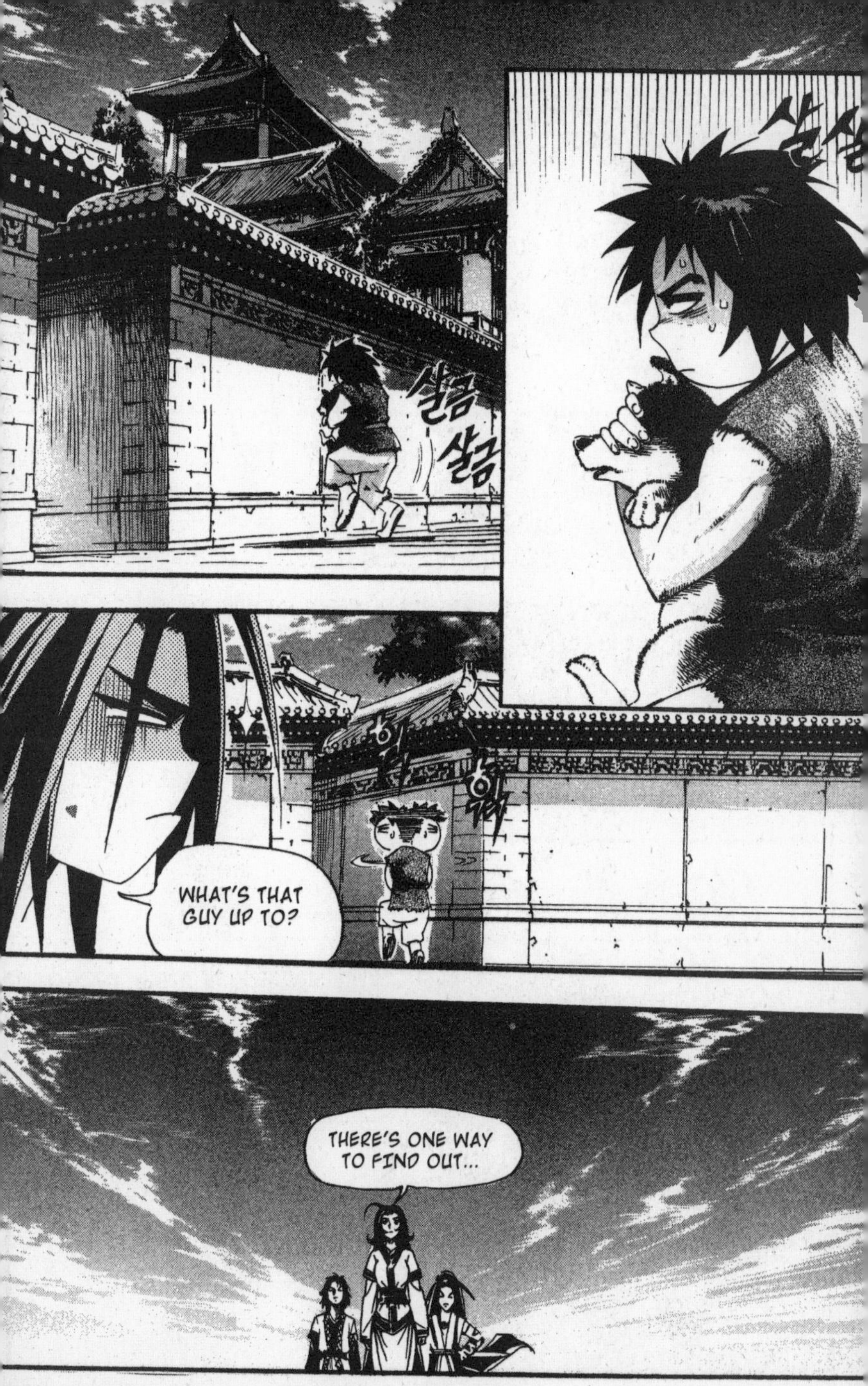
살금 살금
WHAT'S THAT GUY UP TO?
THERE'S ONE WAY TO FIND OUT...

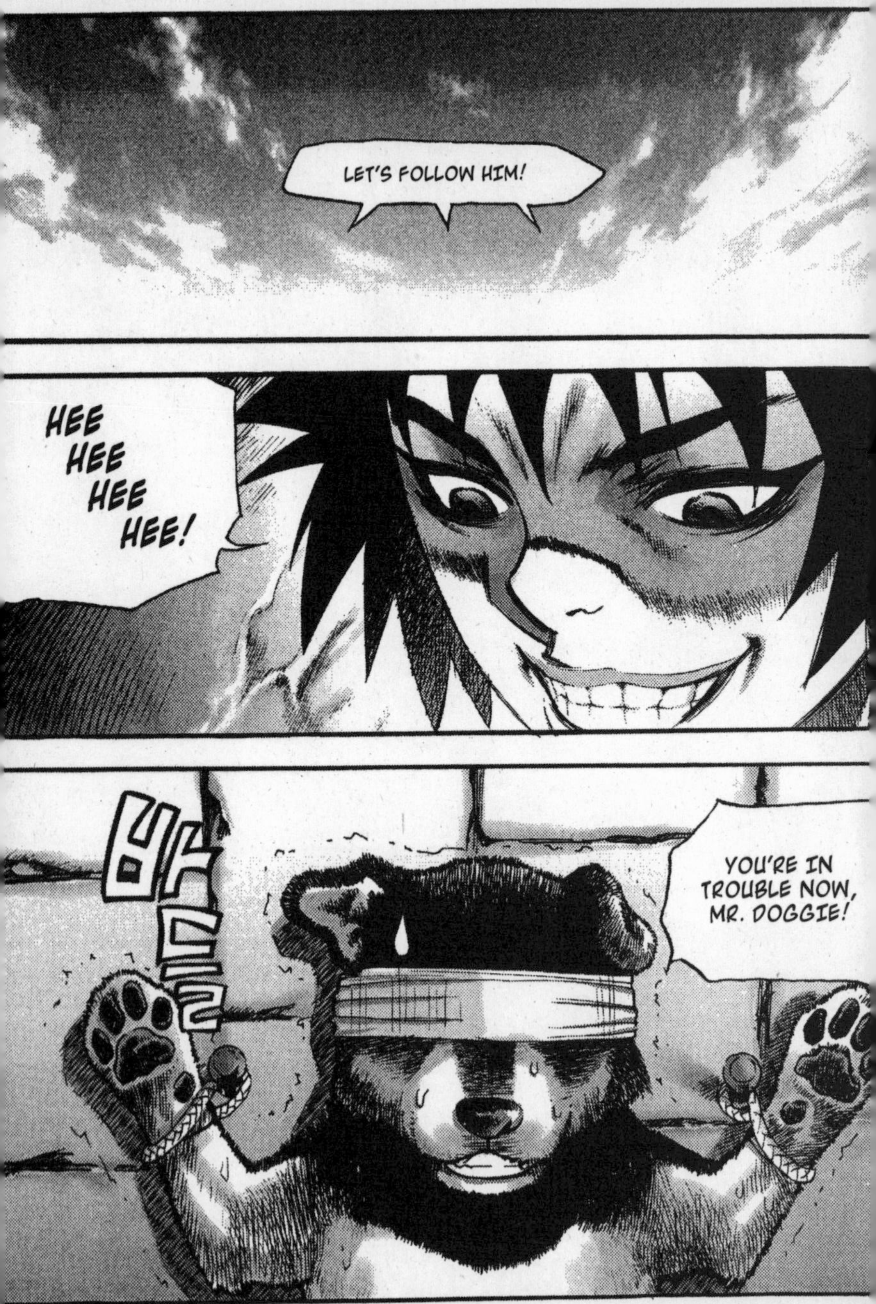
LET'S FOLLOW HIM!
HEE HEE HEE HEE!
YOU'RE IN TROUBLE NOW, MR. DOGGIE!

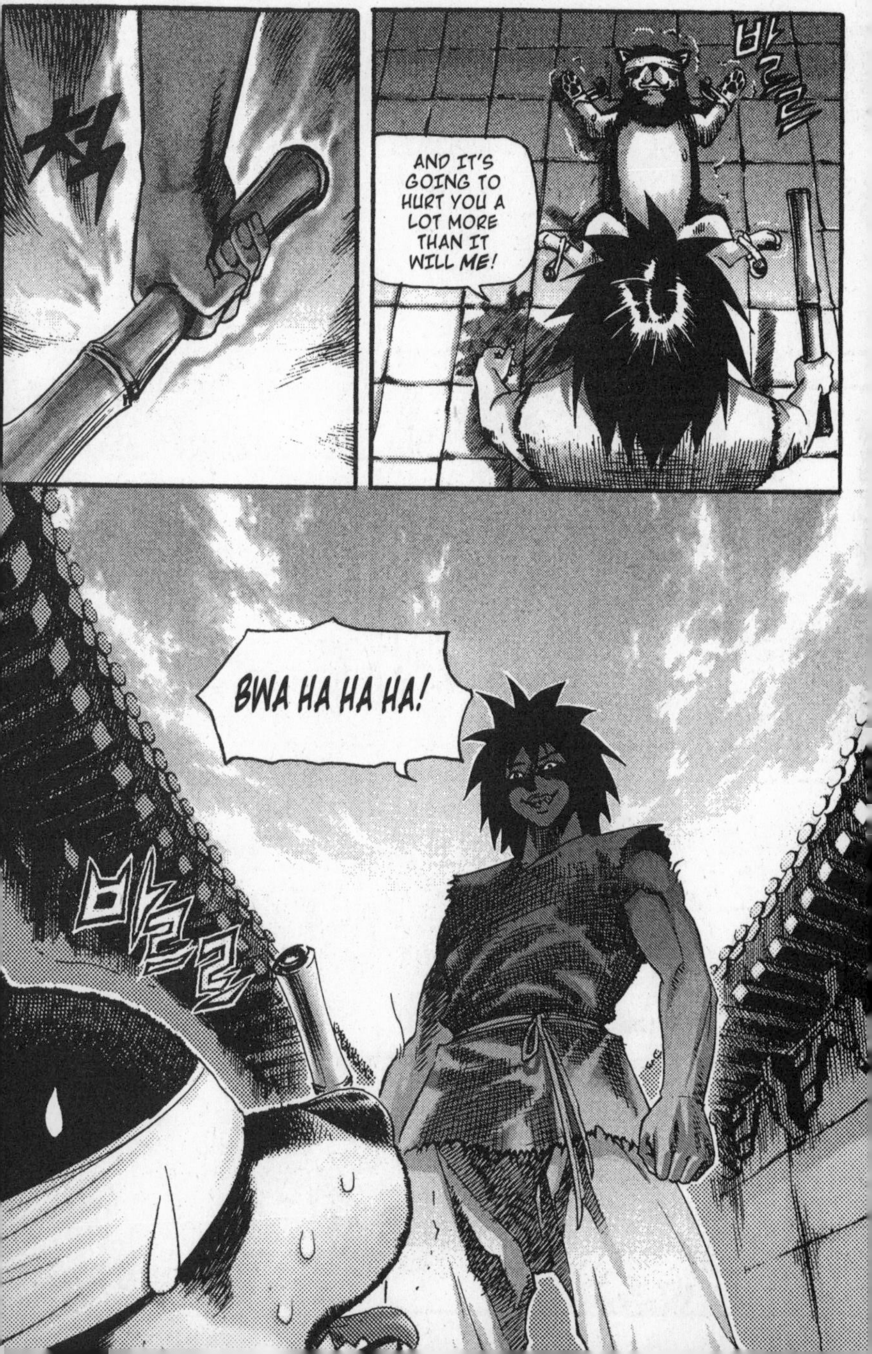
AND IT'S GOING TO HURT YOU A LOT MORE THAN IT WILL ME!
BWA HA HA HA!

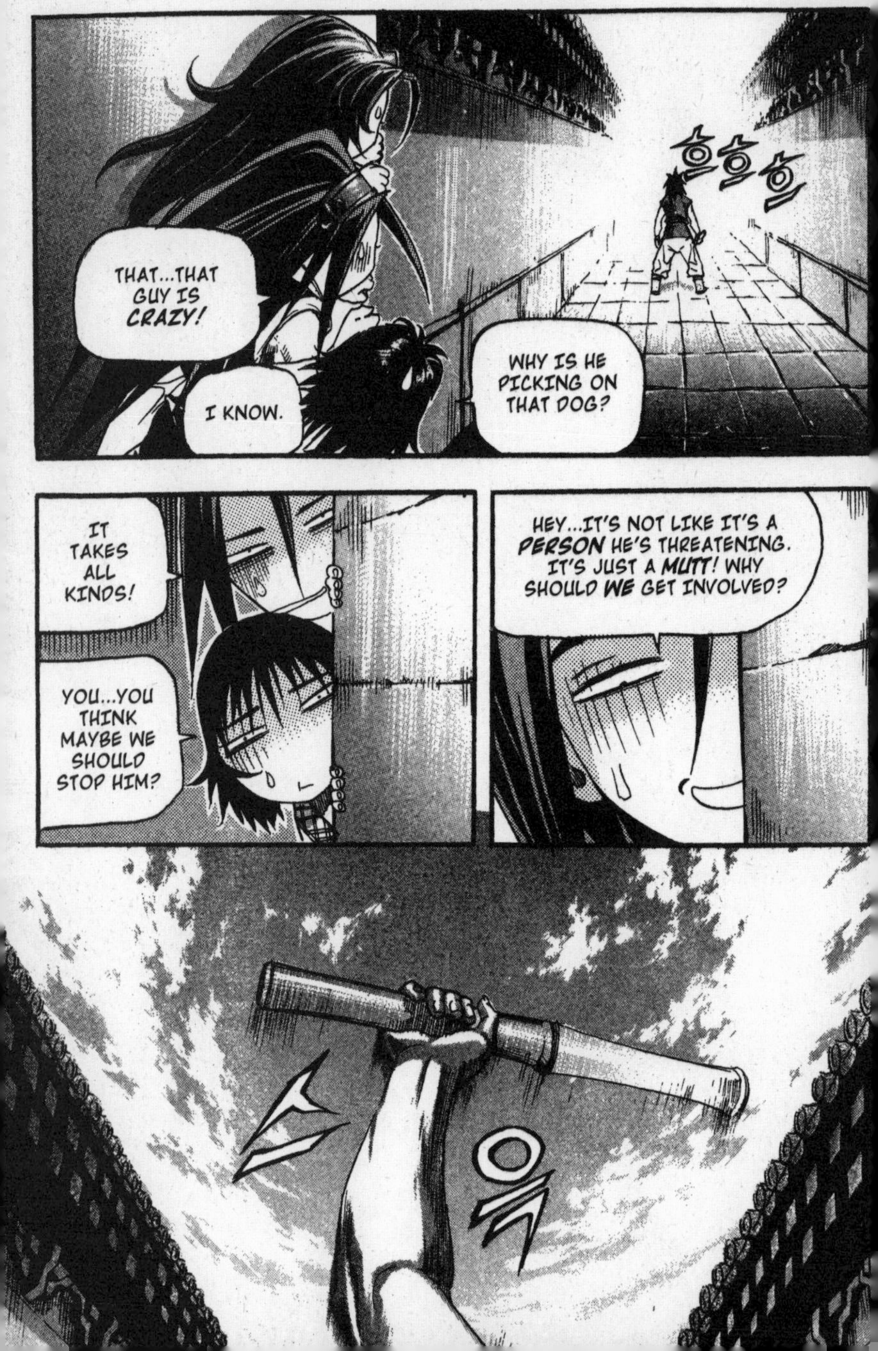
THAT...THAT GUY IS CRAZY!
I KNOW.
WHY IS HE PICKING ON THAT DOG?
IT TAKES ALL KINDS!
YOU...YOU THINK MAYBE WE SHOULD STOP HIM?
HEY...IT'S NOT LIKE IT'S A PERSON HE'S THREATENING. IT'S JUST A MUTT! WHY SHOULD WE GET INVOLVED?

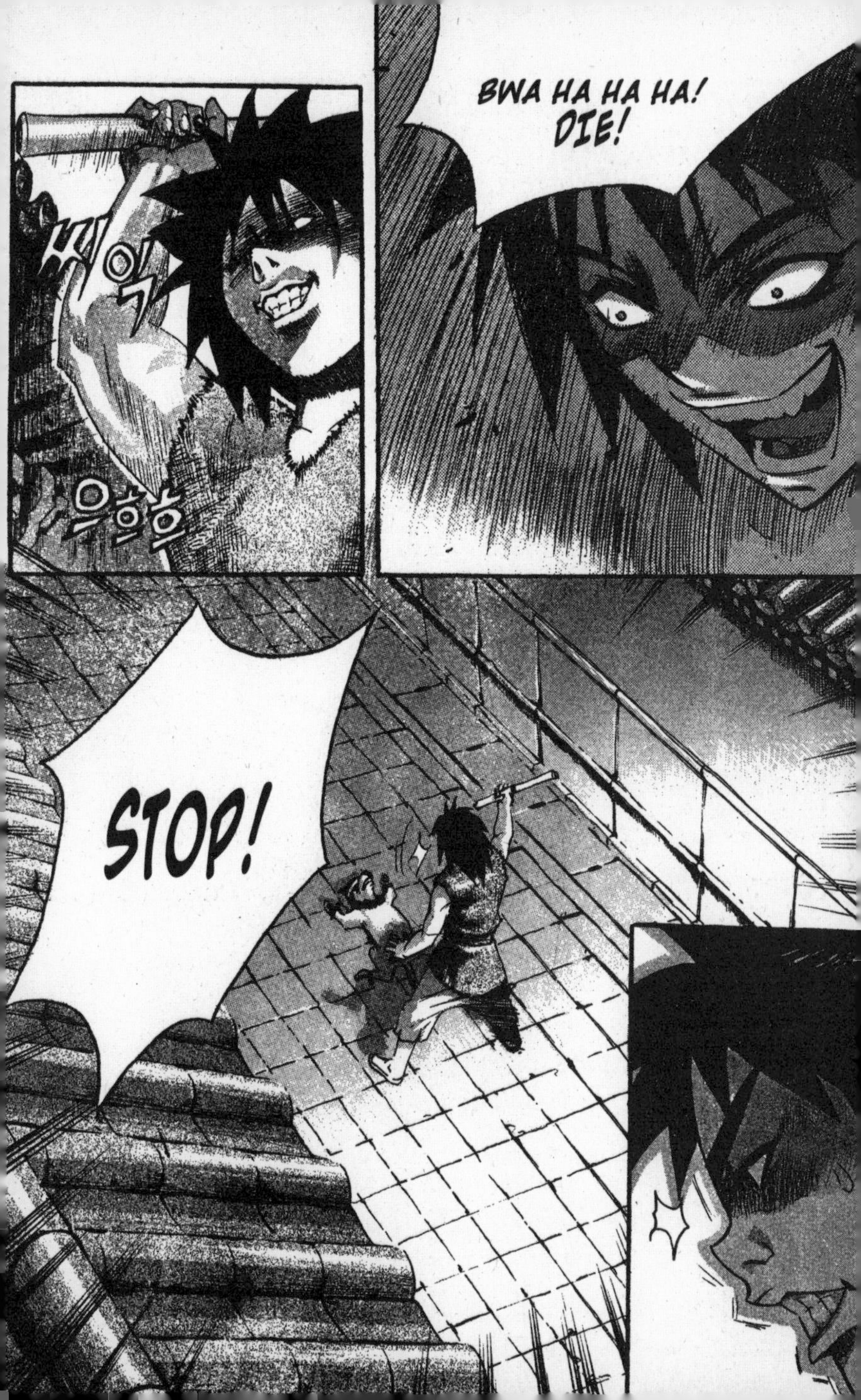
씨익
으흐흐
BWA HA HA HA!
DIE!
STOP!

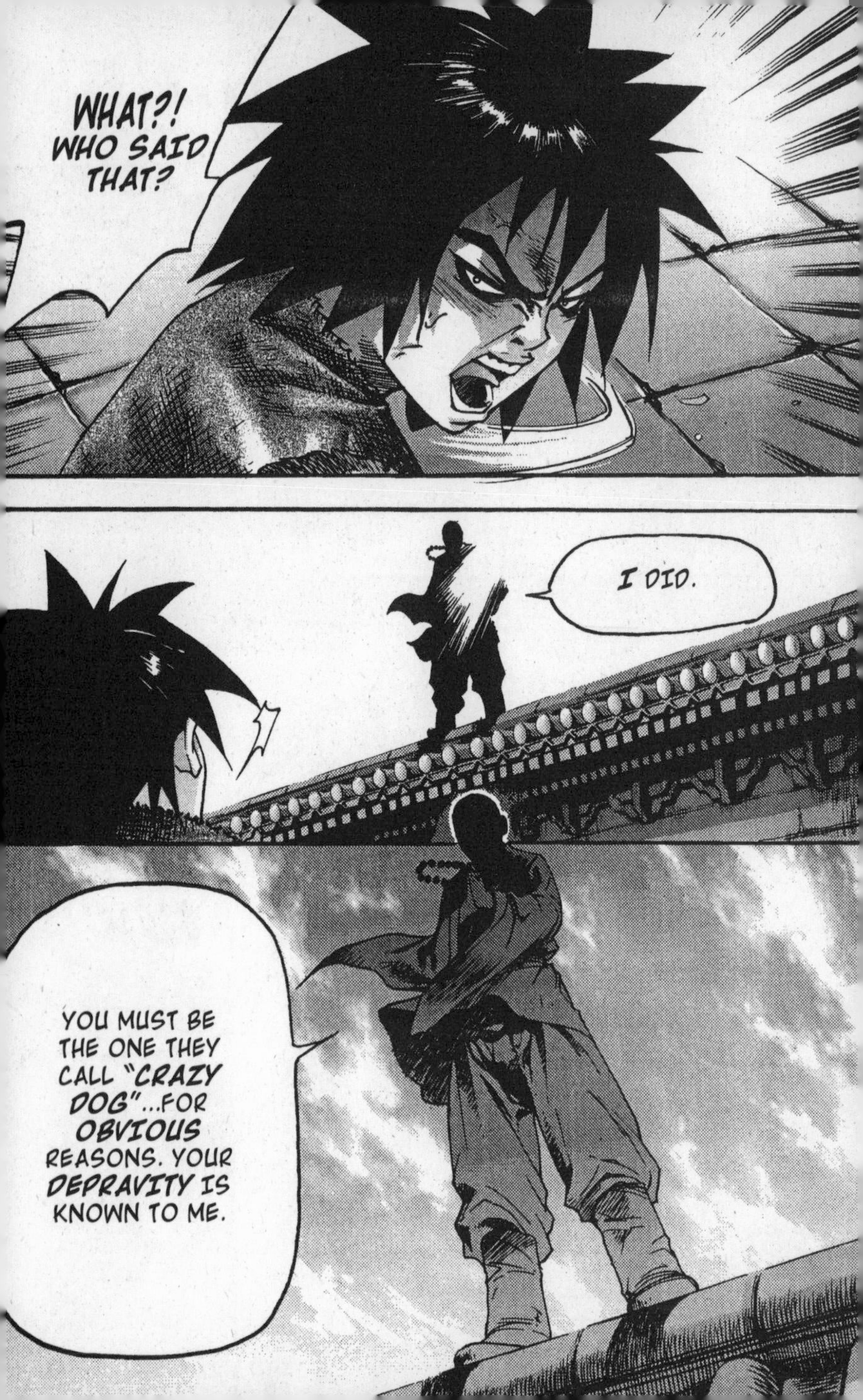
WHAT?! WHO SAID THAT?
I DID.
YOU MUST BE THE ONE THEY CALL "CRAZY DOG"...FOR OBVIOUS REASONS. YOUR DEPRAVITY IS KNOWN TO ME.

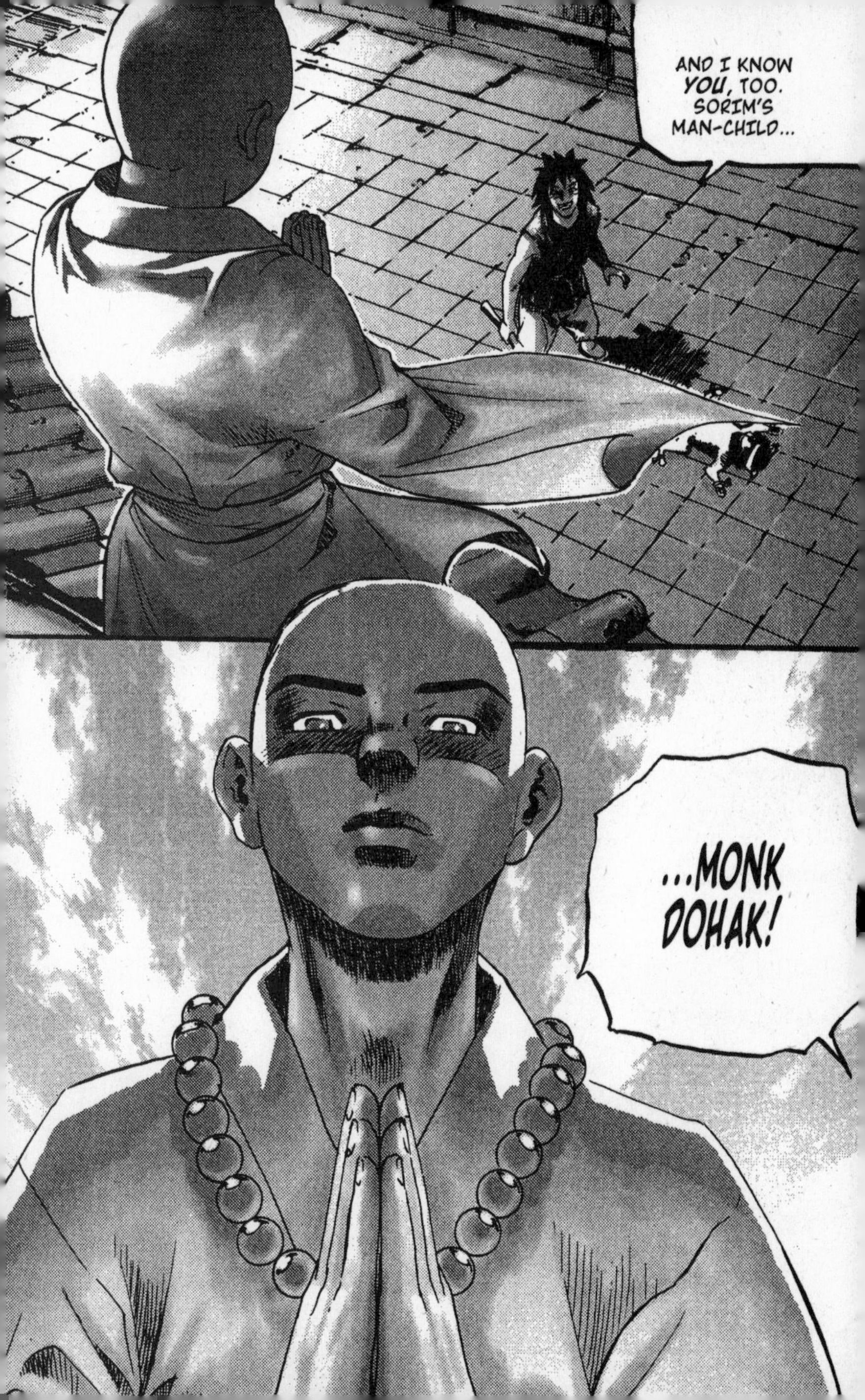
AND I KNOW YOU, TOO. SORIM'S MAN-CHILD...
...MONK DOHAK!

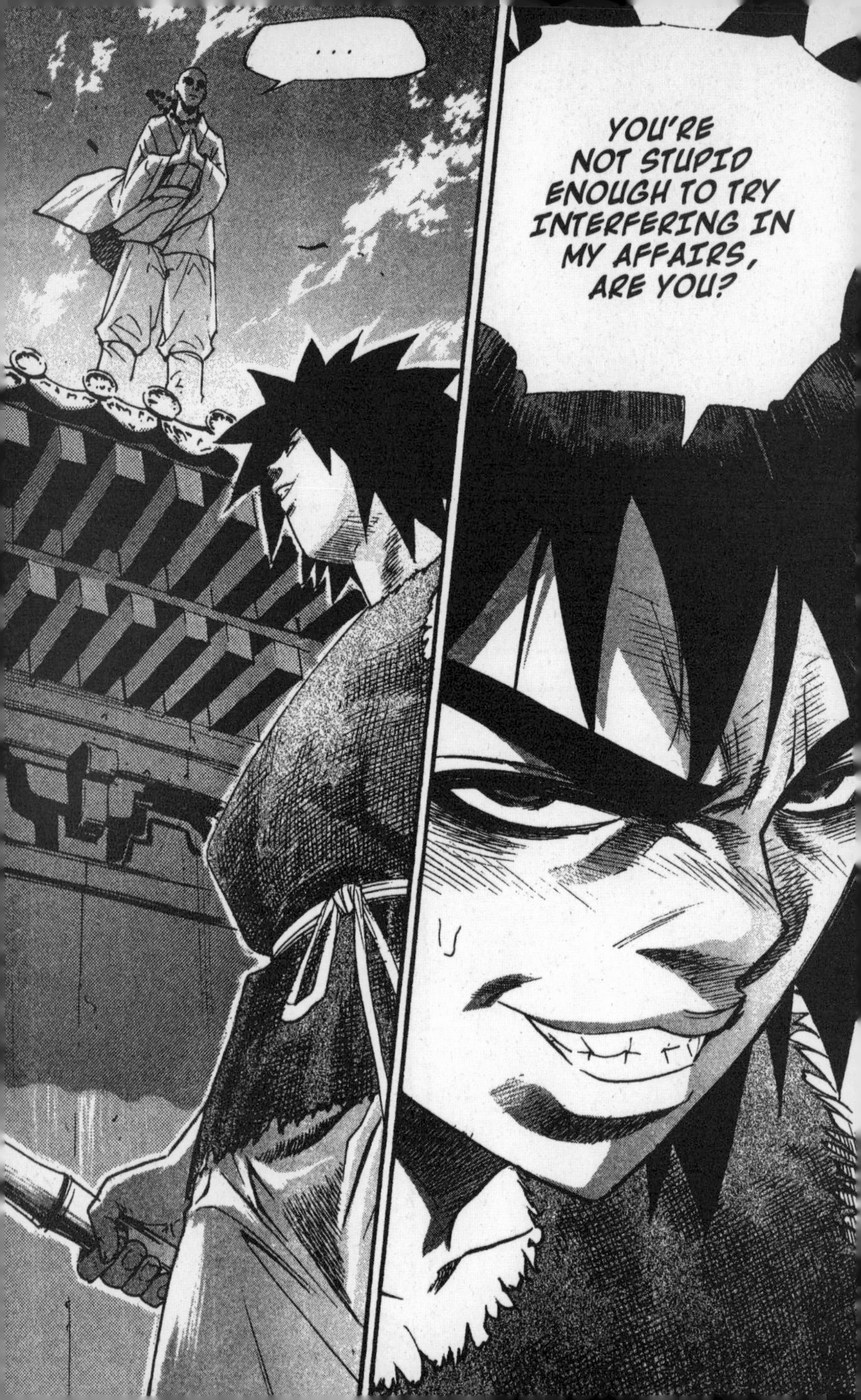
...
YOU'RE NOT STUPID ENOUGH TO TRY INTERFERING IN MY AFFAIRS, ARE YOU?

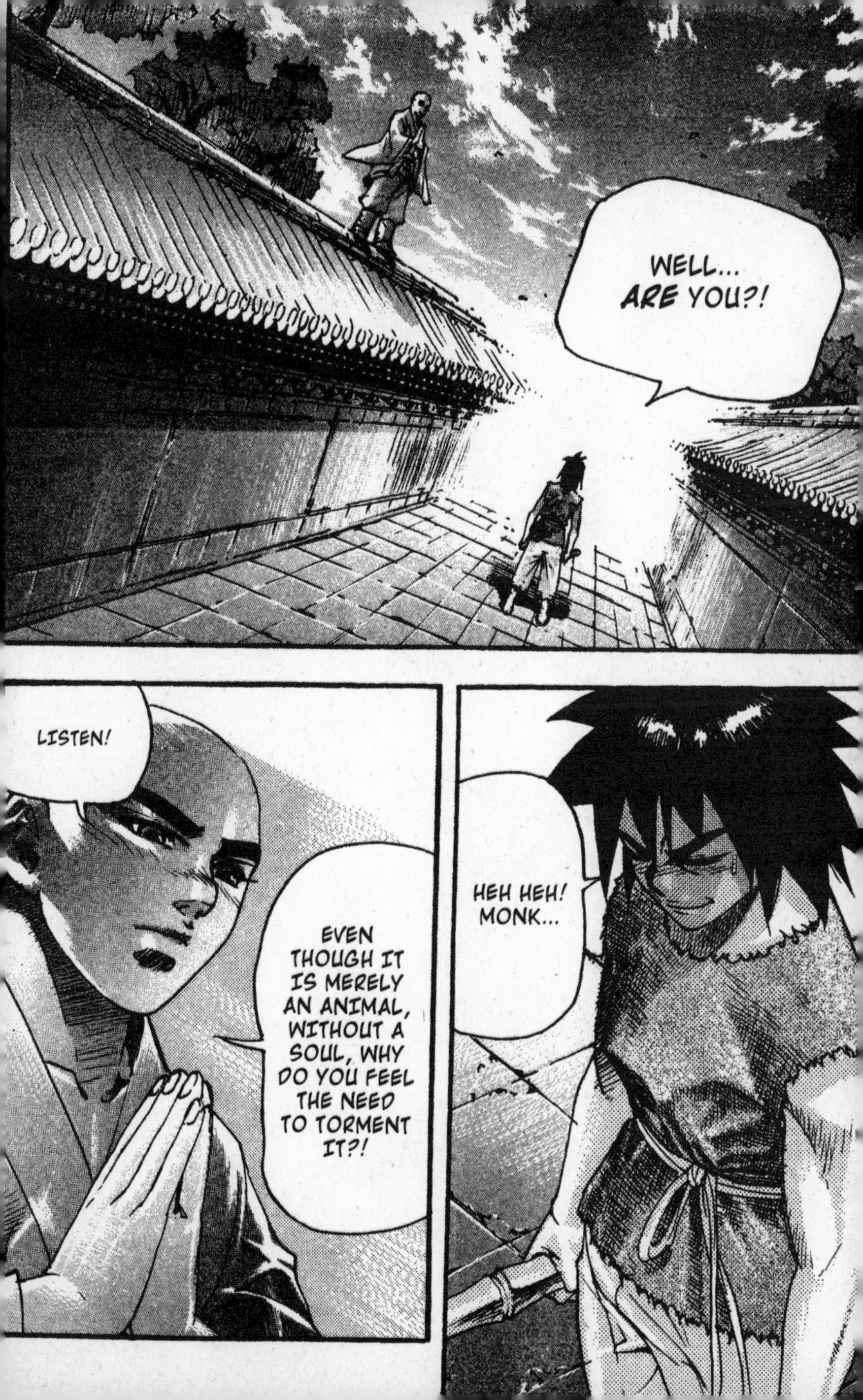
WELL... ARE YOU?!
LISTEN!
EVEN THOUGH IT IS MERELY AN ANIMAL, WITHOUT A SOUL, WHY DO YOU FEEL THE NEED TO TORMENT IT?!
HEH HEH! MONK...

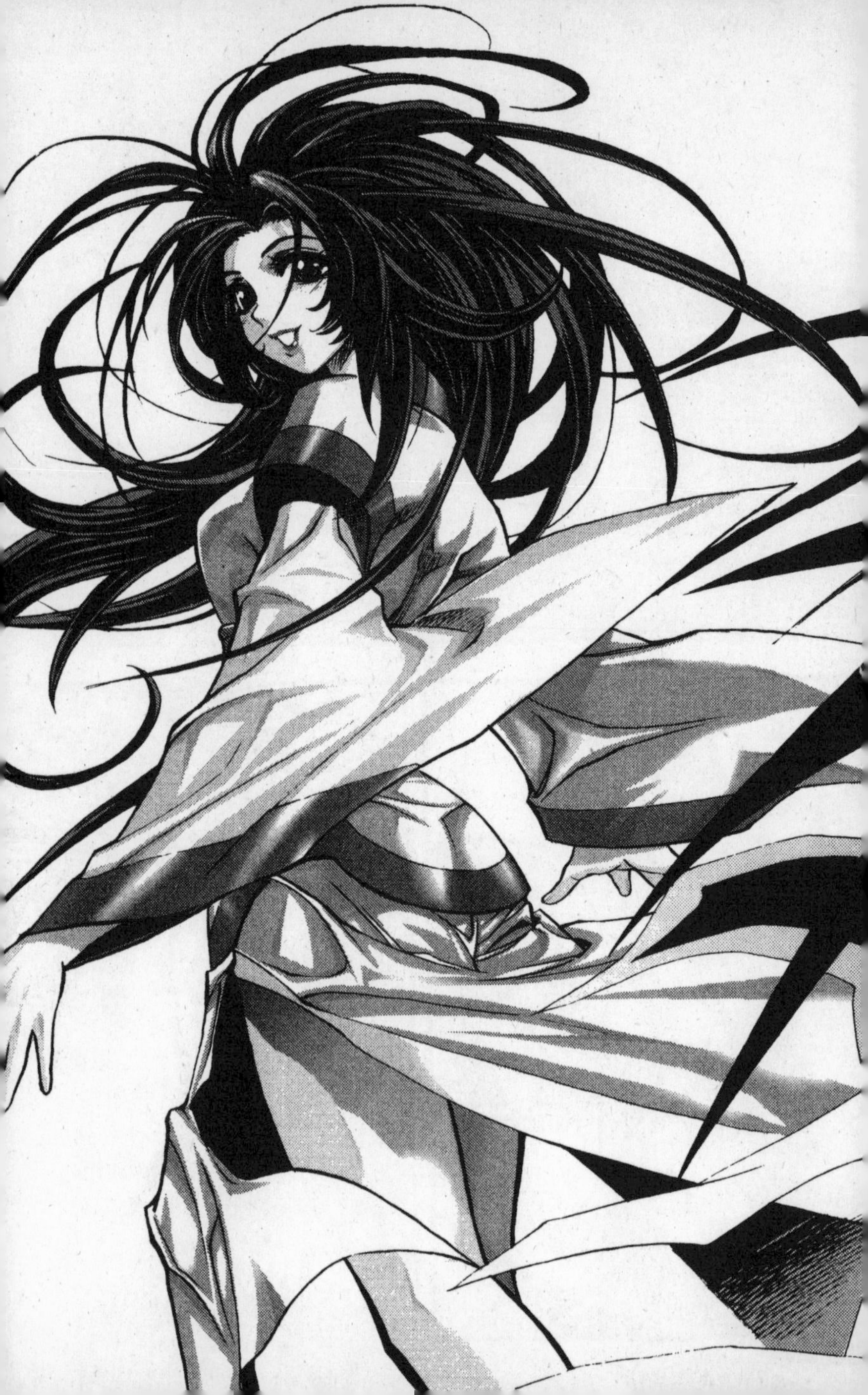

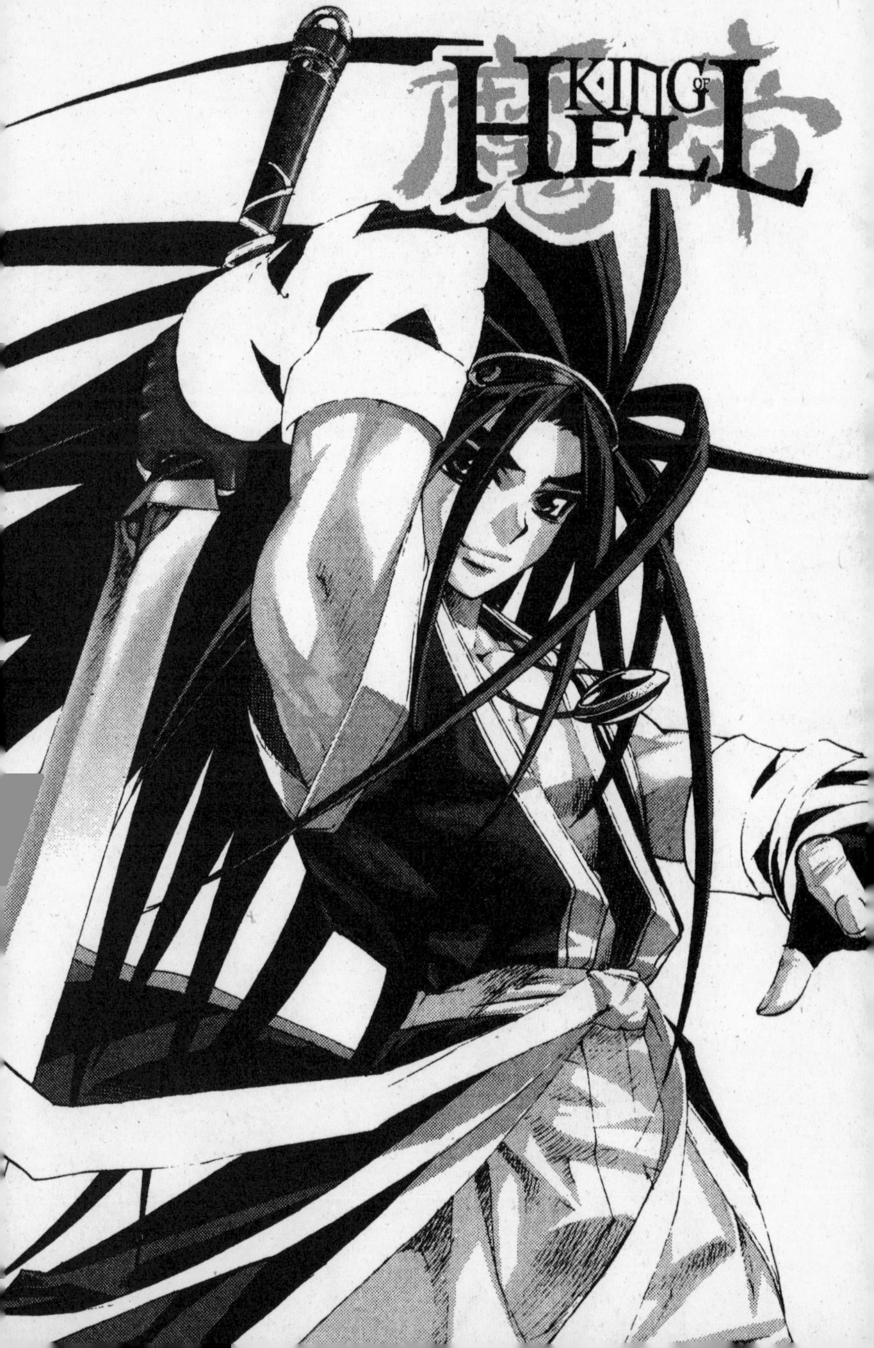
KING OF HELL

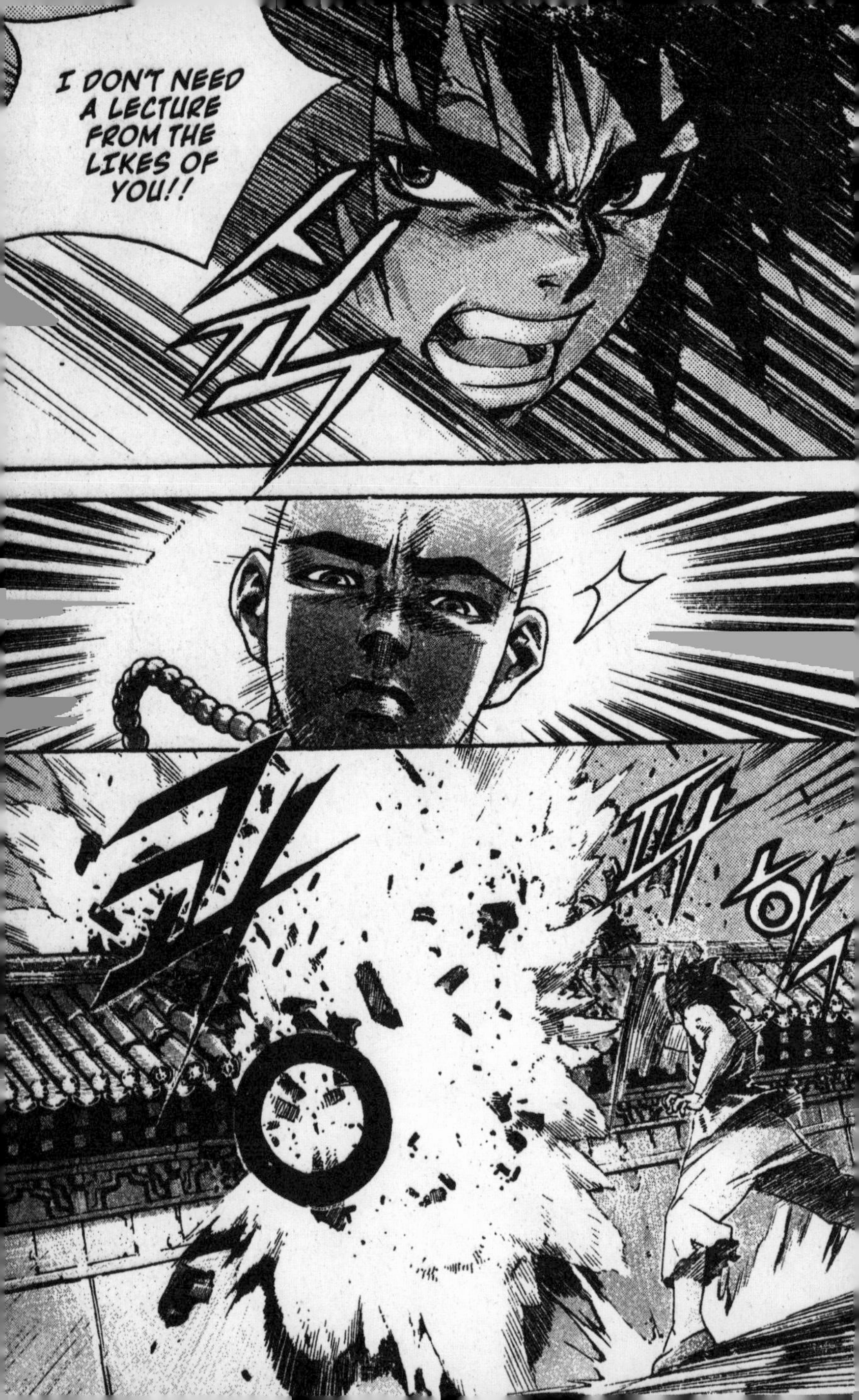
I DON'T NEED A LECTURE FROM THE LIKES OF YOU!!

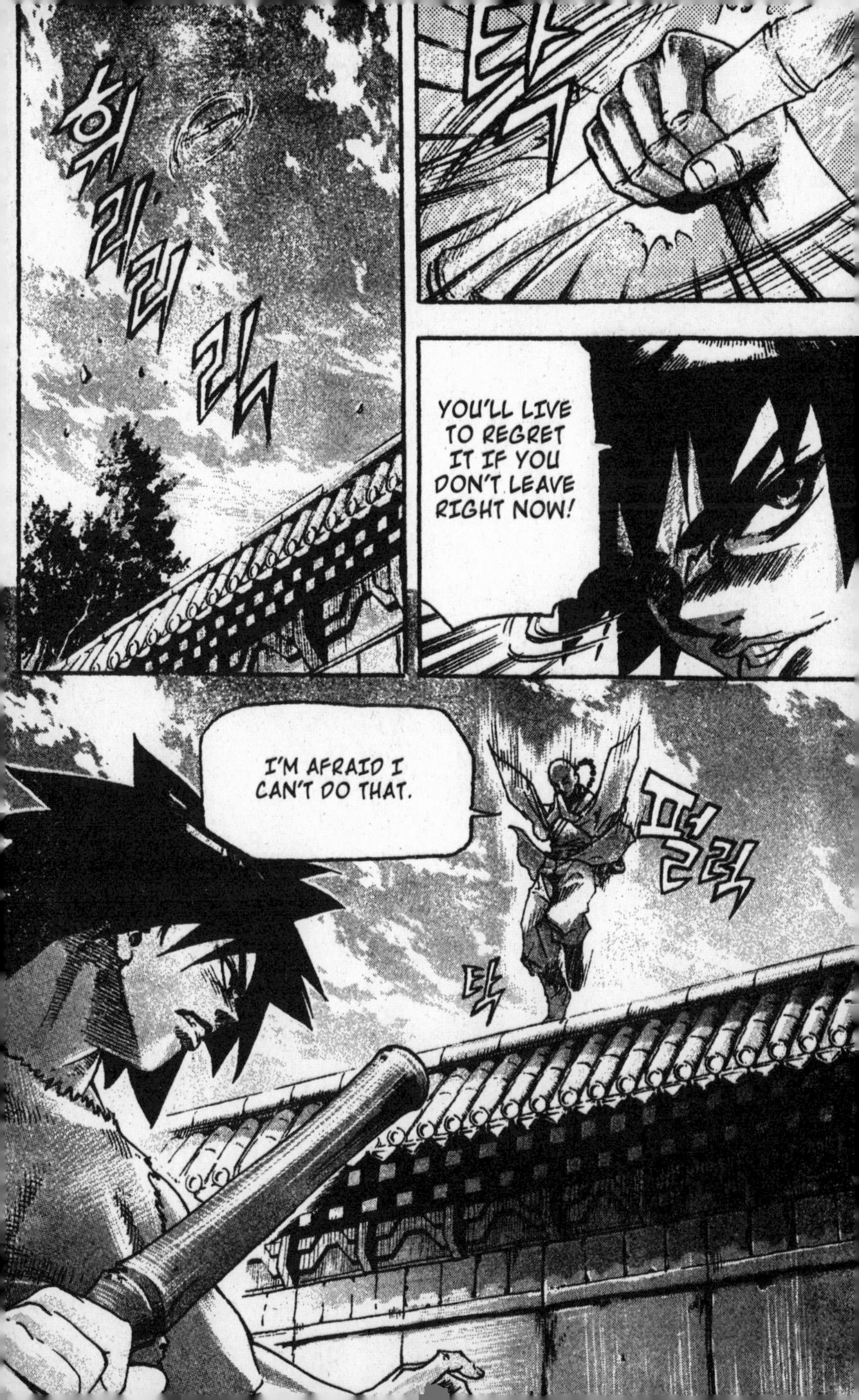
YOU'LL LIVE TO REGRET IT IF YOU DON'T LEAVE RIGHT NOW!
I'M AFRAID I CAN'T DO THAT.

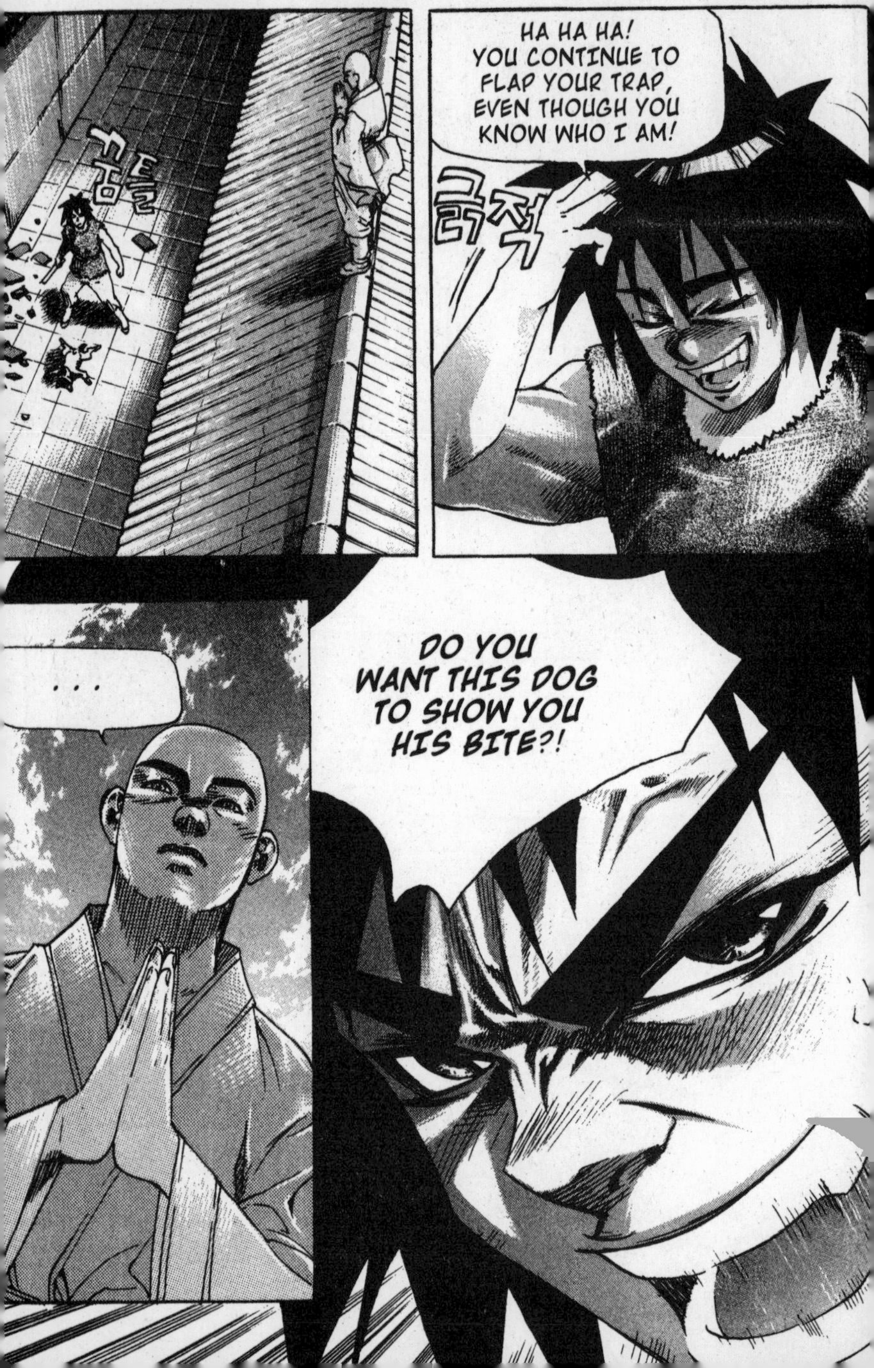
굼틀
HA HA HA! YOU CONTINUE TO FLAP YOUR TRAP, EVEN THOUGH YOU KNOW WHO I AM!
긁적
. . .
DO YOU WANT THIS DOG TO SHOW YOU HIS BITE?!

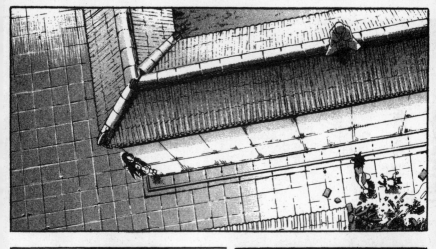

CHUNG POONG! ARE THOSE TWO OF THE MARTIAL ARTS *PRODIGIES* I'VE HEARD ABOUT?

I–I THINK SO.

EH?

SIRS!

WHO... WHO SAID THAT?

PLEASE DON'T BE FRIGHTENED. I AM SPEAKING TO ALL OF YOU THROUGH *TELEPATHY*.

I BESEECH YOU...

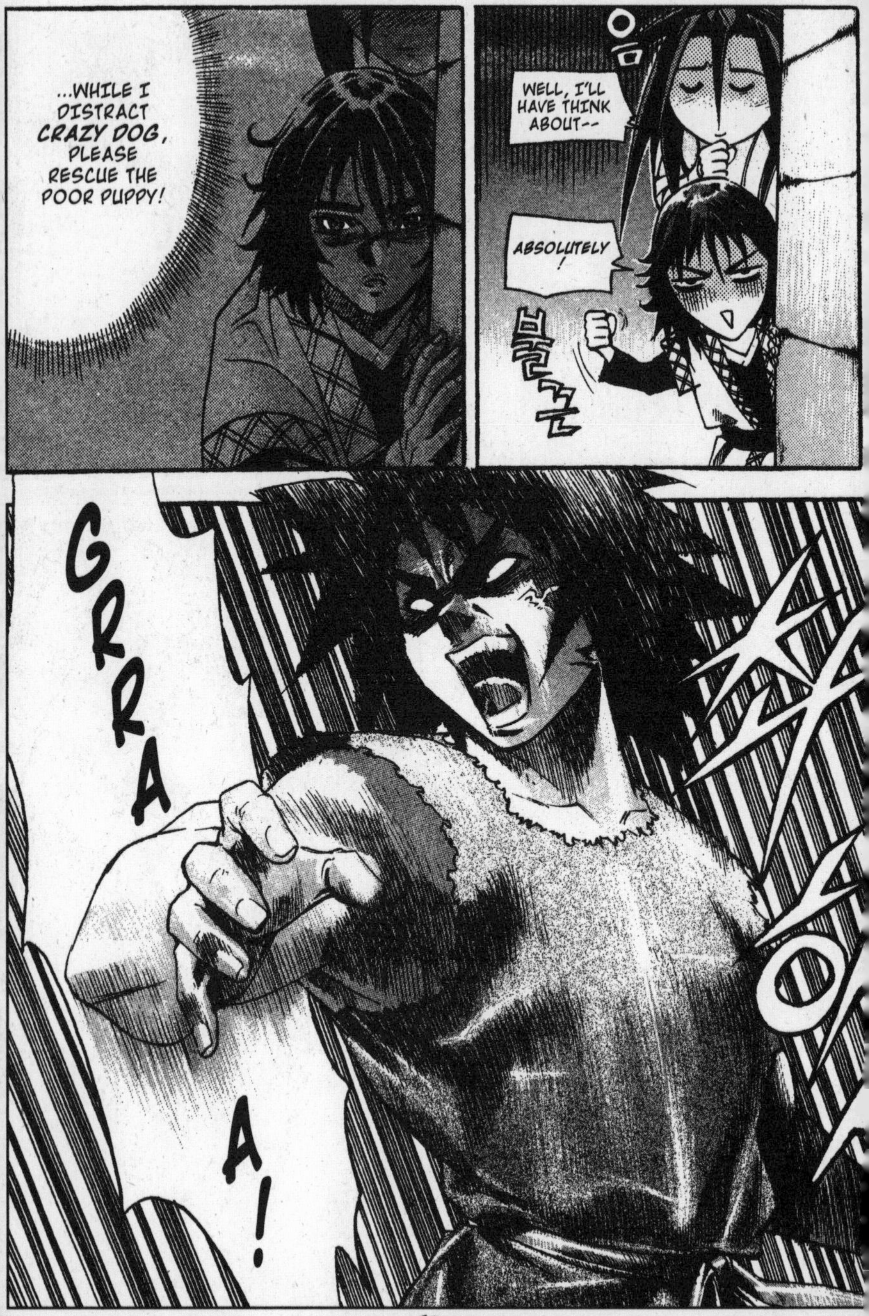
...WHILE I DISTRACT CRAZY DOG, PLEASE RESCUE THE POOR PUPPY!
WELL, I'LL HAVE THINK ABOUT--
ABSOLUTELY!
GRRA
A!

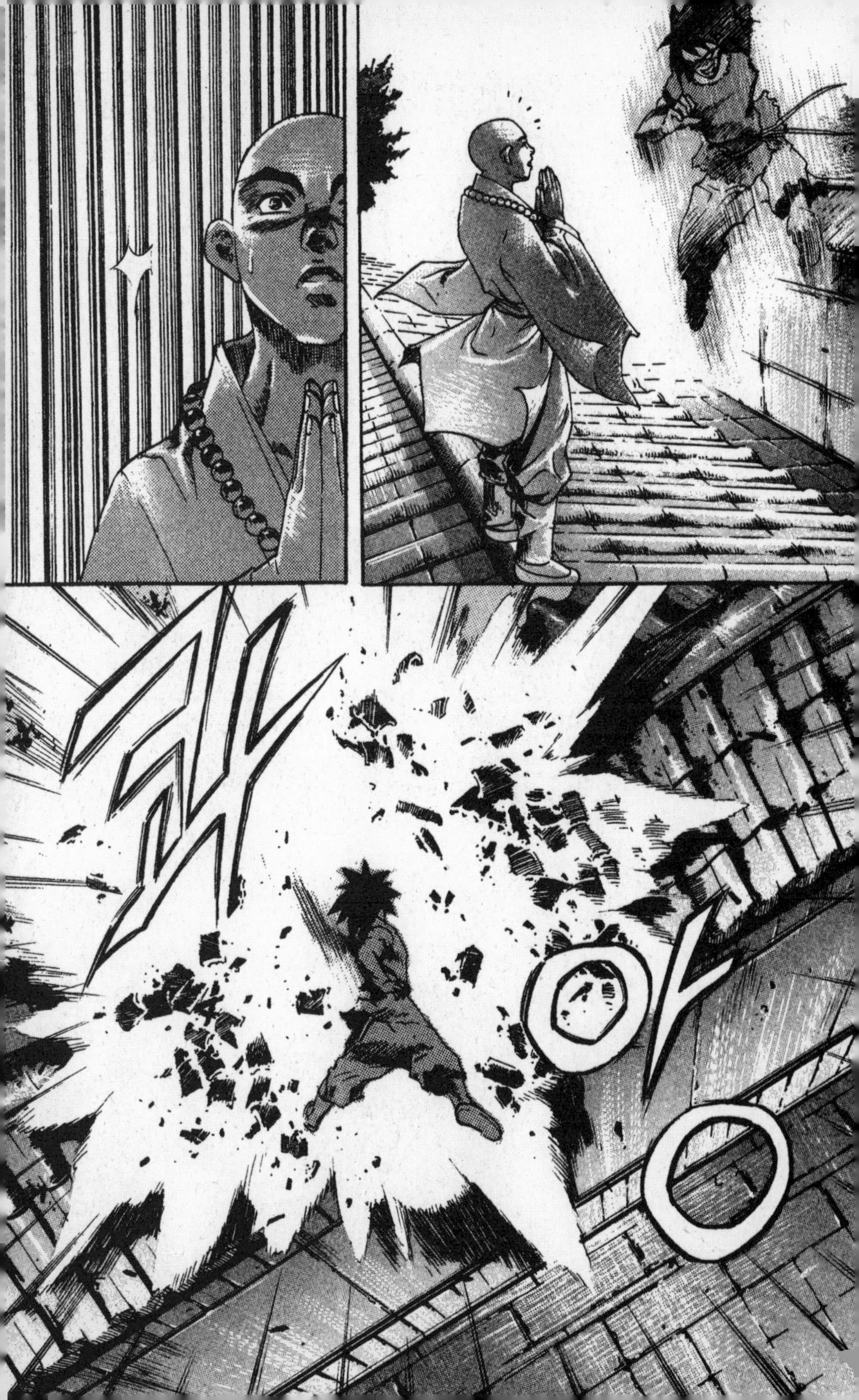

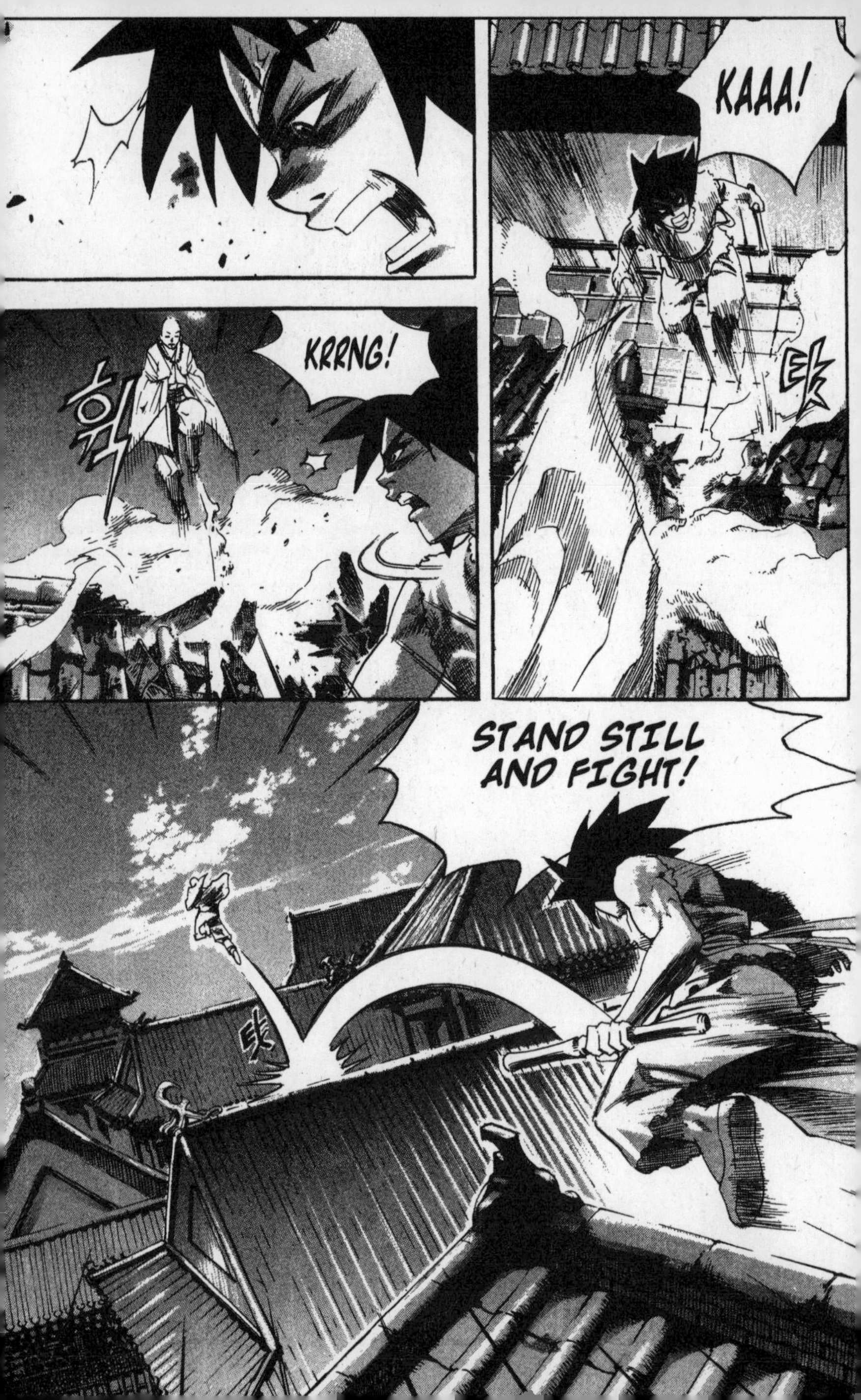
KRRNG!
KAAA!
STAND STILL AND FIGHT!

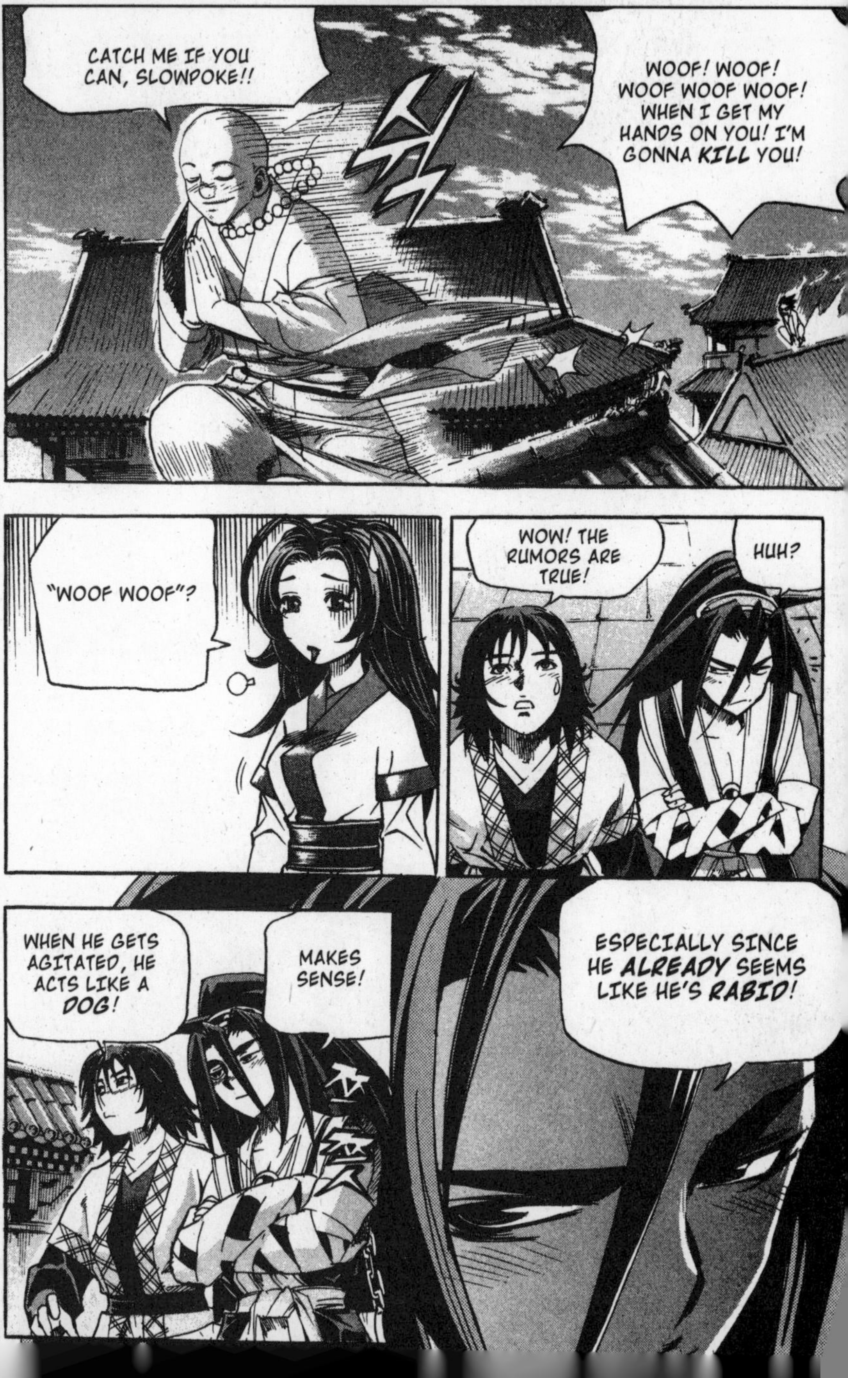
CATCH ME IF YOU CAN, SLOWPOKE!!
WOOF! WOOF! WOOF WOOF WOOF! WHEN I GET MY HANDS ON YOU! I'M GONNA KILL YOU!
"WOOF WOOF"?
WOW! THE RUMORS ARE TRUE!
HUH?
WHEN HE GETS AGITATED, HE ACTS LIKE A DOG!
MAKES SENSE!
ESPECIALLY SINCE HE ALREADY SEEMS LIKE HE'S RABID!

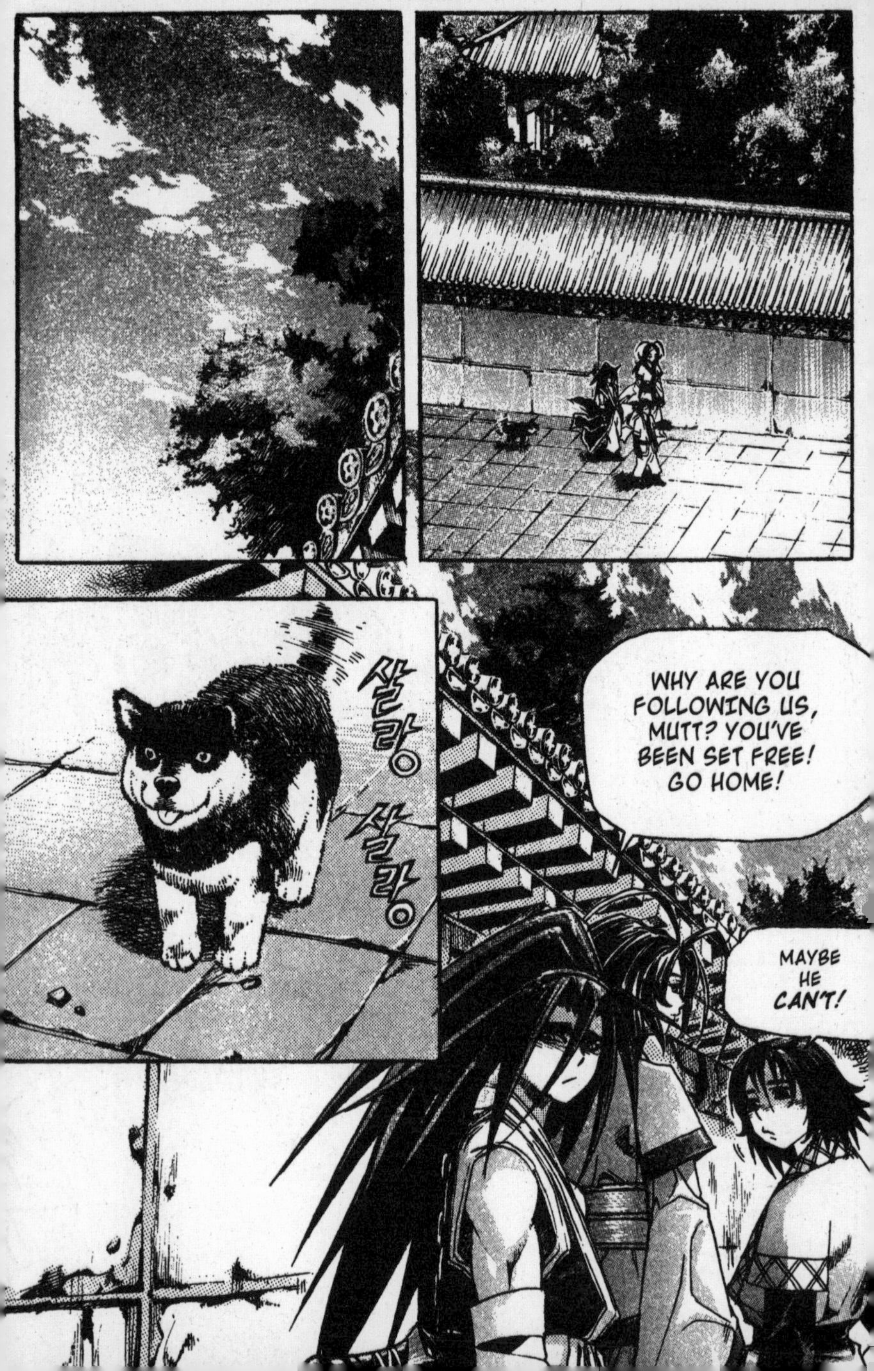
샬랑 샬랑
WHY ARE YOU FOLLOWING US, MUTT? YOU'VE BEEN SET FREE! GO HOME!
MAYBE HE CAN'T!

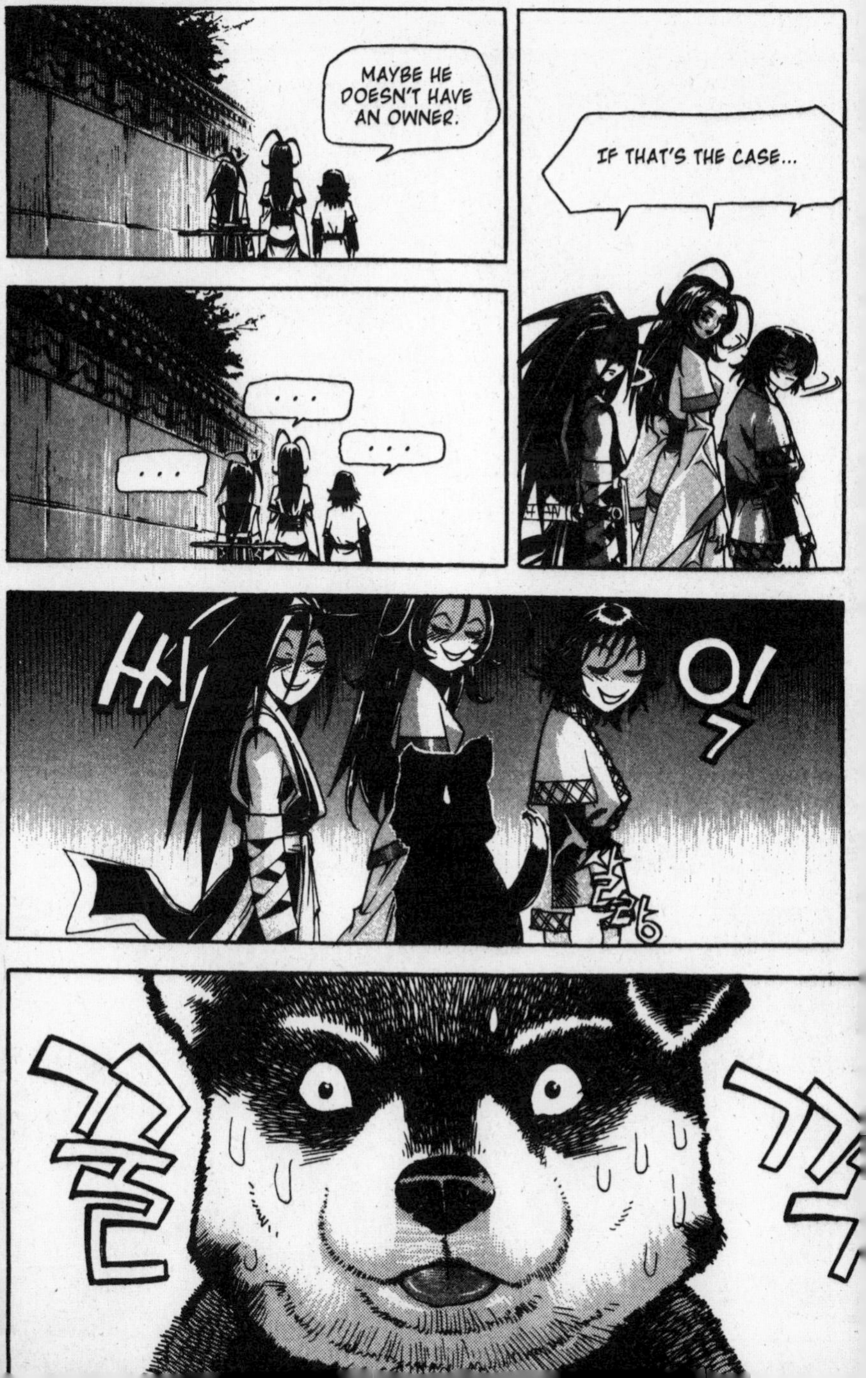

MAYBE HE DOESN'T HAVE AN OWNER.
...
...
...
IF THAT'S THE CASE...
씨익

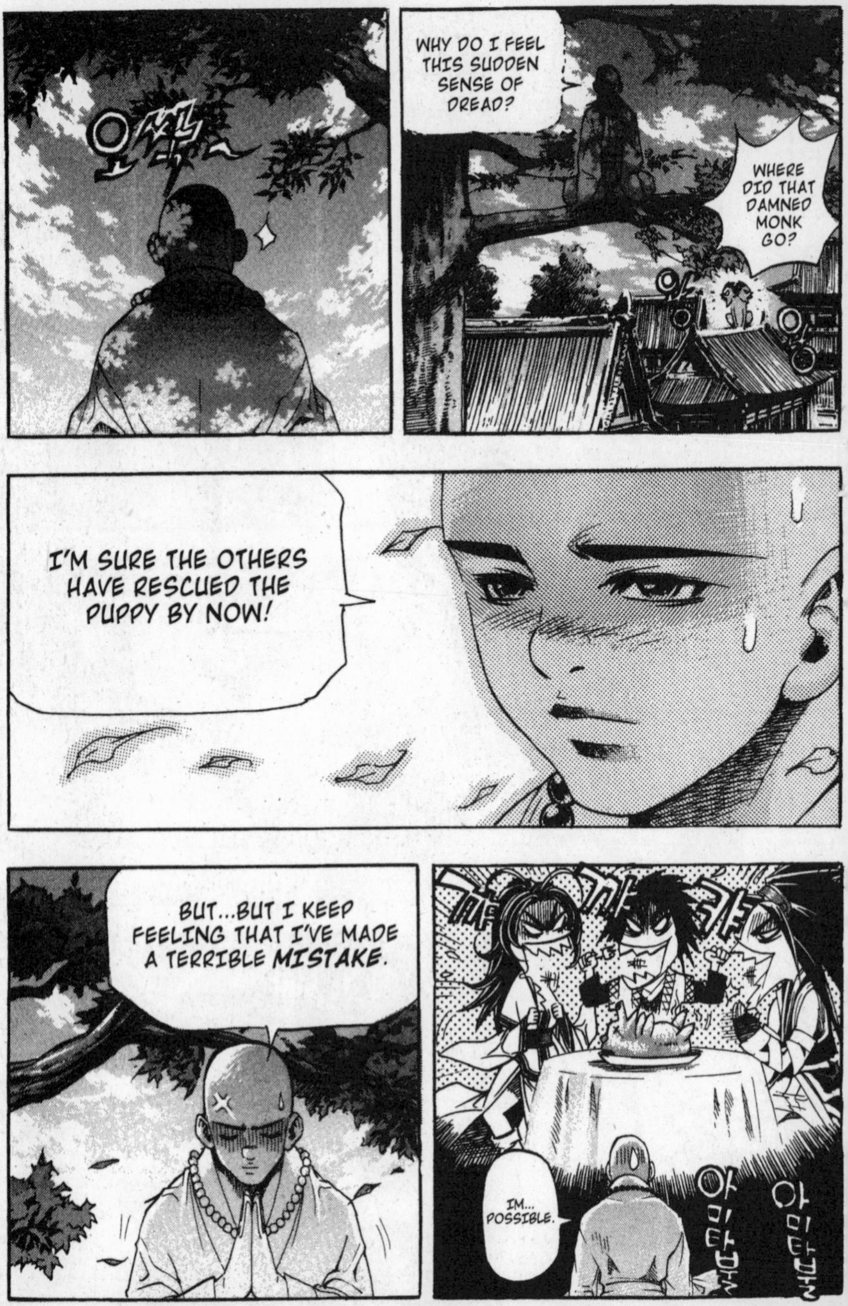
오싹
WHY DO I FEEL THIS SUDDEN SENSE OF DREAD?
WHERE DID THAT DAMNED MONK GO?
I'M SURE THE OTHERS HAVE RESCUED THE PUPPY BY NOW!
BUT...BUT I KEEP FEELING THAT I'VE MADE A TERRIBLE MISTAKE.
IM... POSSIBLE.
아미타불
아미타불

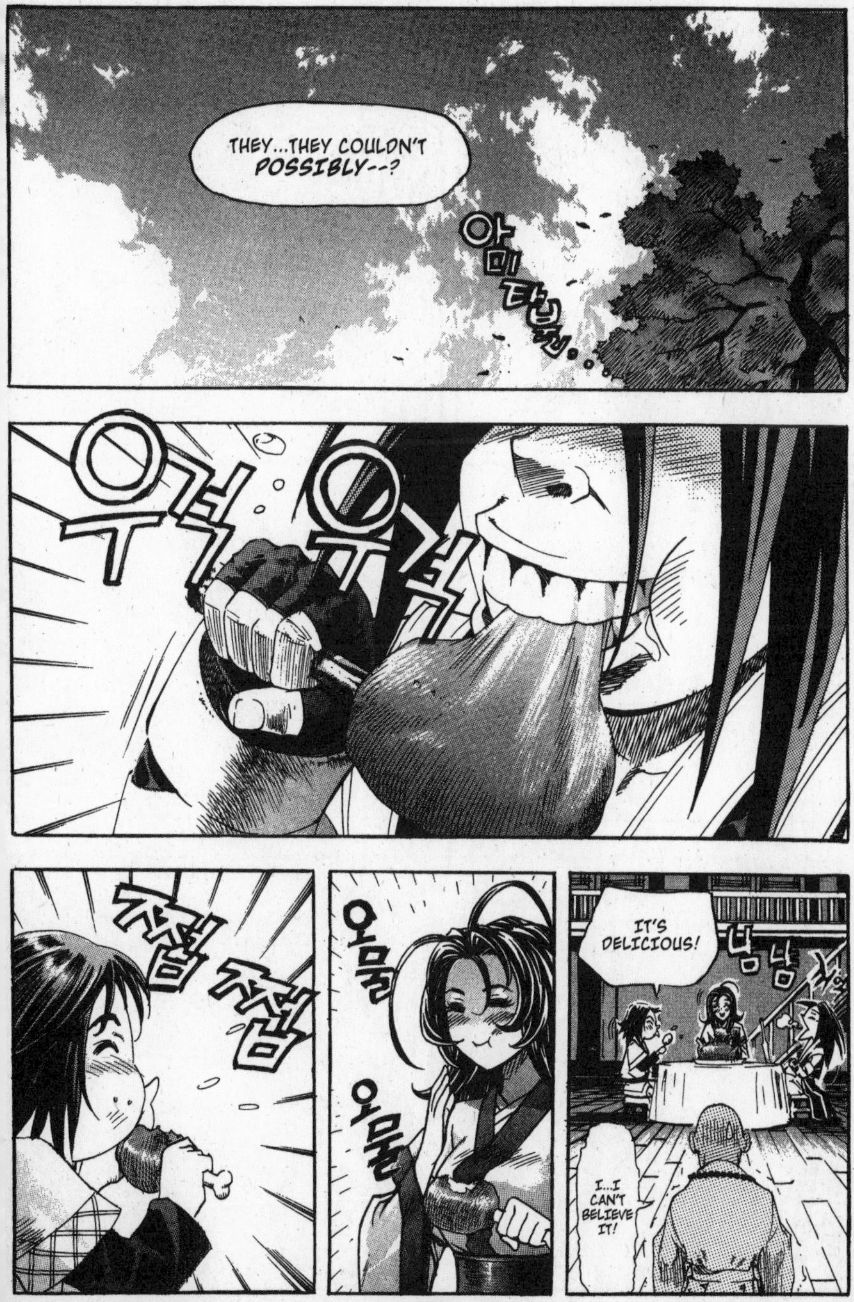

THEY...THEY COULDN'T POSSIBLY--?
오물
오물
IT'S DELICIOUS!
냠냠
I...I CAN'T BELIEVE IT!

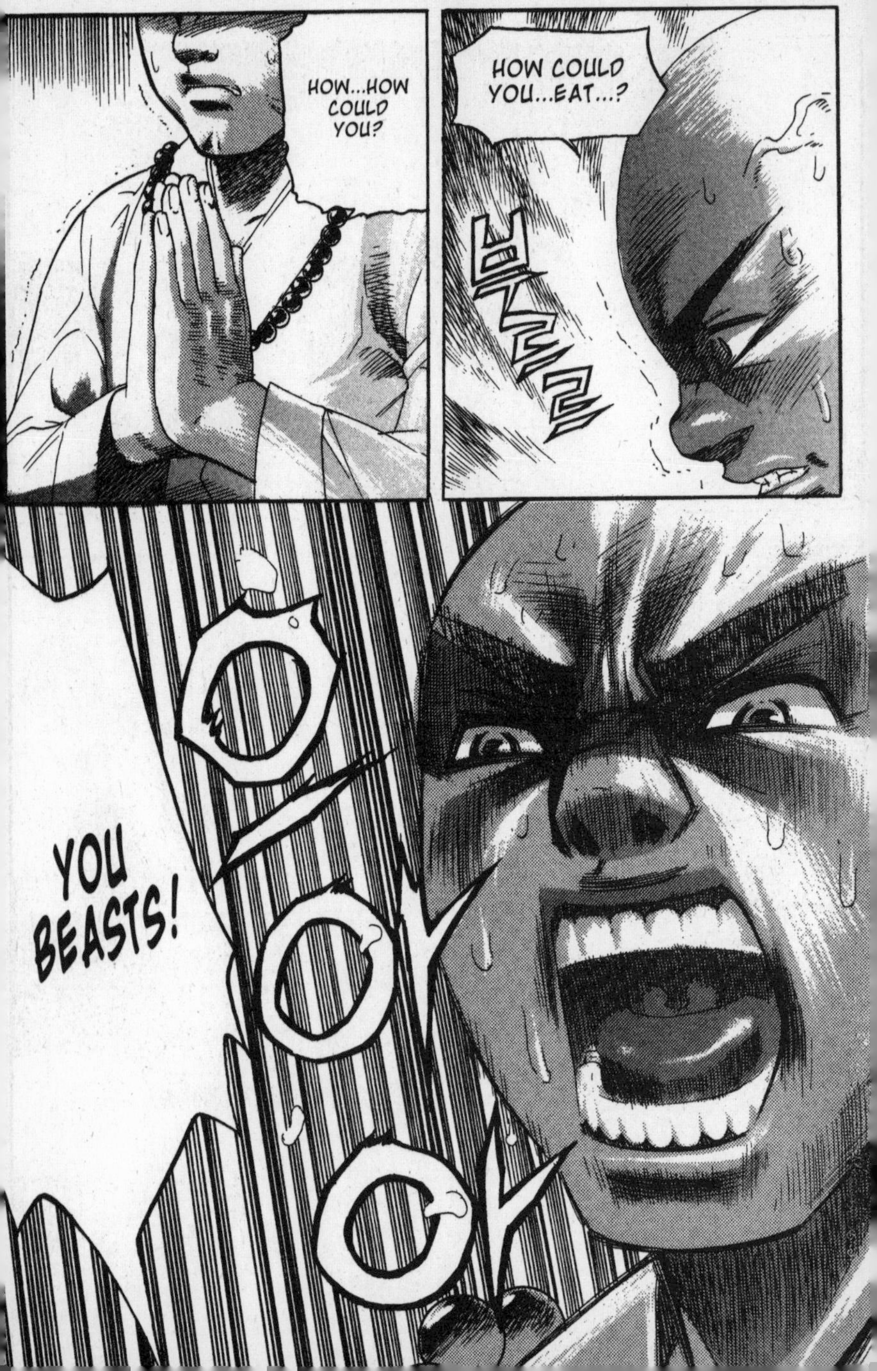
HOW...HOW COULD YOU?
HOW COULD YOU...EAT...?
YOU BEASTS!
OOO

YOU SLAUGHTERED AND ATE THAT HELPLESS ANIMAL!

YOU BASTAR-- EH?!

? ? ? ....

AHK!

?

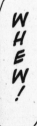

WHEW!

... ...

THAT MONK IS A LITTLE OFF KILTER, TOO!

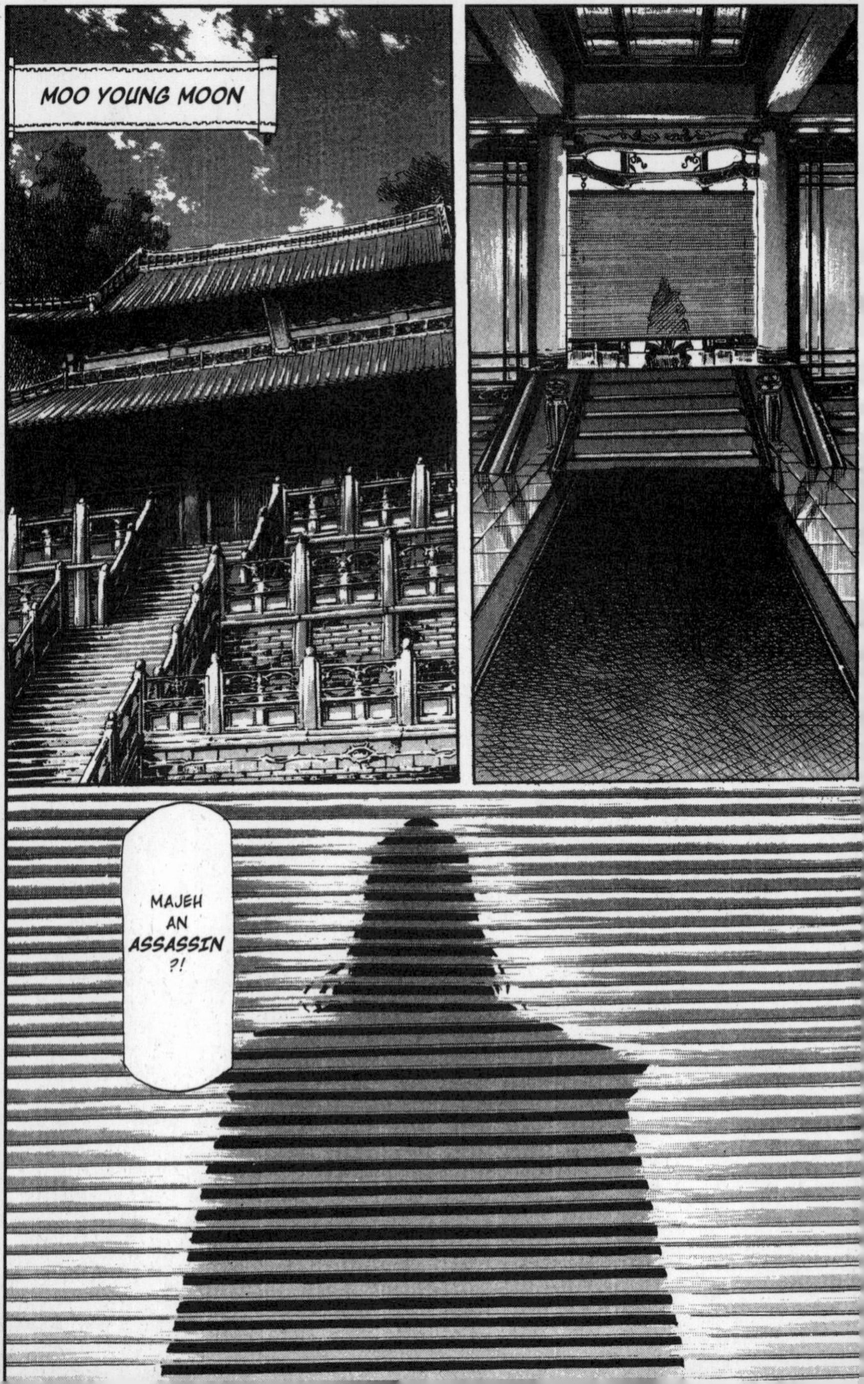
MOO YOUNG MOON
MAJEH AN ASSASSIN ?!

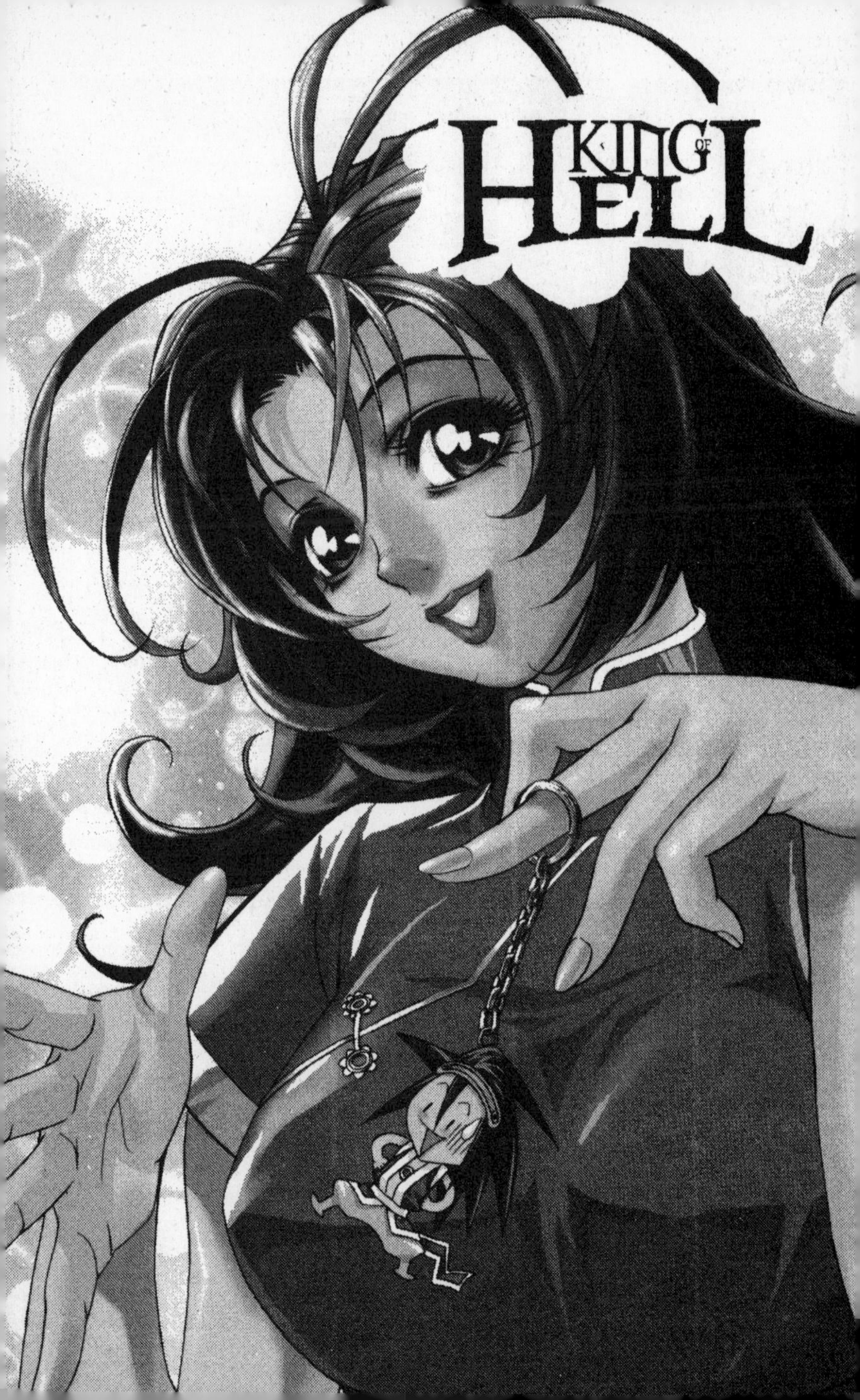
KING OF HELL

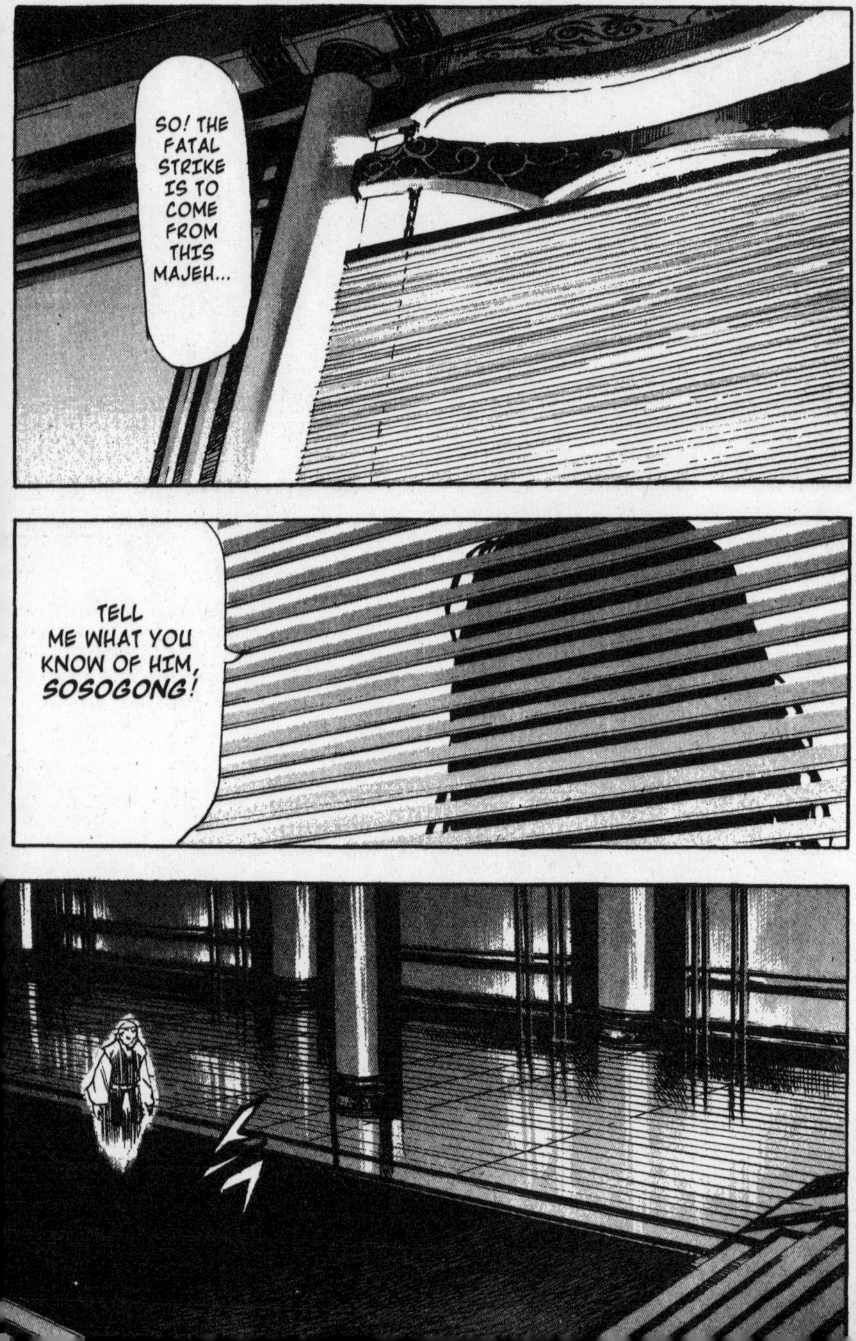
SO! THE FATAL STRIKE IS TO COME FROM THIS MAJEH...
TELL ME WHAT YOU KNOW OF HIM, SOSOGONG!

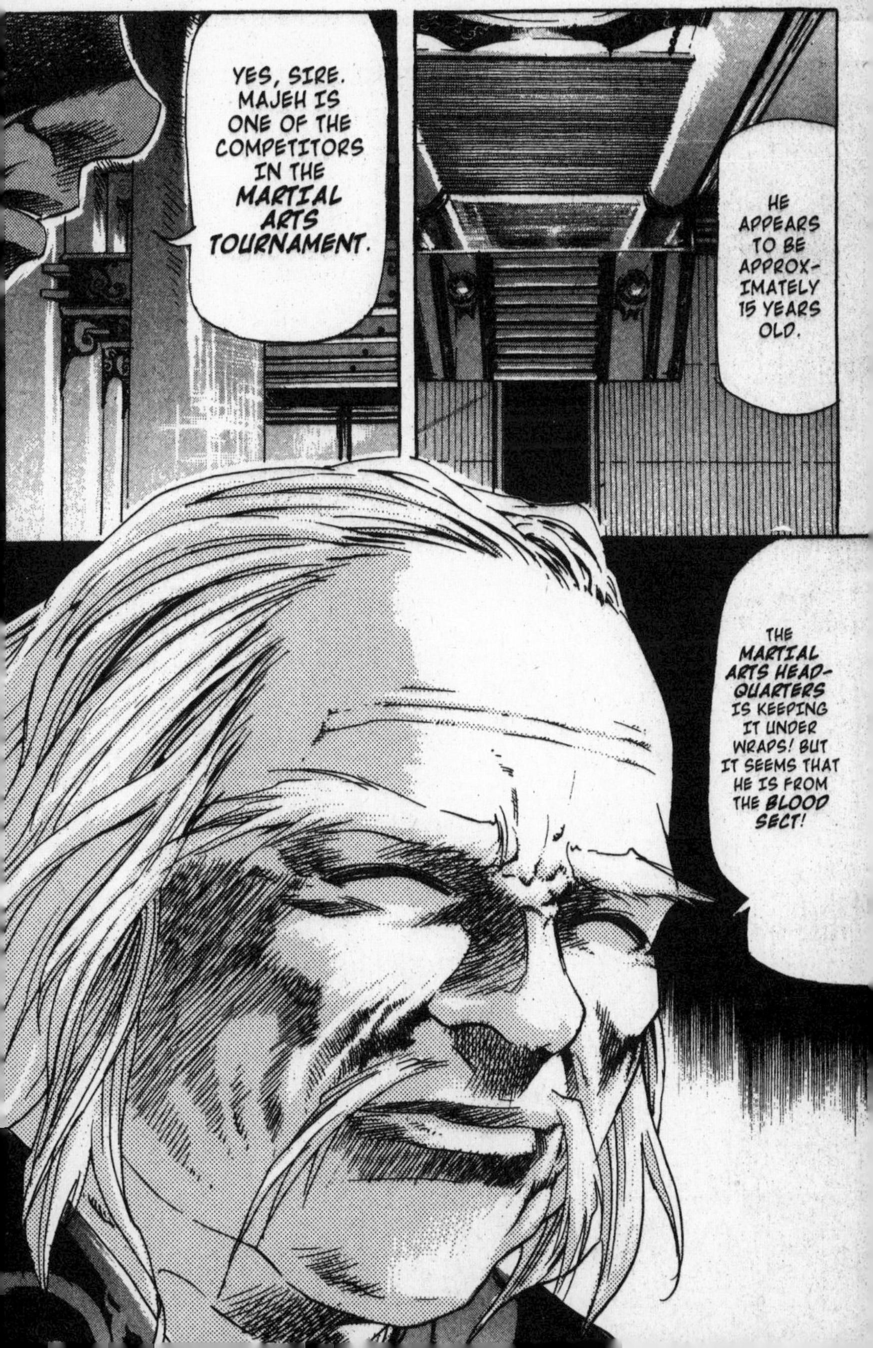
YES, SIRE. MAJEH IS ONE OF THE COMPETITORS IN THE MARTIAL ARTS TOURNAMENT.
HE APPEARS TO BE APPROX-IMATELY 15 YEARS OLD.
THE MARTIAL ARTS HEAD-QUARTERS IS KEEPING IT UNDER WRAPS! BUT IT SEEMS THAT HE IS FROM THE BLOOD SECT!

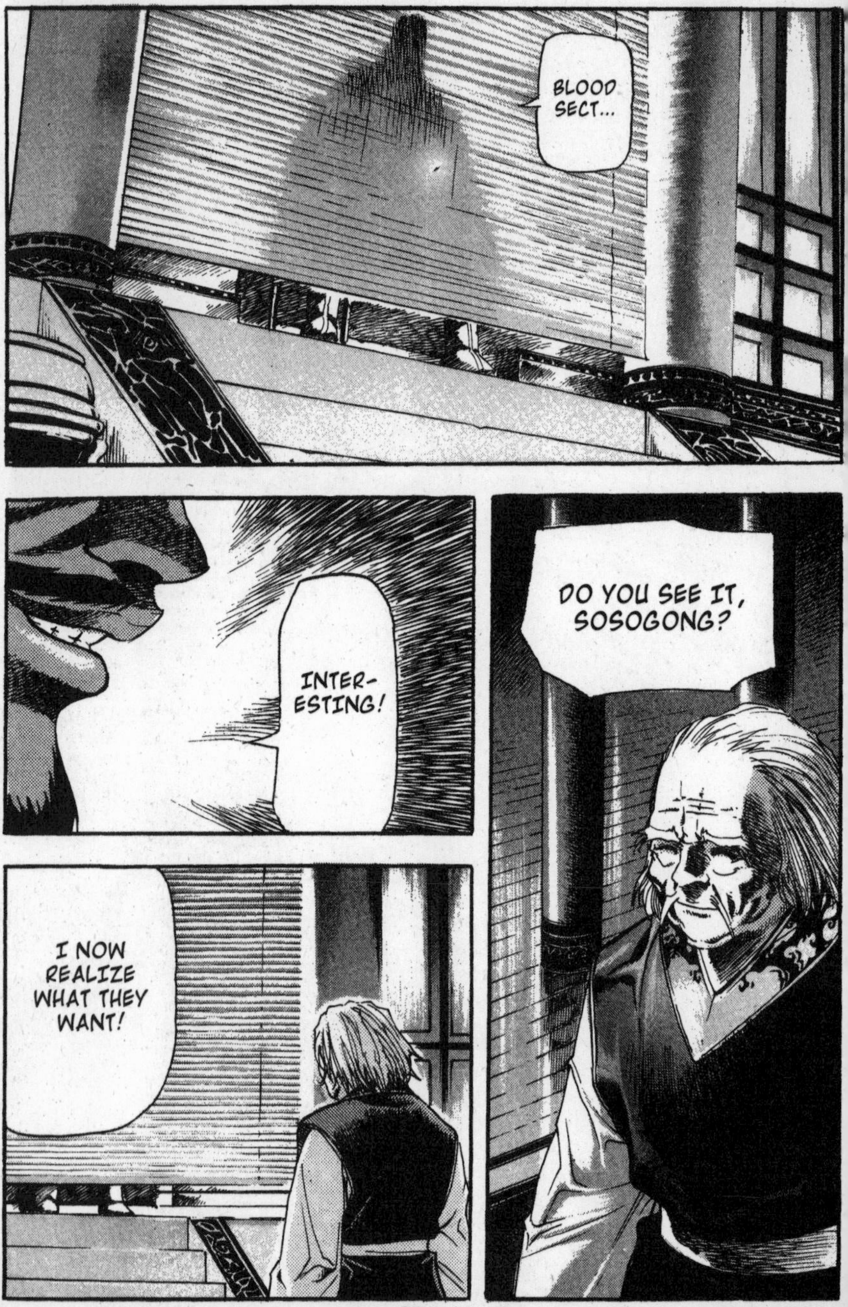
BLOOD SECT...
INTER-ESTING!
I NOW REALIZE WHAT THEY WANT!
DO YOU SEE IT, SOSOGONG?

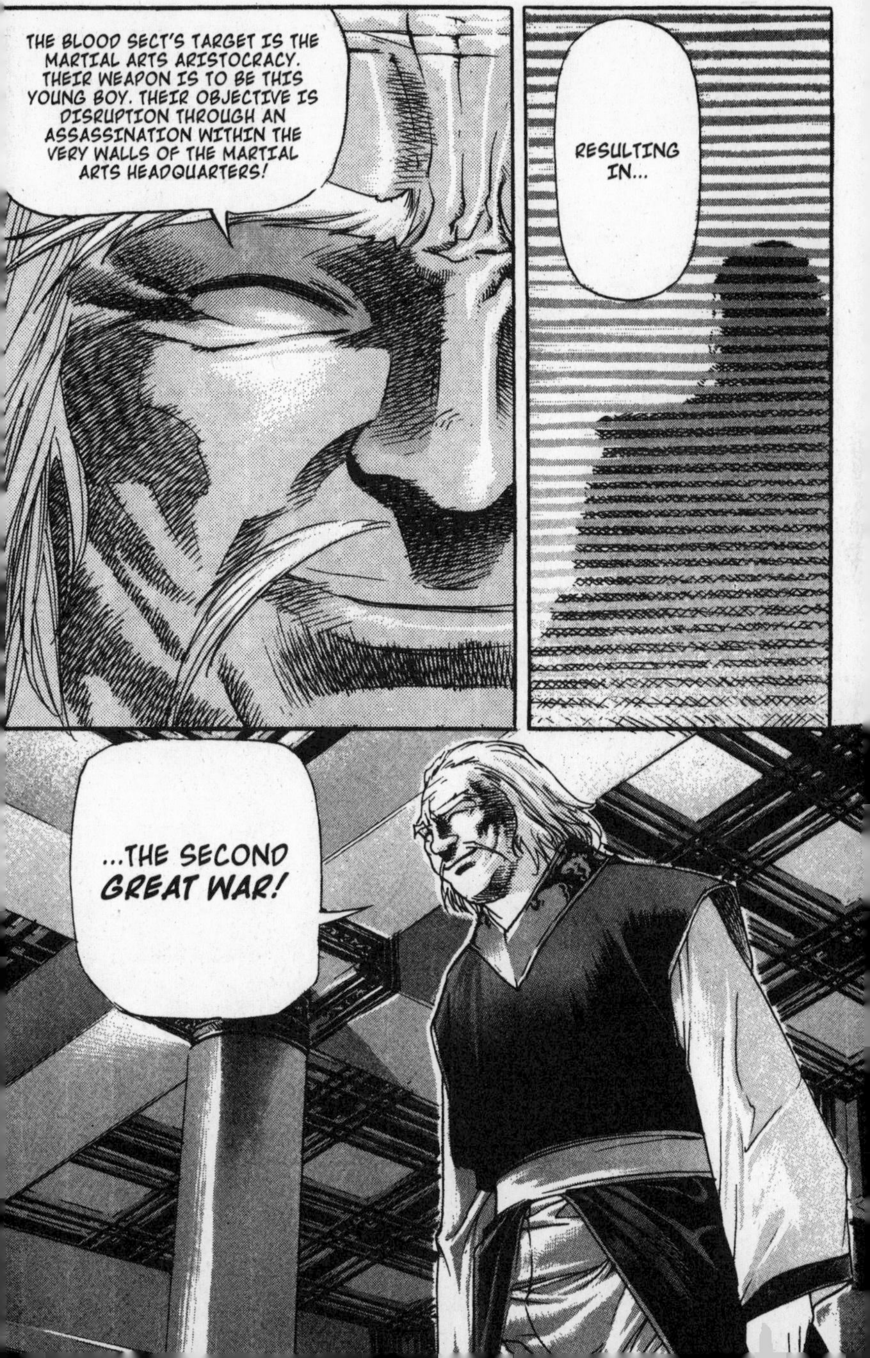
THE BLOOD SECT'S TARGET IS THE MARTIAL ARTS ARISTOCRACY. THEIR WEAPON IS TO BE THIS YOUNG BOY. THEIR OBJECTIVE IS DISRUPTION THROUGH AN ASSASSINATION WITHIN THE VERY WALLS OF THE MARTIAL ARTS HEADQUARTERS!
RESULTING IN...
...THE SECOND GREAT WAR!

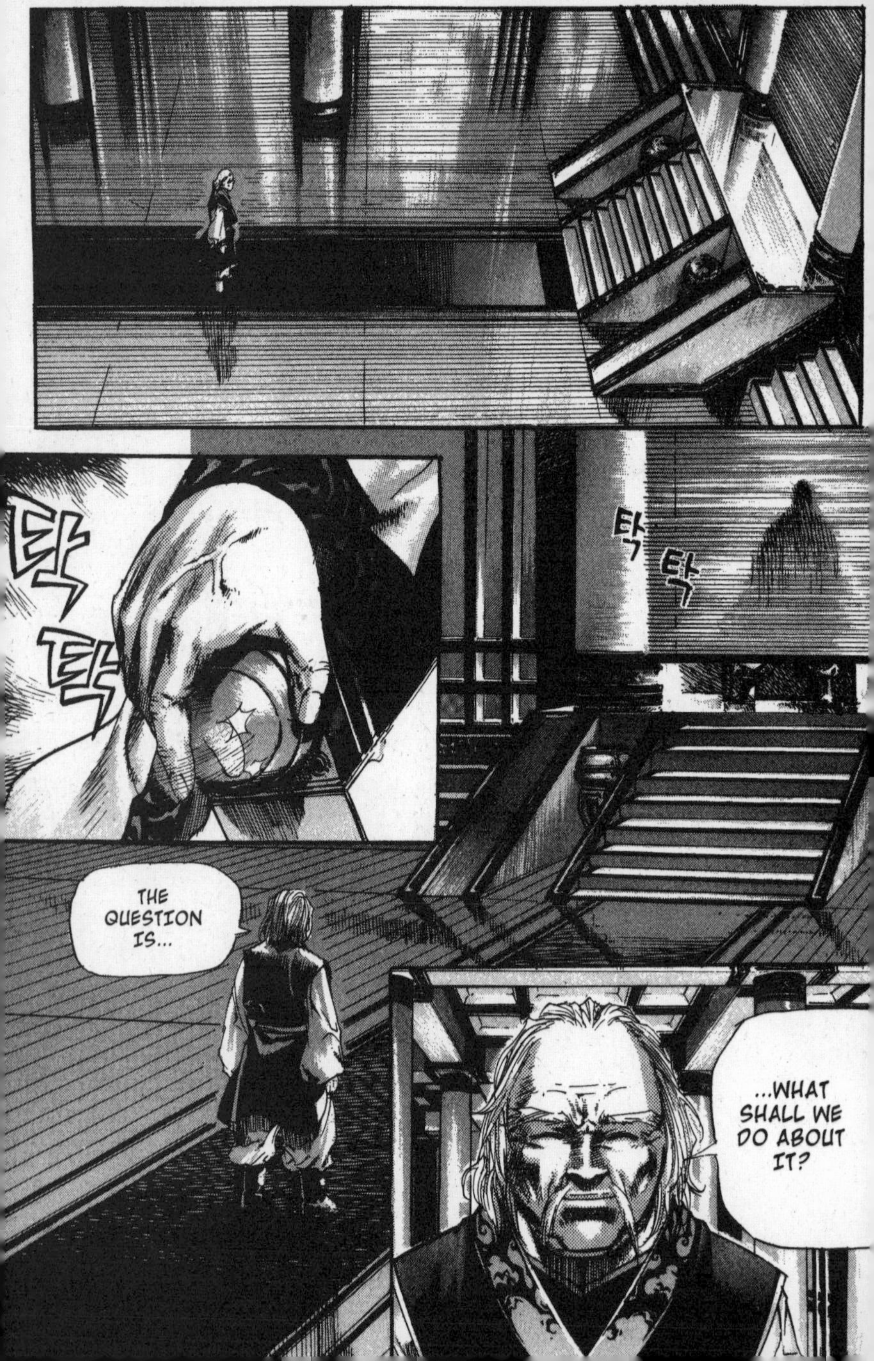
탁
탁
탁
탁
THE QUESTION IS...
...WHAT SHALL WE DO ABOUT IT?

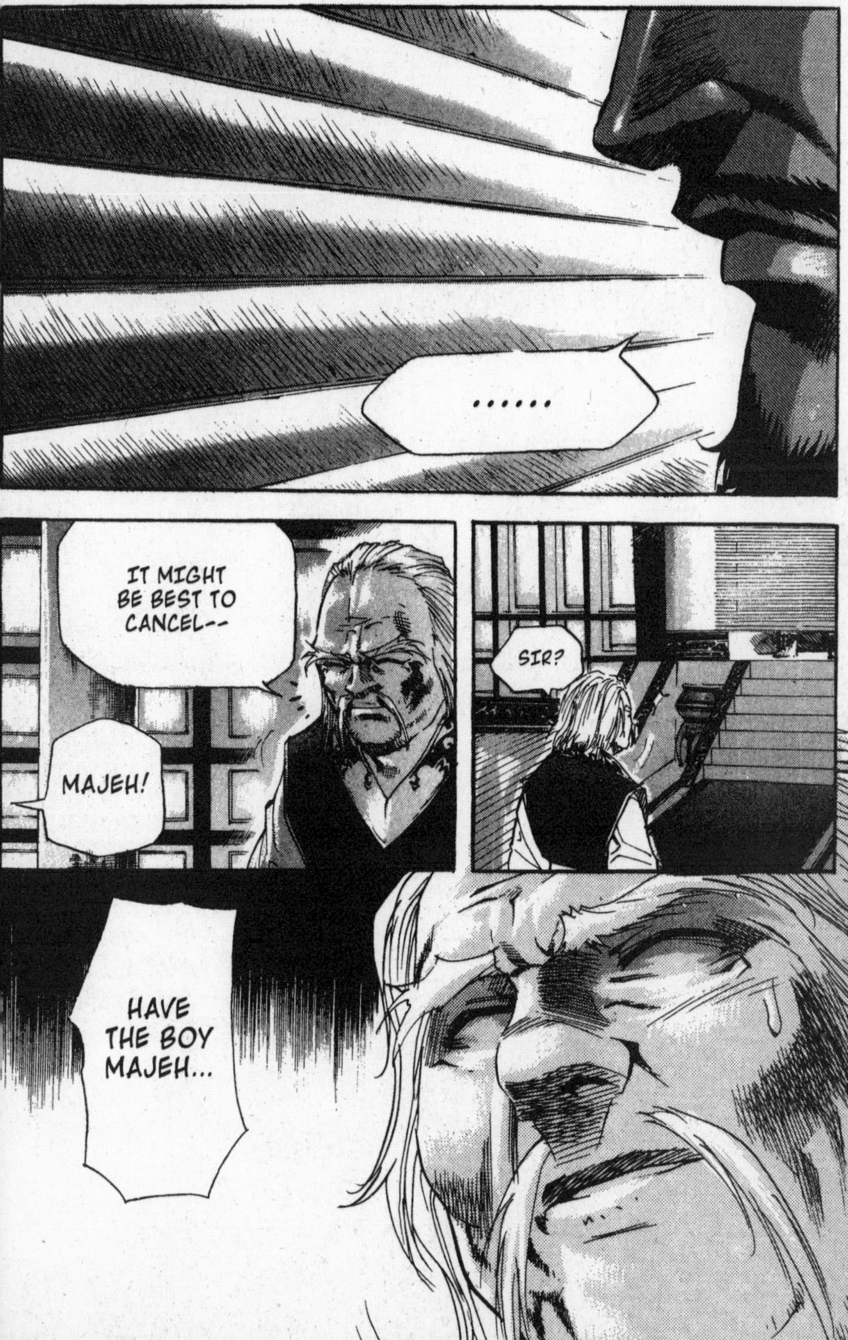
......
IT MIGHT BE BEST TO CANCEL--
MAJEH!
SIR?
HAVE THE BOY MAJEH...

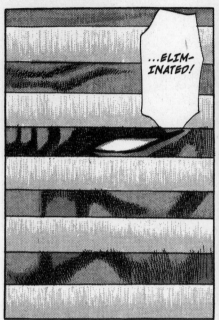

...ELIM-
INATED!

AS
YOU
COM-
MAND!

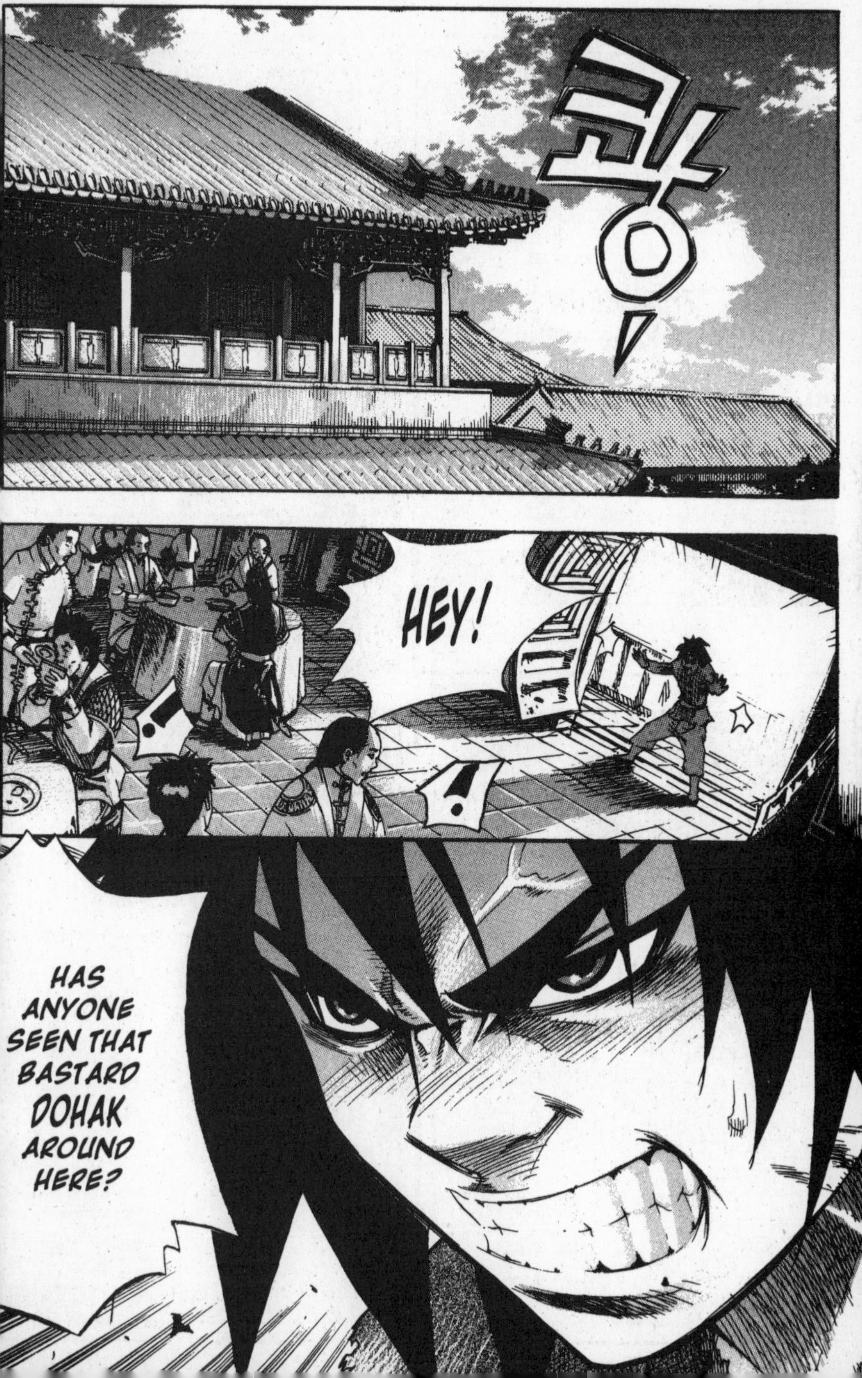

쾅
HEY!
HAS ANYONE SEEN THAT BASTARD DOHAK AROUND HERE?

WOW! THIS PUPPY MUST HAVE BEEN *REALLY* HUNGRY!

THAT DOG...

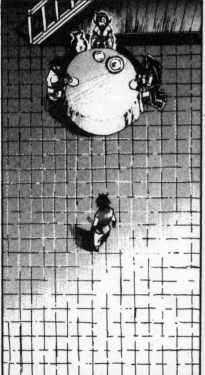

YOU THREE...

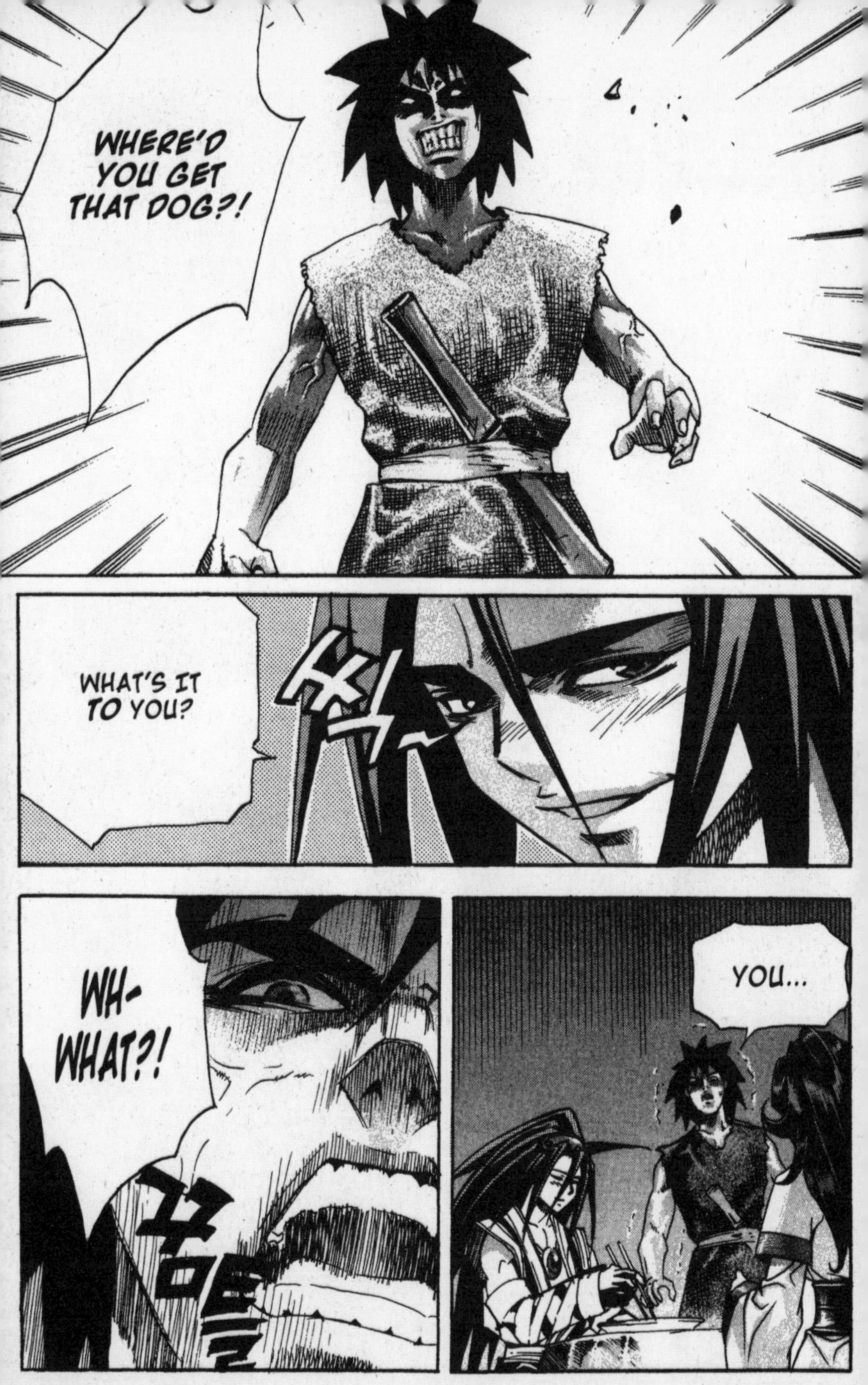
WHERE'D YOU GET THAT DOG?!
WHAT'S IT TO YOU?
WH- WHAT?!
YOU...

DO YOU REALIZE WHO I *AM*?!

I DON'T *CARE* WHO YOU ARE. BUT YOU'D BETTER *LEAVE*-- YOU'RE DISTURBING MY MEAL!

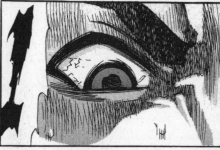

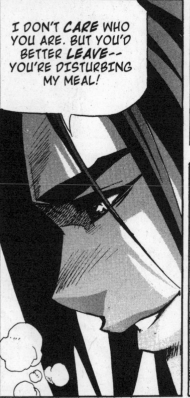

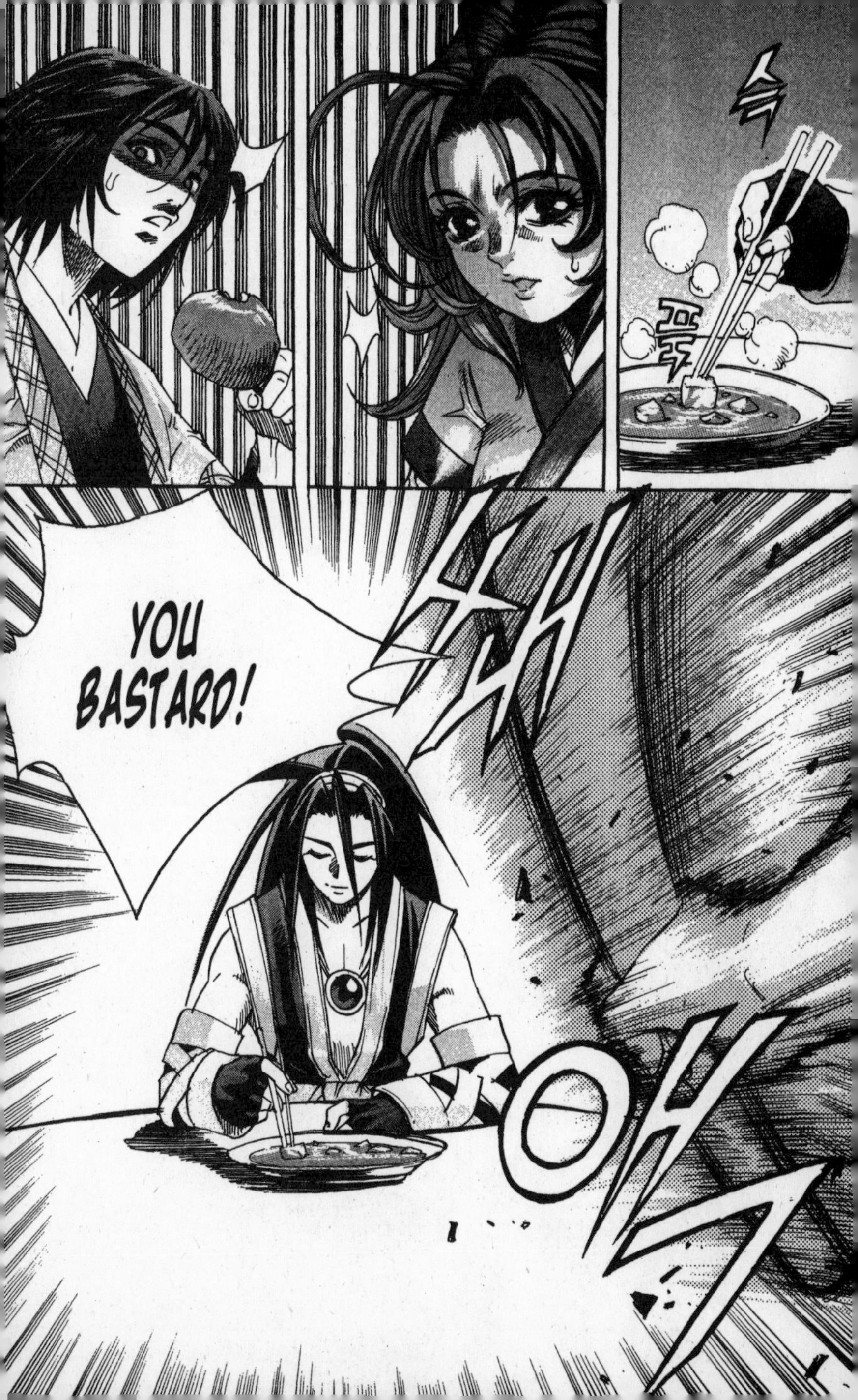
YOU BASTARD!

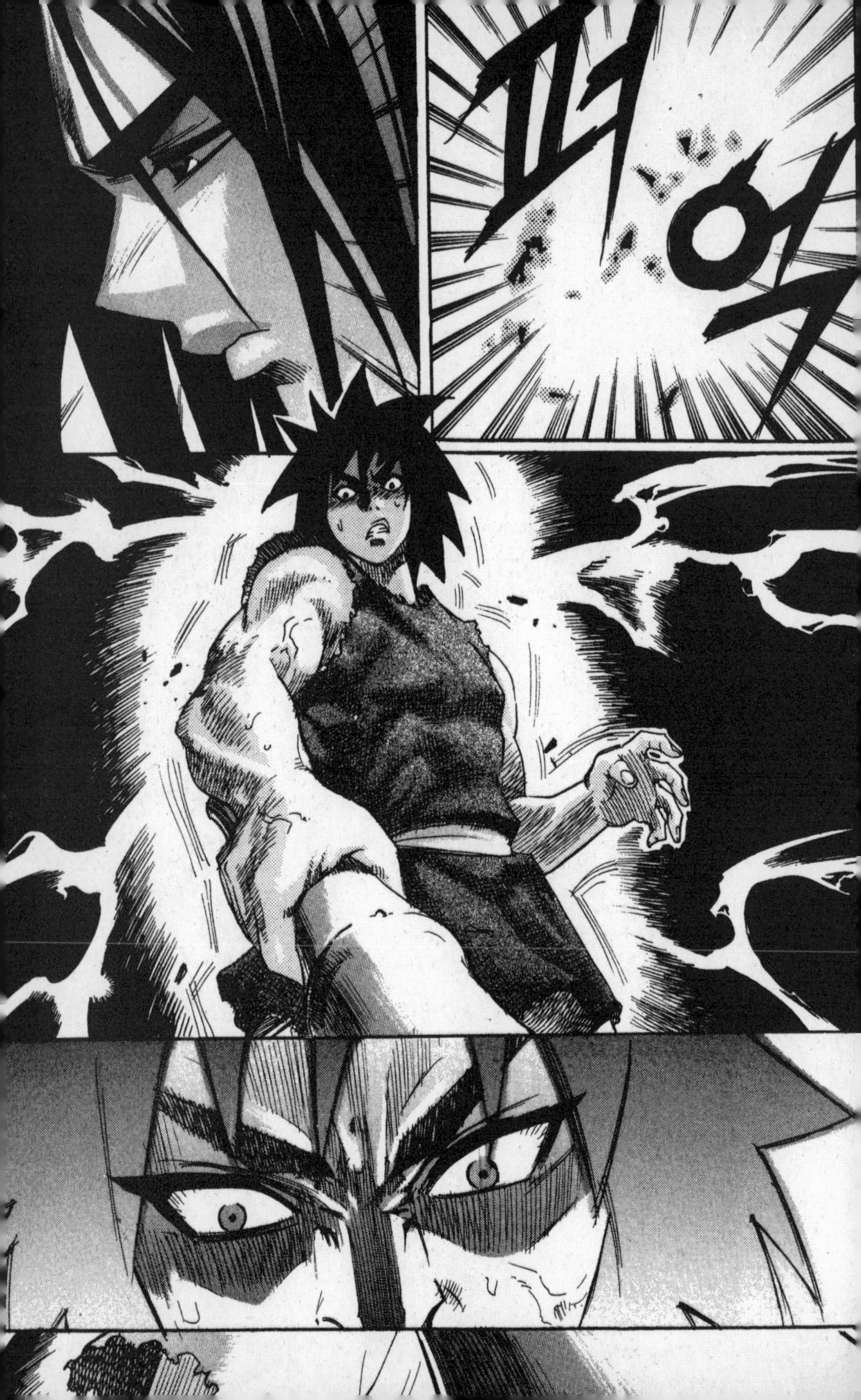
꺼어

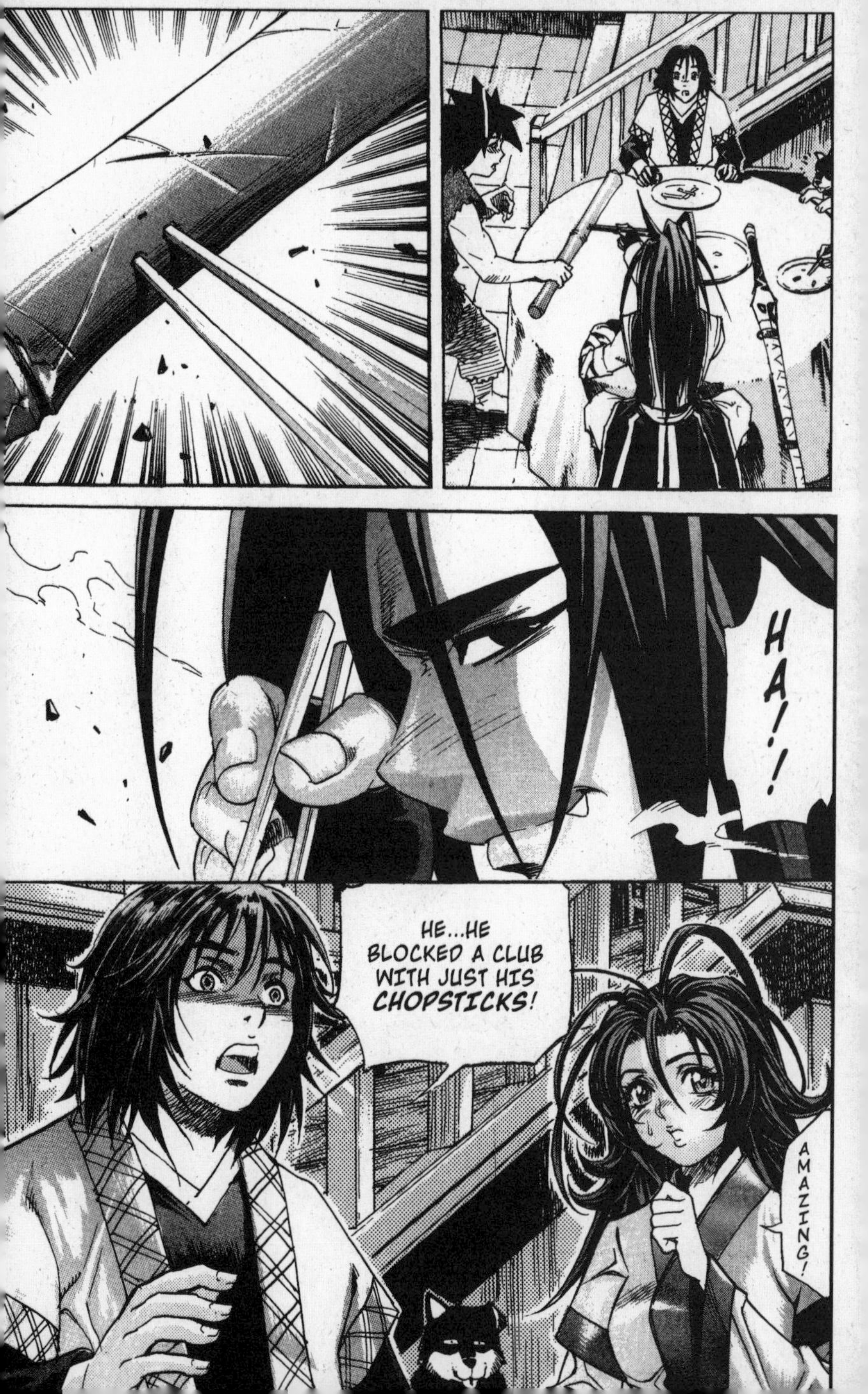
HA!!
HE...HE BLOCKED A CLUB WITH JUST HIS CHOPSTICKS!
AMAZING!

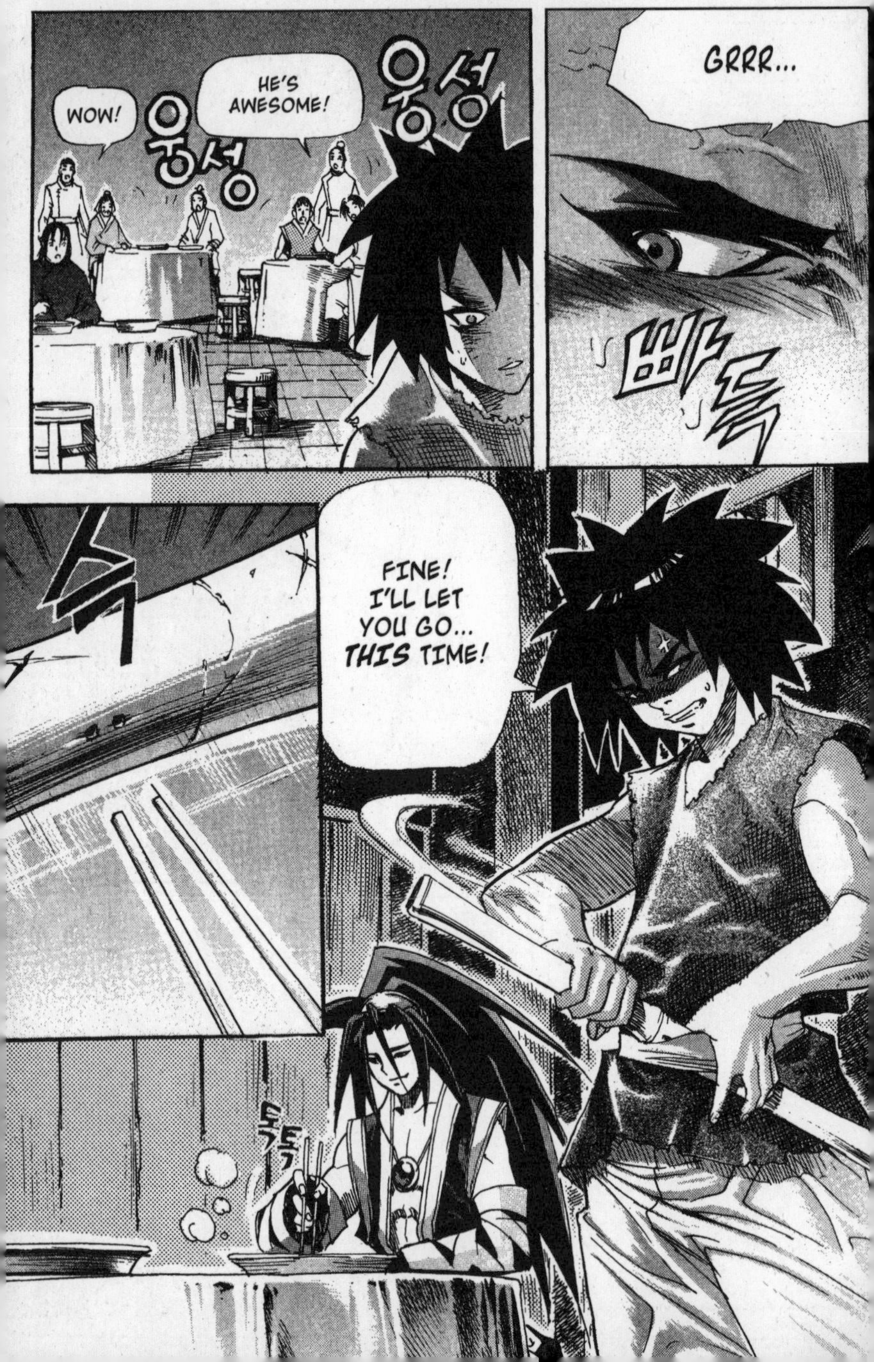

WOW!
HE'S AWESOME!
웅성
웅성
GRRR...
빠득
FINE! I'LL LET YOU GO... THIS TIME!

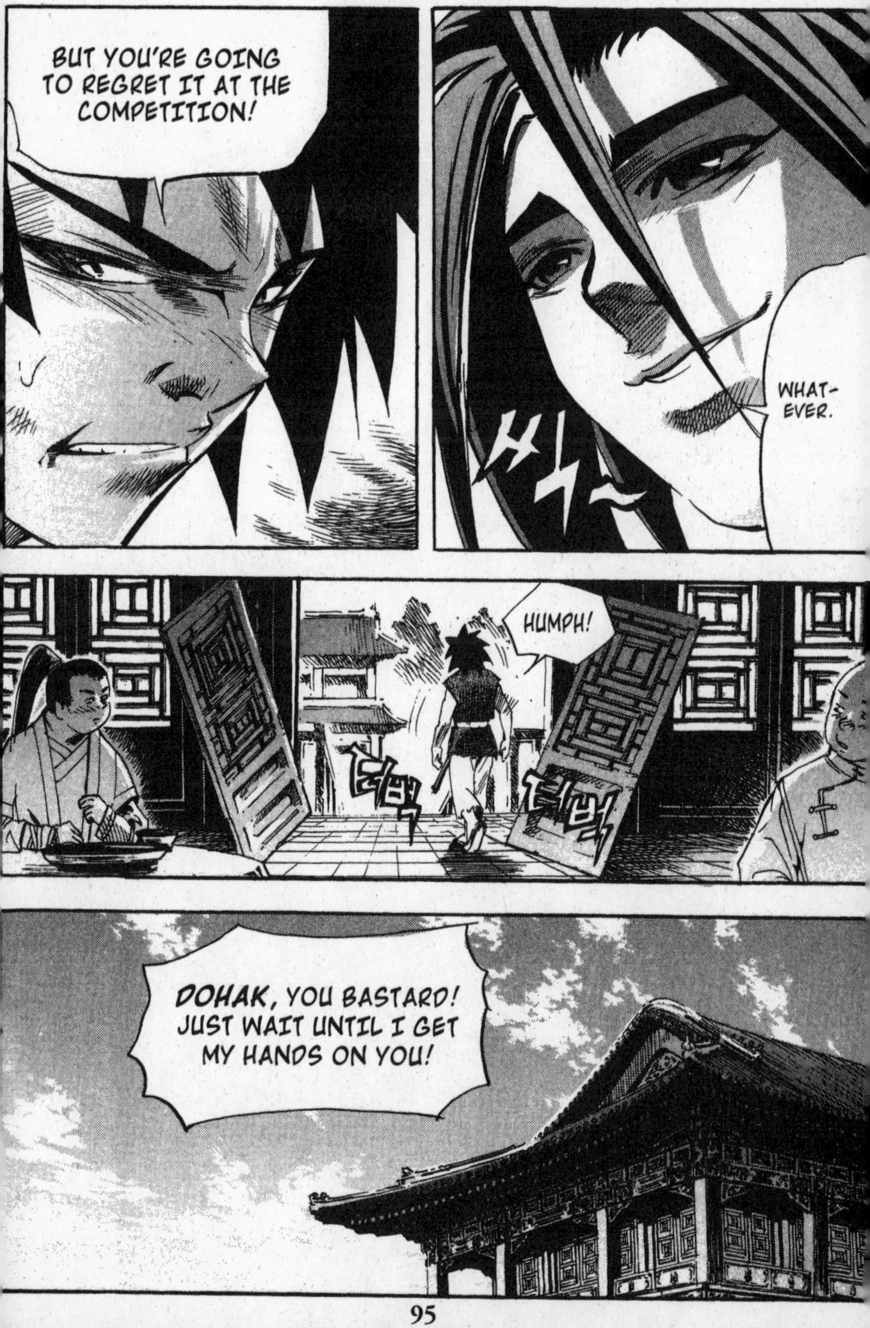
BUT YOU'RE GOING TO REGRET IT AT THE COMPETITION!
WHAT-EVER.
HUMPH!
DOHAK, YOU BASTARD! JUST WAIT UNTIL I GET MY HANDS ON YOU!

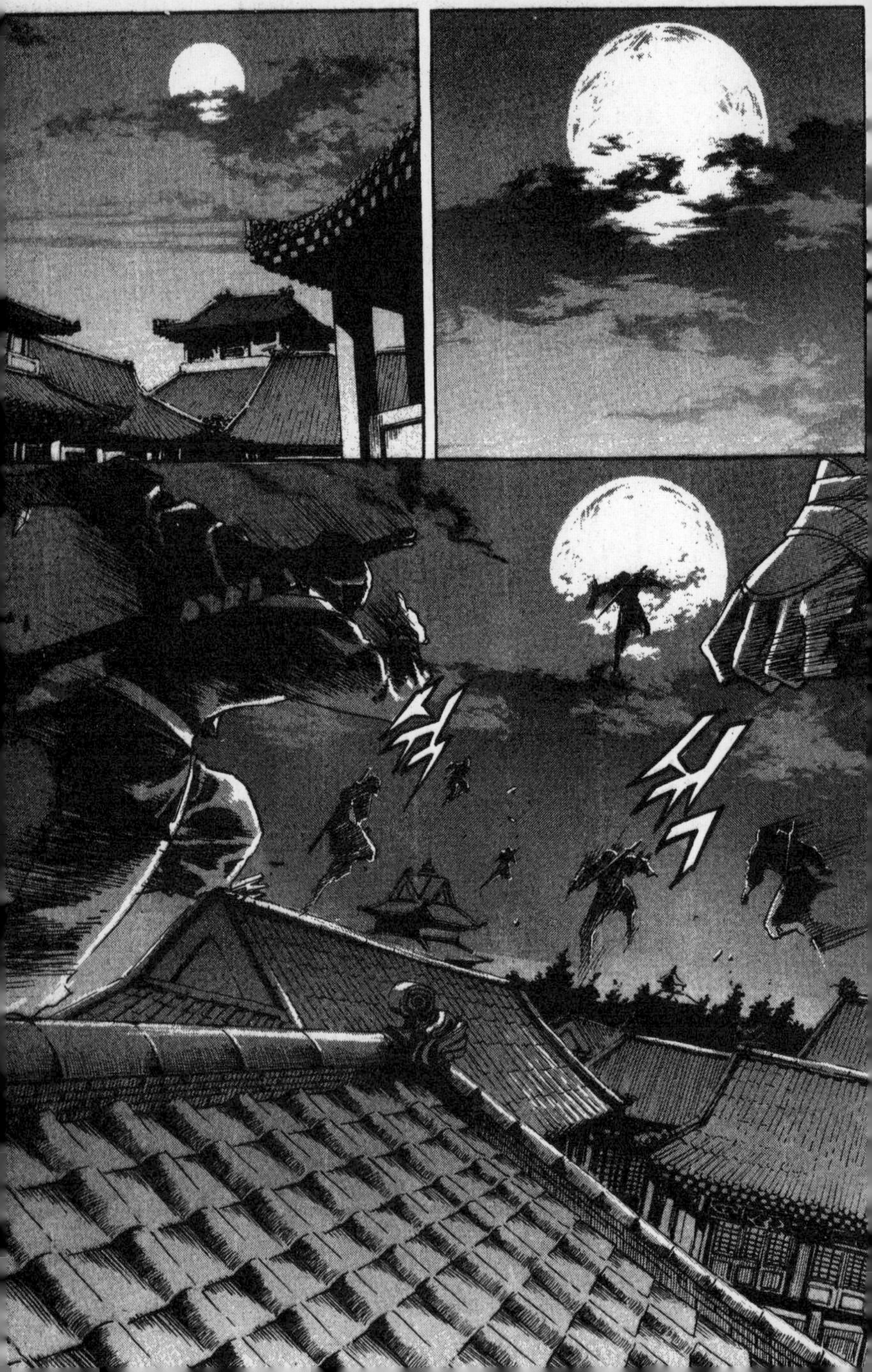

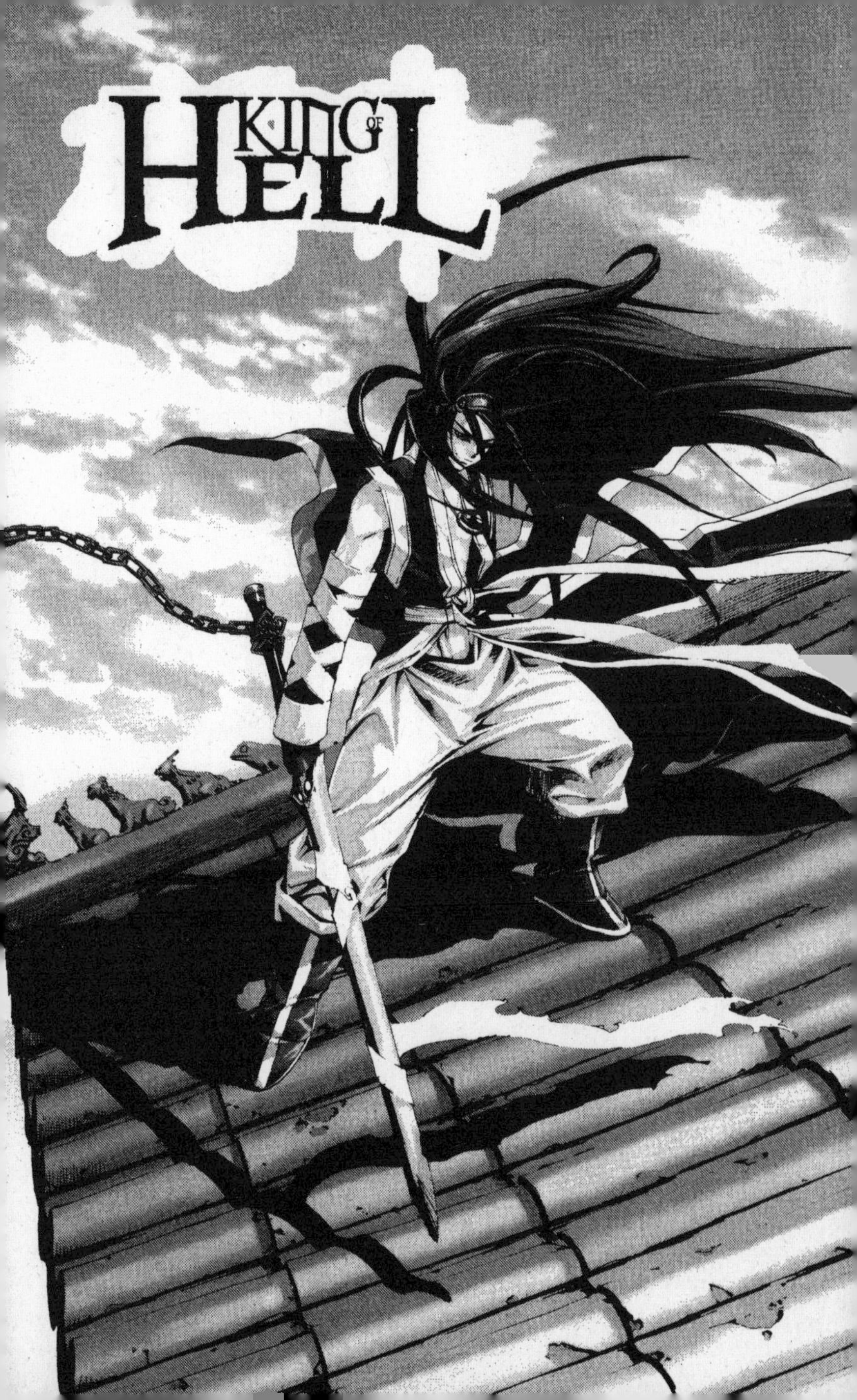
KING OF HELL

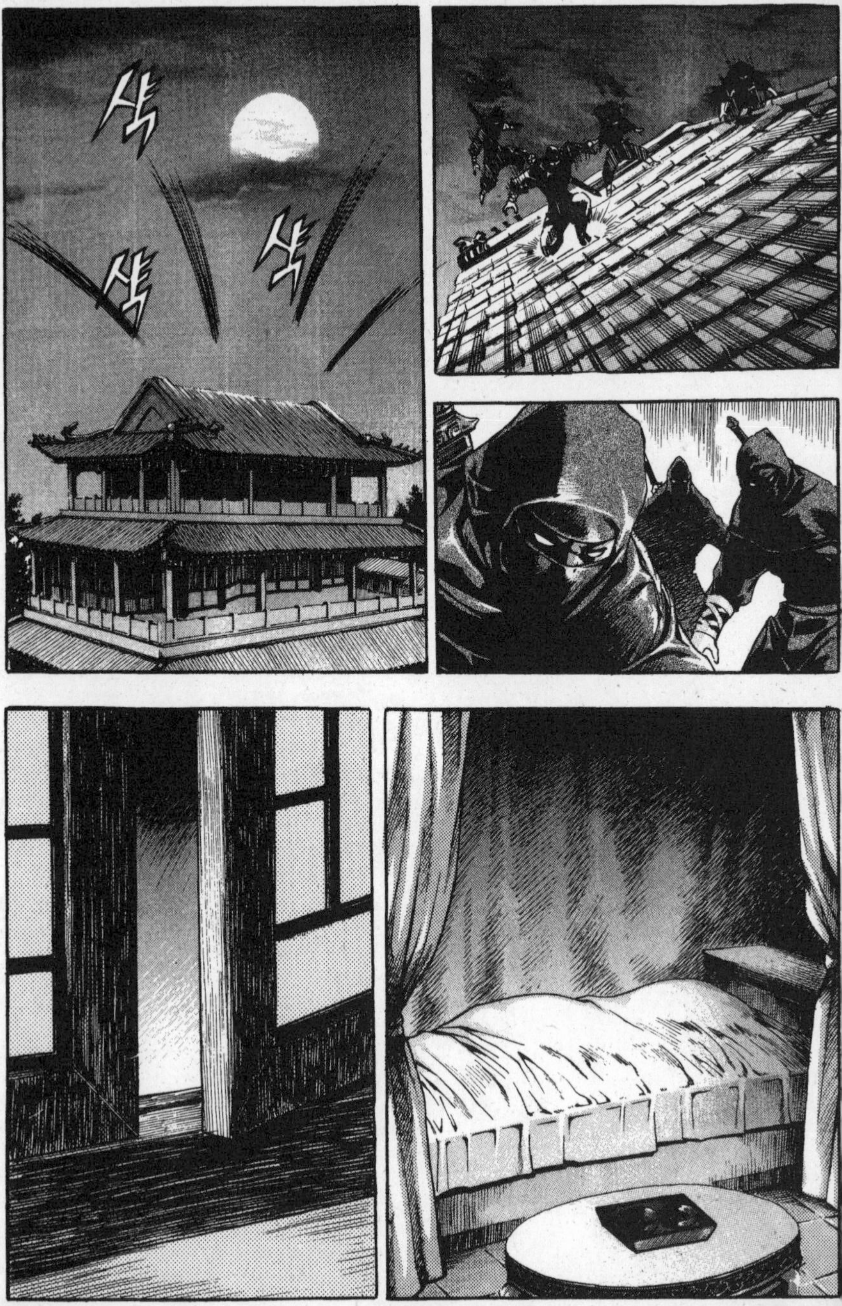
샥
샥
샥

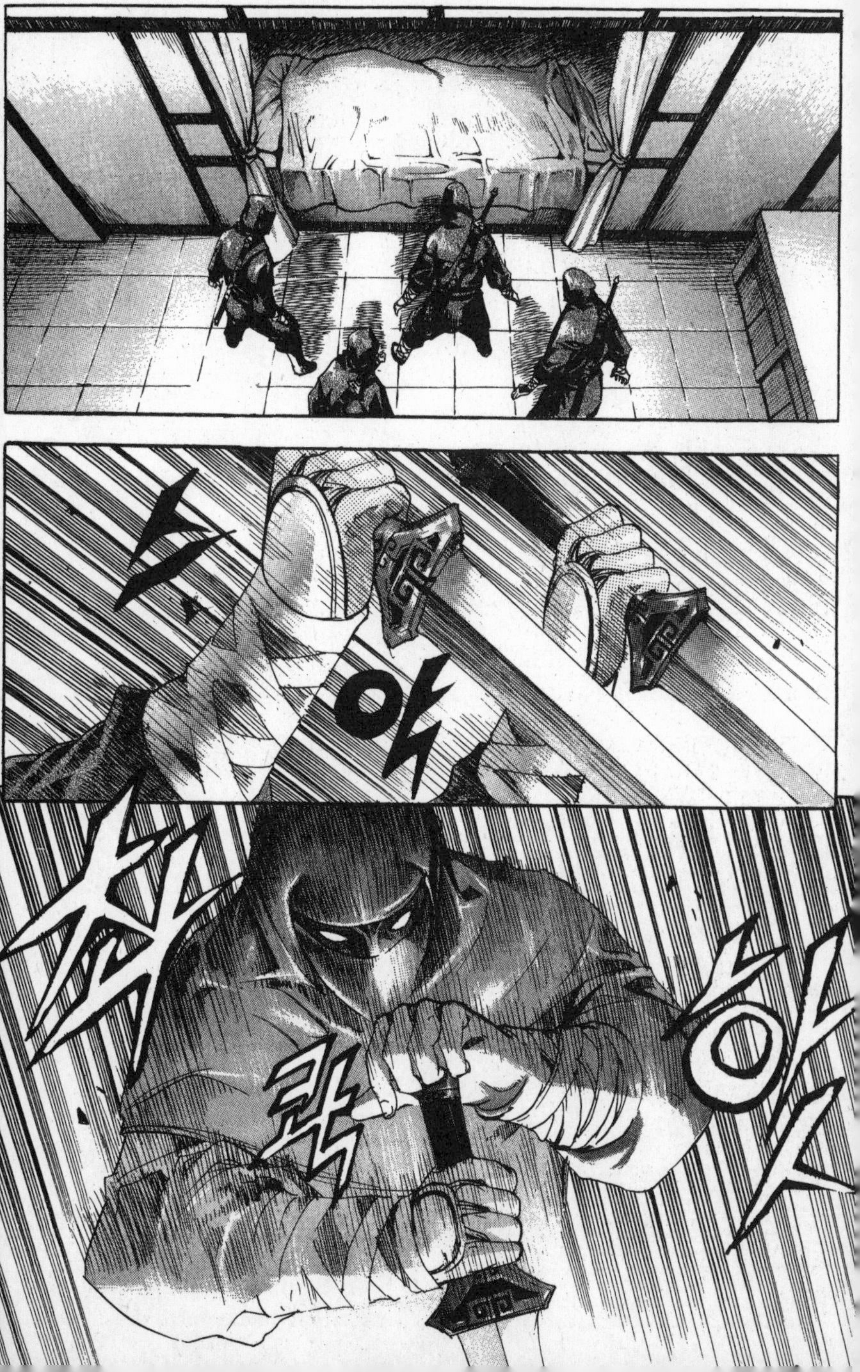

아

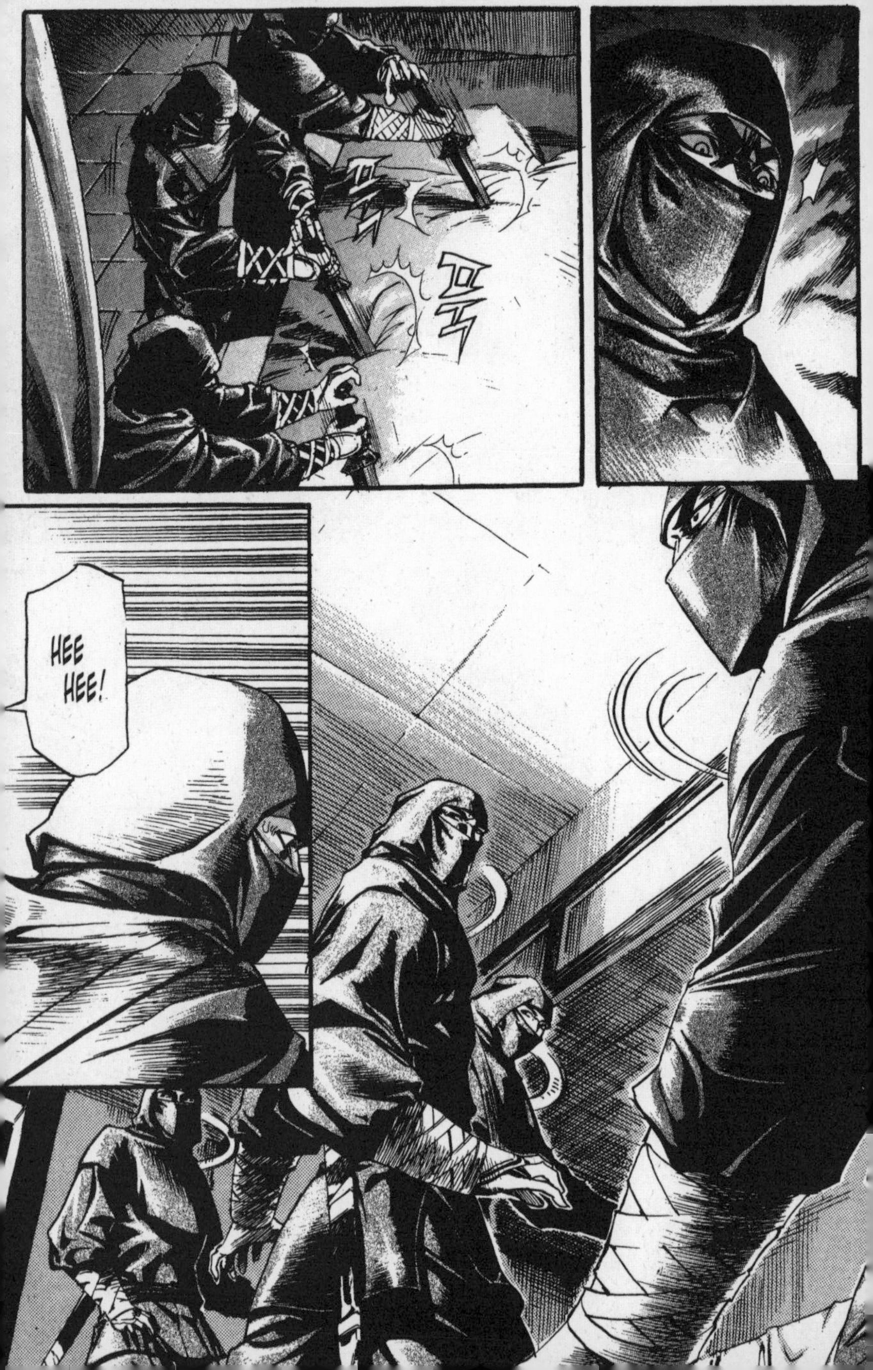
HEE HEE!

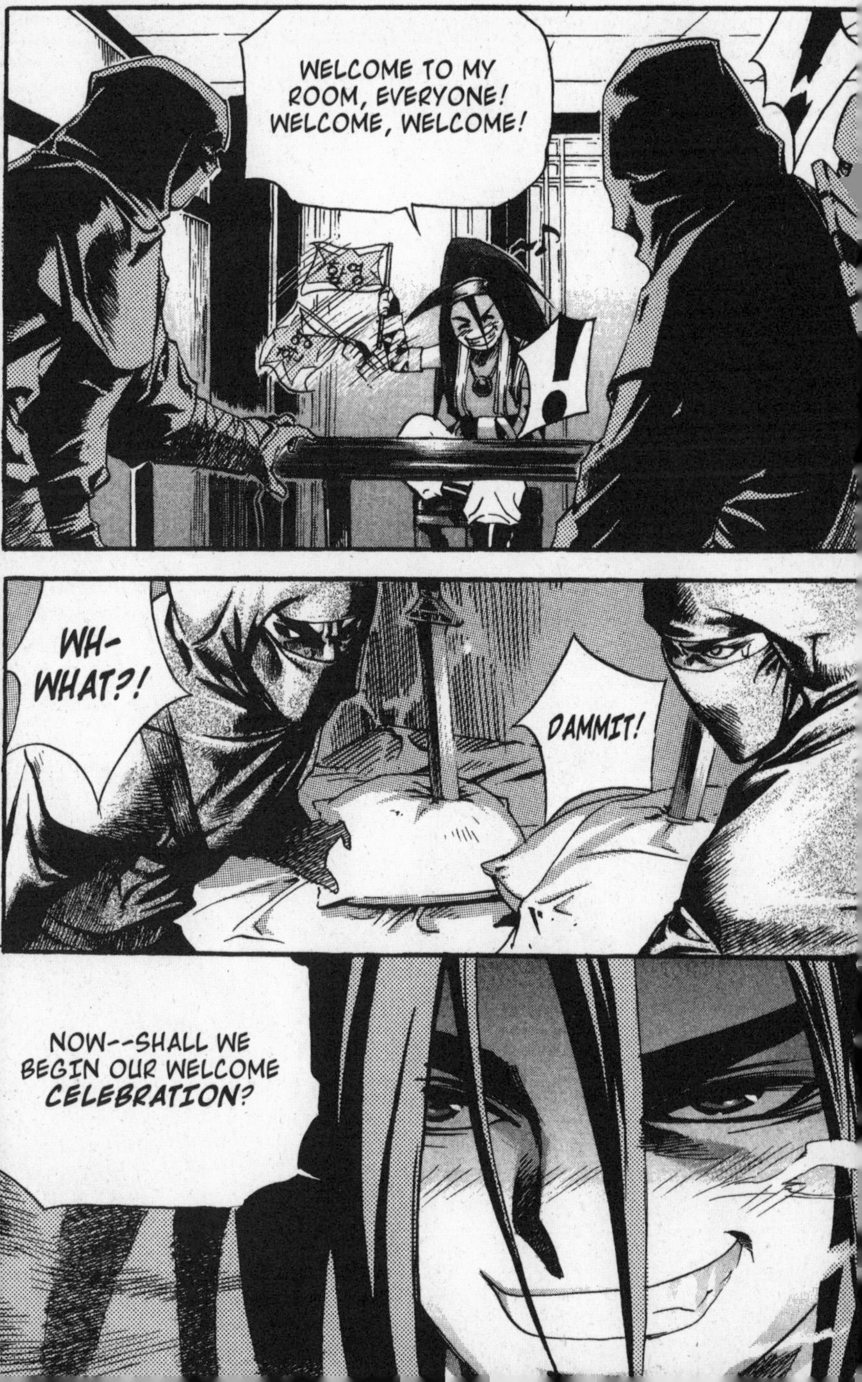
WELCOME TO MY ROOM, EVERYONE! WELCOME, WELCOME!
WH- WHAT?!
DAMMIT!
NOW--SHALL WE BEGIN OUR WELCOME CELEBRATION?

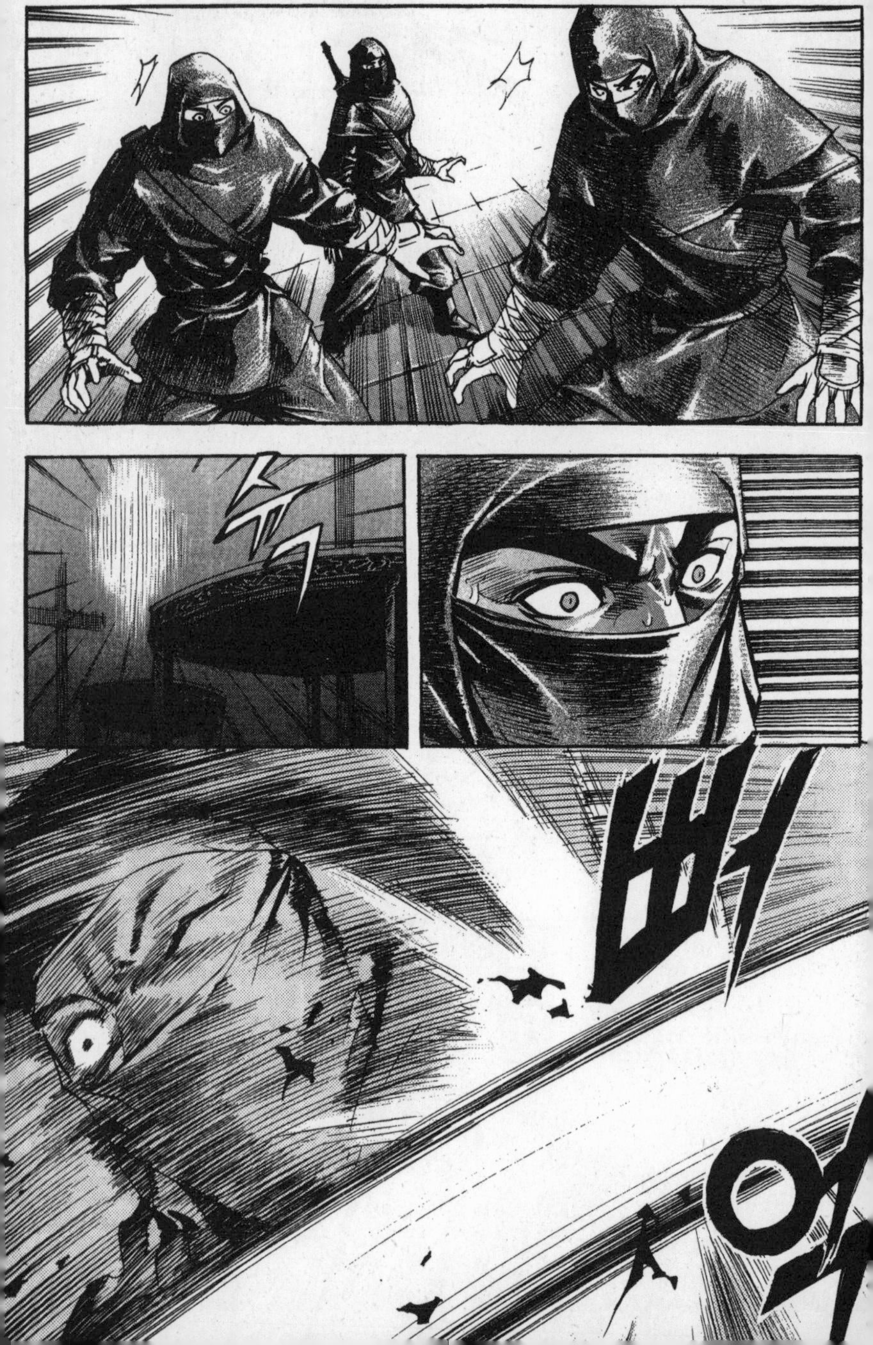

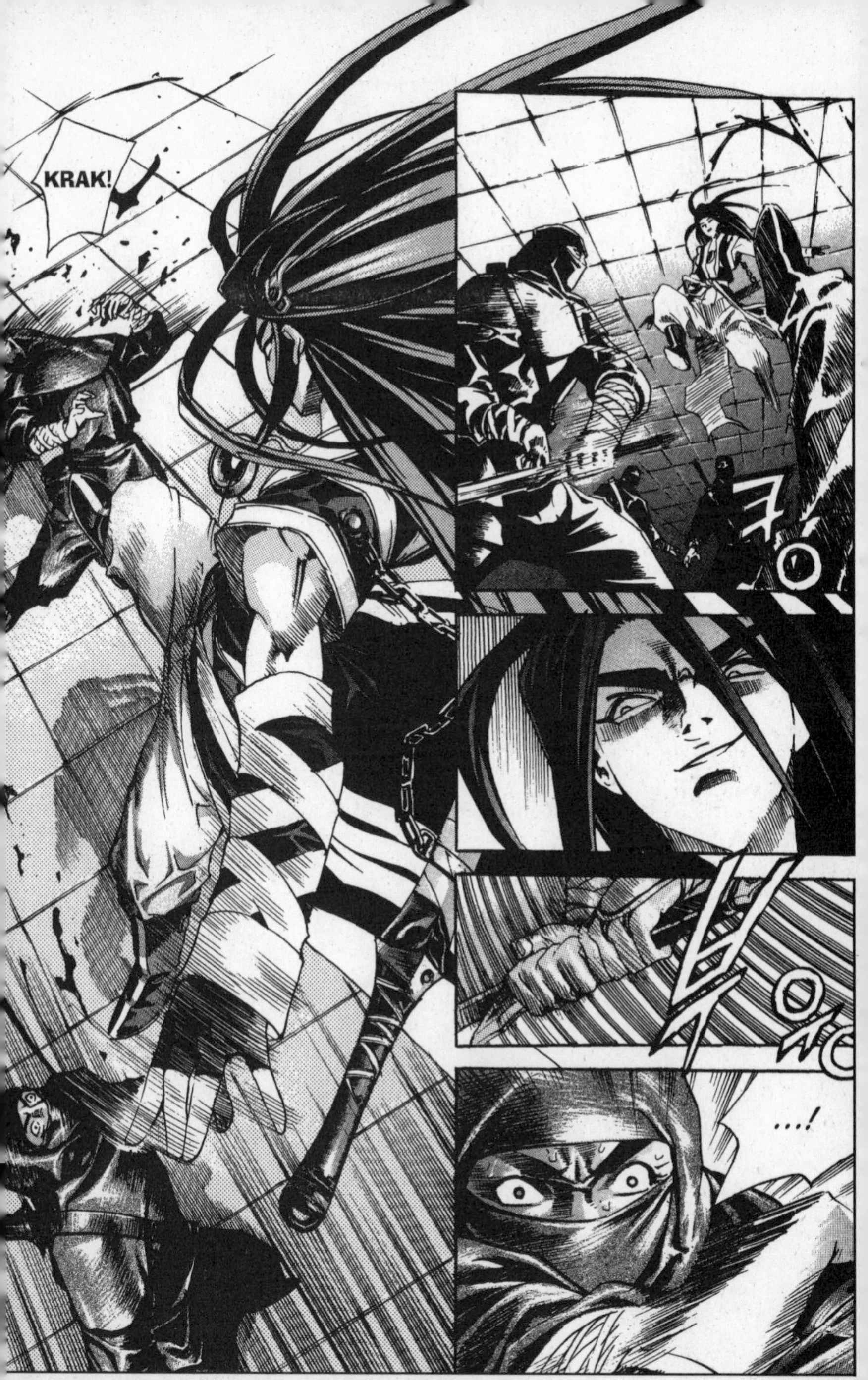
KRAK!
...!

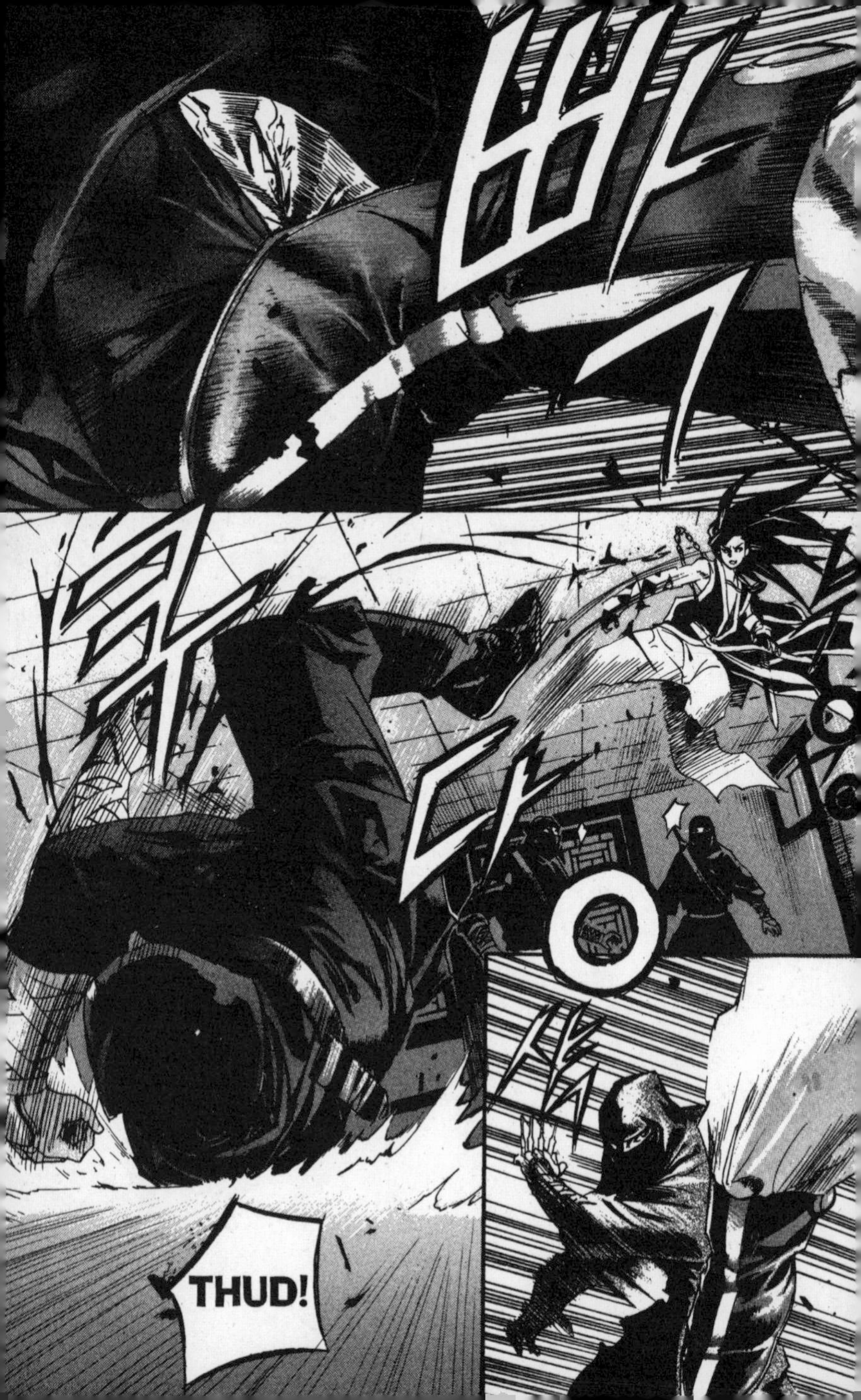
THUD!

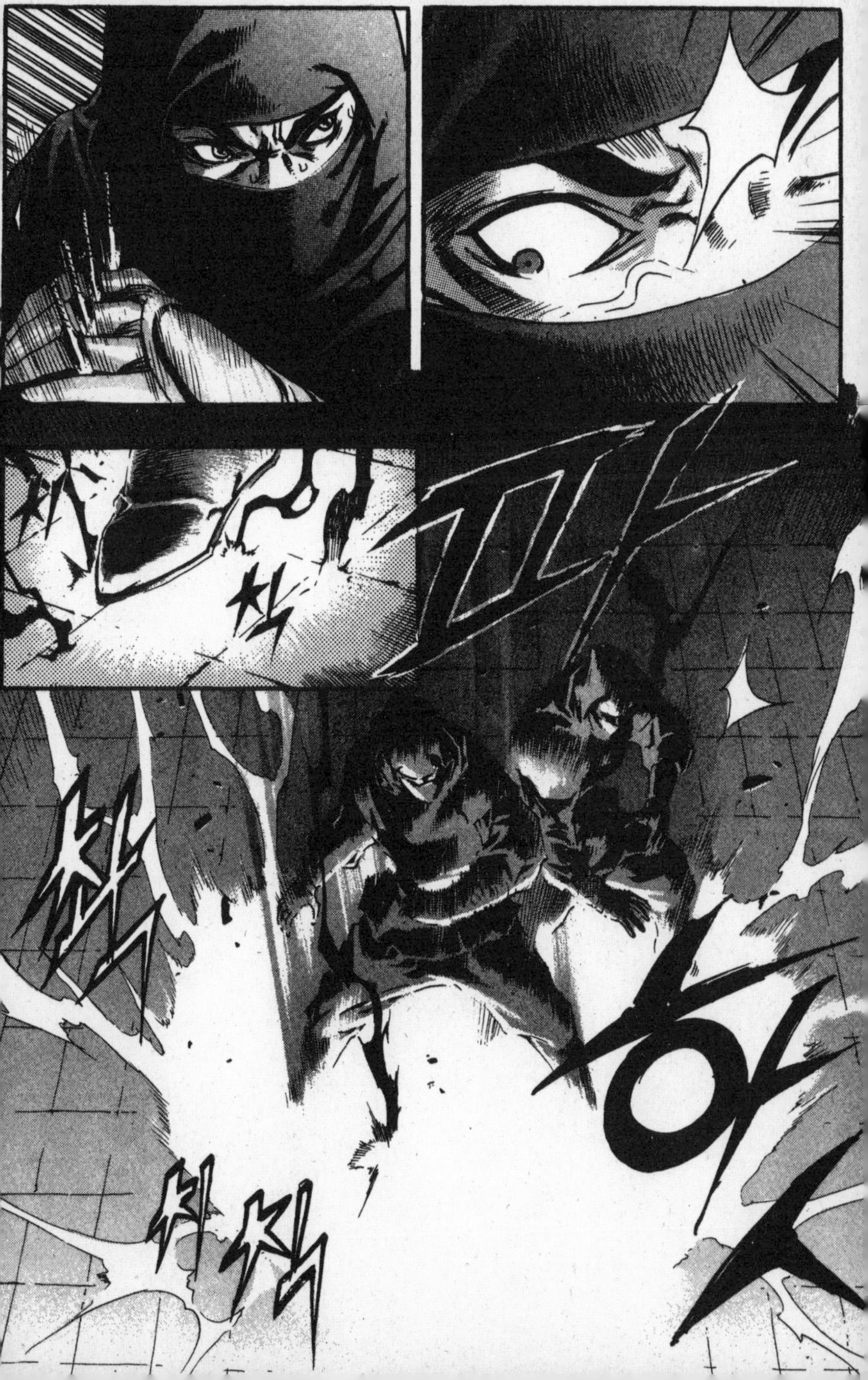
치
치칫

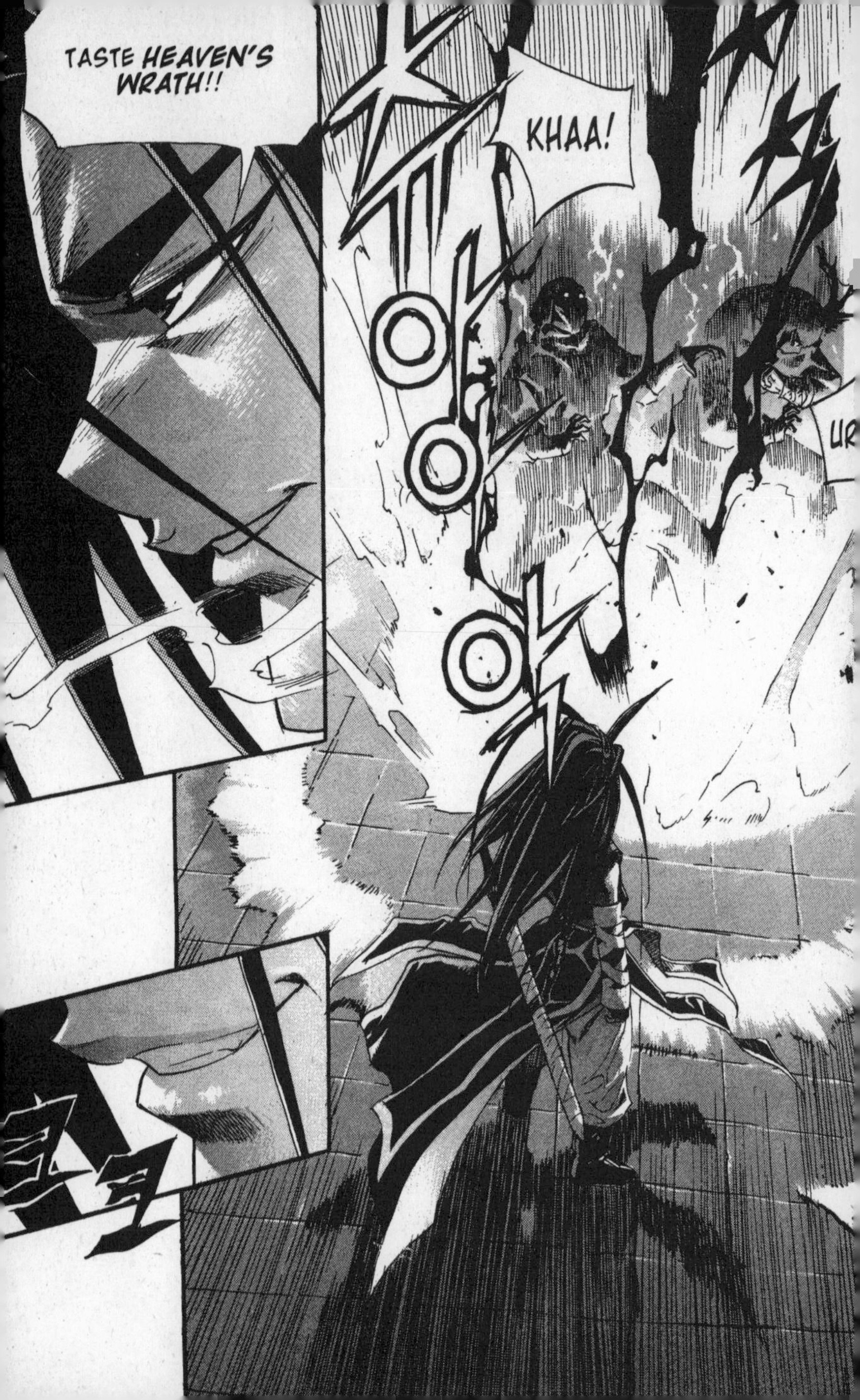
TASTE HEAVEN'S WRATH!!
KHAA!
UR

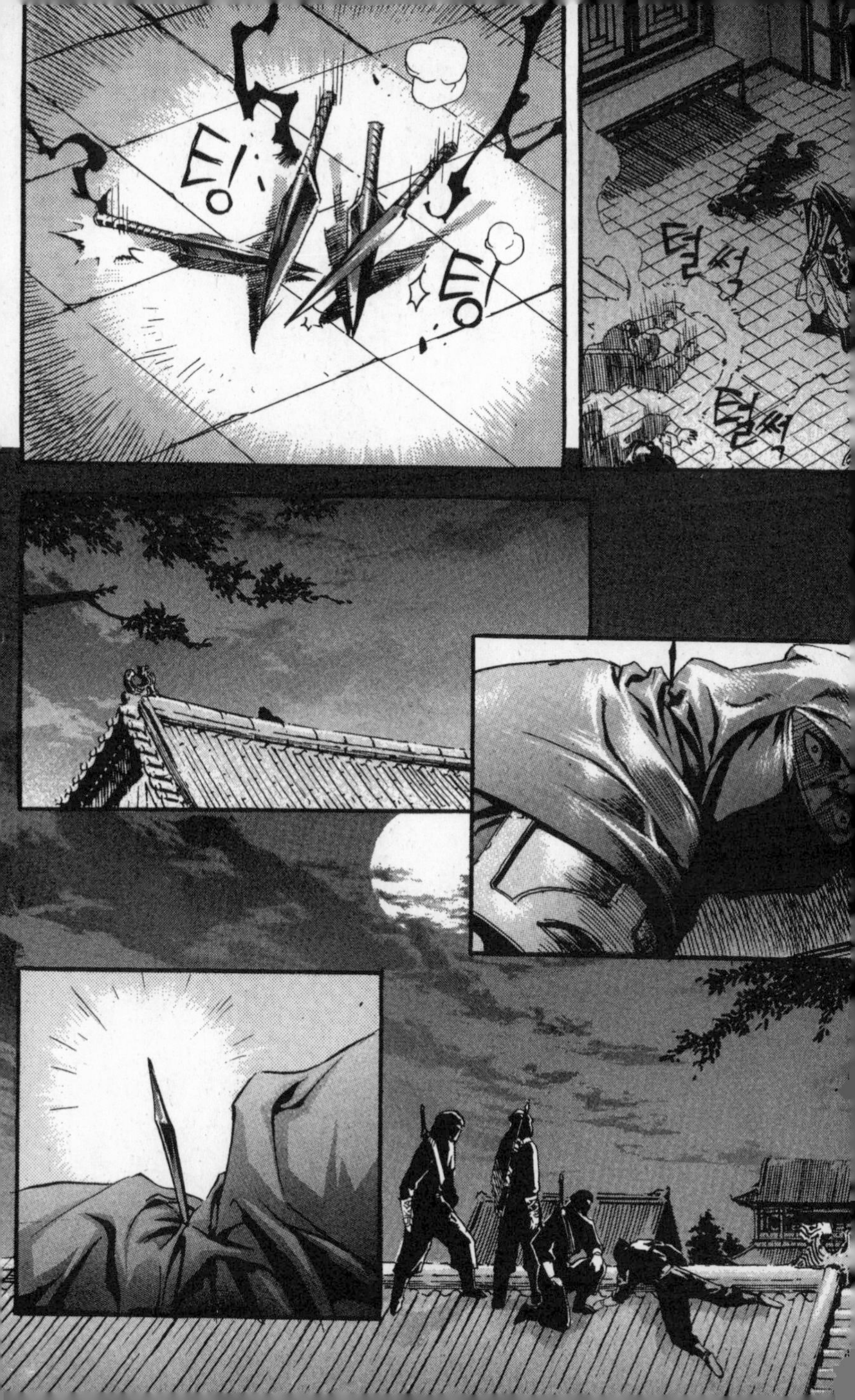
팅!
팅
털썩
털썩

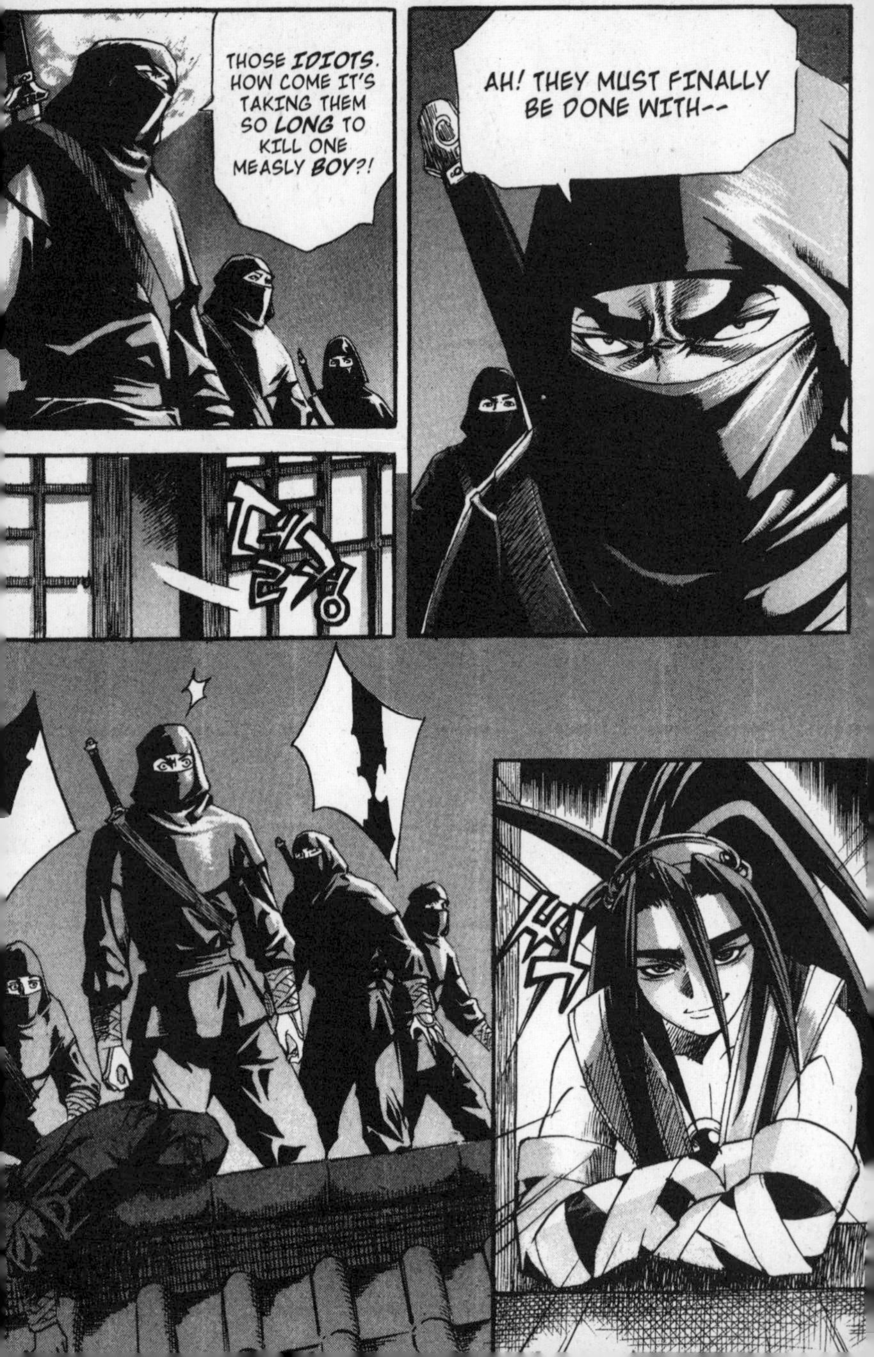
THOSE IDIOTS. HOW COME IT'S TAKING THEM SO LONG TO KILL ONE MEASLY BOY?!
AH! THEY MUST FINALLY BE DONE WITH--

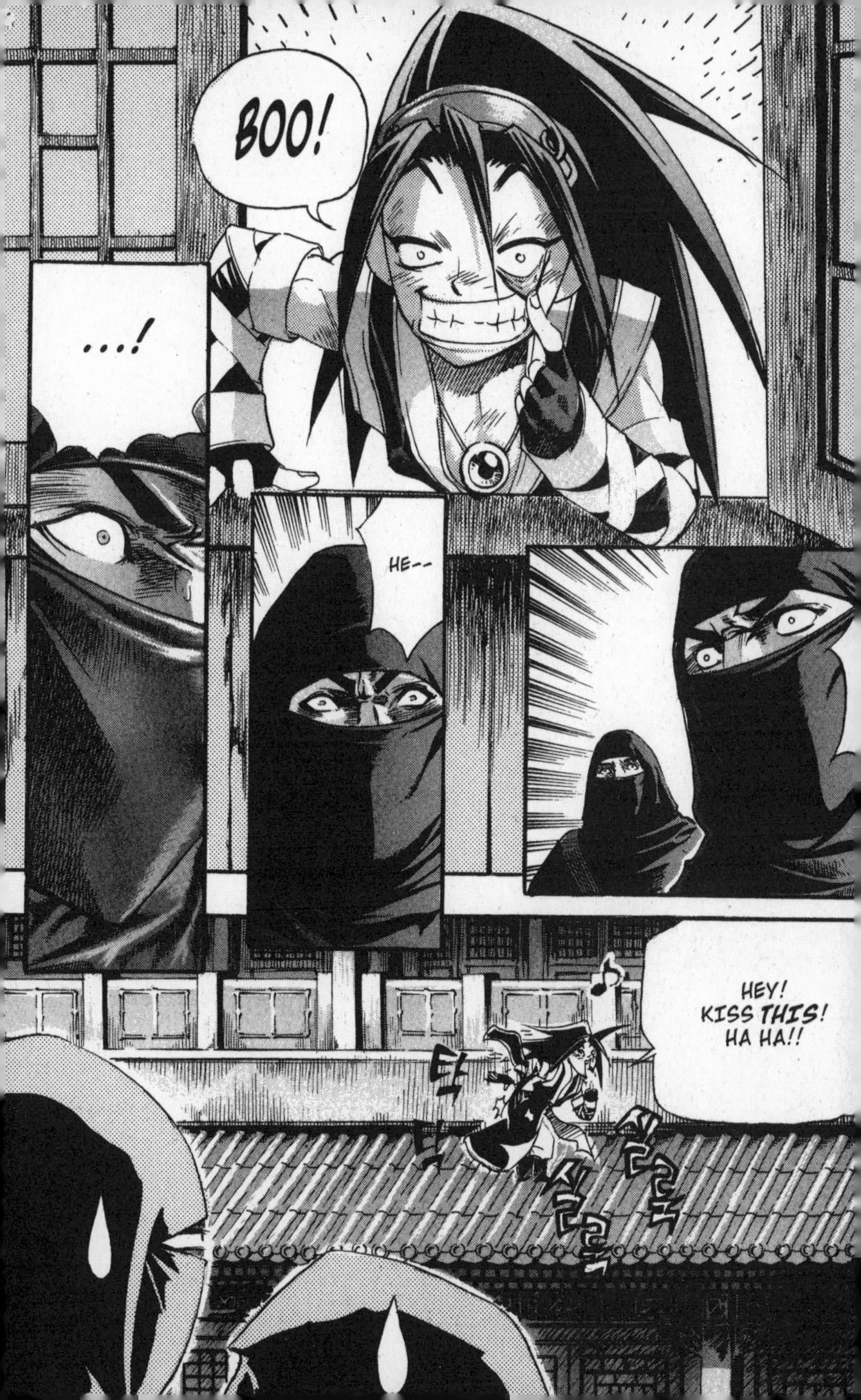
BOO!
...!
HE--
HEY! KISS THIS! HA HA!!

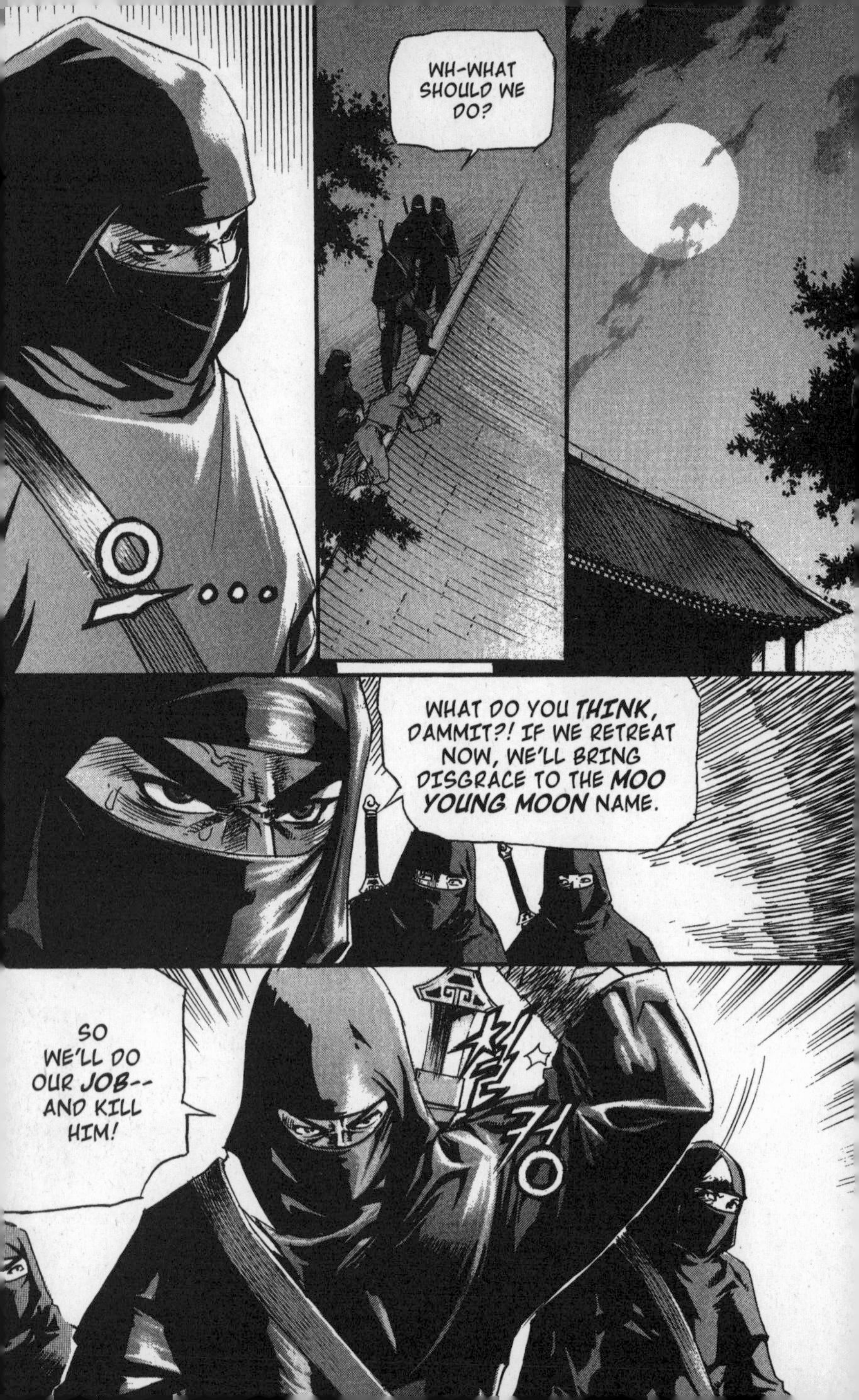
...
WH-WHAT SHOULD WE DO?
WHAT DO YOU THINK, DAMMIT?! IF WE RETREAT NOW, WE'LL BRING DISGRACE TO THE MOO YOUNG MOON NAME.
SO WE'LL DO OUR JOB-- AND KILL HIM!

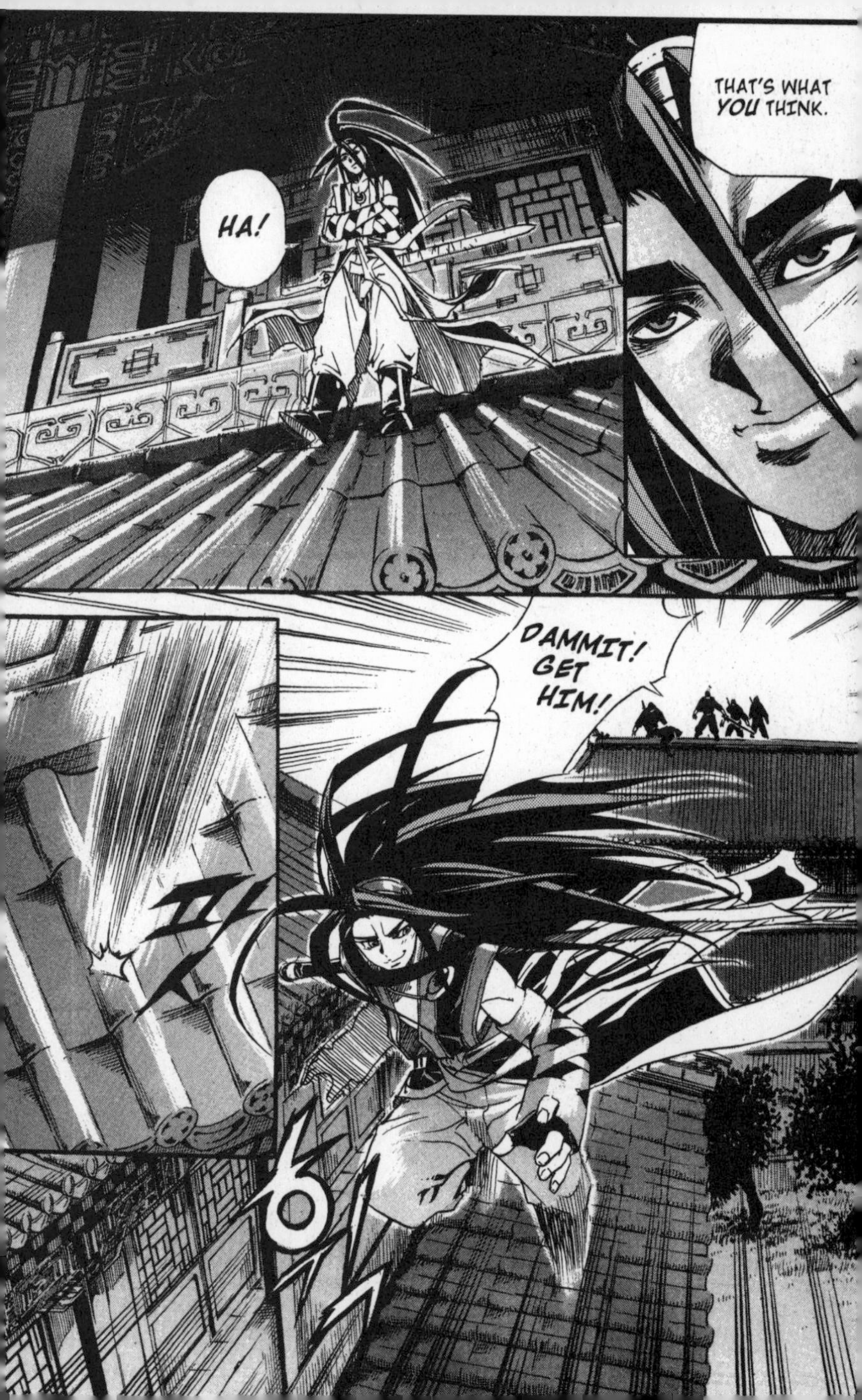
HA!
THAT'S WHAT *YOU* THINK.
DAMMIT! GET HIM!

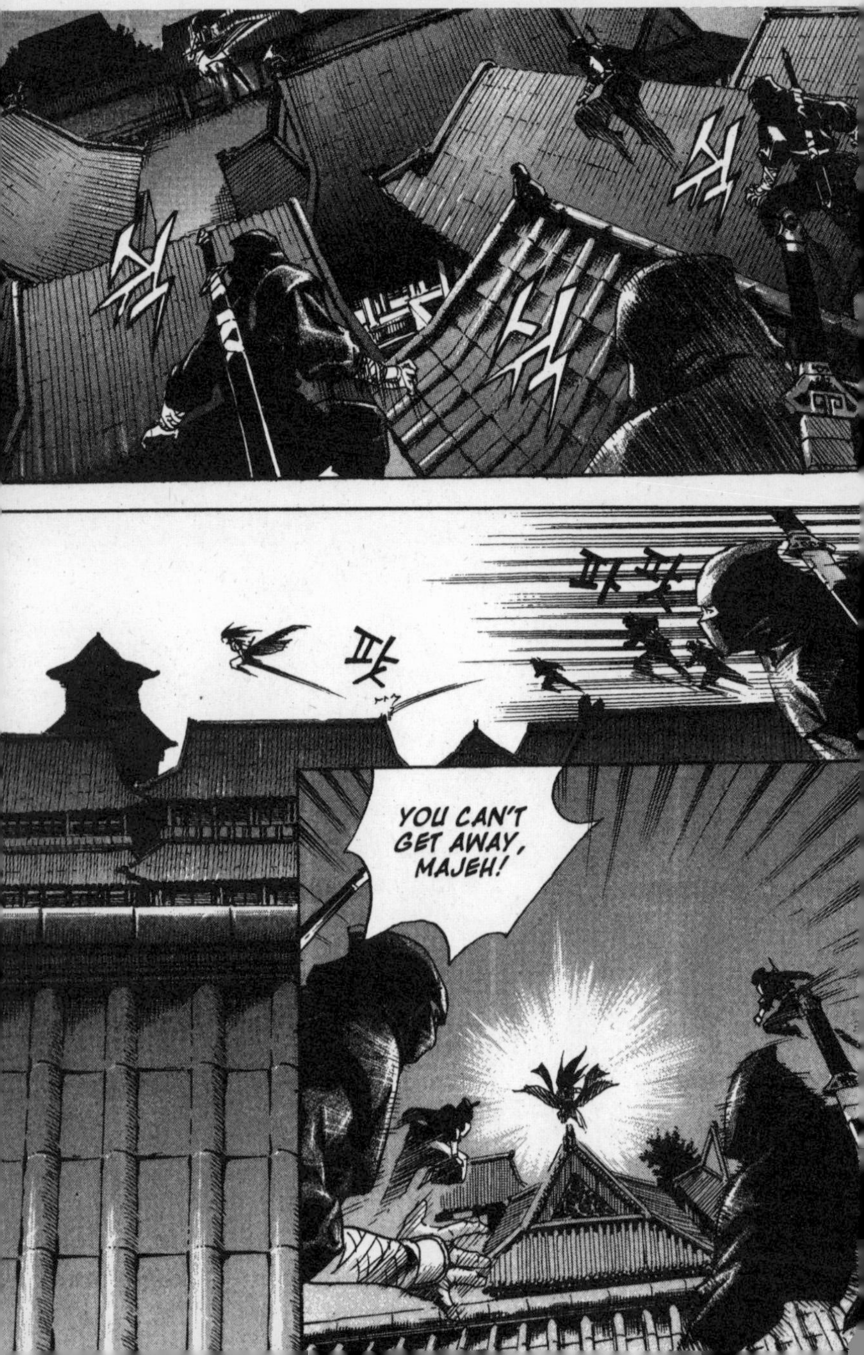
팟
파팟
YOU CAN'T GET AWAY, MAJEH!

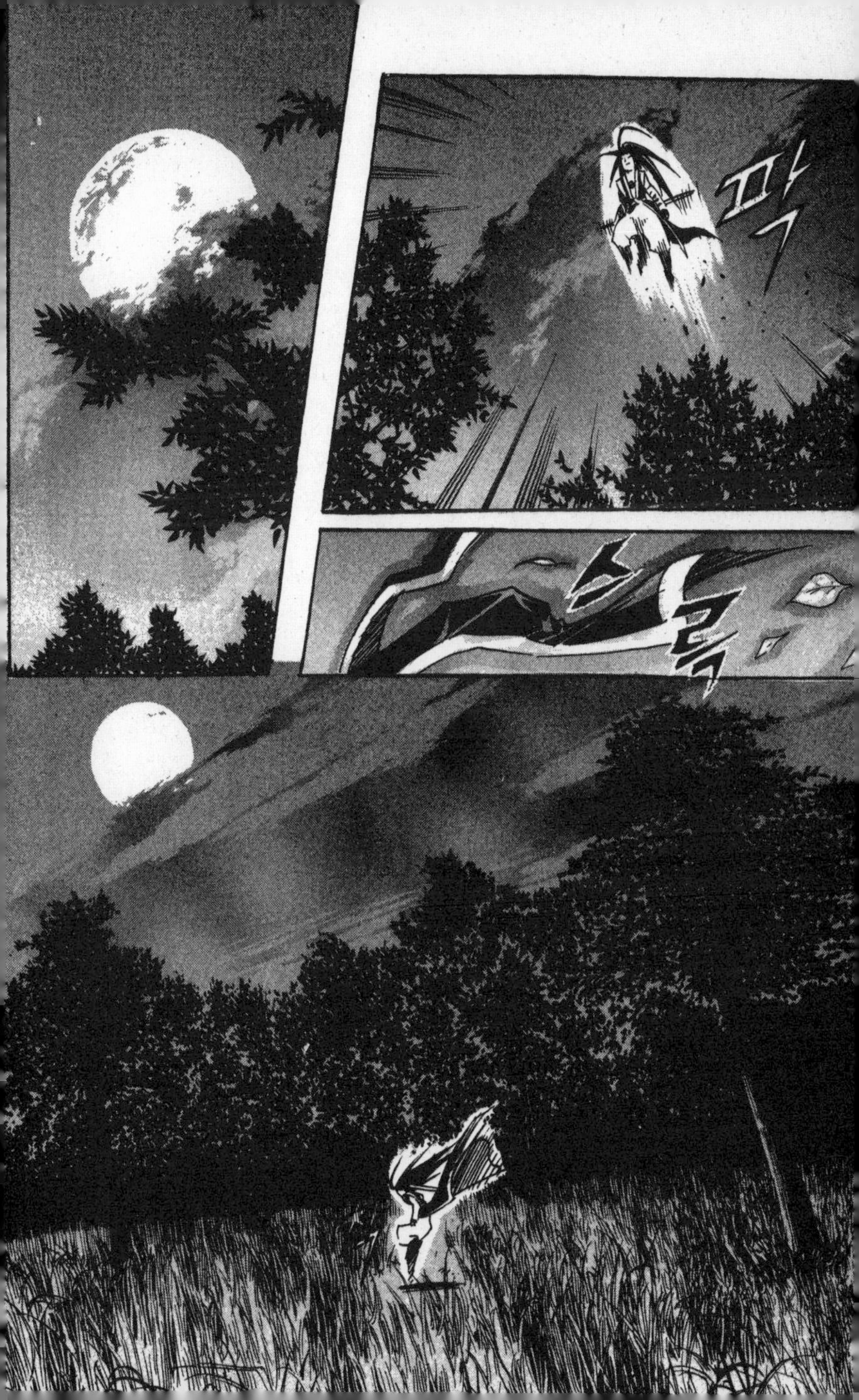

팍
스륵

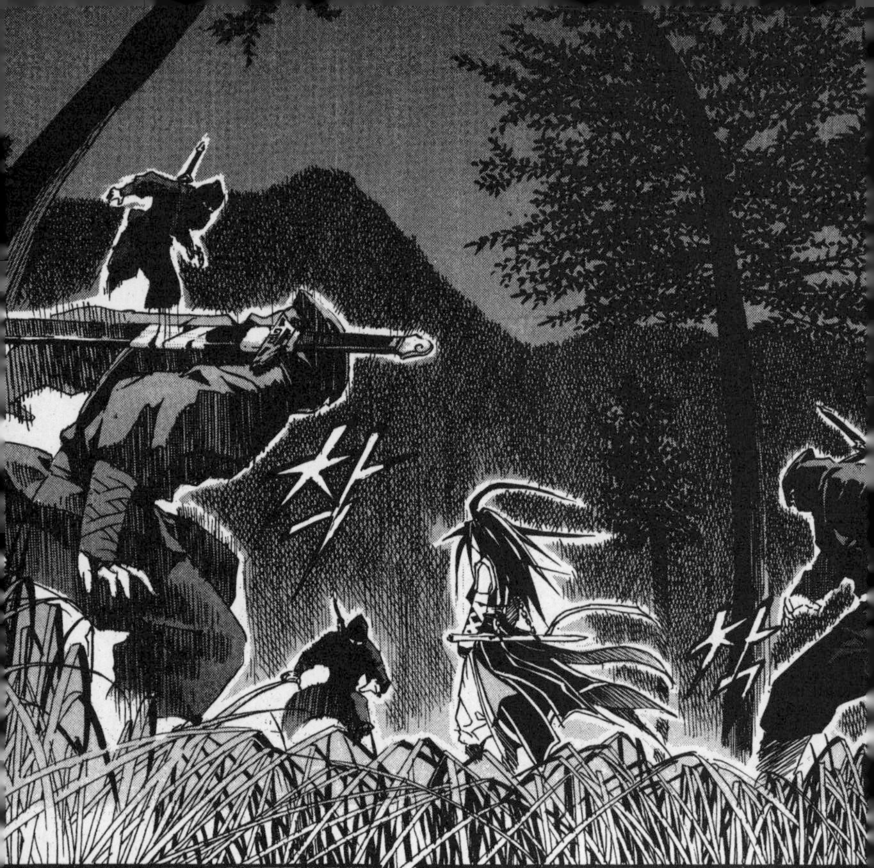

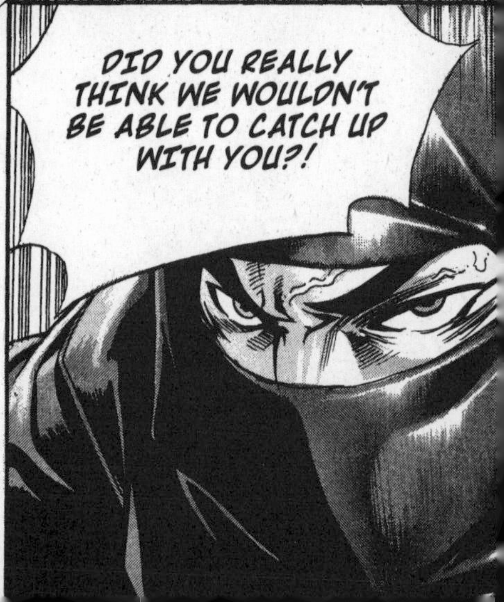
DID YOU REALLY THINK WE WOULDN'T BE ABLE TO CATCH UP WITH YOU?!

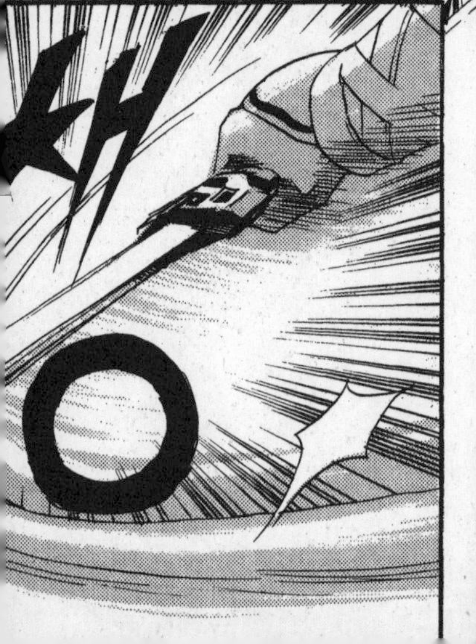

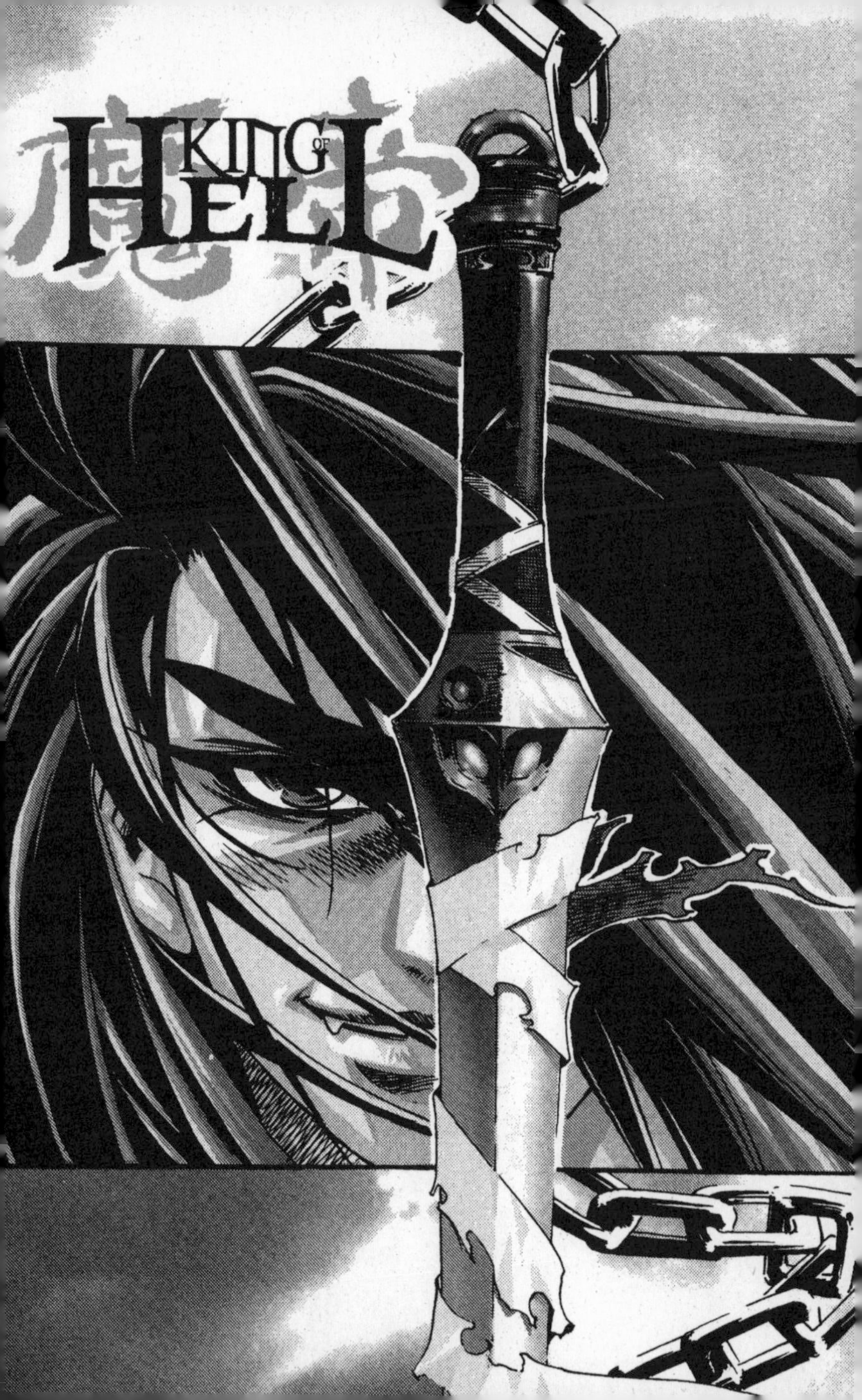
KING OF HELL
魔夜

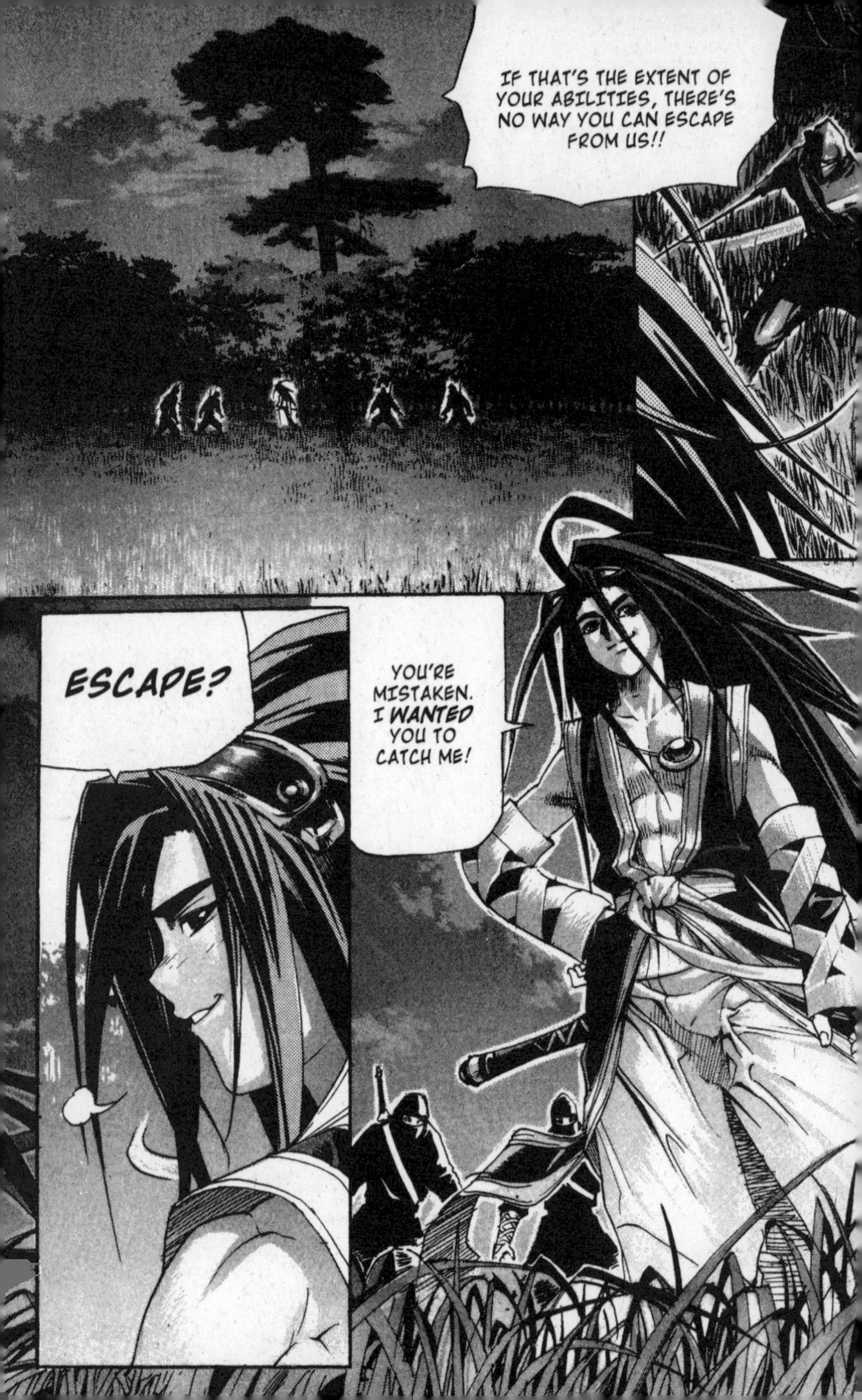
IF THAT'S THE EXTENT OF YOUR ABILITIES, THERE'S NO WAY YOU CAN ESCAPE FROM US!!
ESCAPE?
YOU'RE MISTAKEN. I WANTED YOU TO CATCH ME!

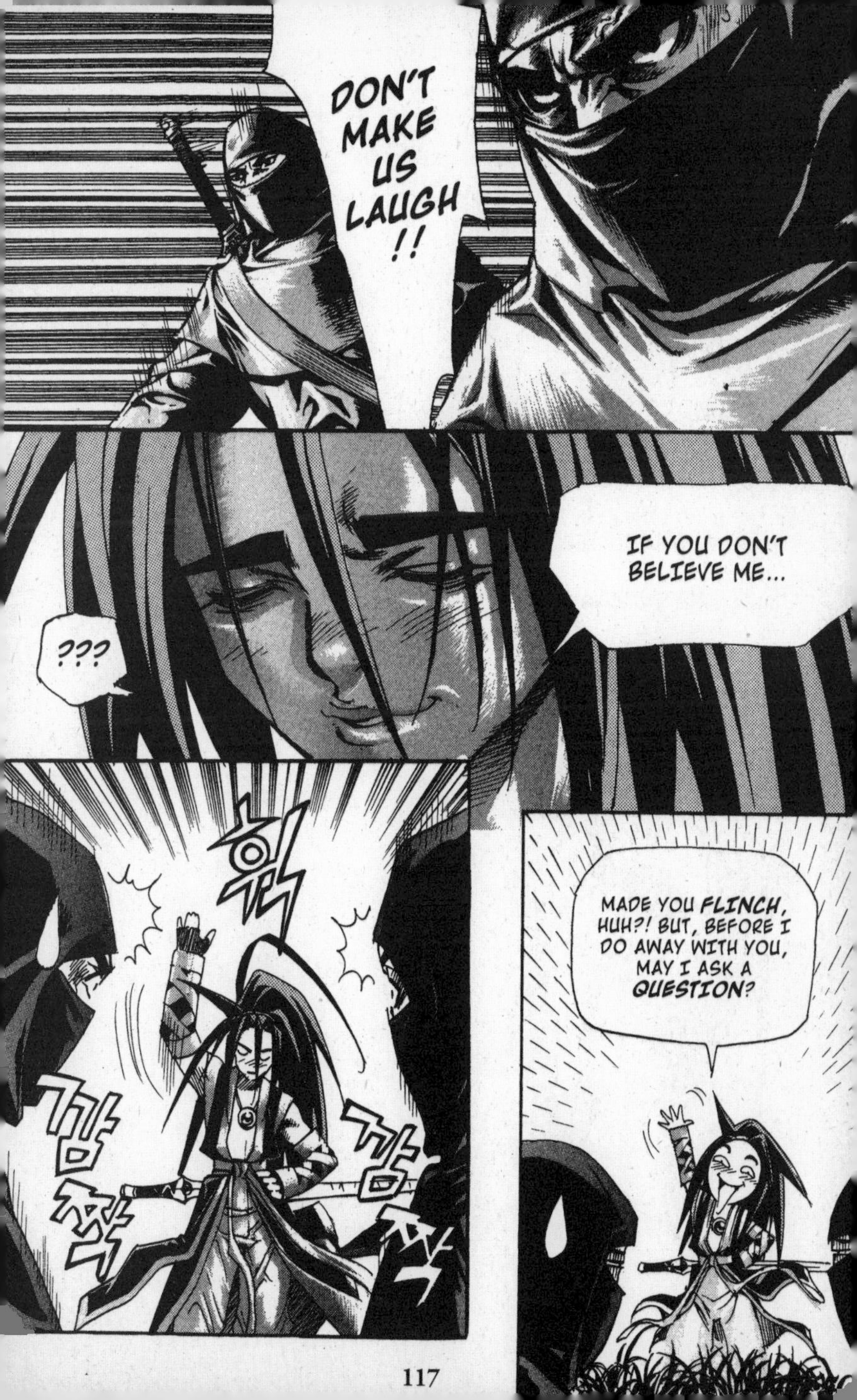
DON'T MAKE US LAUGH !!
IF YOU DON'T BELIEVE ME...
???
MADE YOU **FLINCH**, HUH?! BUT, BEFORE I DO AWAY WITH YOU, MAY I ASK A **QUESTION**?

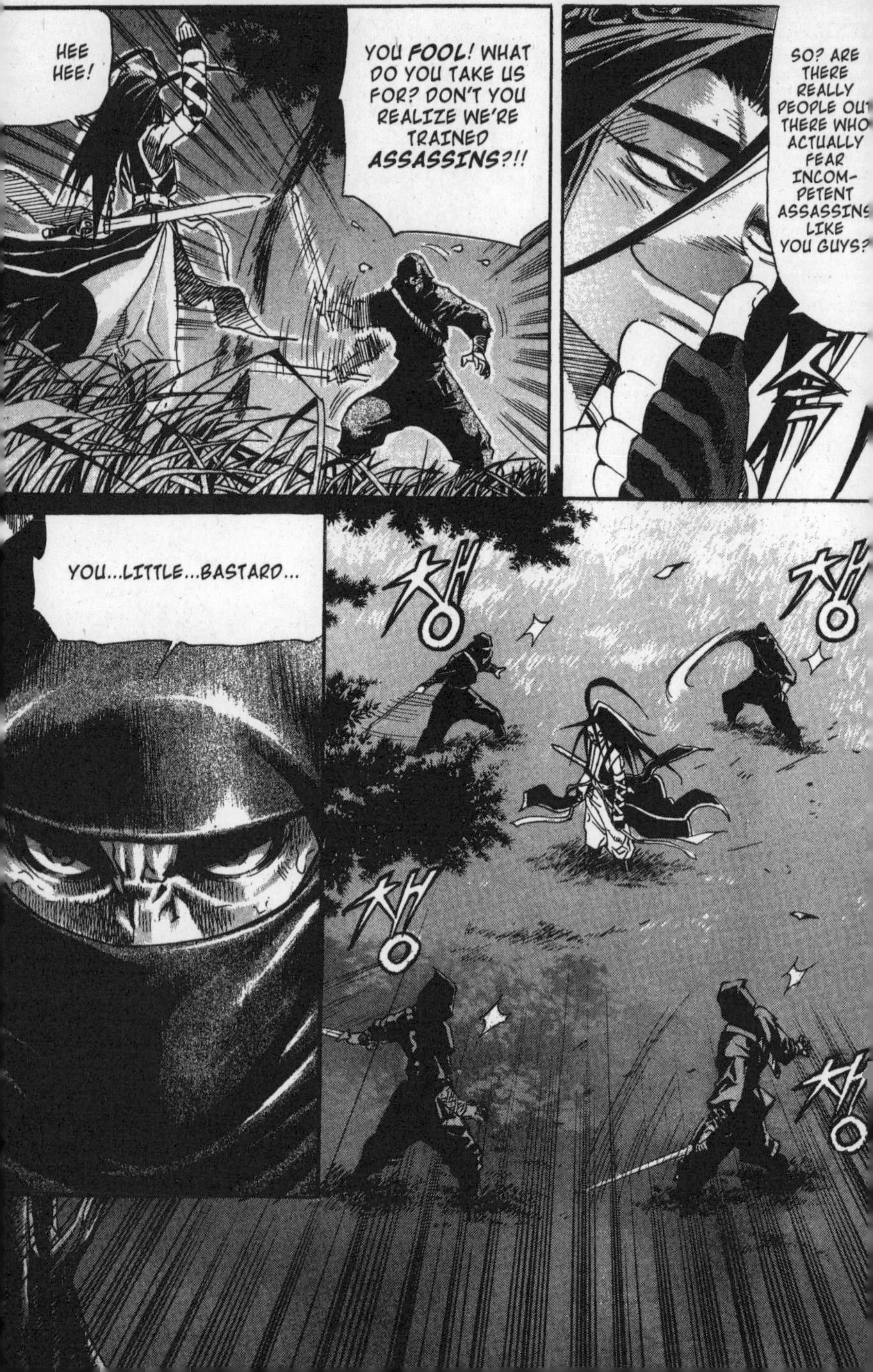
HEE HEE!
YOU FOOL! WHAT DO YOU TAKE US FOR? DON'T YOU REALIZE WE'RE TRAINED ASSASSINS?!!
SO? ARE THERE REALLY PEOPLE OUT THERE WHO ACTUALLY FEAR INCOMPETENT ASSASSINS LIKE YOU GUYS?
YOU...LITTLE...BASTARD...

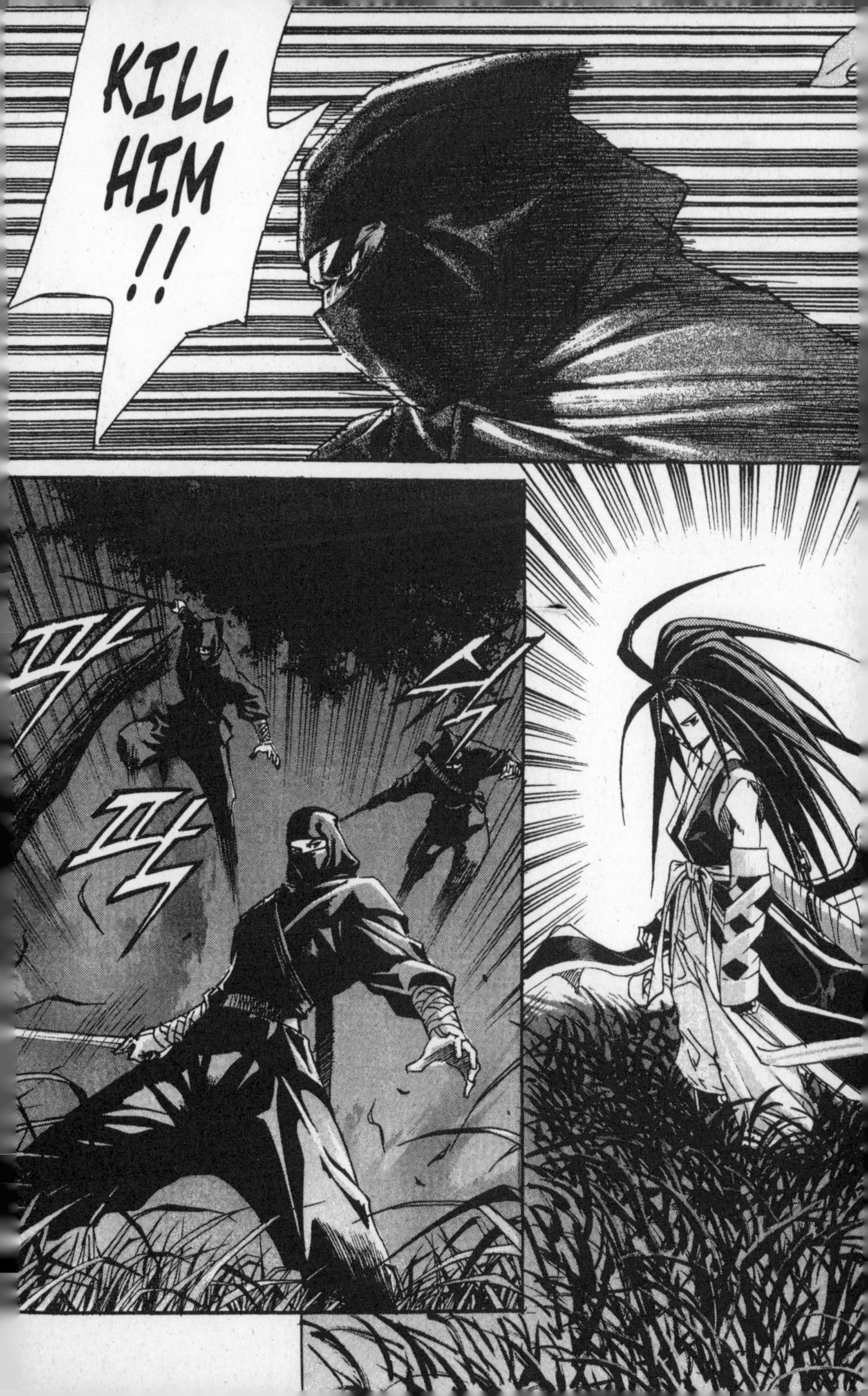
KILL HIM!!

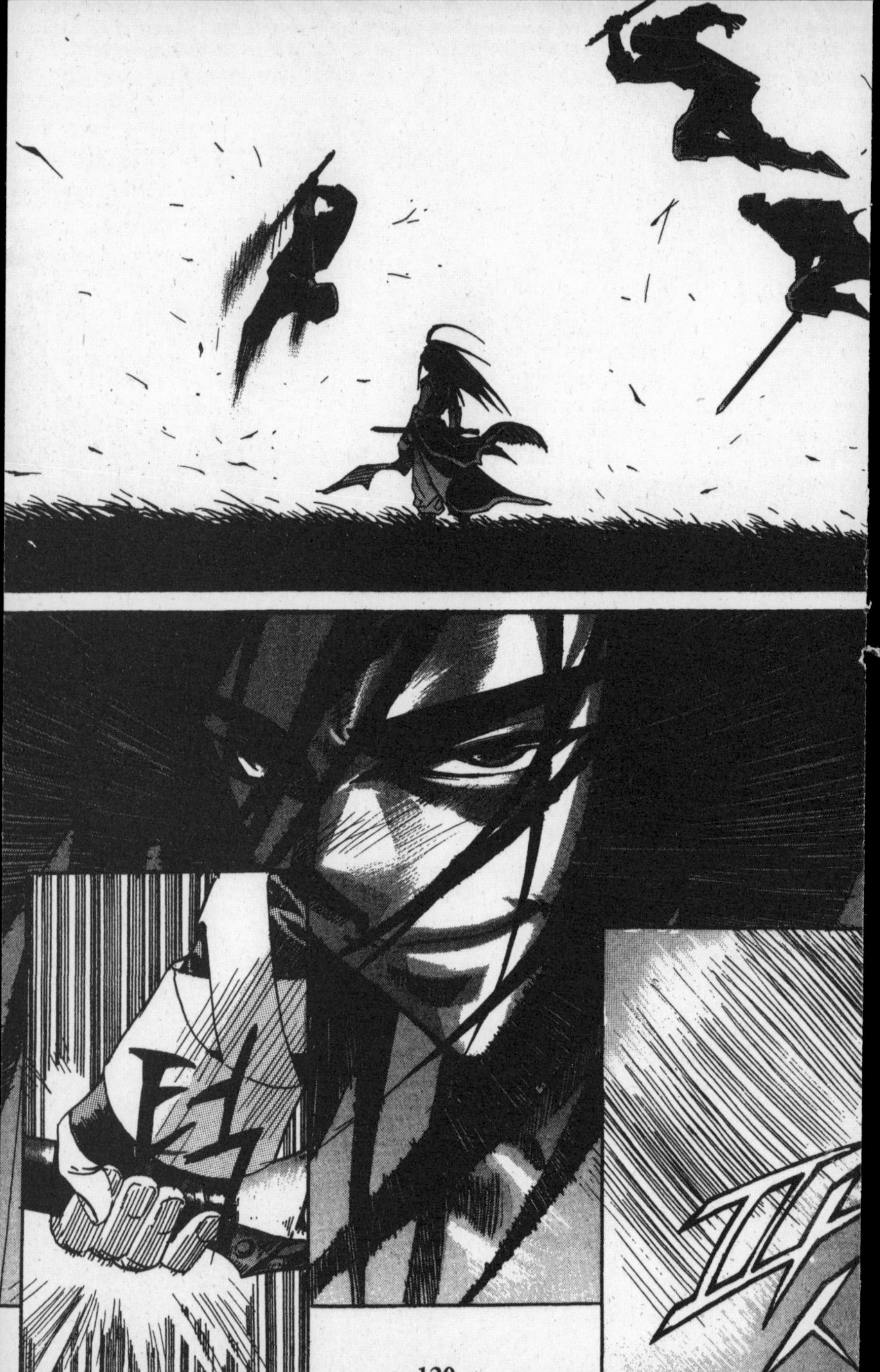

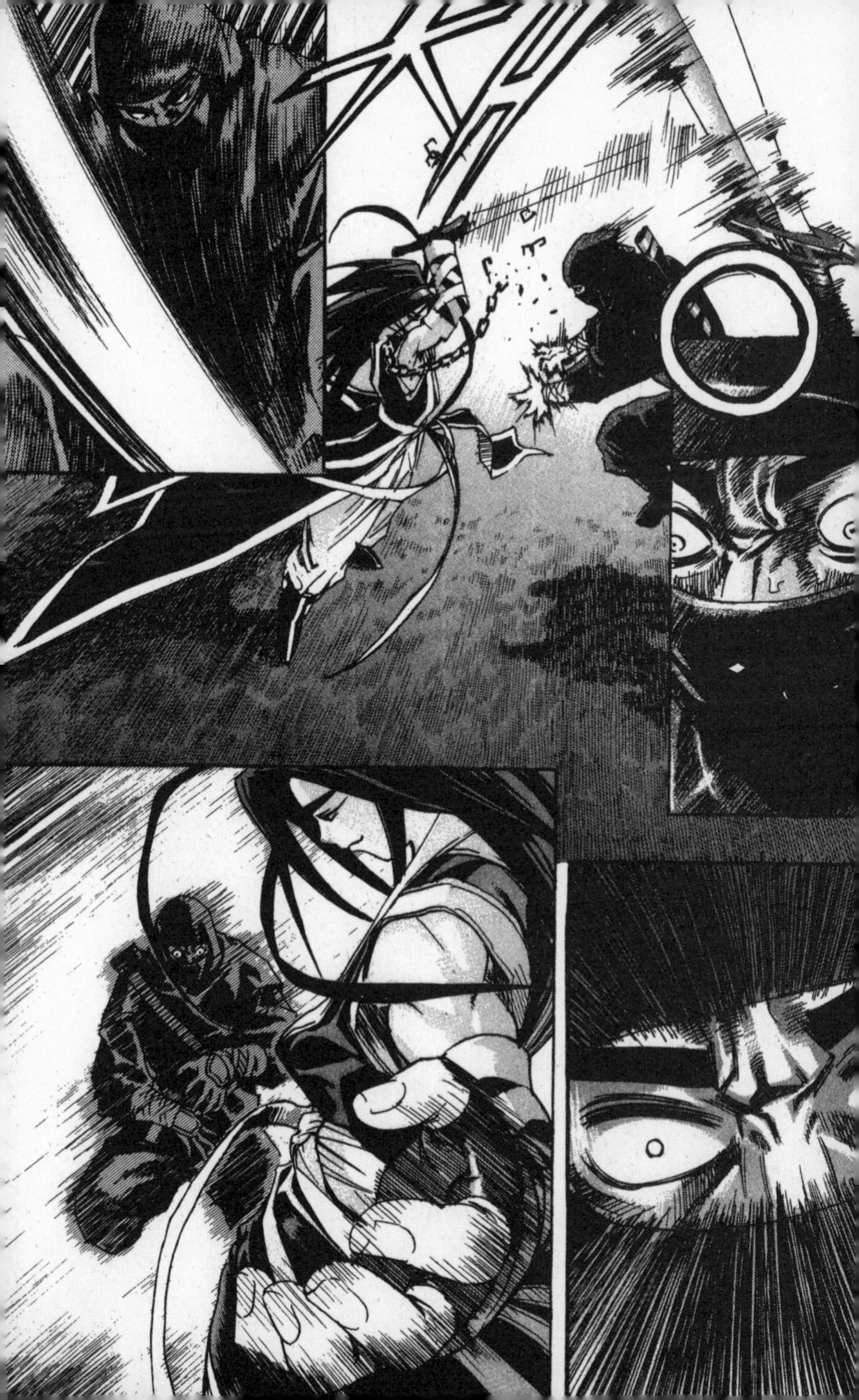

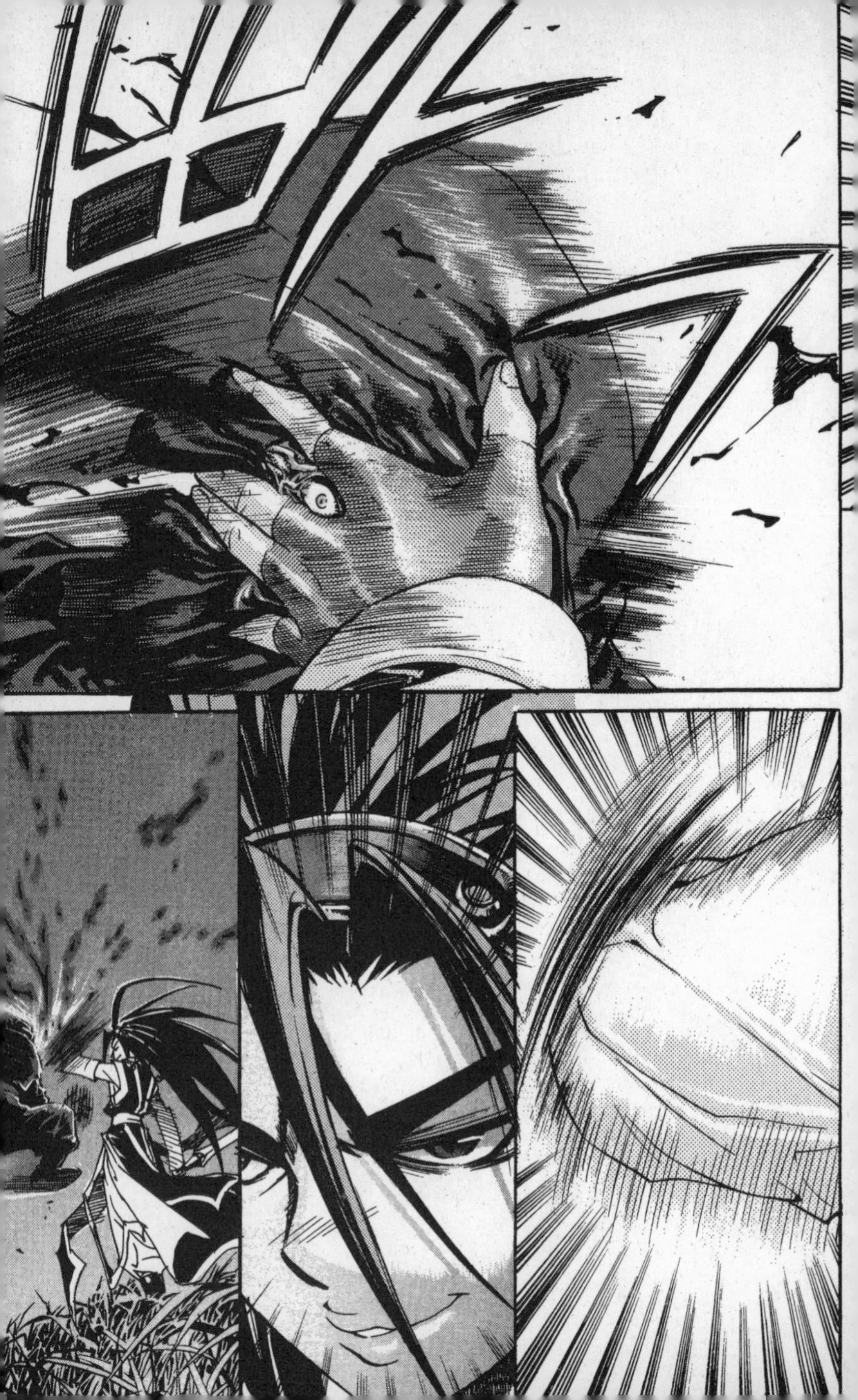

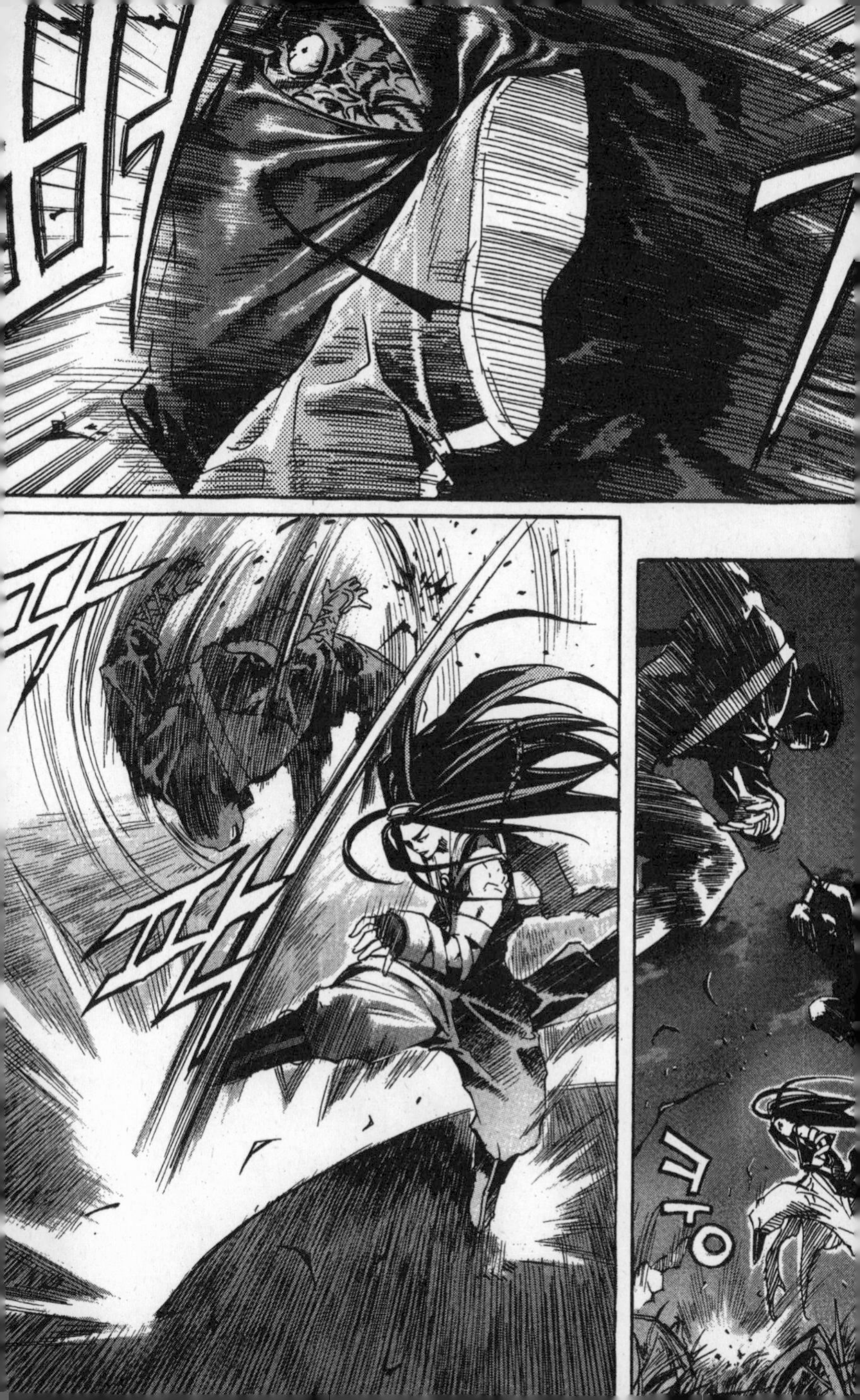

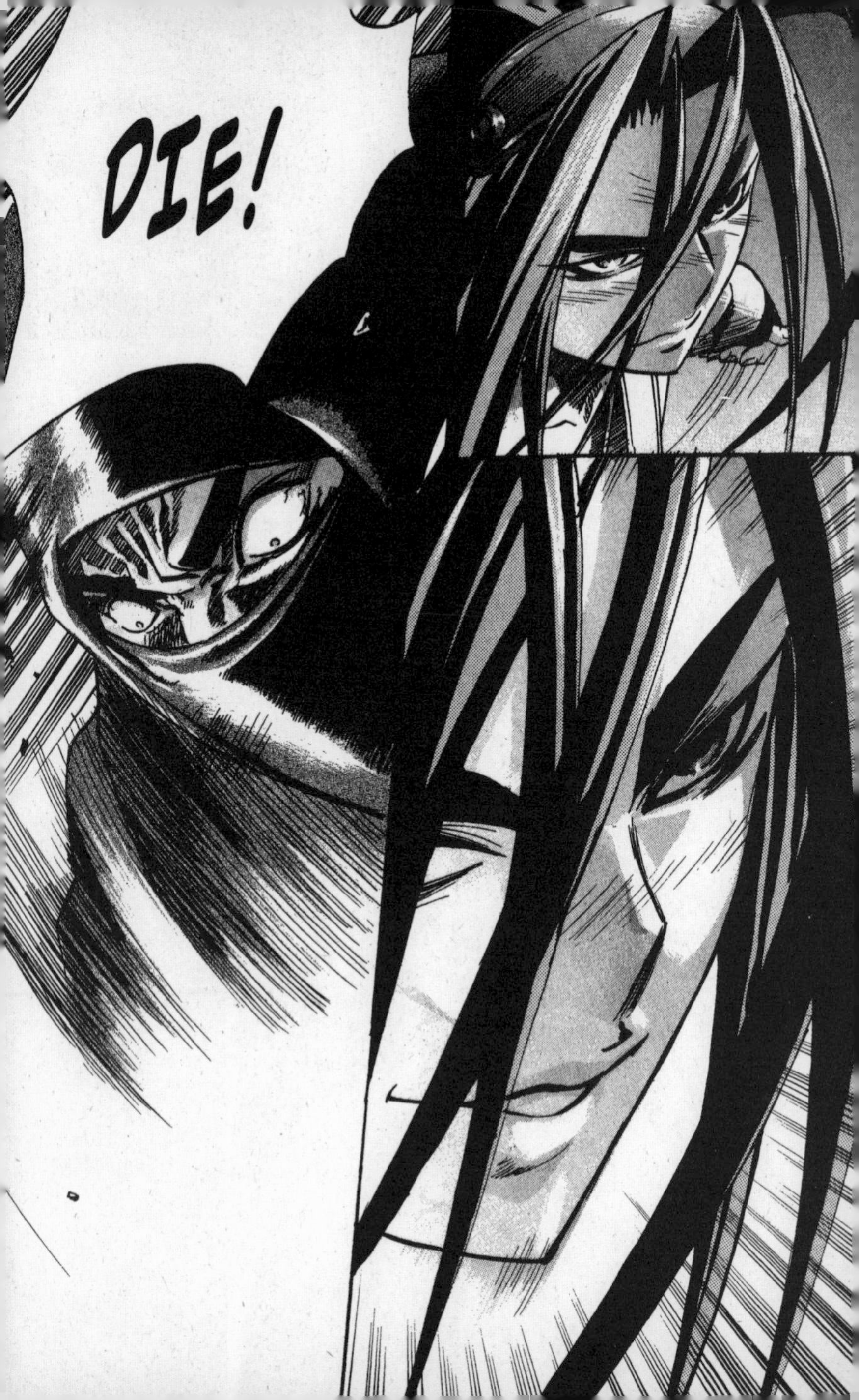
DIE!

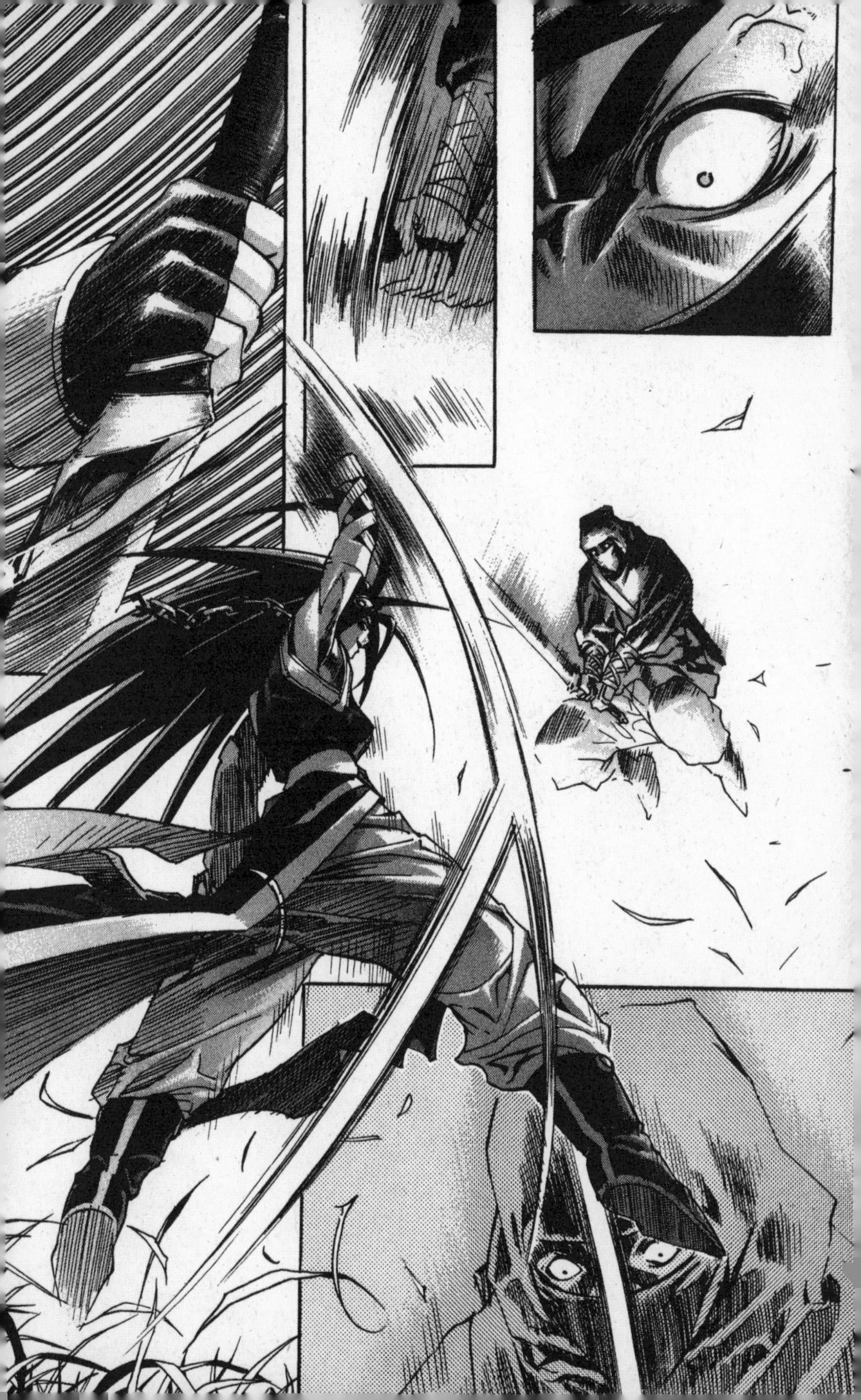

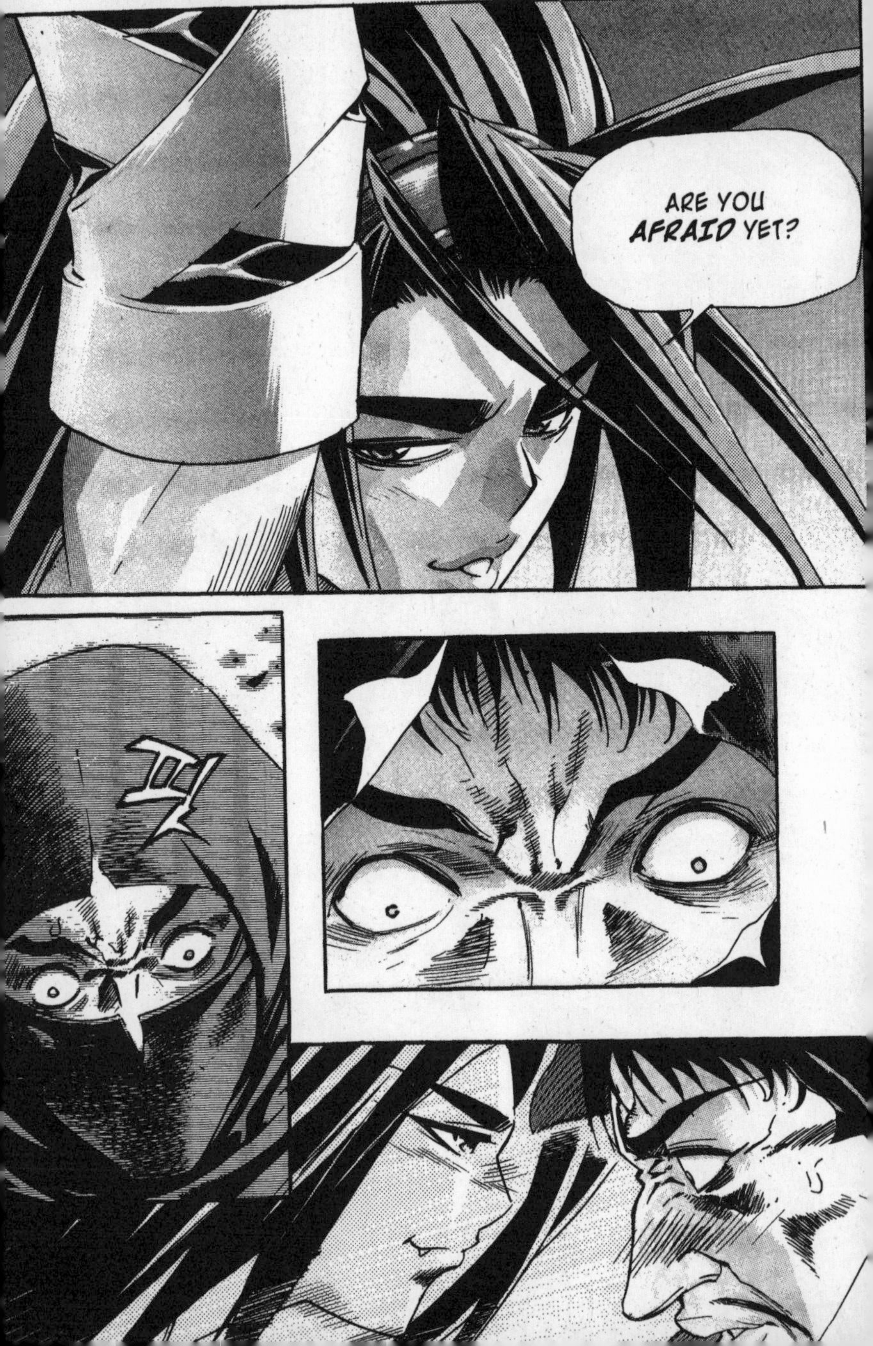
ARE YOU AFRAID YET?

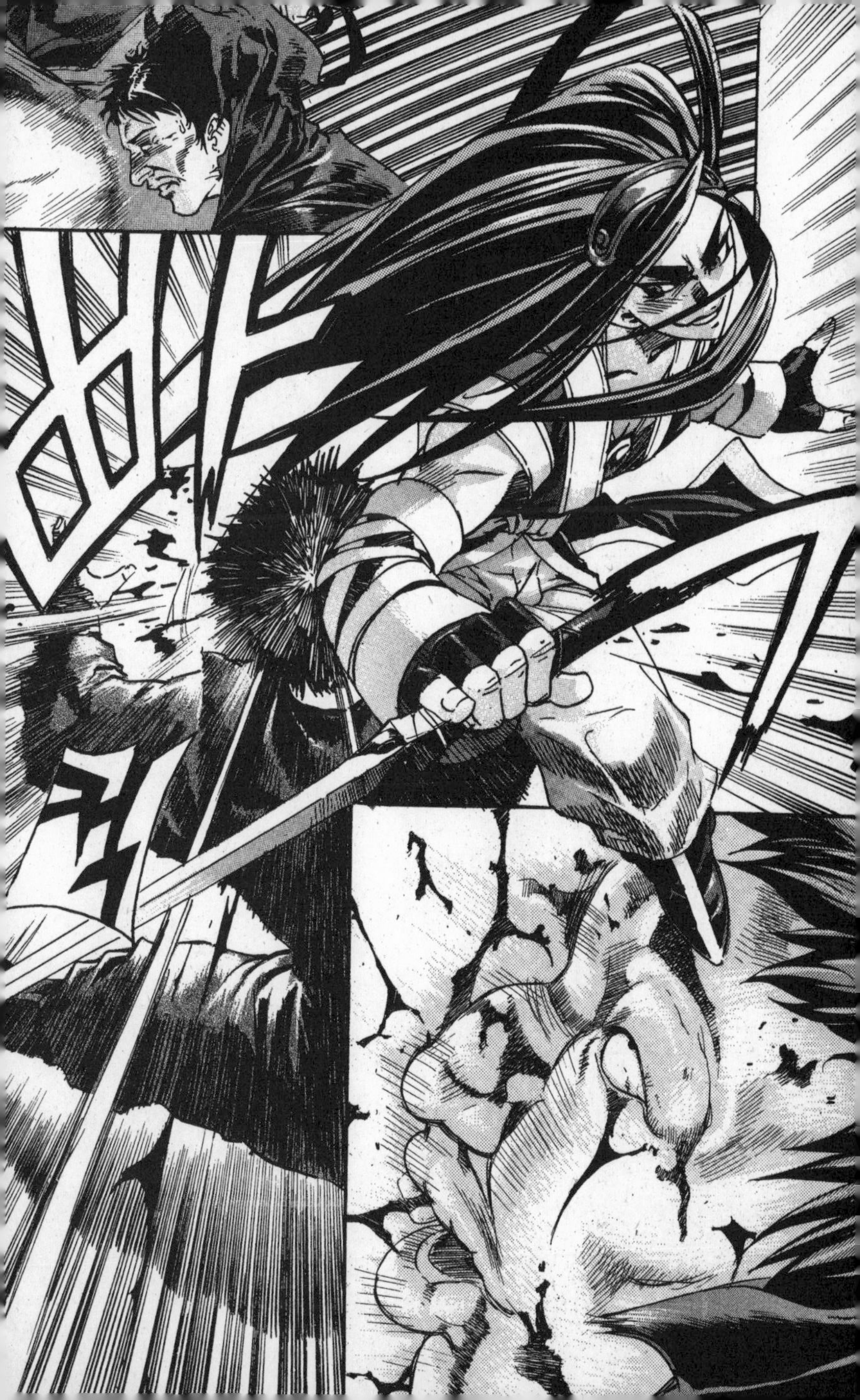

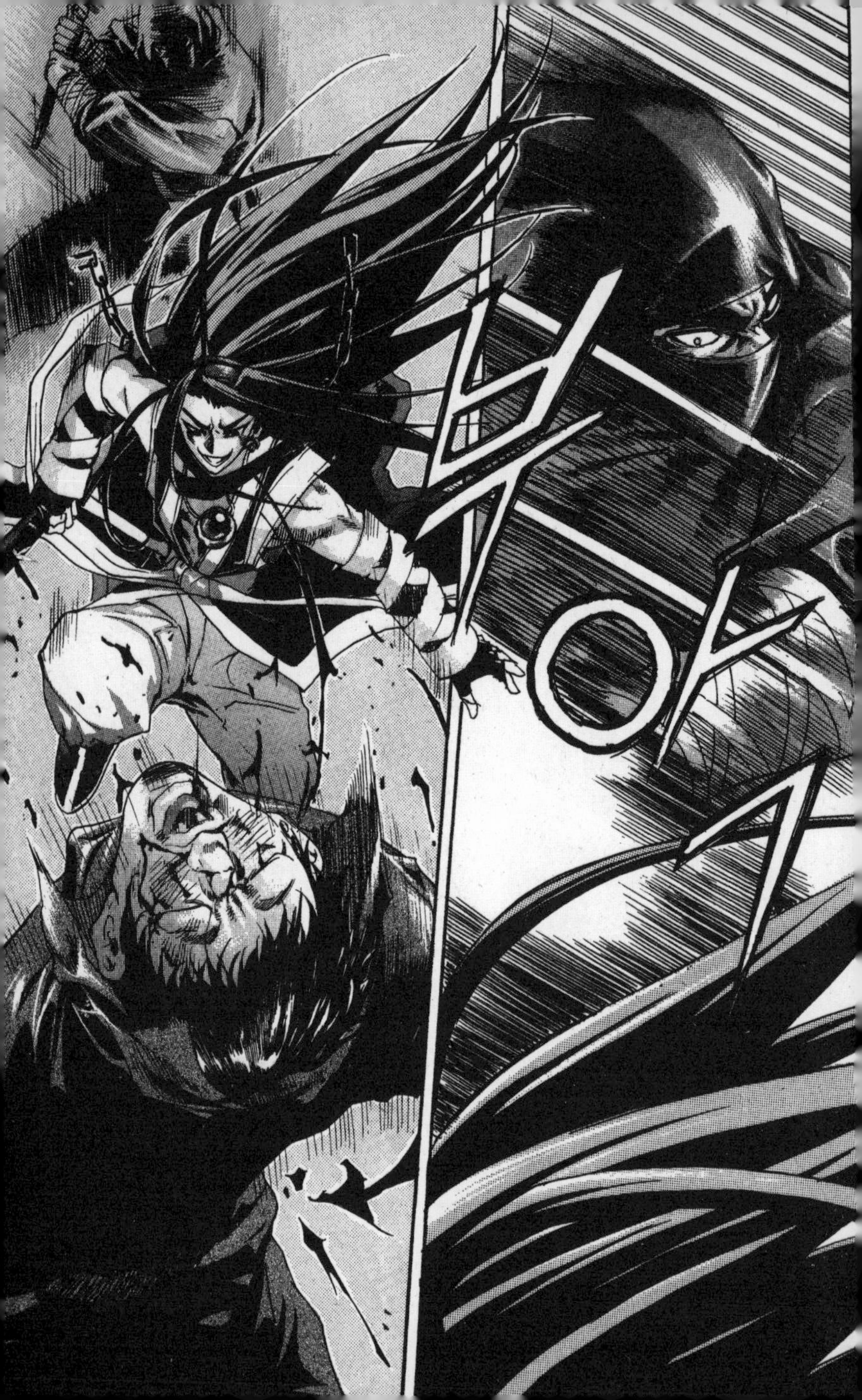

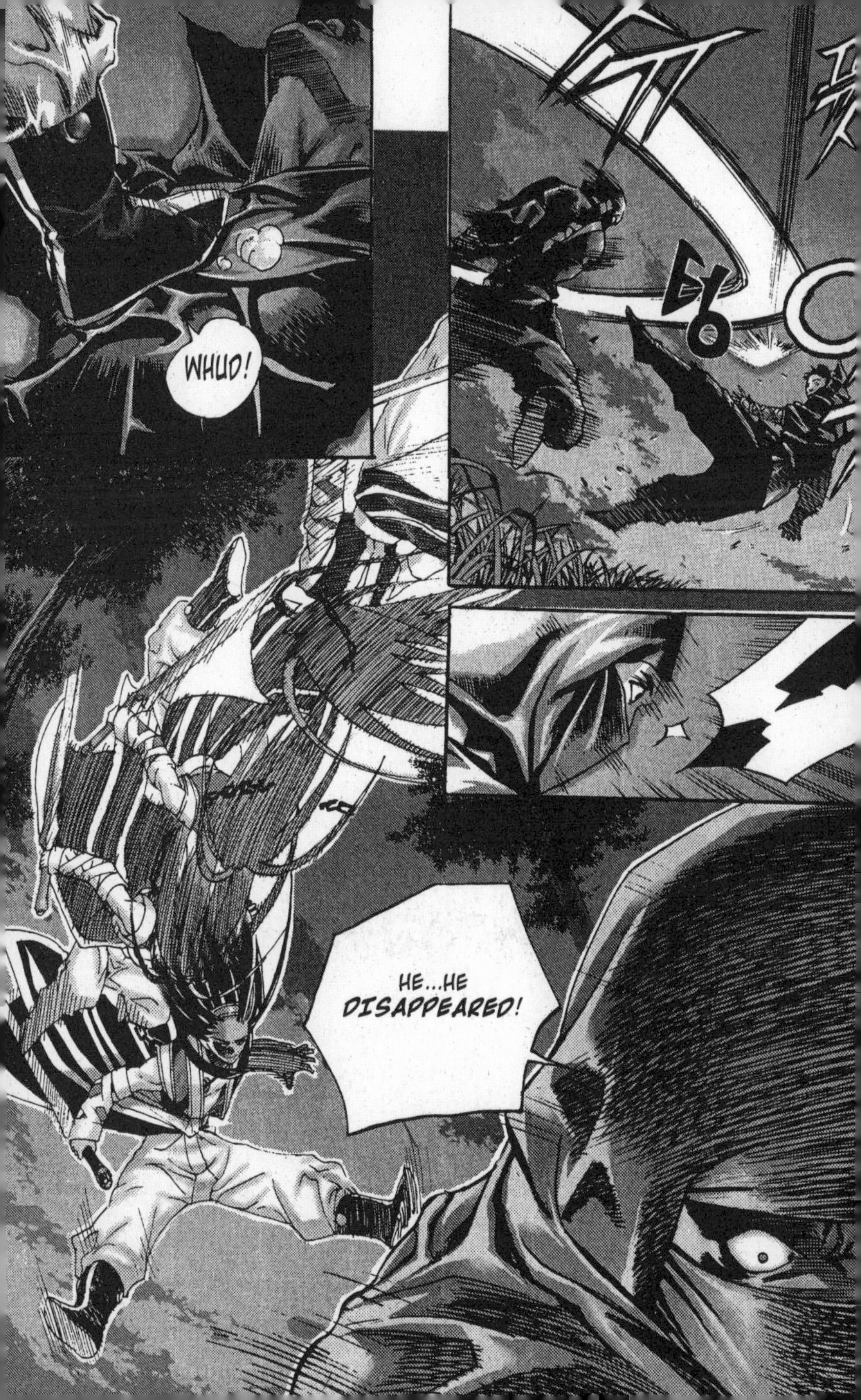
WHUD!
HE...HE DISAPPEARED!

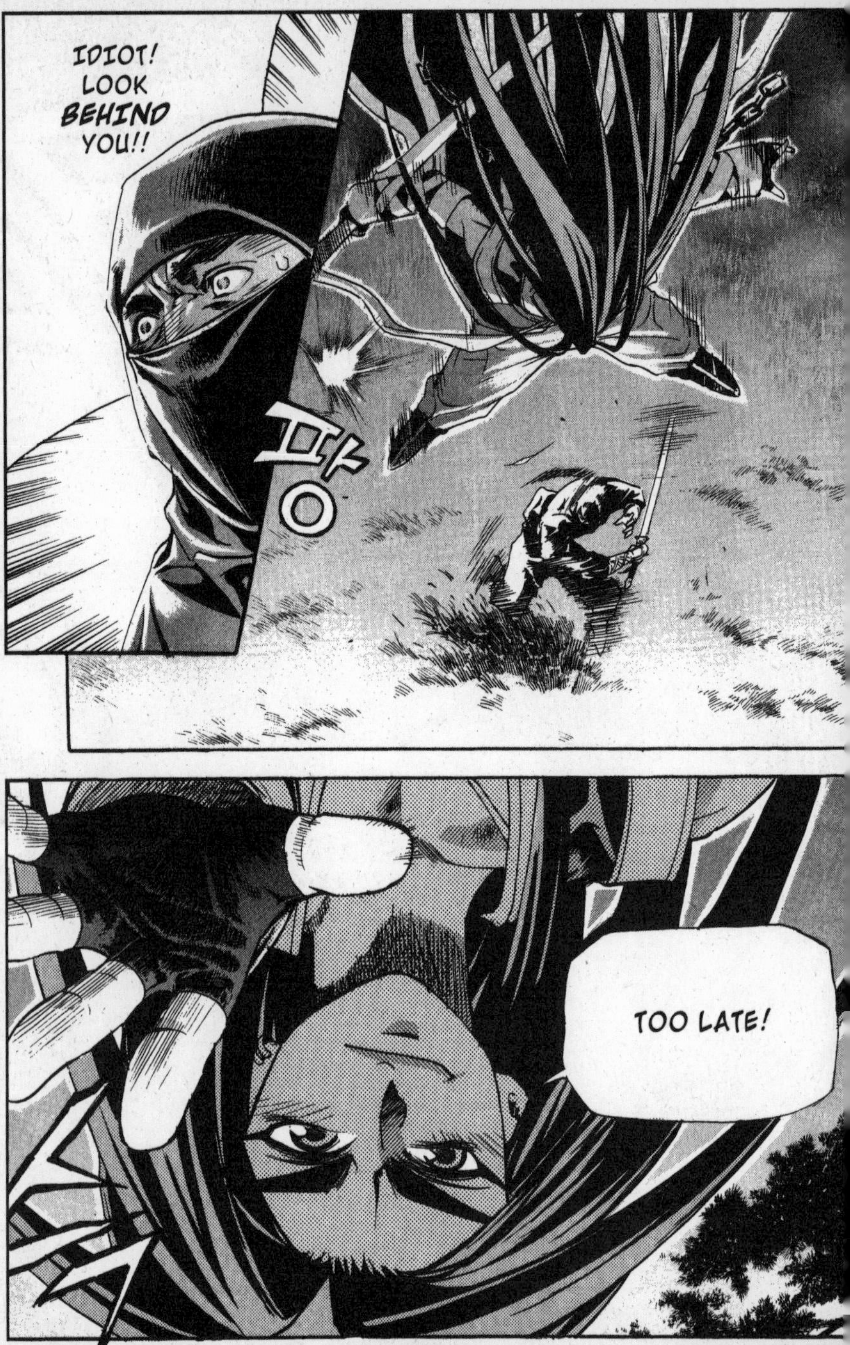
IDIOT! LOOK BEHIND YOU!!
TOO LATE!

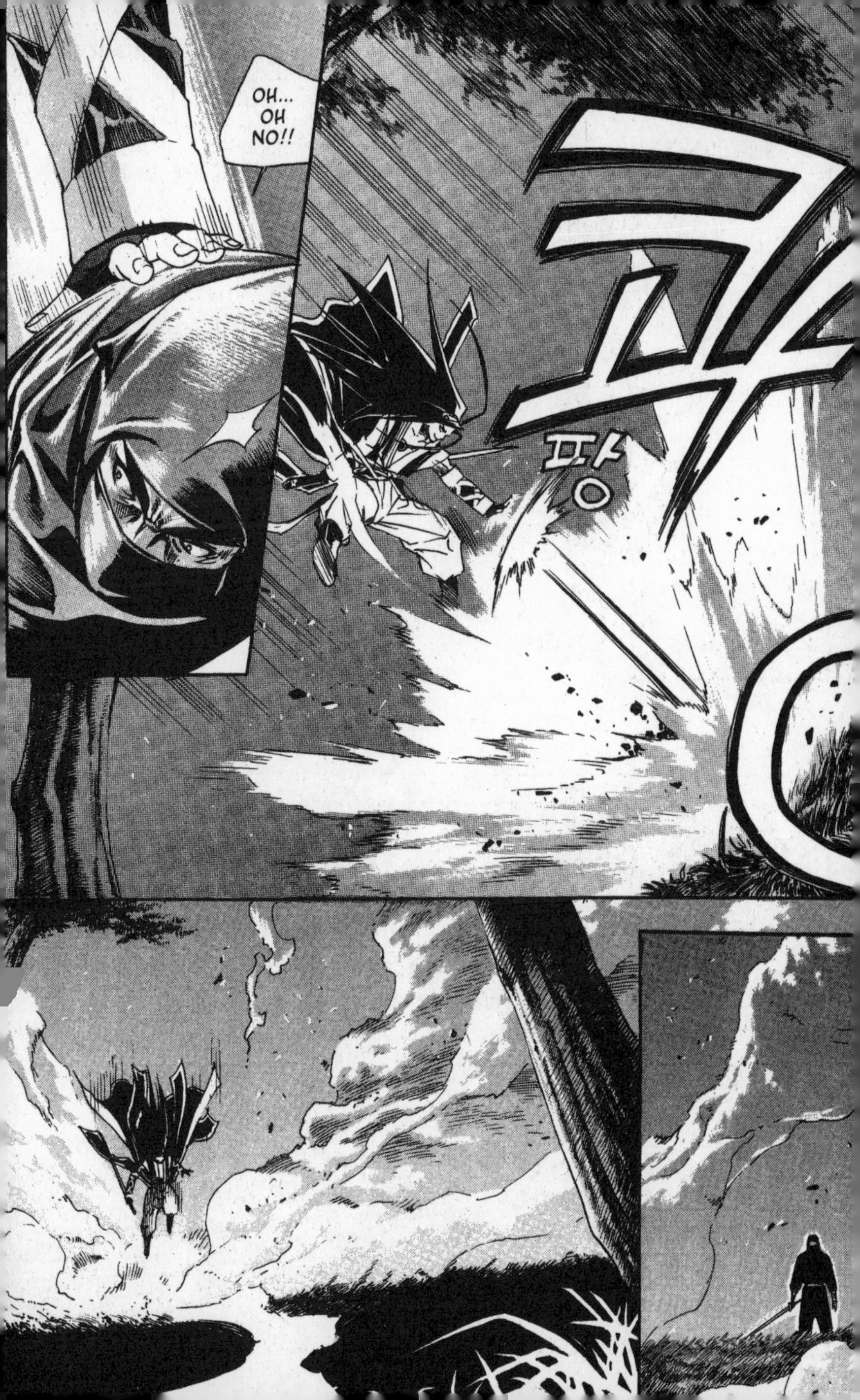
OH... OH NO!!

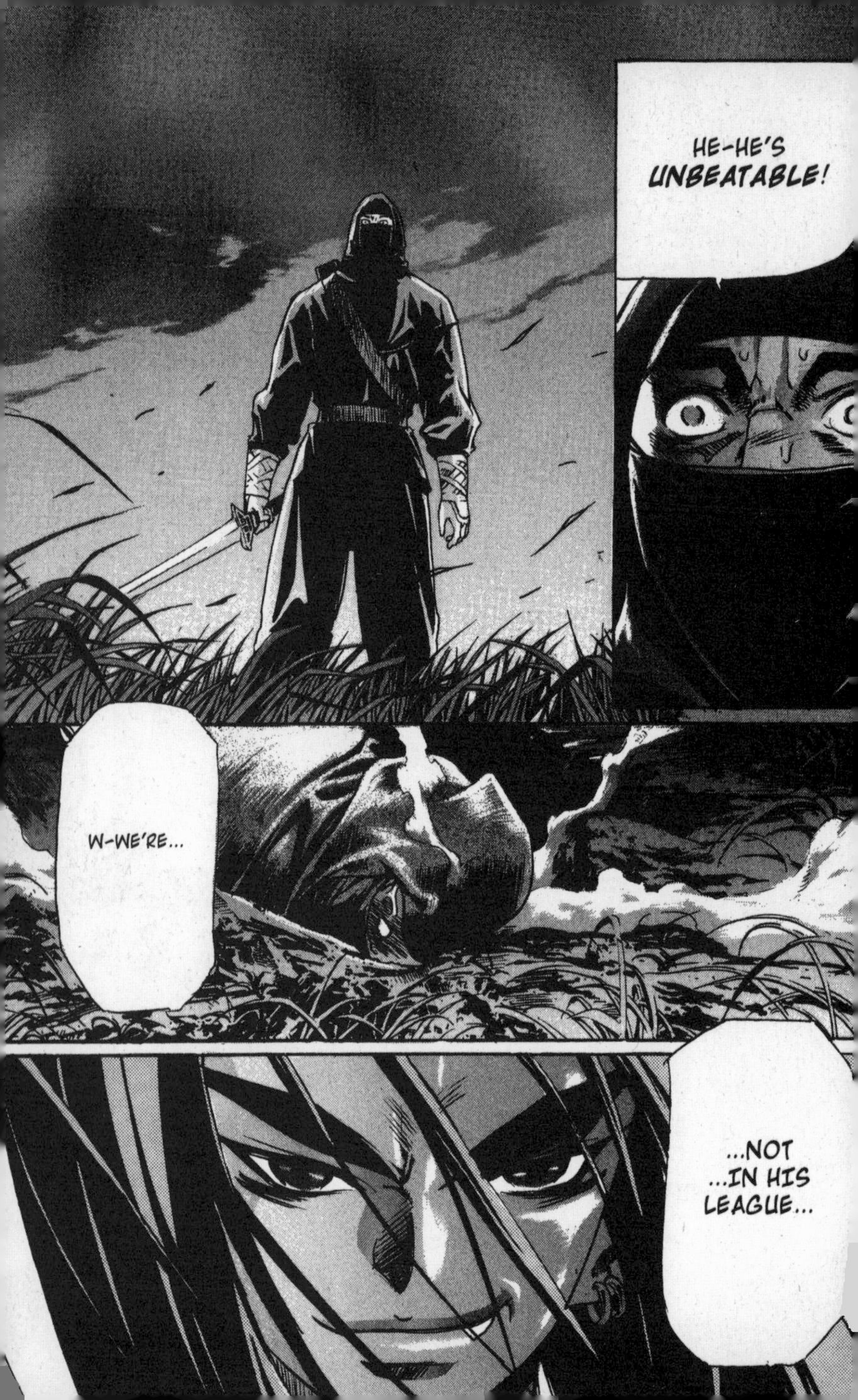
HE-HE'S UNBEATABLE!
W-WE'RE...
...NOT ...IN HIS LEAGUE...

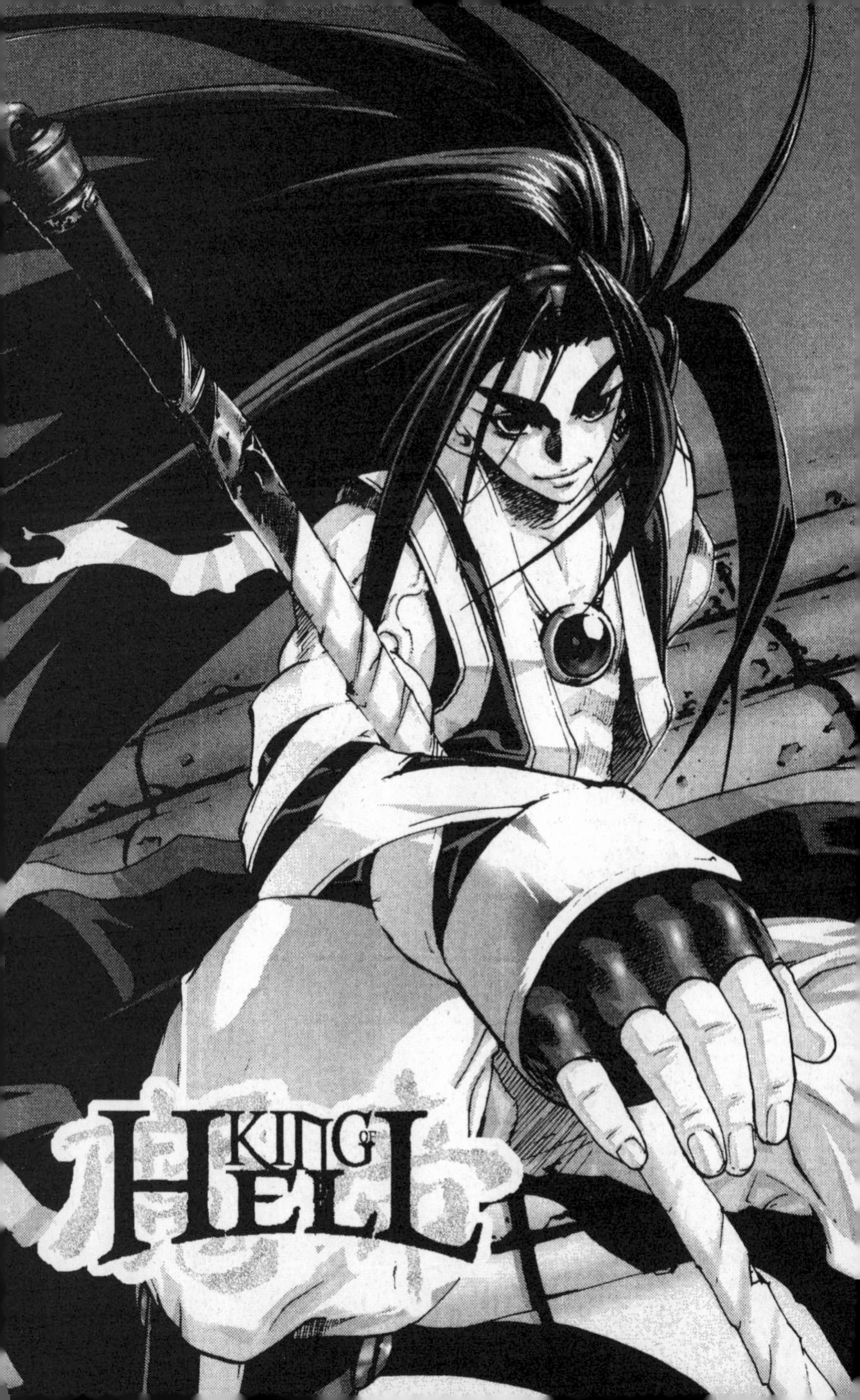
KING OF HELL

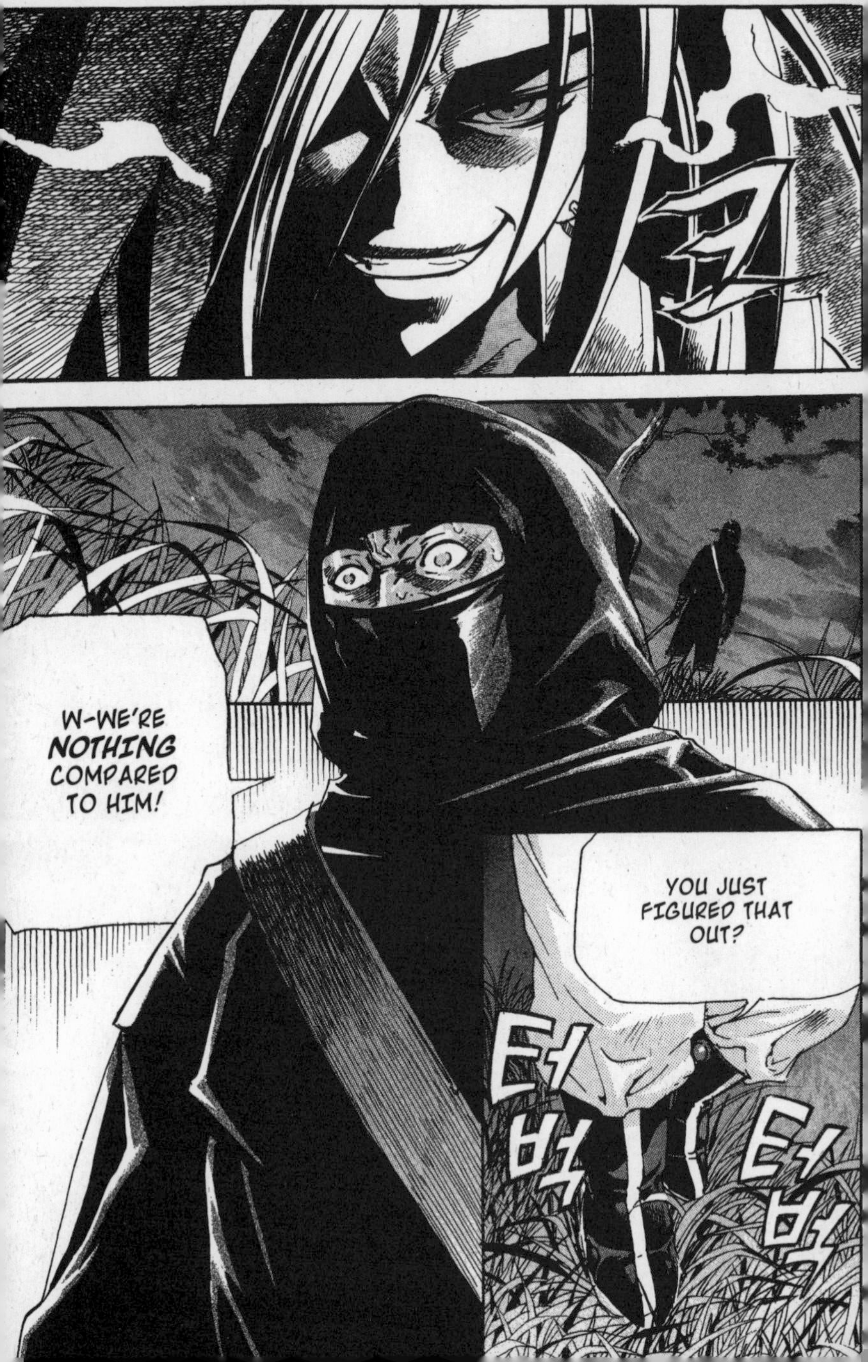
W-WE'RE **NOTHING** COMPARED TO HIM!
YOU JUST FIGURED THAT OUT?

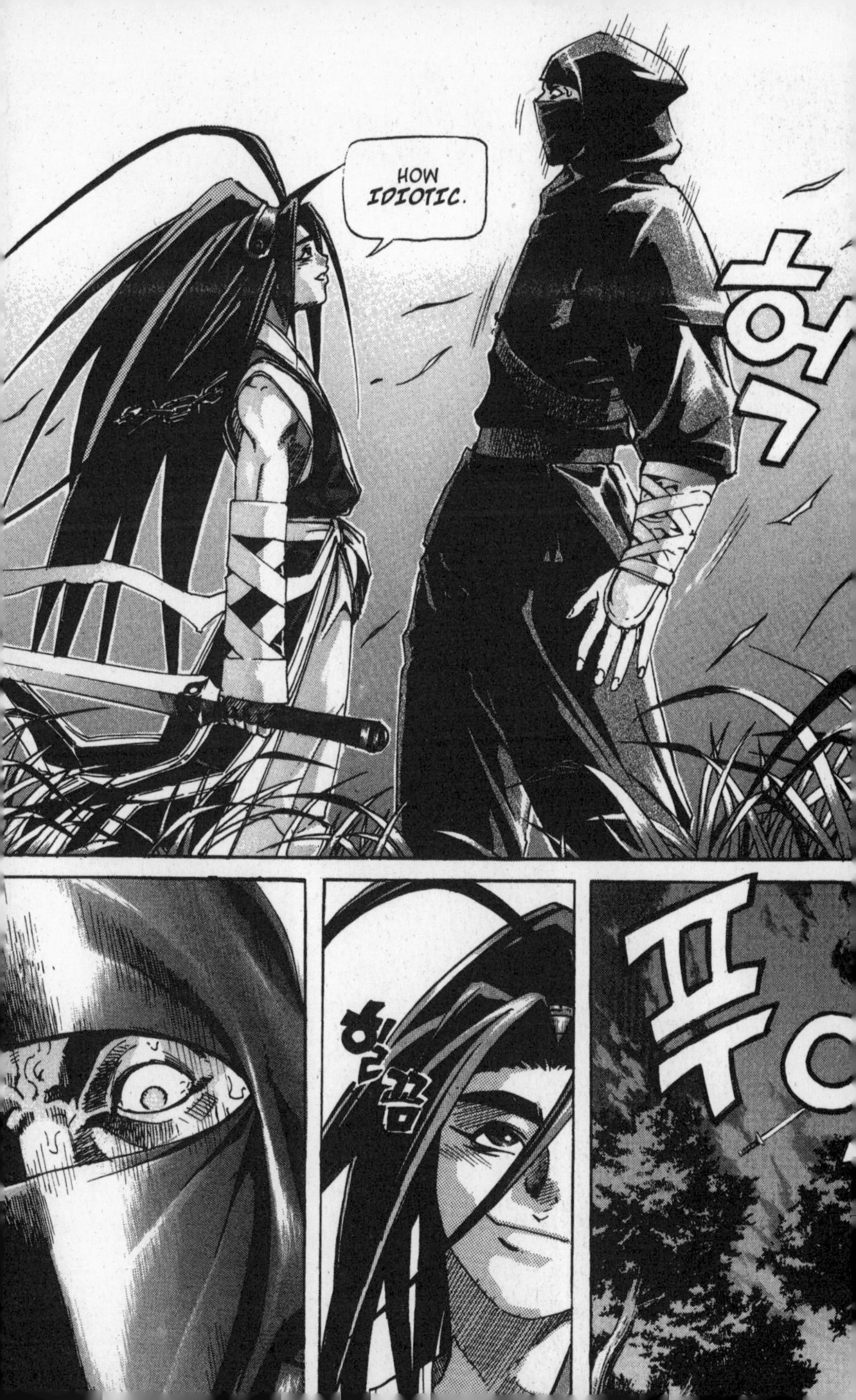
HOW IDIOTIC.
헉
힐끔

뚝, 뚝..

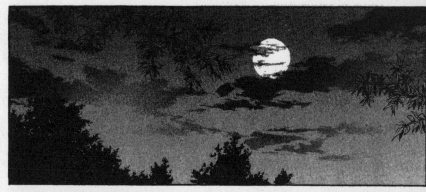

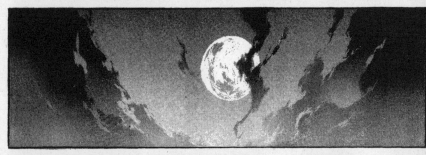

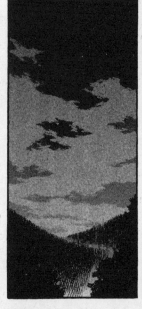

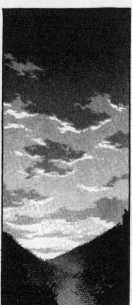

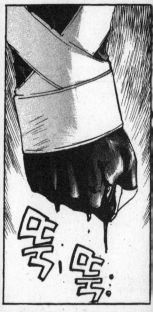

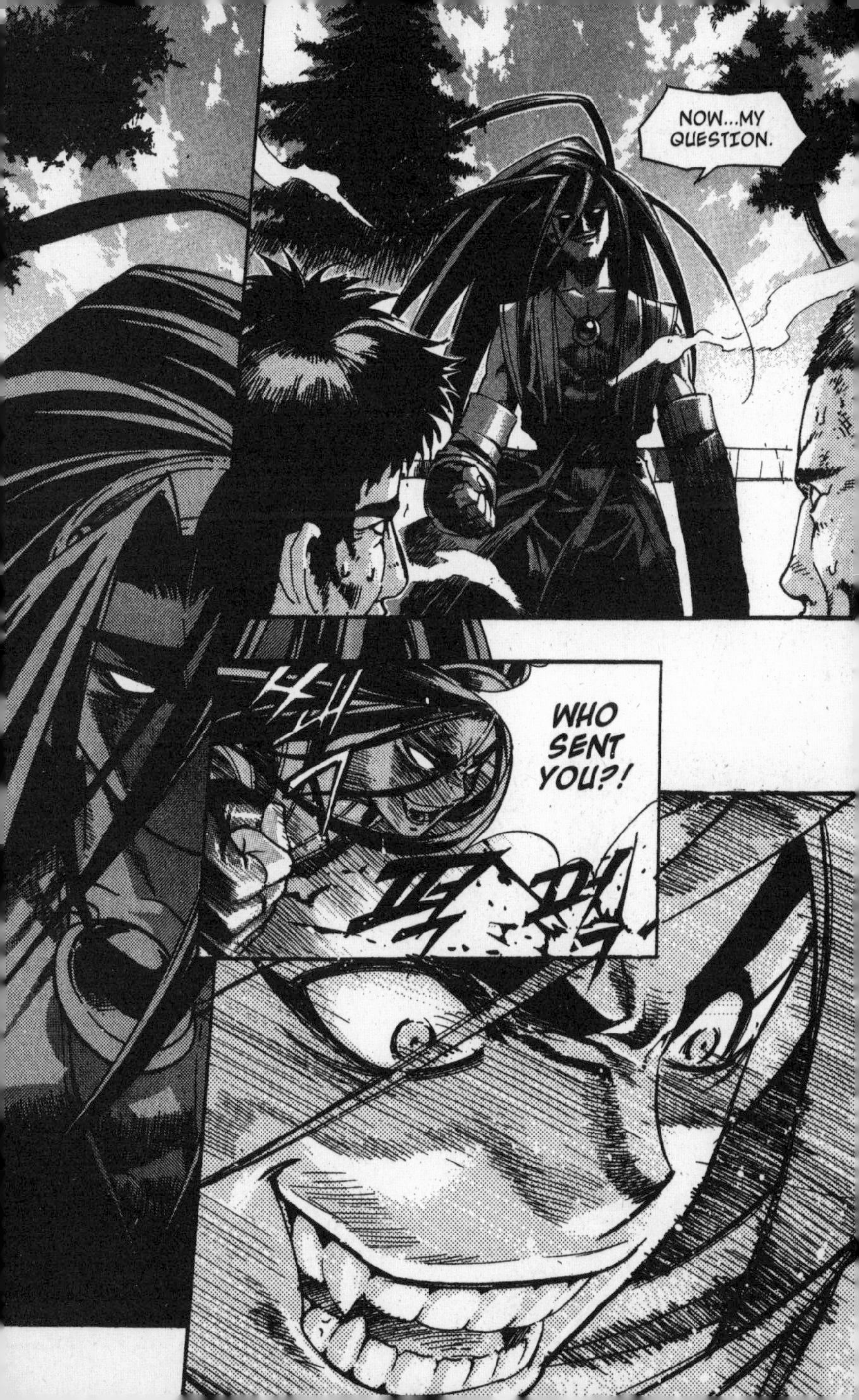
NOW...MY QUESTION.
WHO SENT YOU?!

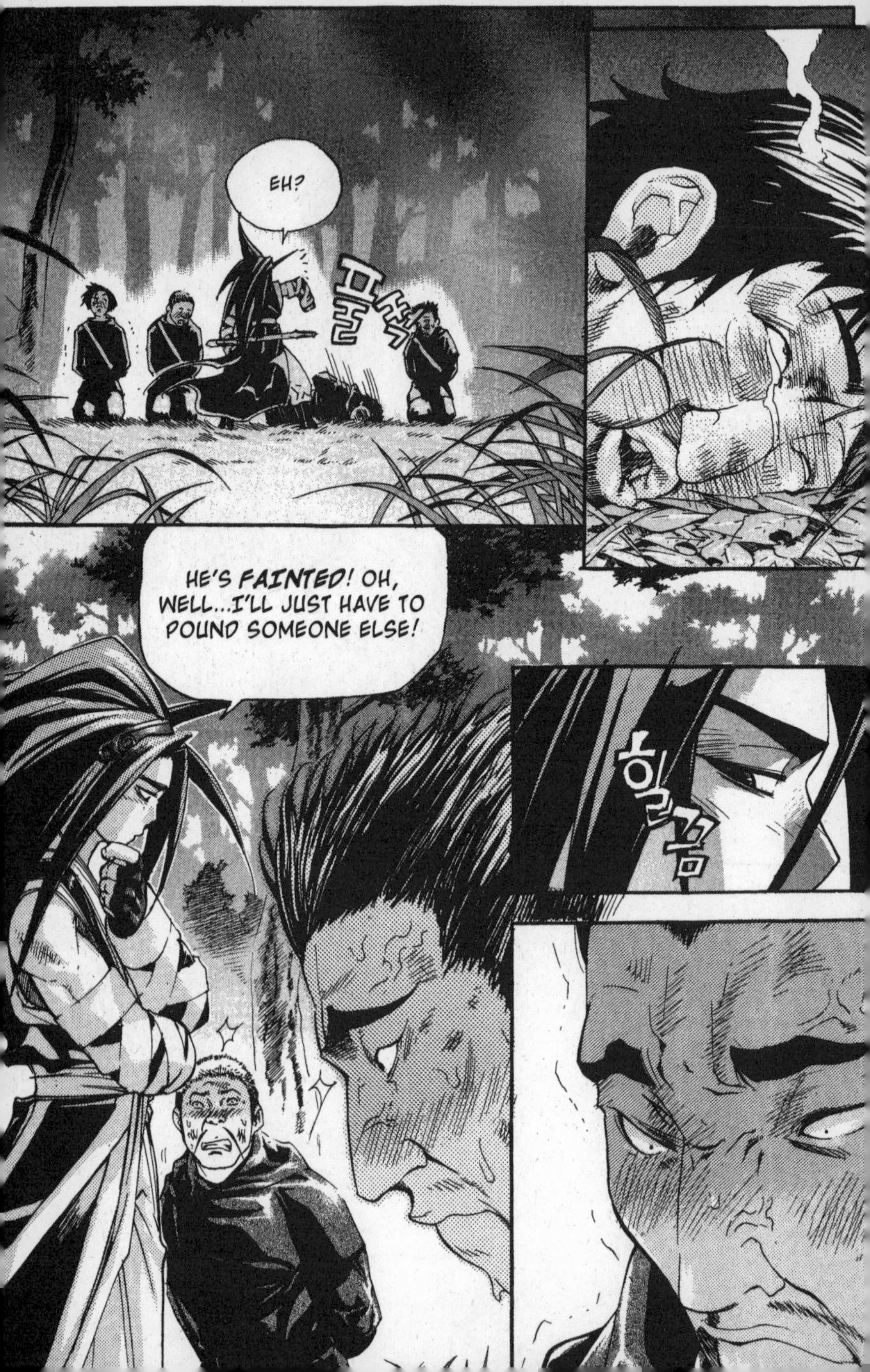
EH?
HE'S FAINTED! OH, WELL...I'LL JUST HAVE TO POUND SOMEONE ELSE!

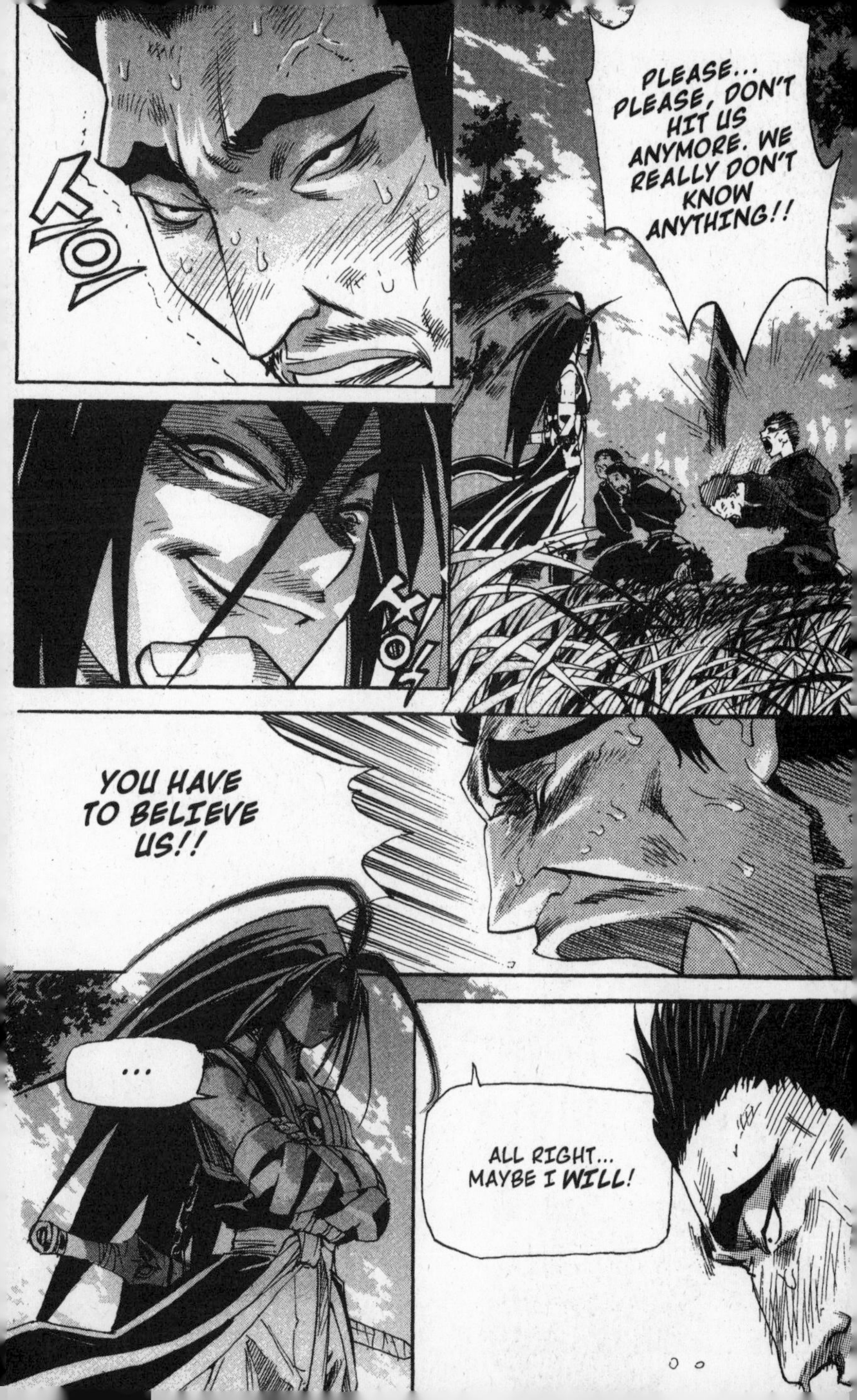
PLEASE... PLEASE, DON'T HIT US ANYMORE. WE REALLY DON'T KNOW ANYTHING!!
YOU HAVE TO BELIEVE US!!
...
ALL RIGHT... MAYBE I WILL!

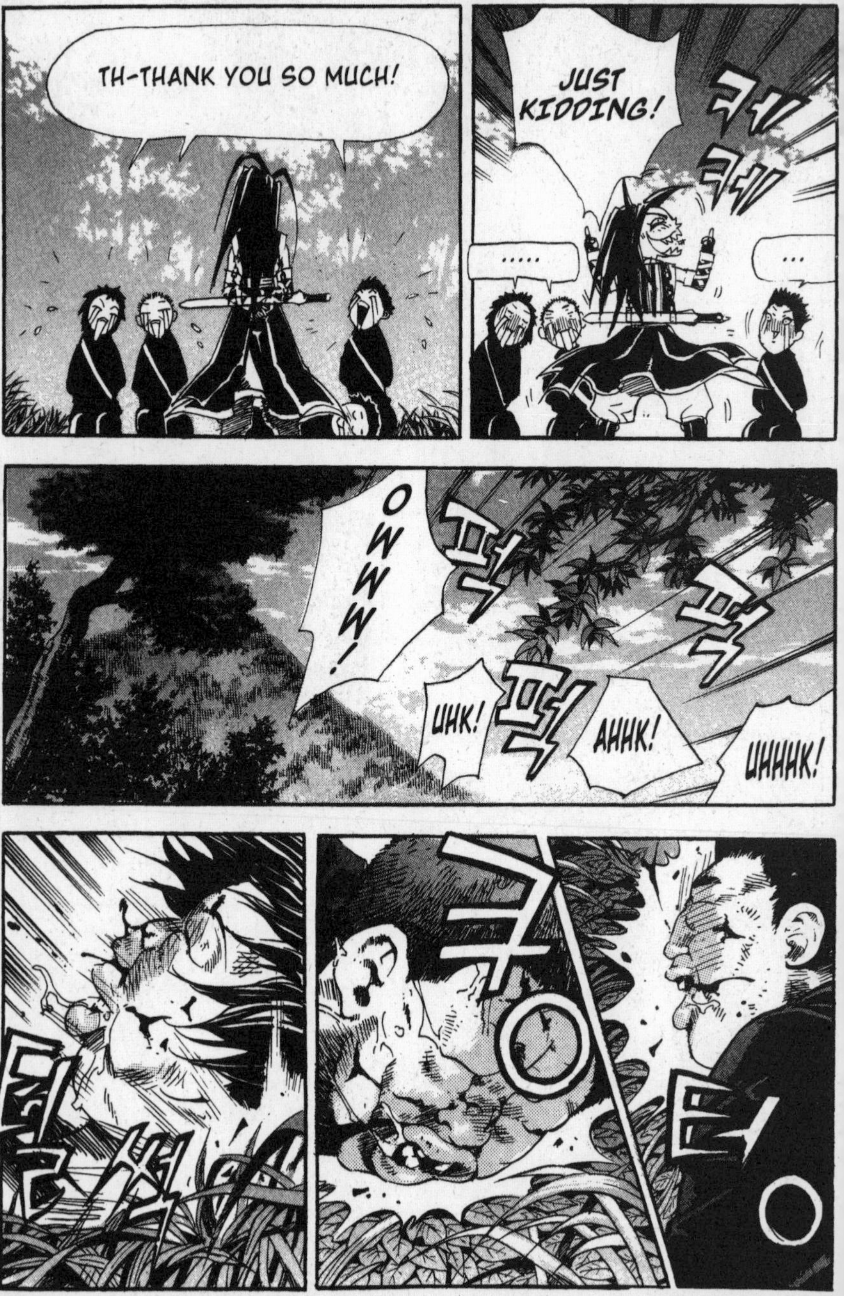
TH-THANK YOU SO MUCH!
JUST KIDDING!
.....
...
OWWWW!
UHK!
AHHK!
UHHHK!

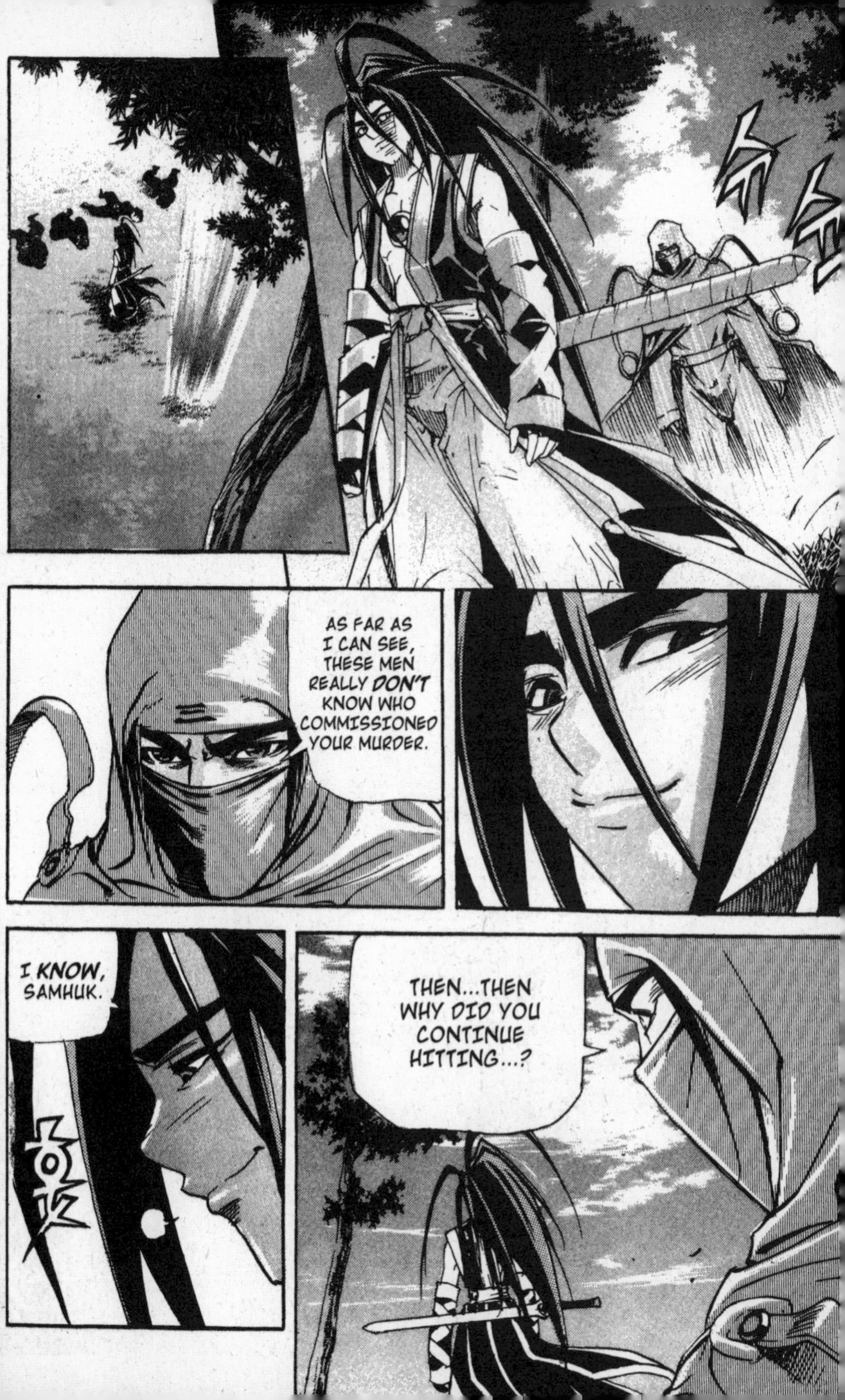
KYE KYEH
AS FAR AS I CAN SEE, THESE MEN REALLY DON'T KNOW WHO COMMISSIONED YOUR MURDER.
I KNOW, SAMHUK.
THEN...THEN WHY DID YOU CONTINUE HITTING...?

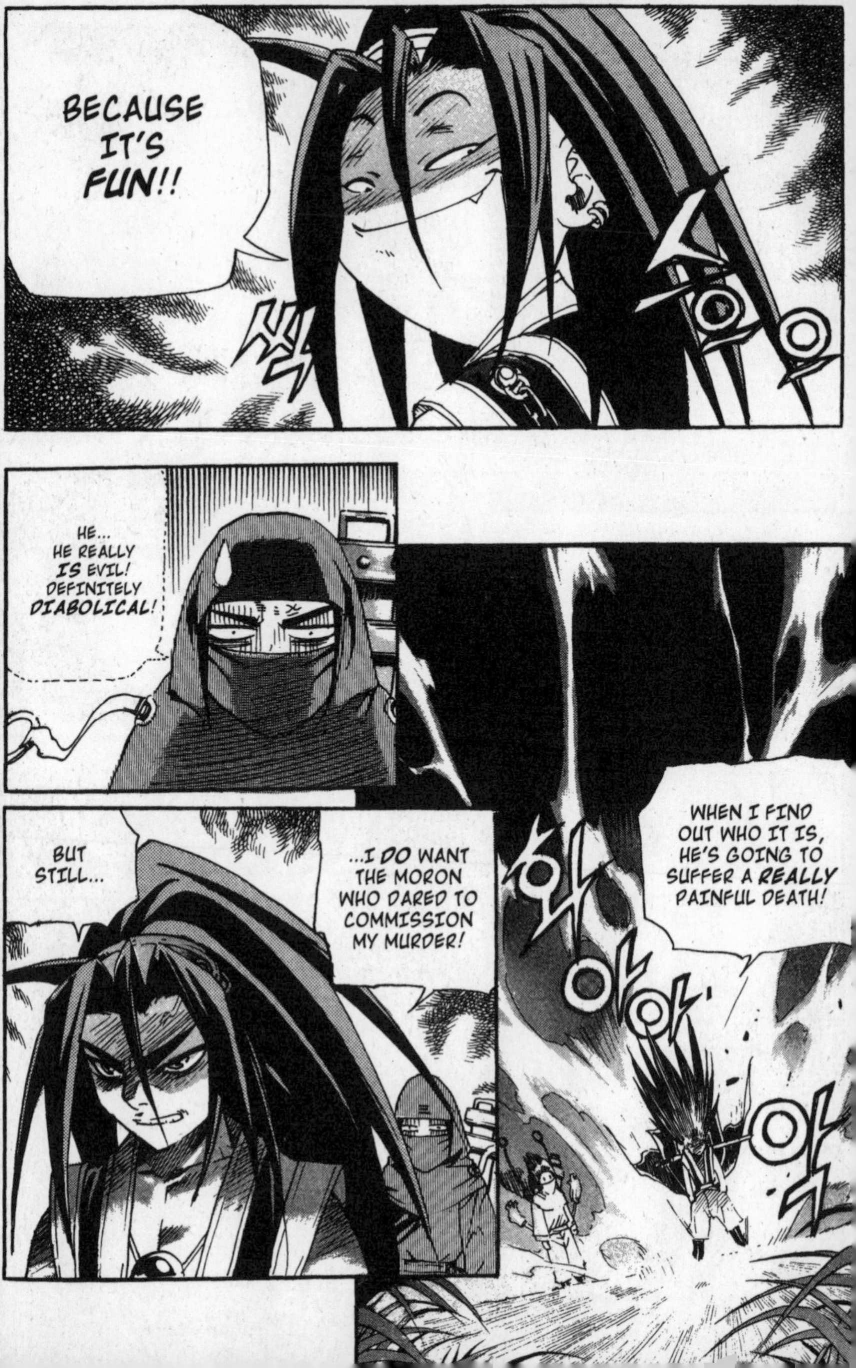
BECAUSE IT'S FUN!!
HE... HE REALLY IS EVIL! DEFINITELY DIABOLICAL!
BUT STILL...
...I DO WANT THE MORON WHO DARED TO COMMISSION MY MURDER!
WHEN I FIND OUT WHO IT IS, HE'S GOING TO SUFFER A REALLY PAINFUL DEATH!

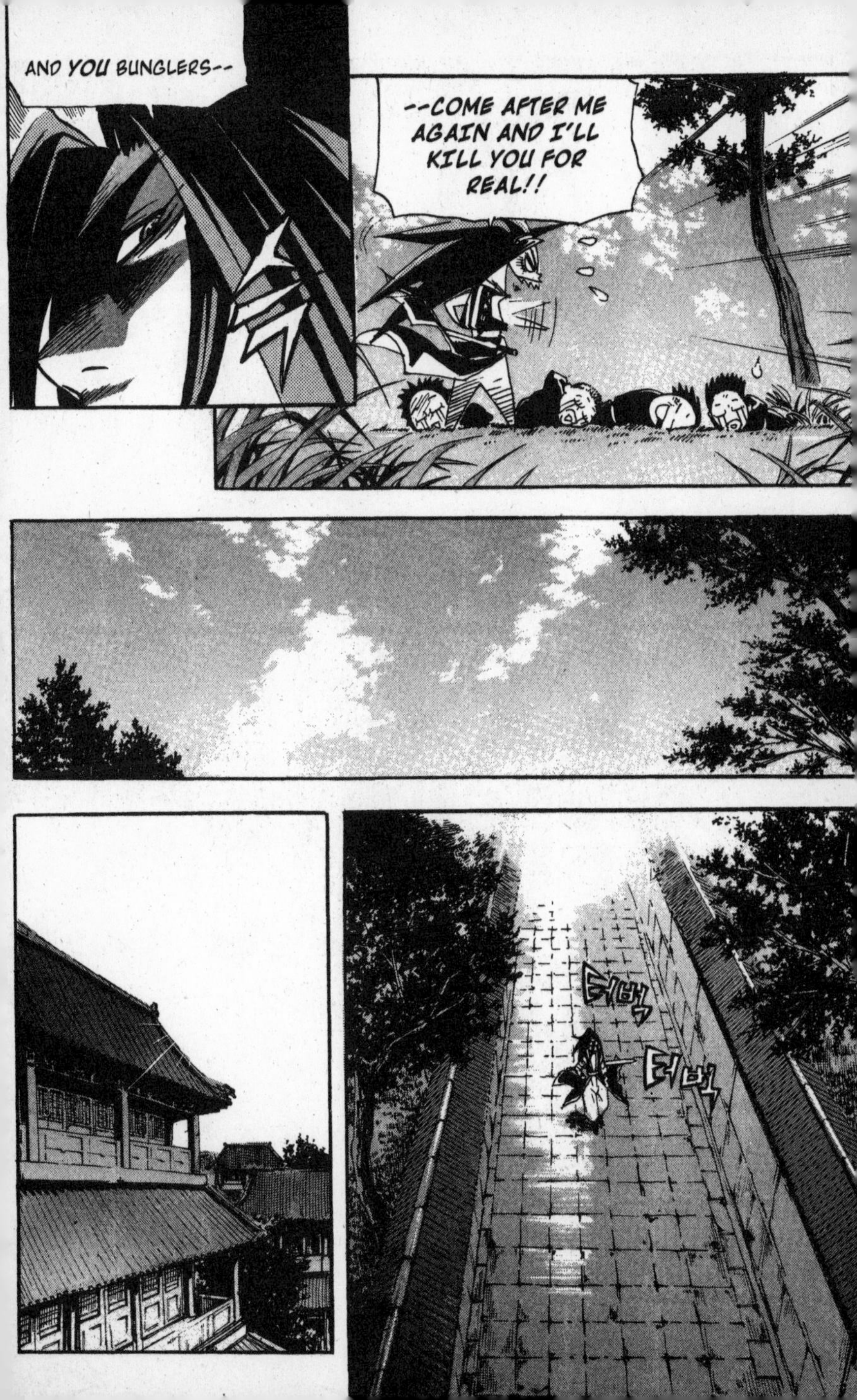
AND *YOU* BUNGLERS--
--COME AFTER ME AGAIN AND I'LL KILL YOU FOR REAL!!
터벅
터벅

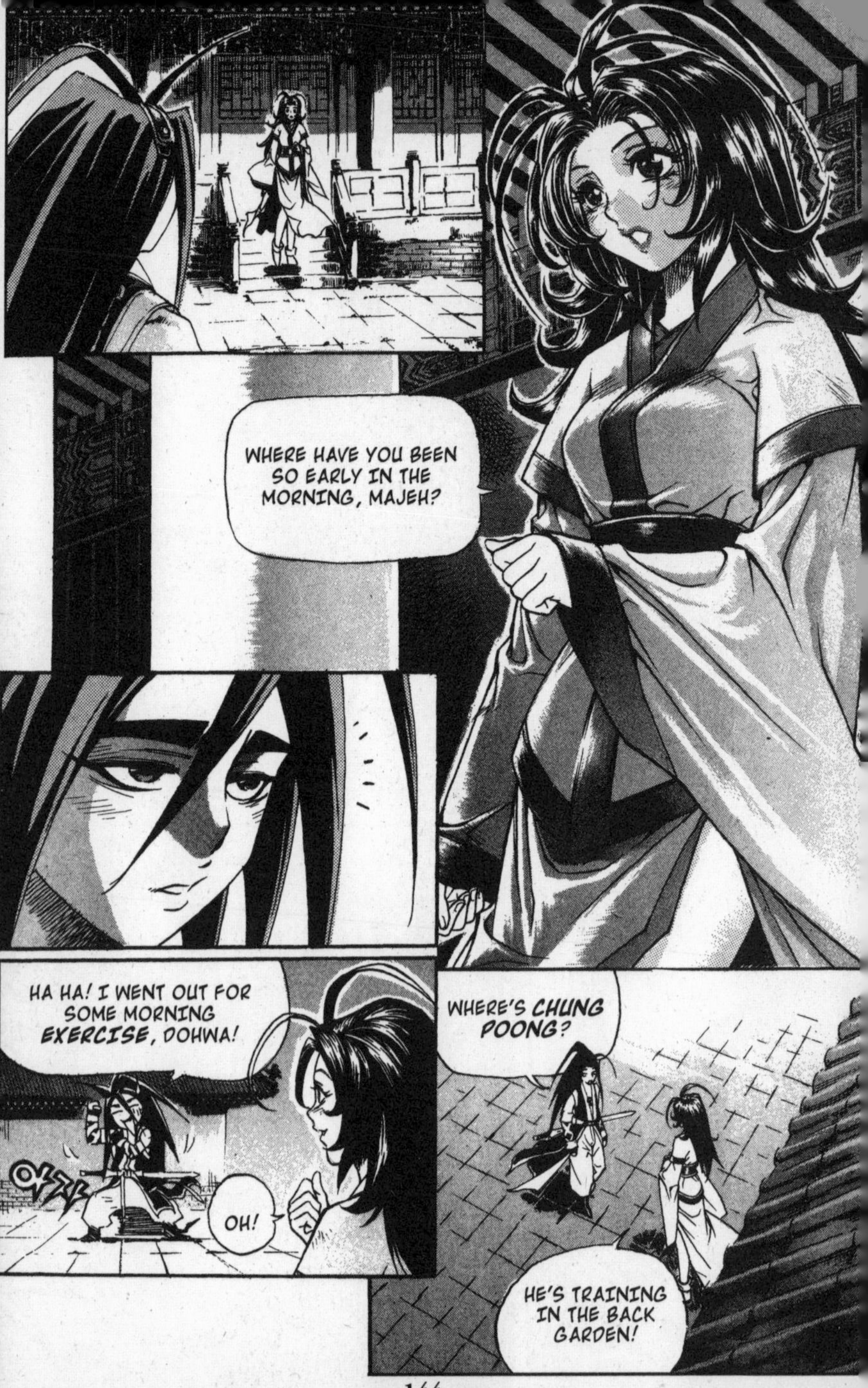
WHERE HAVE YOU BEEN SO EARLY IN THE MORNING, MAJEH?
HA HA! I WENT OUT FOR SOME MORNING EXERCISE, DOHWA!
OH!
WHERE'S CHUNG POONG?
HE'S TRAINING IN THE BACK GARDEN!

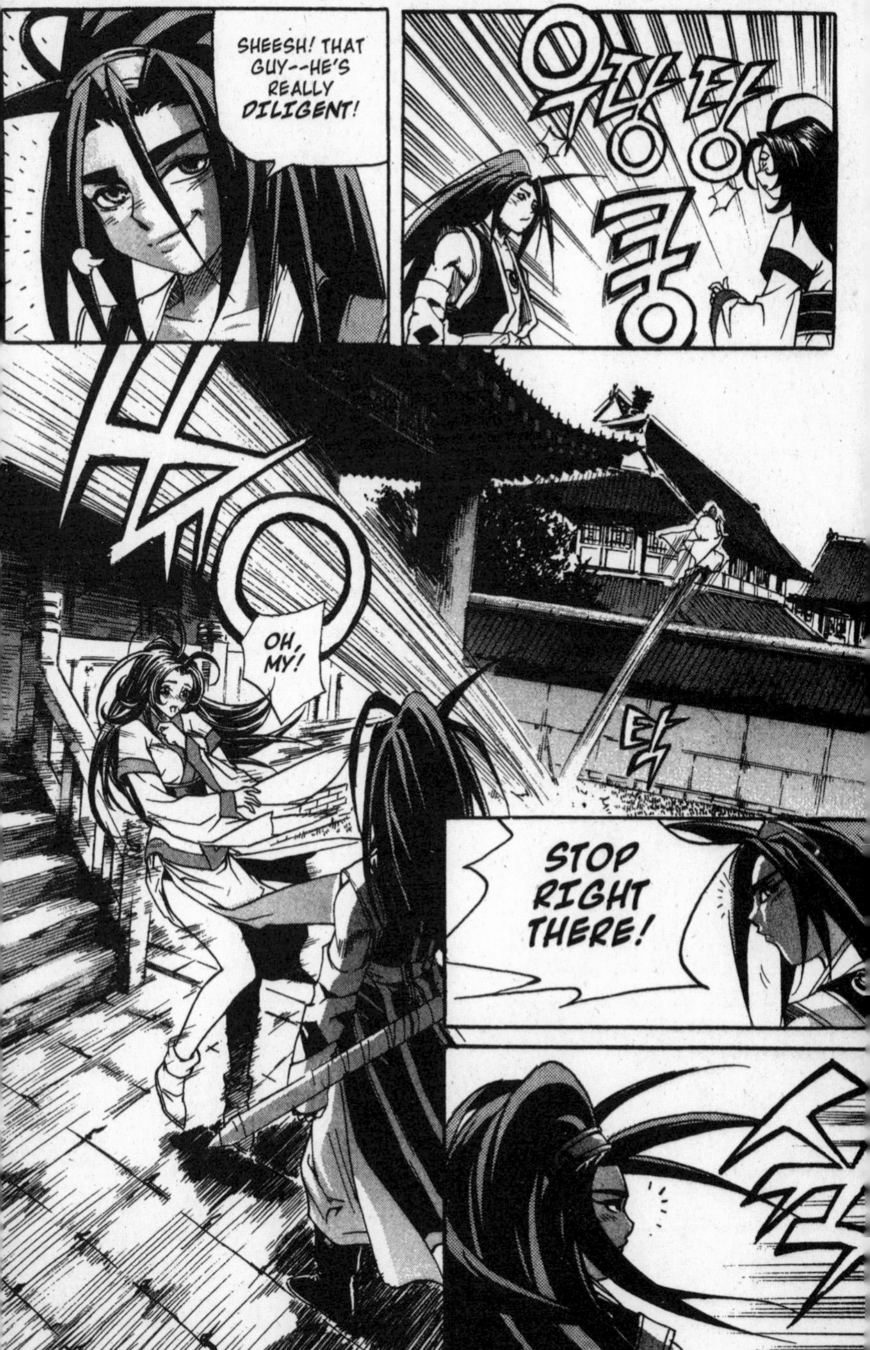
SHEESH! THAT GUY--HE'S REALLY DILIGENT!
OH, MY!
탁
STOP RIGHT THERE!

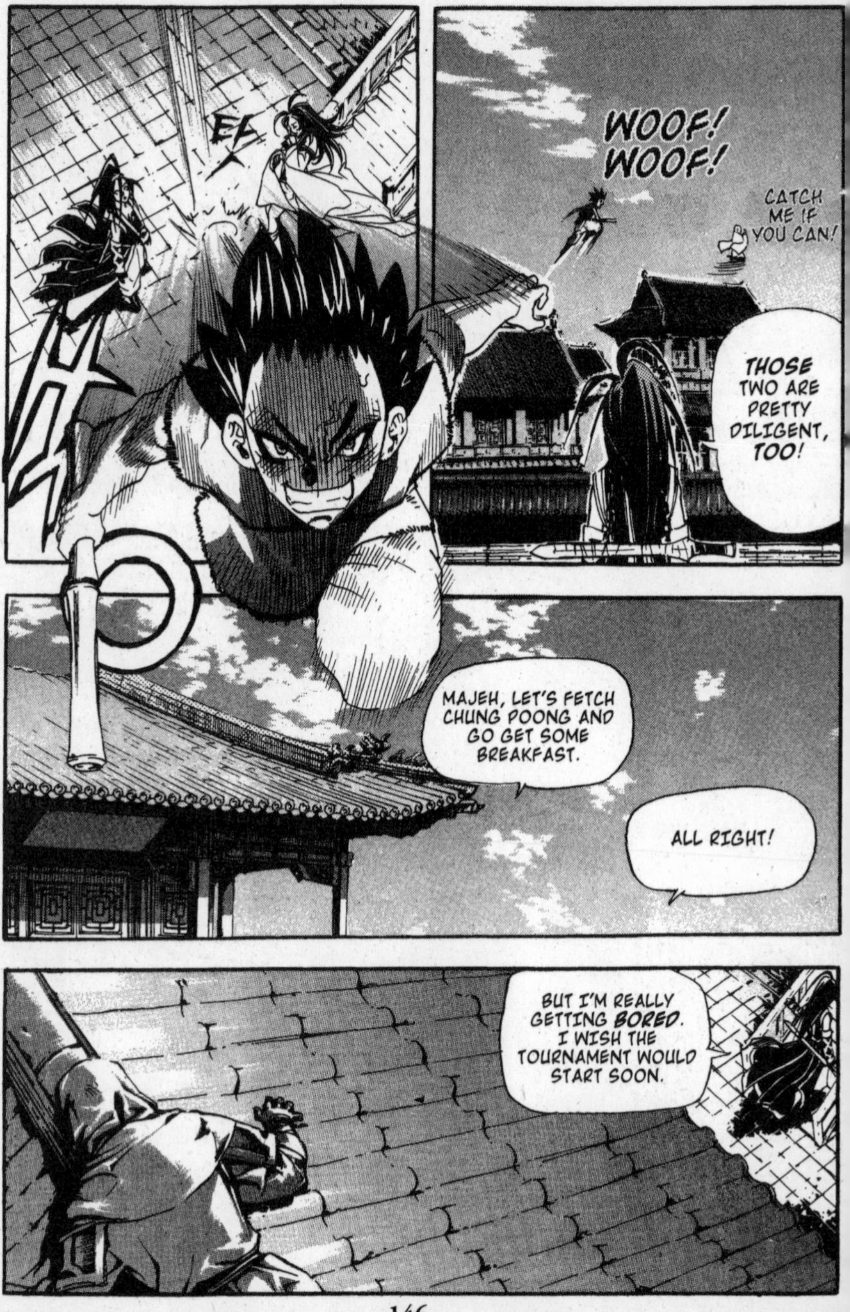
WOOF! WOOF!
CATCH ME IF YOU CAN!
THOSE TWO ARE PRETTY DILIGENT, TOO!
MAJEH, LET'S FETCH CHUNG POONG AND GO GET SOME BREAKFAST.
ALL RIGHT!
BUT I'M REALLY GETTING BORED. I WISH THE TOURNAMENT WOULD START SOON.

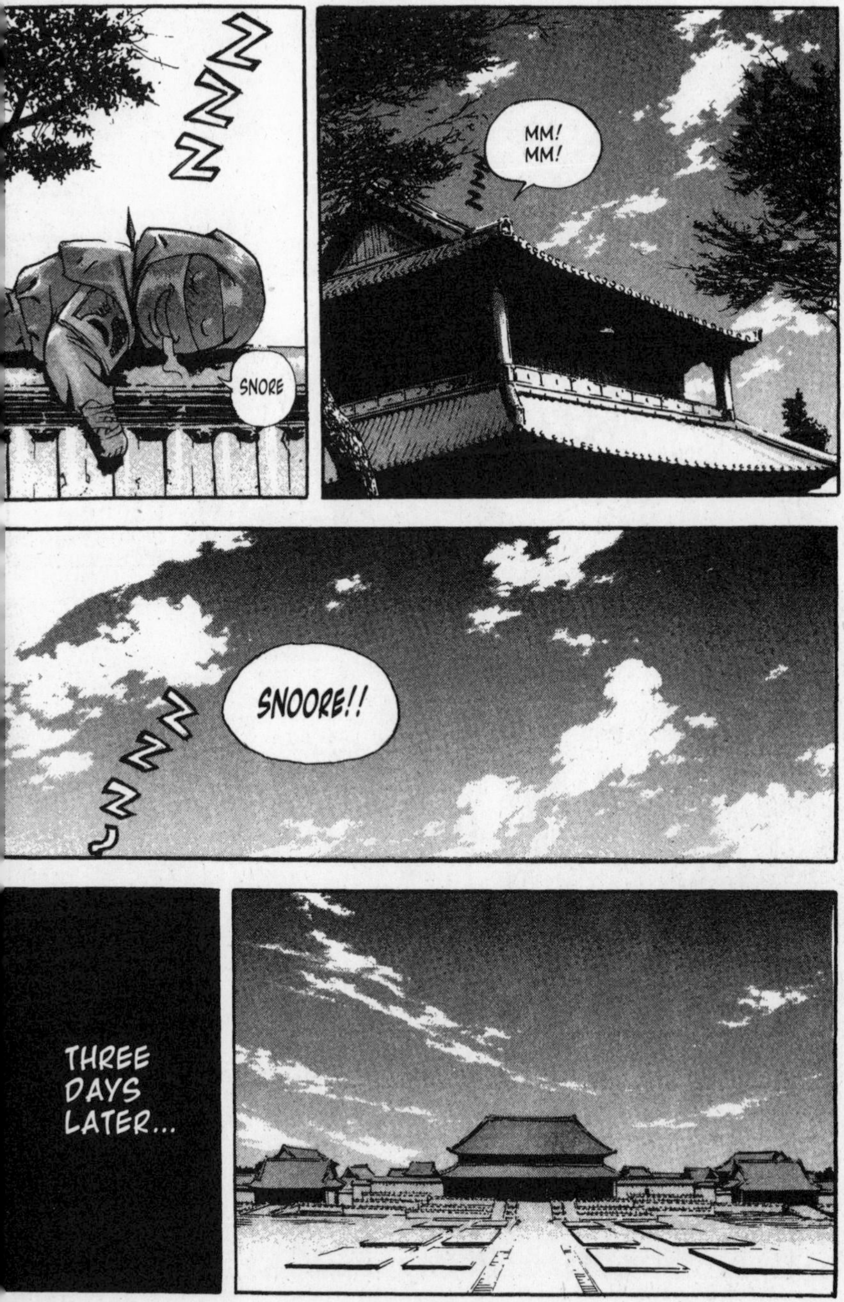
ZZZ
SNORE
MM! MM!
SNOORE!!
THREE DAYS LATER...

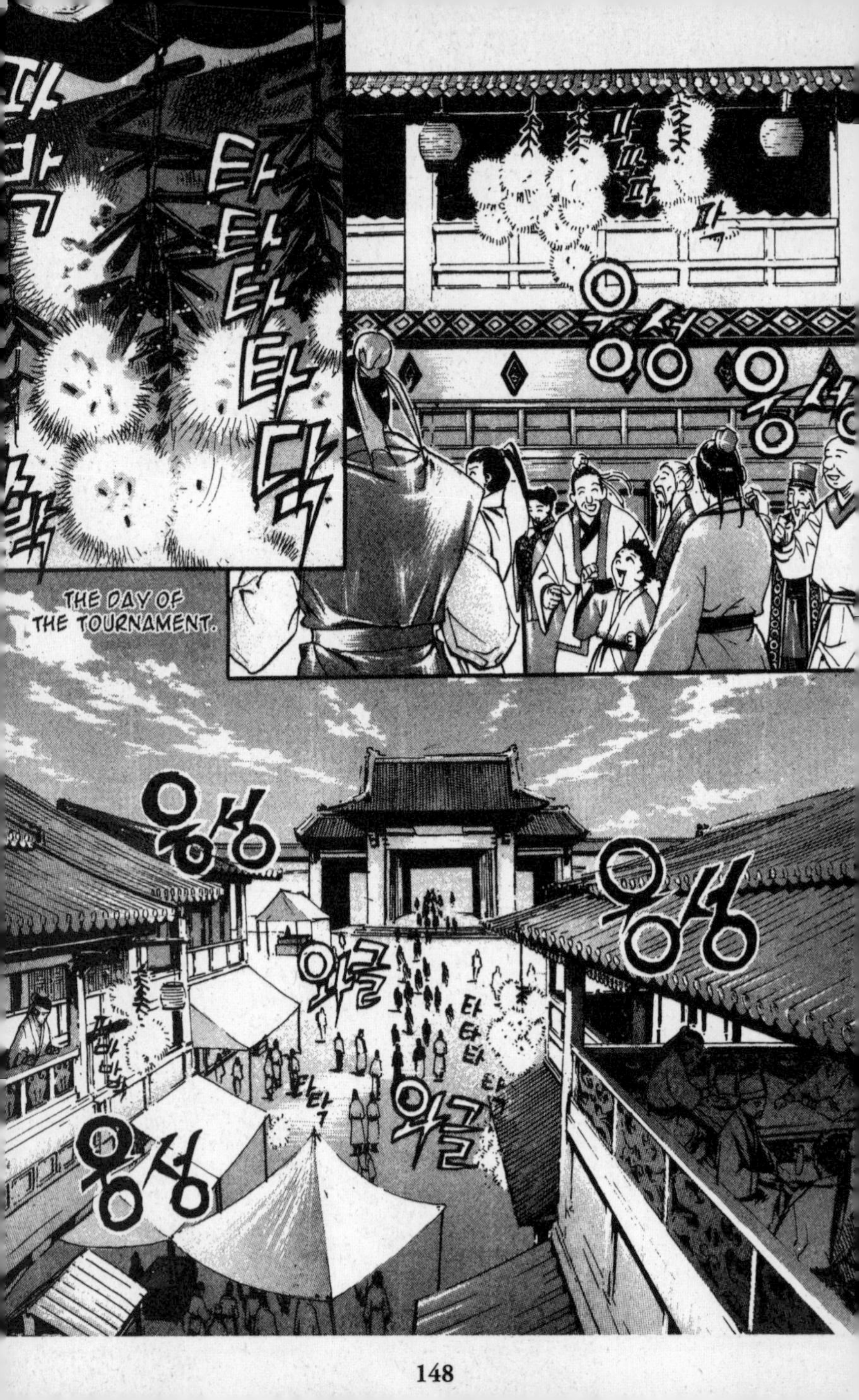
웅성
웅성
THE DAY OF THE TOURNAMENT.
웅성
와글
웅성
와글
웅성

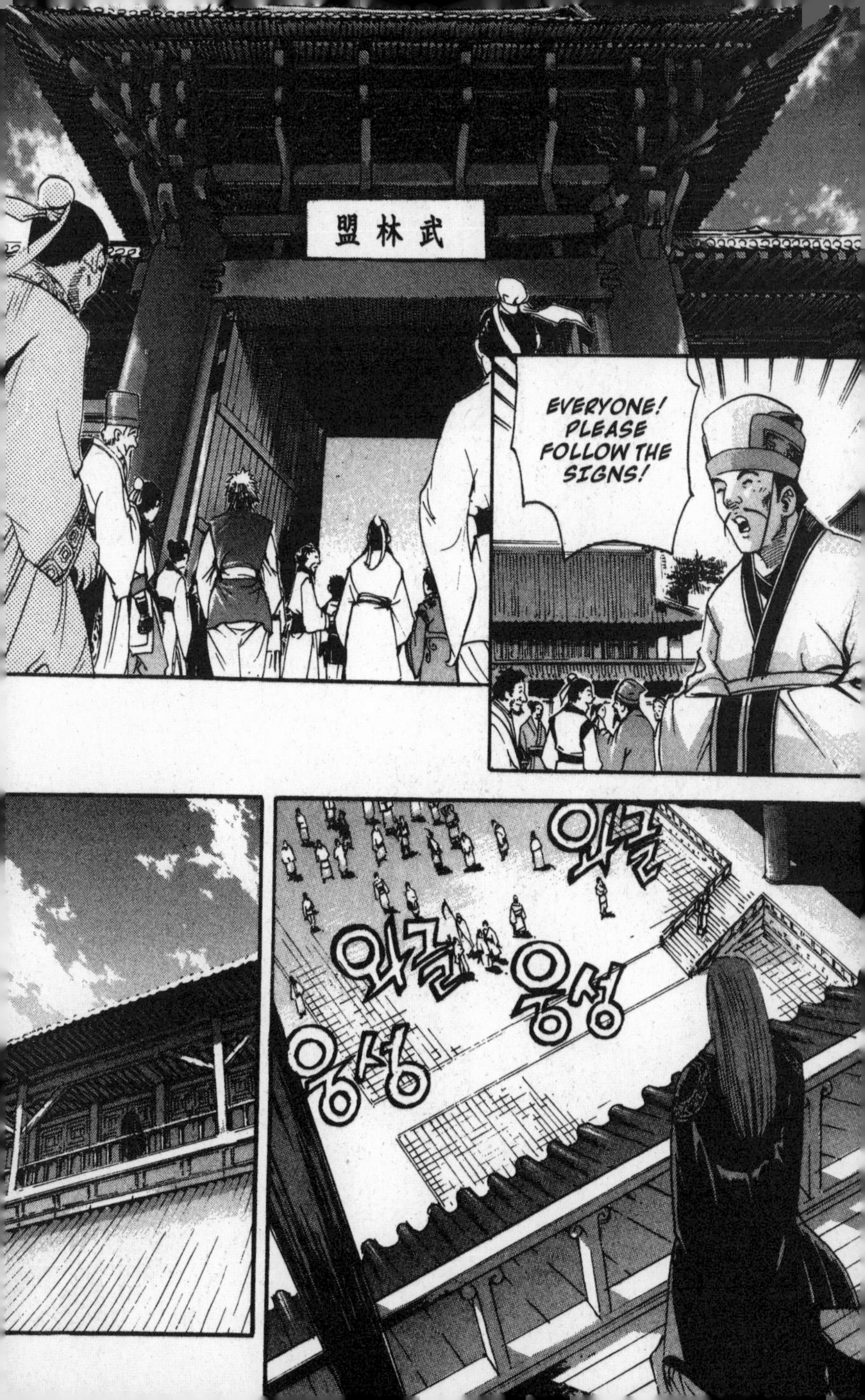
武林盟
EVERYONE! PLEASE FOLLOW THE SIGNS!
와글
와글
웅성
웅성

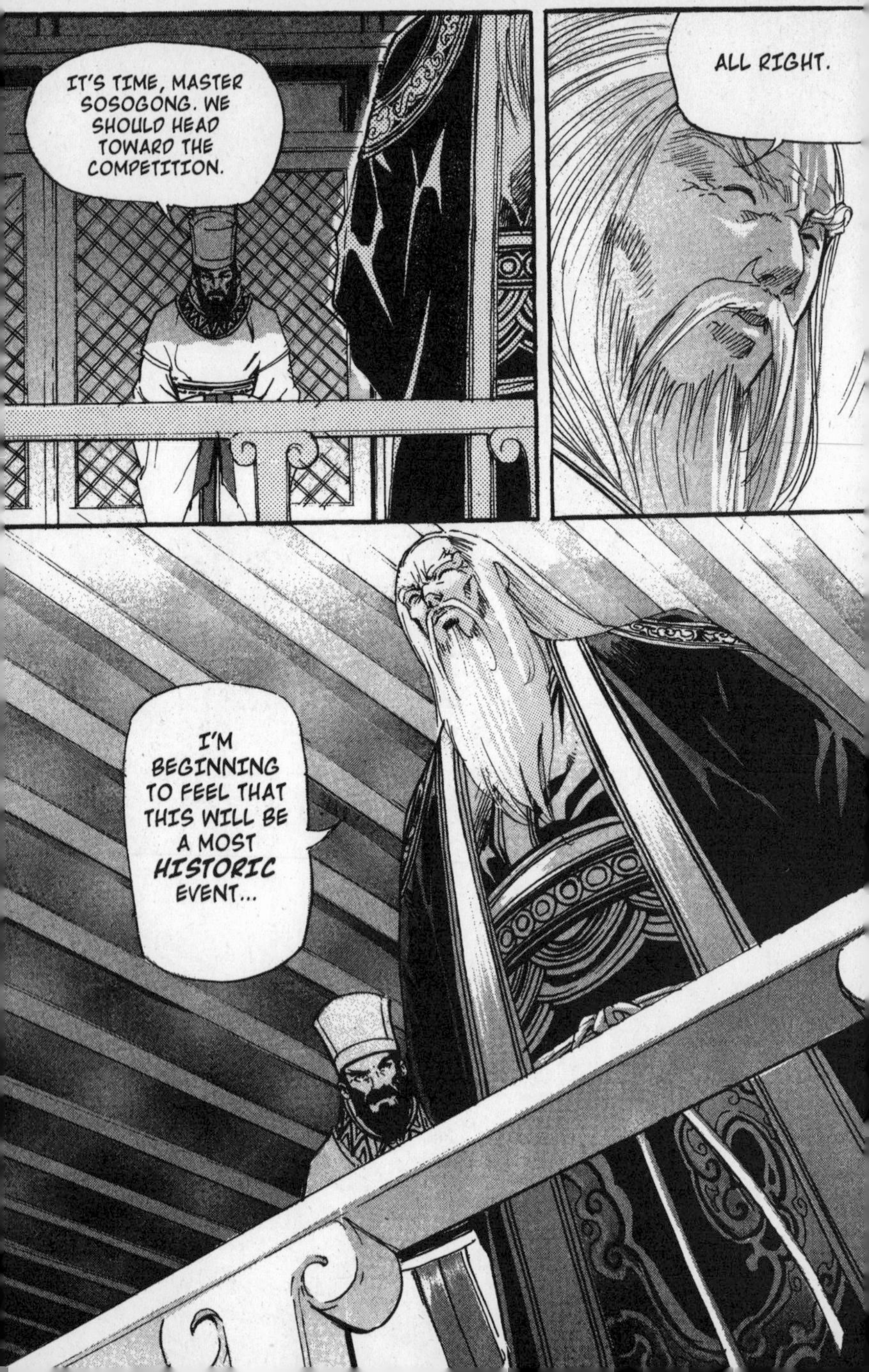
IT'S TIME, MASTER SOSOGONG. WE SHOULD HEAD TOWARD THE COMPETITION.
ALL RIGHT.
I'M BEGINNING TO FEEL THAT THIS WILL BE A MOST HISTORIC EVENT...

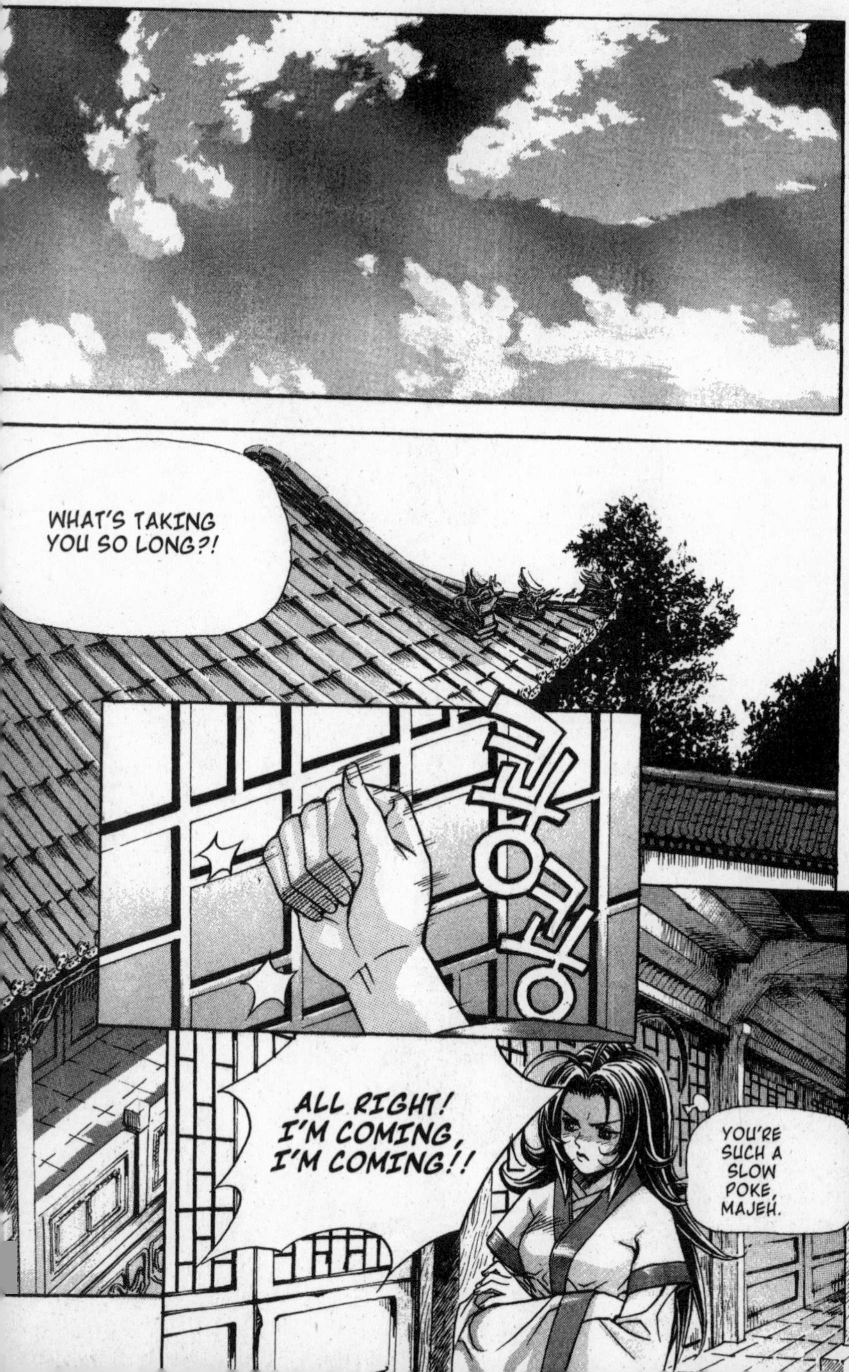
WHAT'S TAKING YOU SO LONG?!
ALL RIGHT! I'M COMING, I'M COMING!!
YOU'RE SUCH A SLOW POKE, MAJEH.

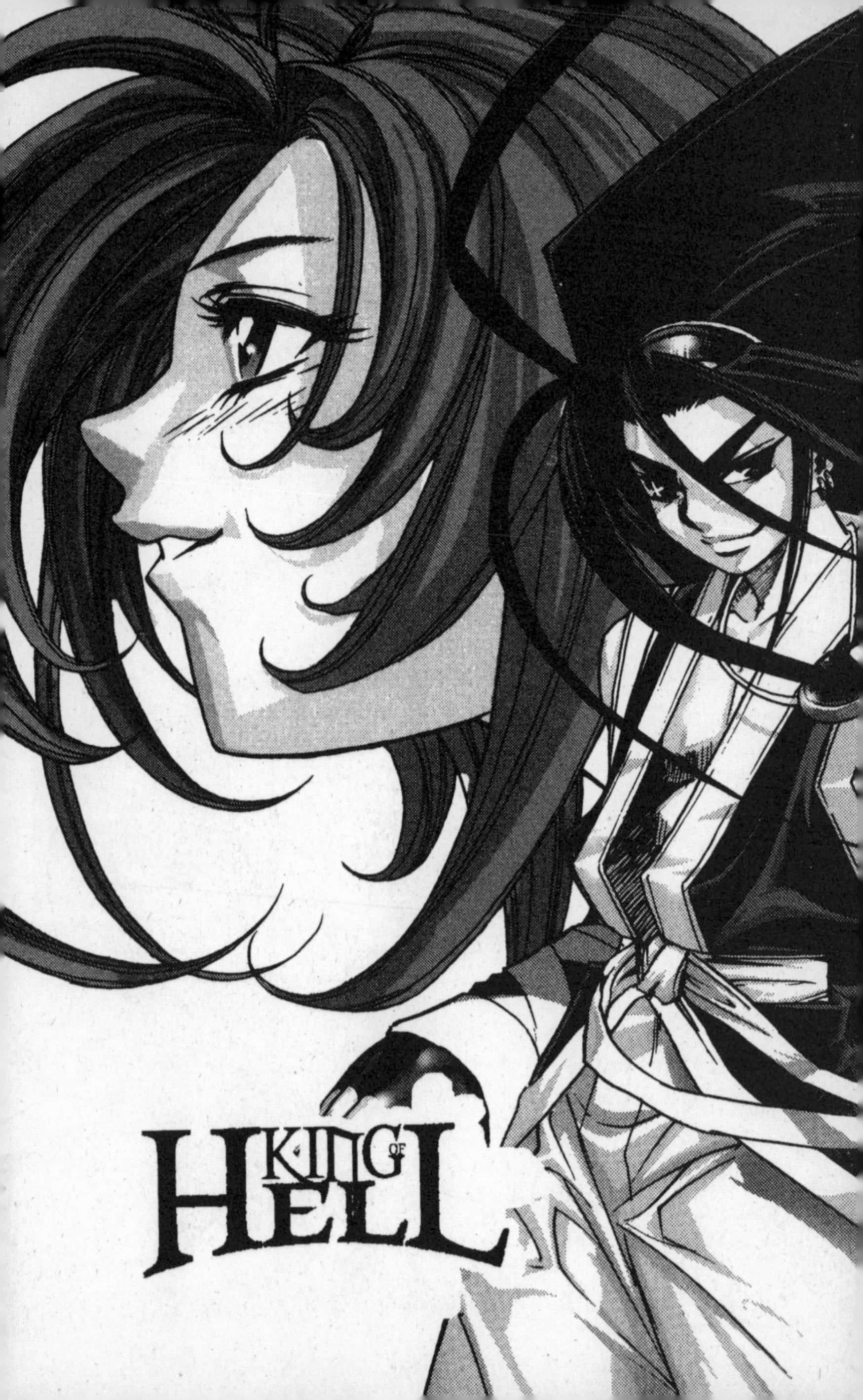
KING OF HELL

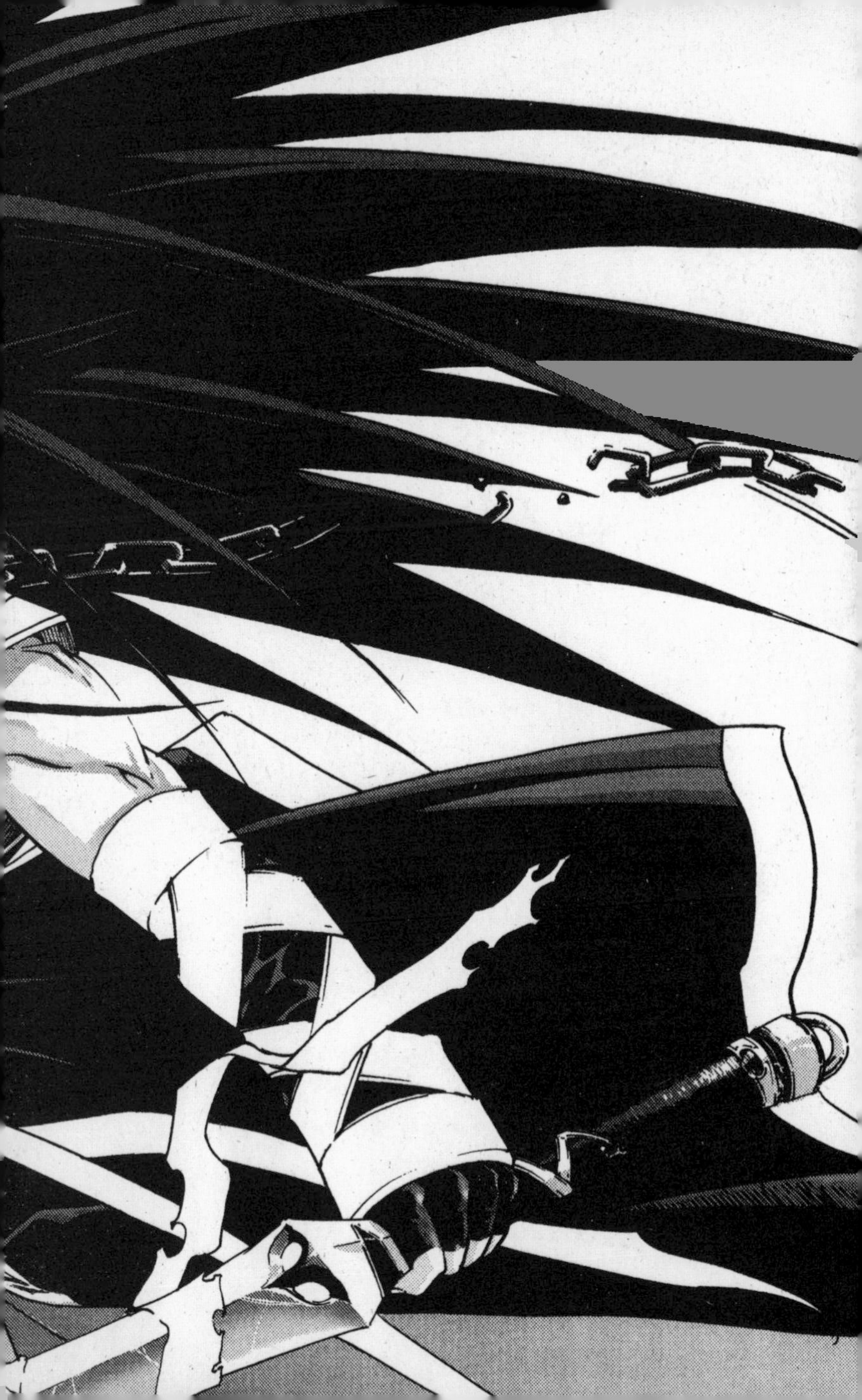

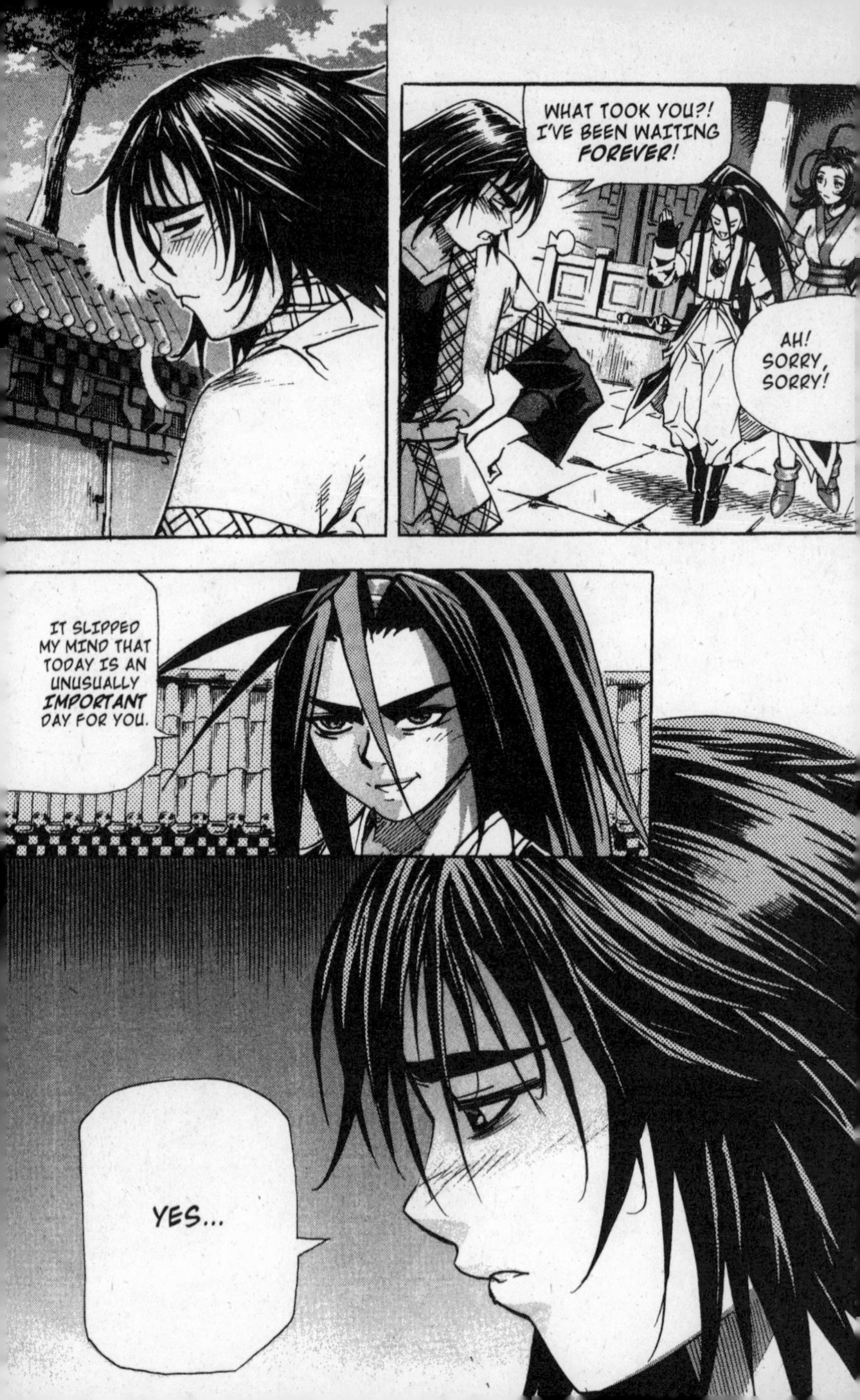
WHAT TOOK YOU?! I'VE BEEN WAITING **FOREVER**!
AH! SORRY, SORRY!
IT SLIPPED MY MIND THAT TODAY IS AN UNUSUALLY **IMPORTANT** DAY FOR YOU.
YES...

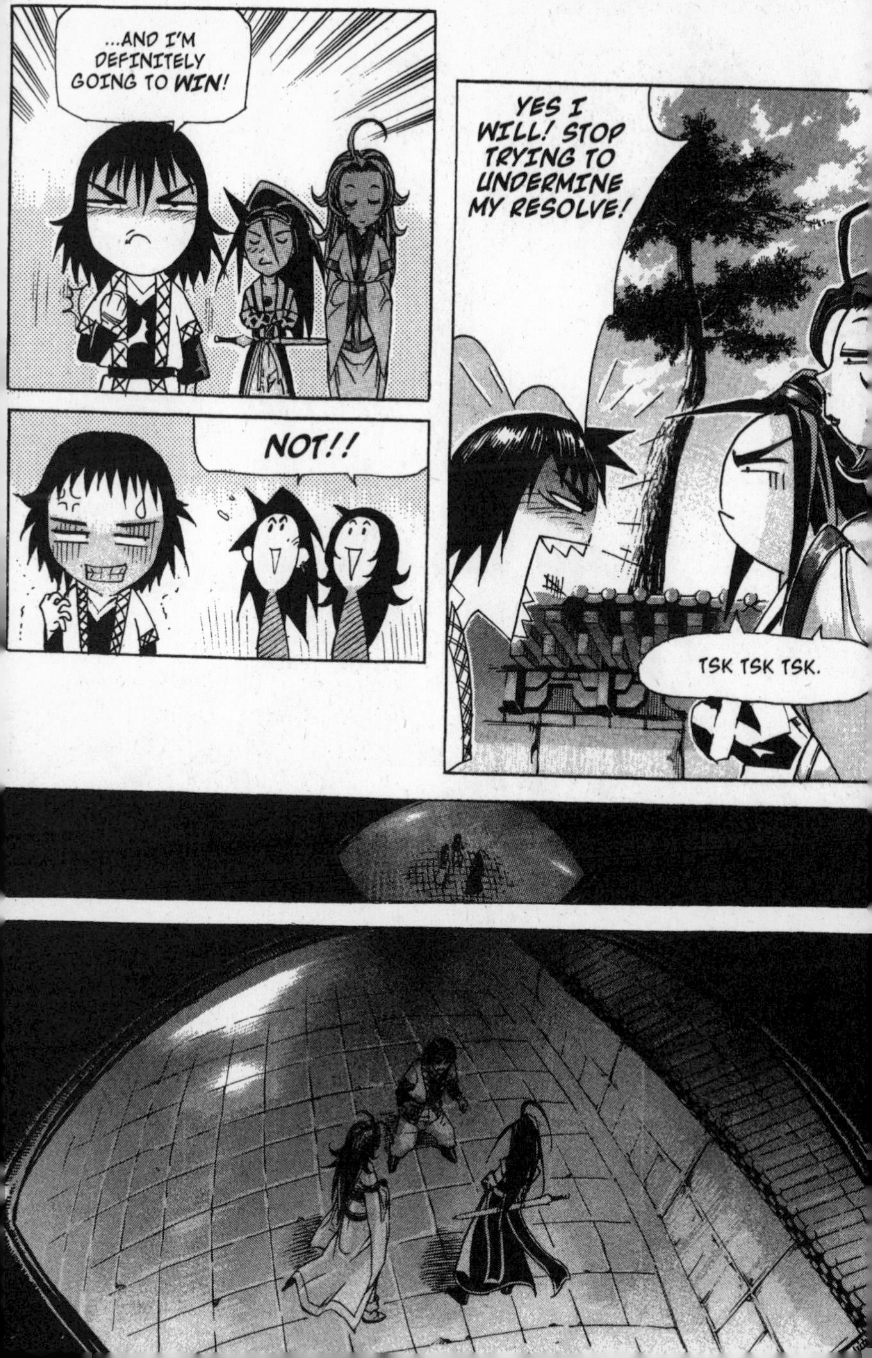
...AND I'M DEFINITELY GOING TO WIN!
NOT!!
YES I WILL! STOP TRYING TO UNDERMINE MY RESOLVE!
TSK TSK TSK.

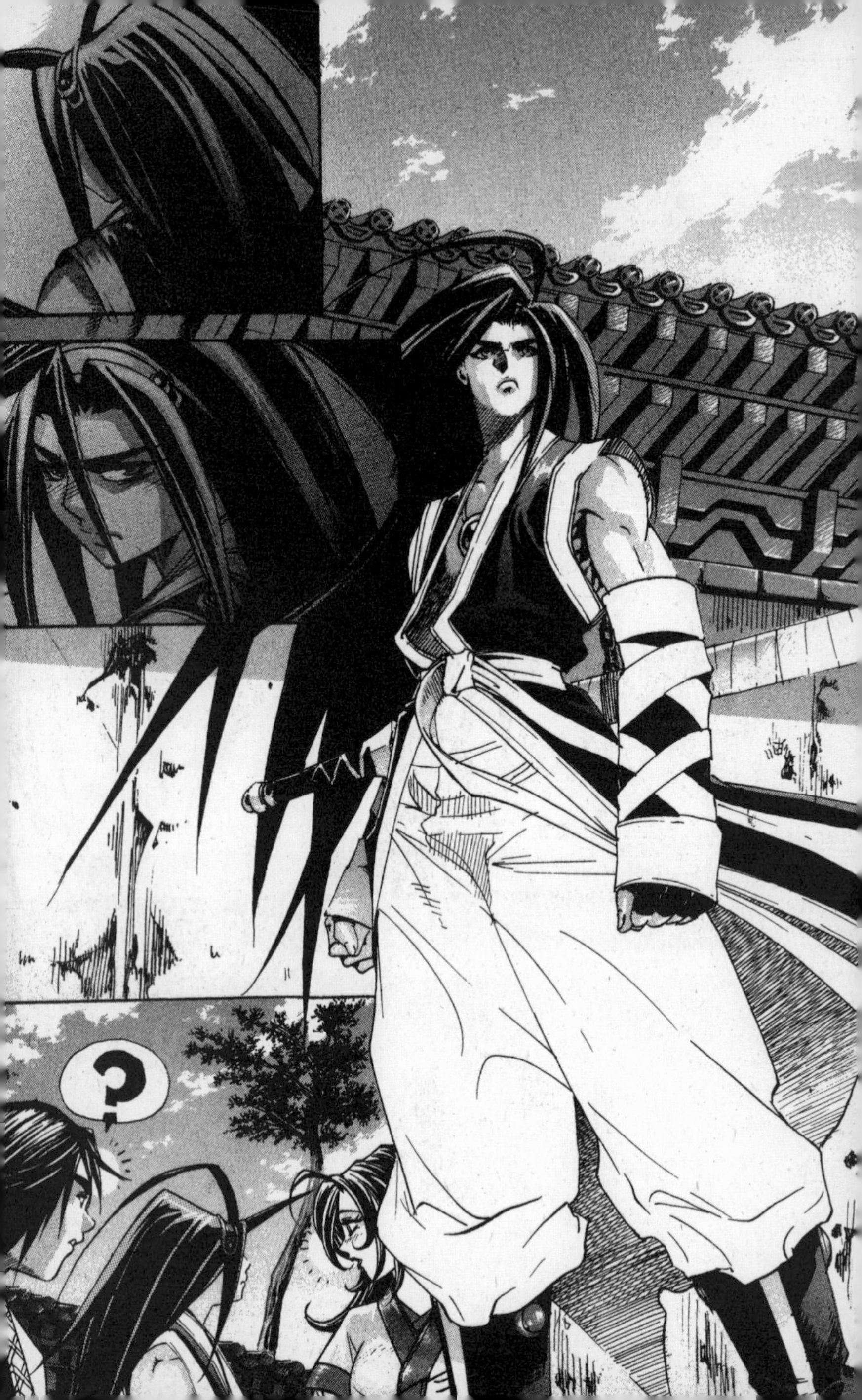
?

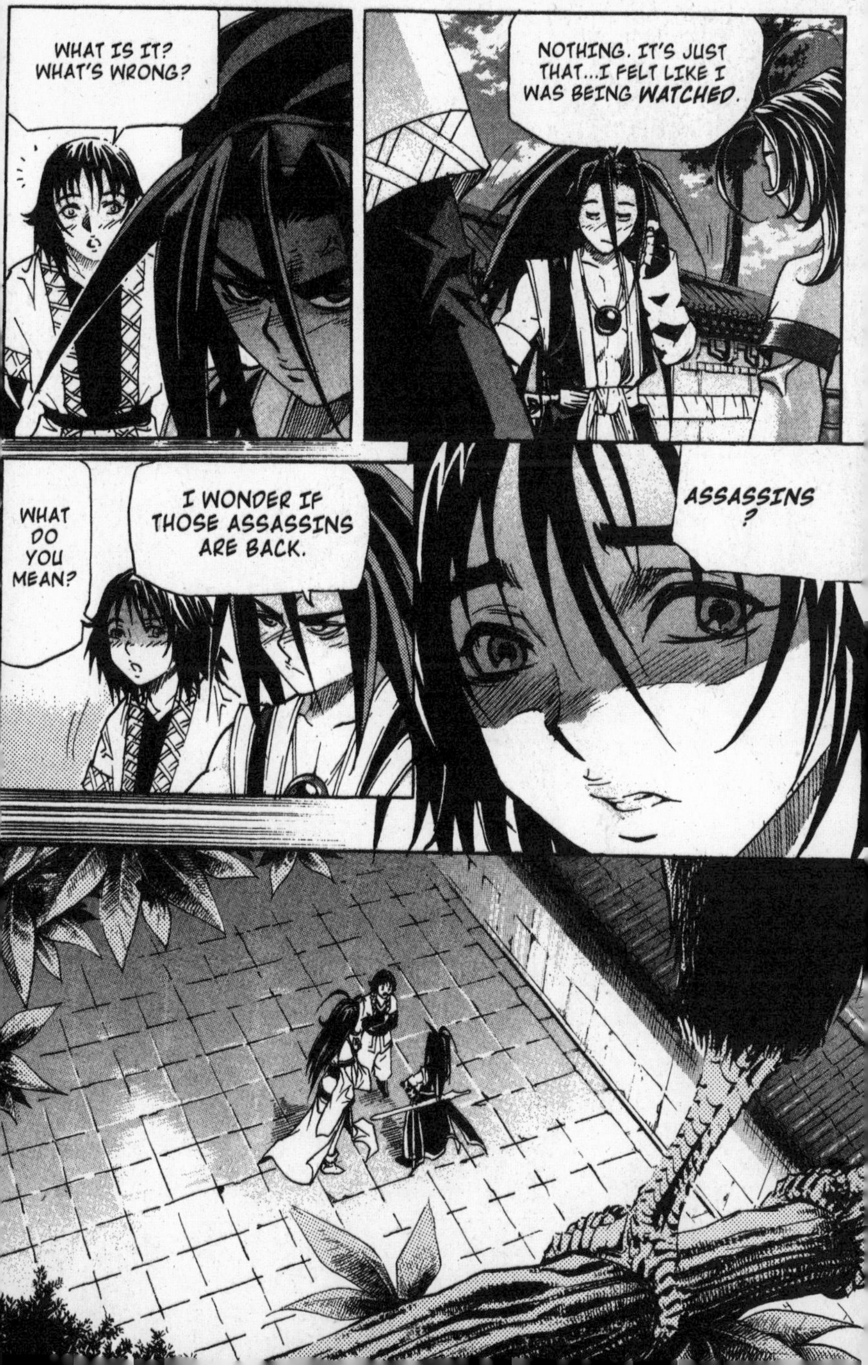
WHAT IS IT? WHAT'S WRONG?
NOTHING. IT'S JUST THAT...I FELT LIKE I WAS BEING **WATCHED**.
WHAT DO YOU MEAN?
I WONDER IF THOSE ASSASSINS ARE BACK.
ASSASSINS?

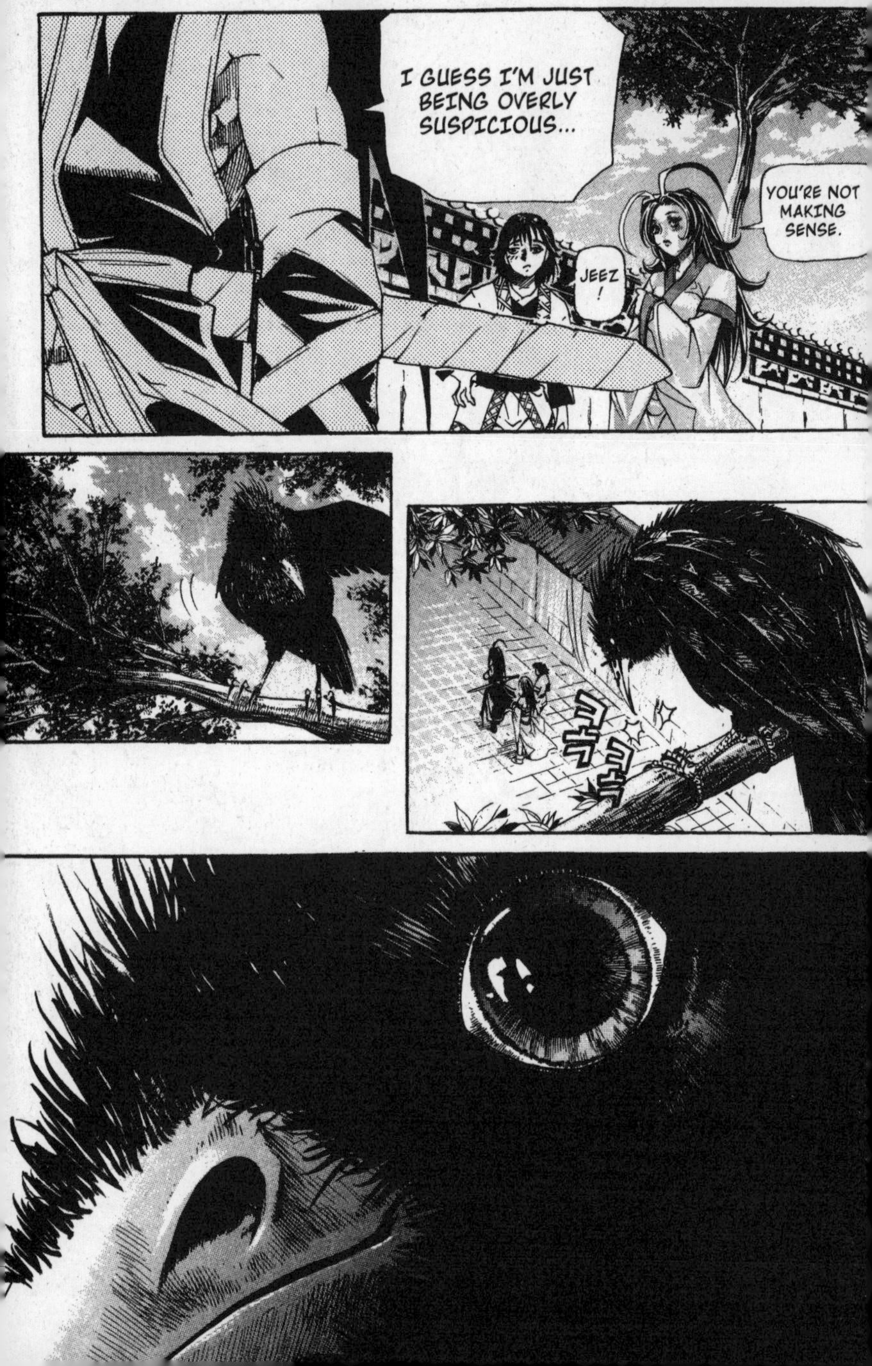
I GUESS I'M JUST BEING OVERLY SUSPICIOUS...
JEEZ!
YOU'RE NOT MAKING SENSE.

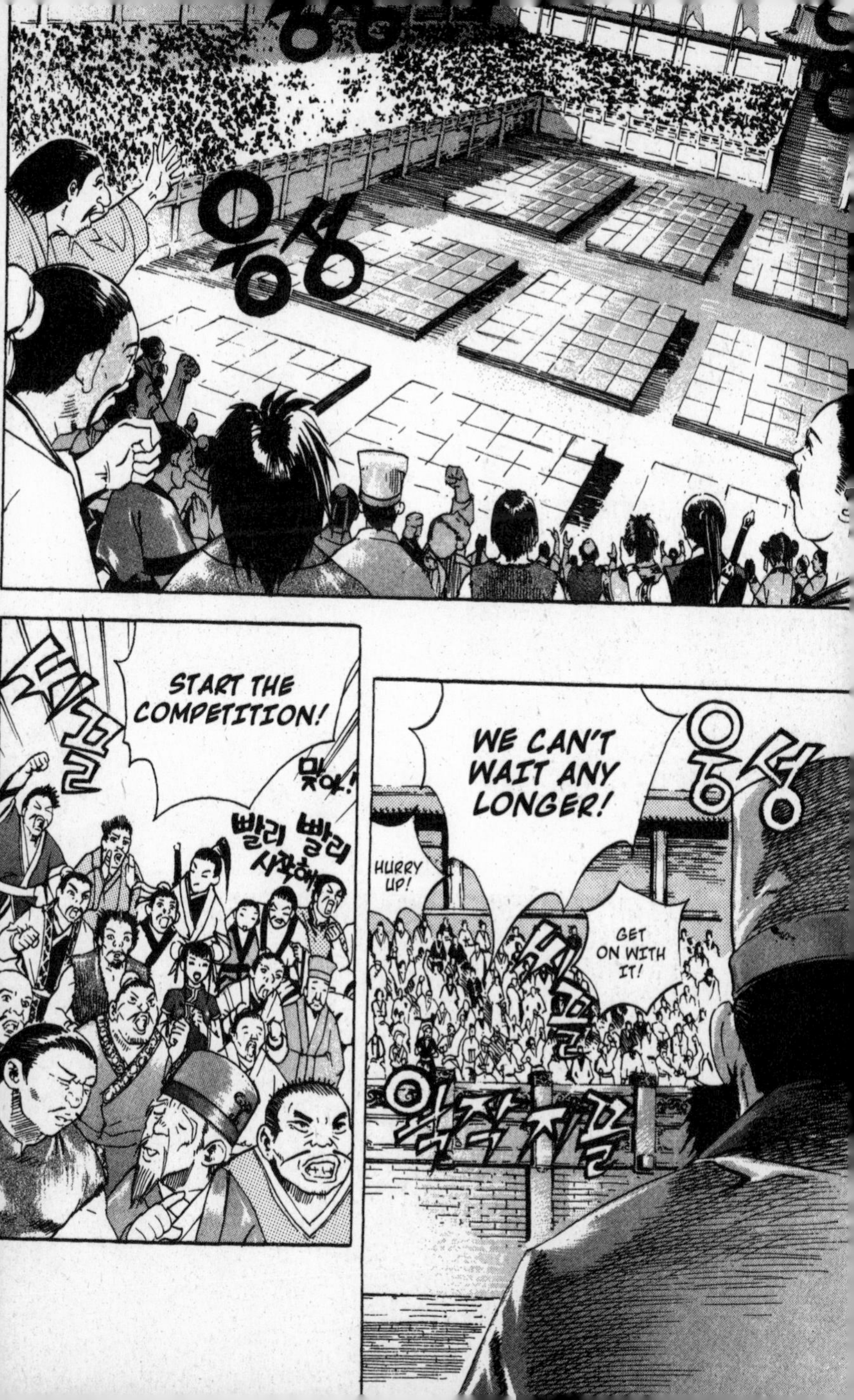
웅성
START THE COMPETITION!
맞아!
빨리 빨리 시작해
WE CAN'T WAIT ANY LONGER!
웅성
HURRY UP!
GET ON WITH IT!

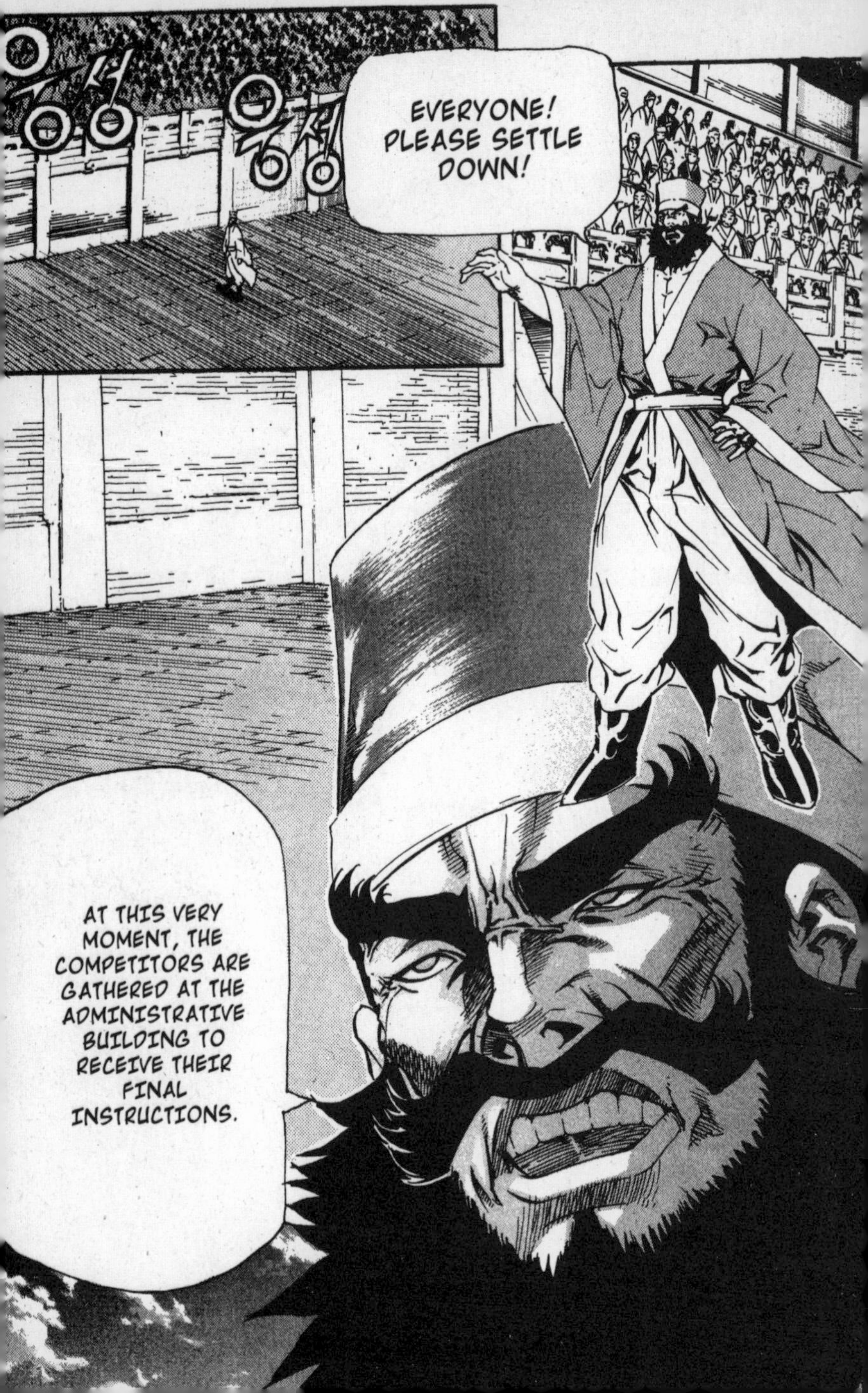
EVERYONE! PLEASE SETTLE DOWN!
AT THIS VERY MOMENT, THE COMPETITORS ARE GATHERED AT THE ADMINISTRATIVE BUILDING TO RECEIVE THEIR FINAL INSTRUCTIONS.

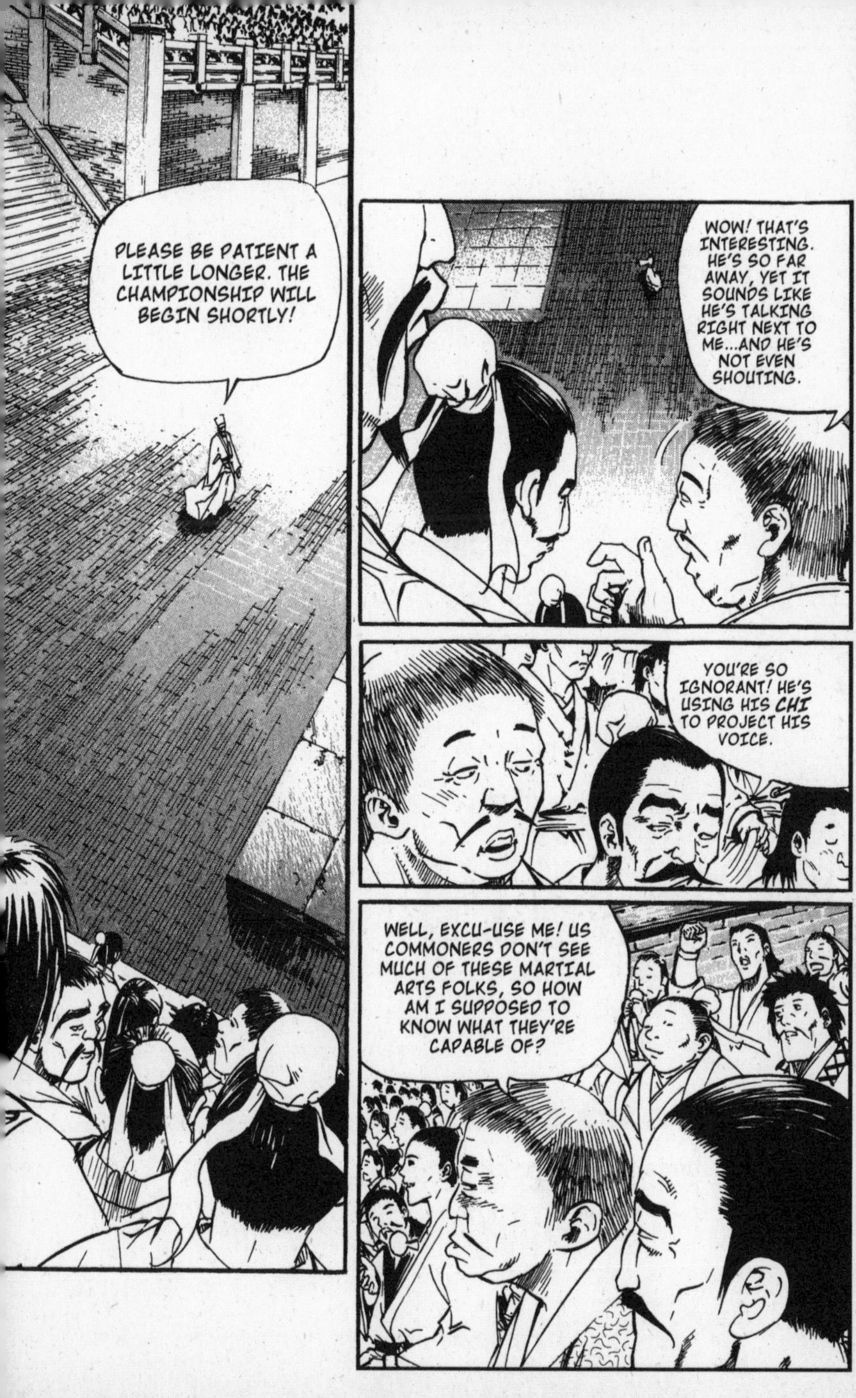
PLEASE BE PATIENT A LITTLE LONGER. THE CHAMPIONSHIP WILL BEGIN SHORTLY!
WOW! THAT'S INTERESTING. HE'S SO FAR AWAY, YET IT SOUNDS LIKE HE'S TALKING RIGHT NEXT TO ME...AND HE'S NOT EVEN SHOUTING.
YOU'RE SO IGNORANT! HE'S USING HIS CHI TO PROJECT HIS VOICE.
WELL, EXCU-USE ME! US COMMONERS DON'T SEE MUCH OF THESE MARTIAL ARTS FOLKS, SO HOW AM I SUPPOSED TO KNOW WHAT THEY'RE CAPABLE OF?

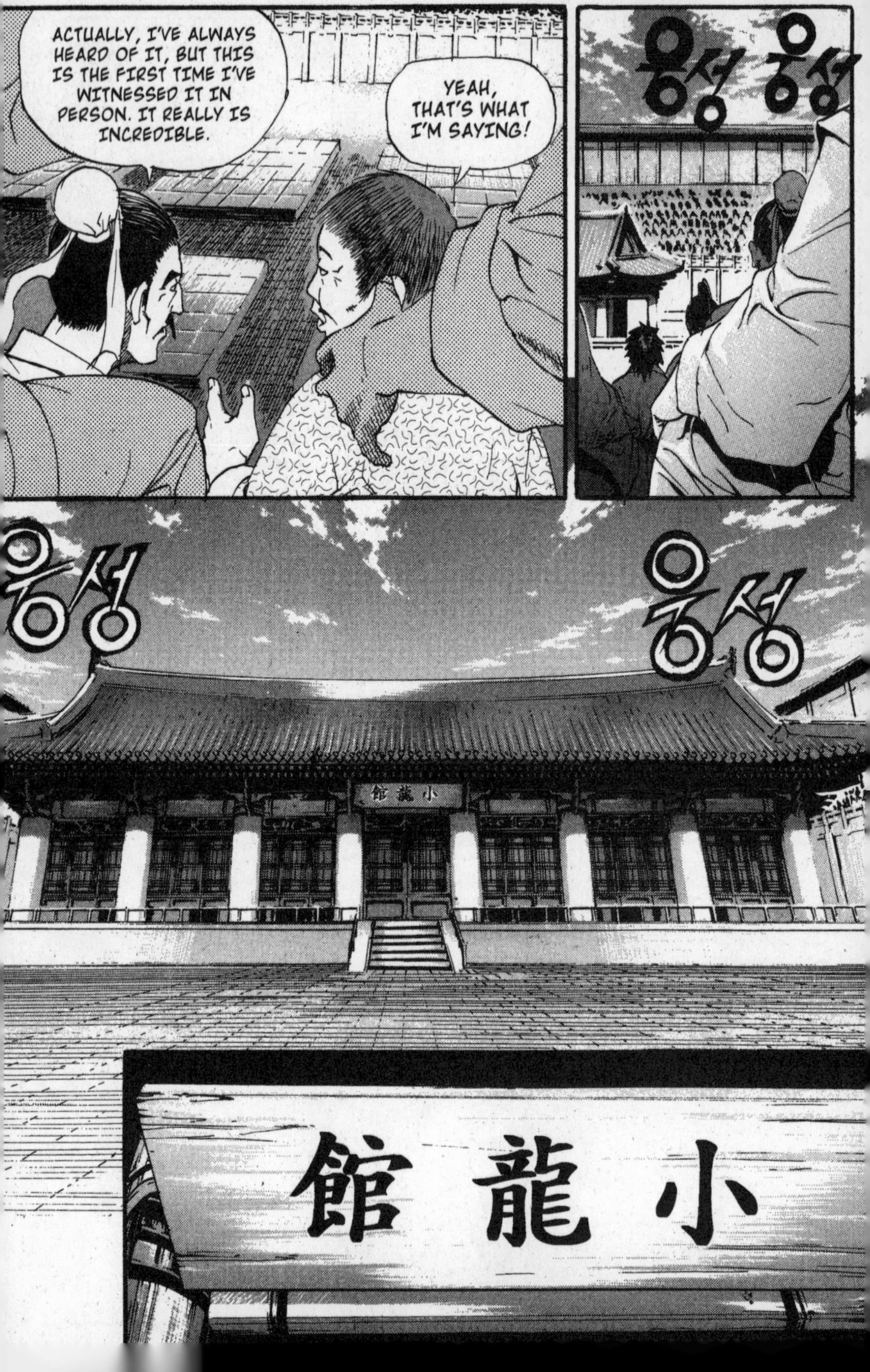
ACTUALLY, I'VE ALWAYS HEARD OF IT, BUT THIS IS THE FIRST TIME I'VE WITNESSED IT IN PERSON. IT REALLY IS INCREDIBLE.
YEAH, THAT'S WHAT I'M SAYING!
웅성 웅성
웅성
웅성
小龍館
小龍館

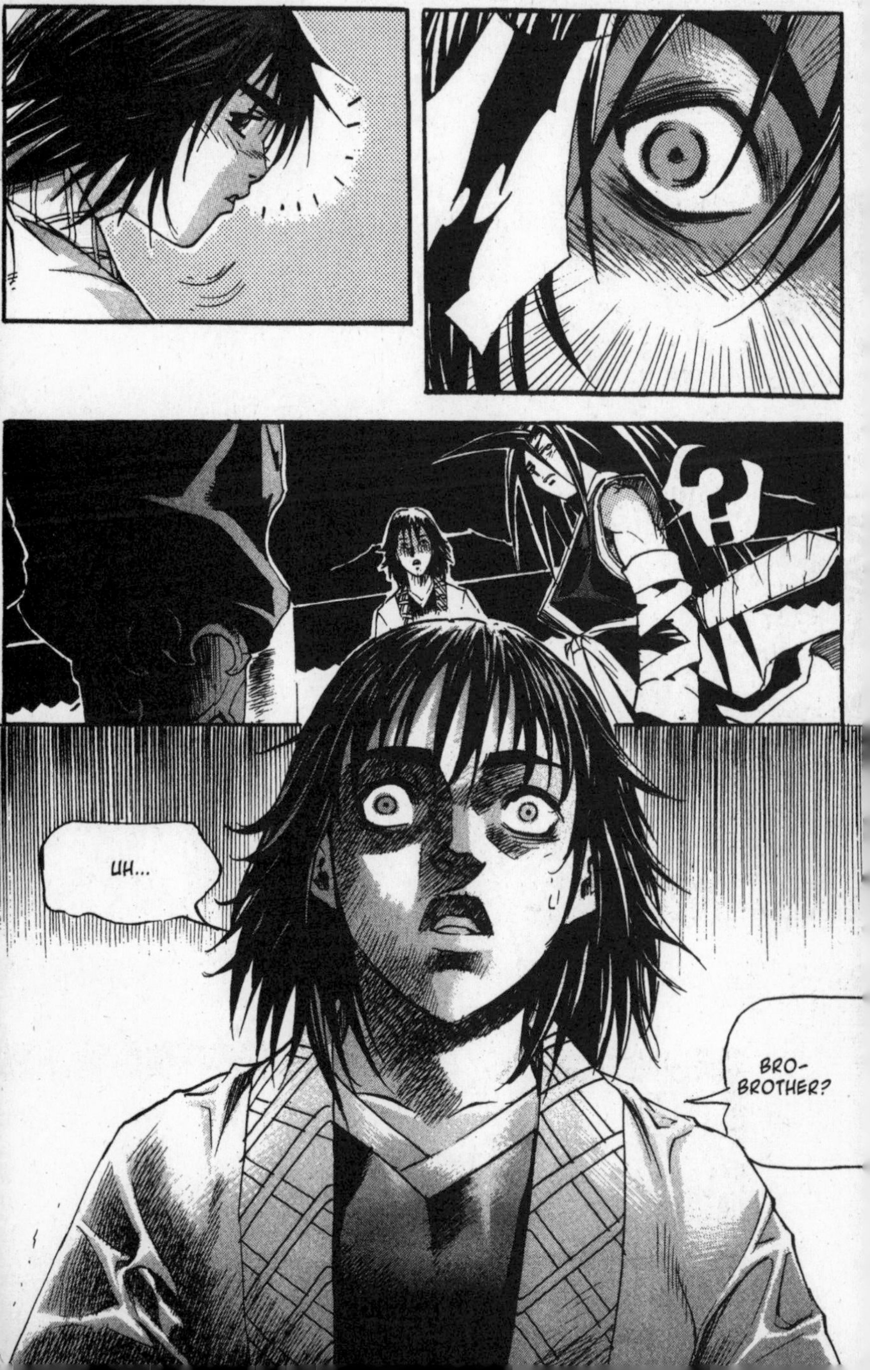
?
UH...
BRO-
BROTHER?

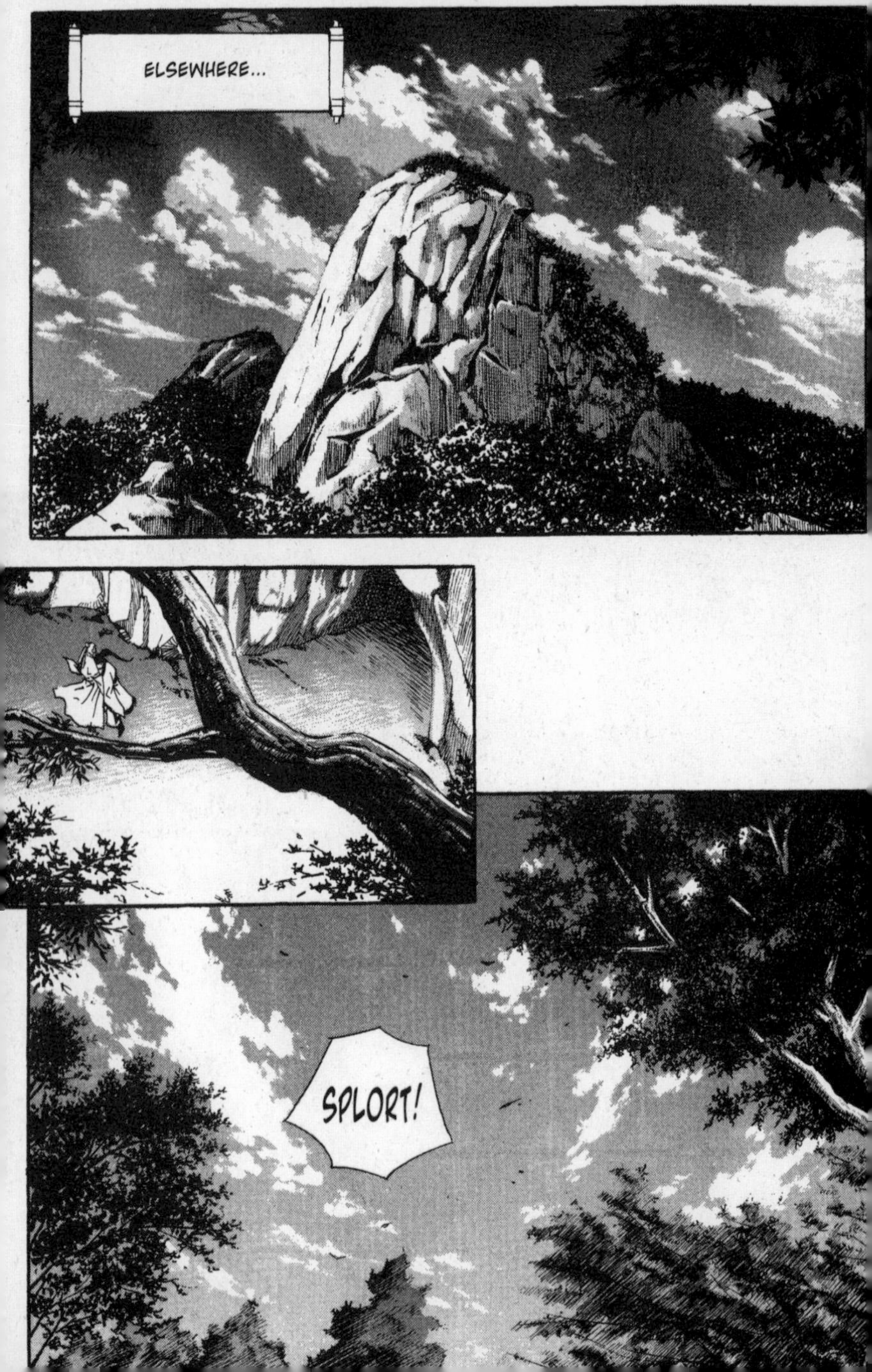
ELSEWHERE...
SPLORT!

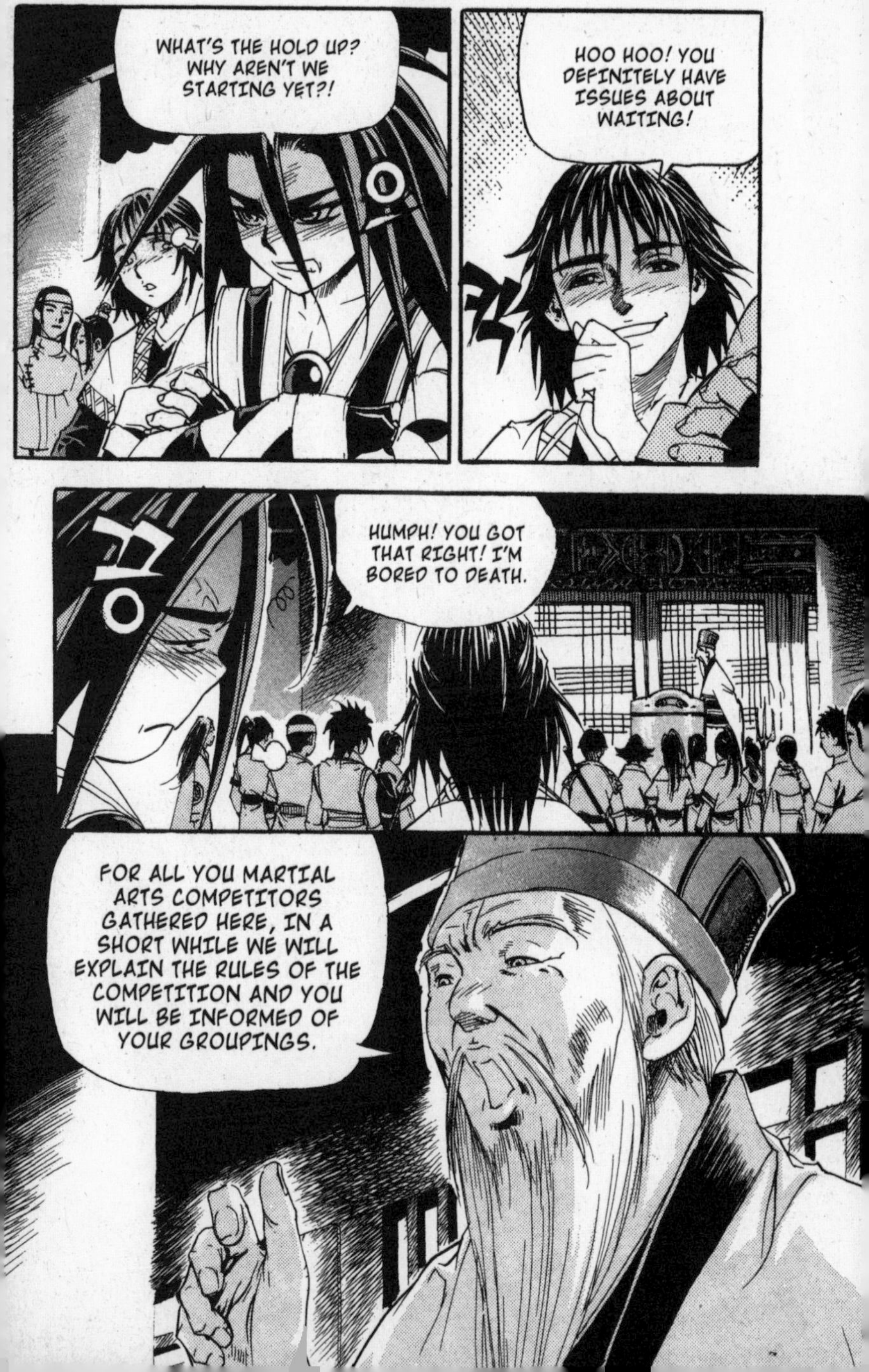
WHAT'S THE HOLD UP? WHY AREN'T WE STARTING YET?!
HOO HOO! YOU DEFINITELY HAVE ISSUES ABOUT WAITING!
HUMPH! YOU GOT THAT RIGHT! I'M BORED TO DEATH.
FOR ALL YOU MARTIAL ARTS COMPETITORS GATHERED HERE, IN A SHORT WHILE WE WILL EXPLAIN THE RULES OF THE COMPETITION AND YOU WILL BE INFORMED OF YOUR GROUPINGS.

I'M GONNA LOSE MY MIND! I HAVE TO WAIT EVEN *LONGER?*

OH...

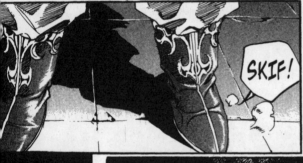

SKIF!

*CHUNG POONG!*

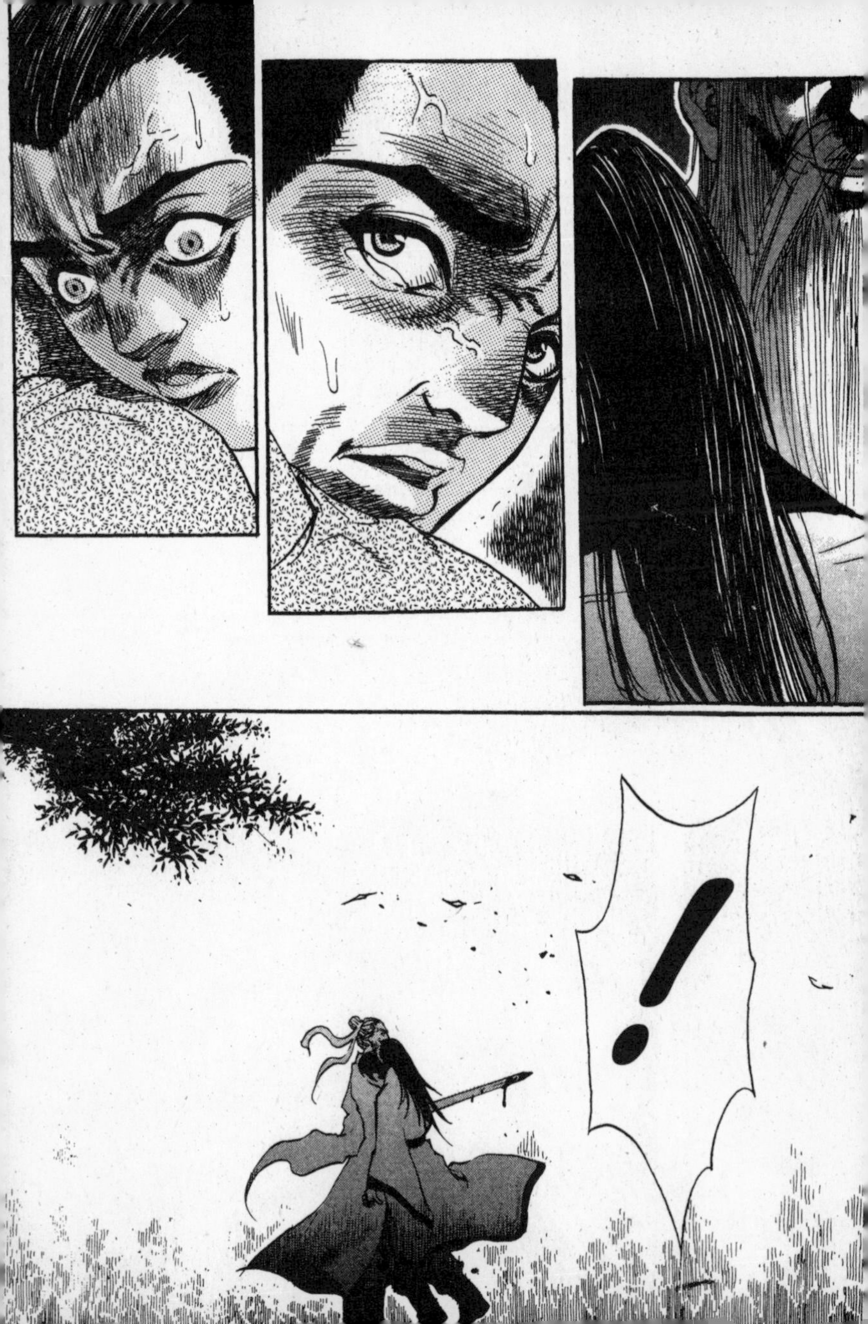
!

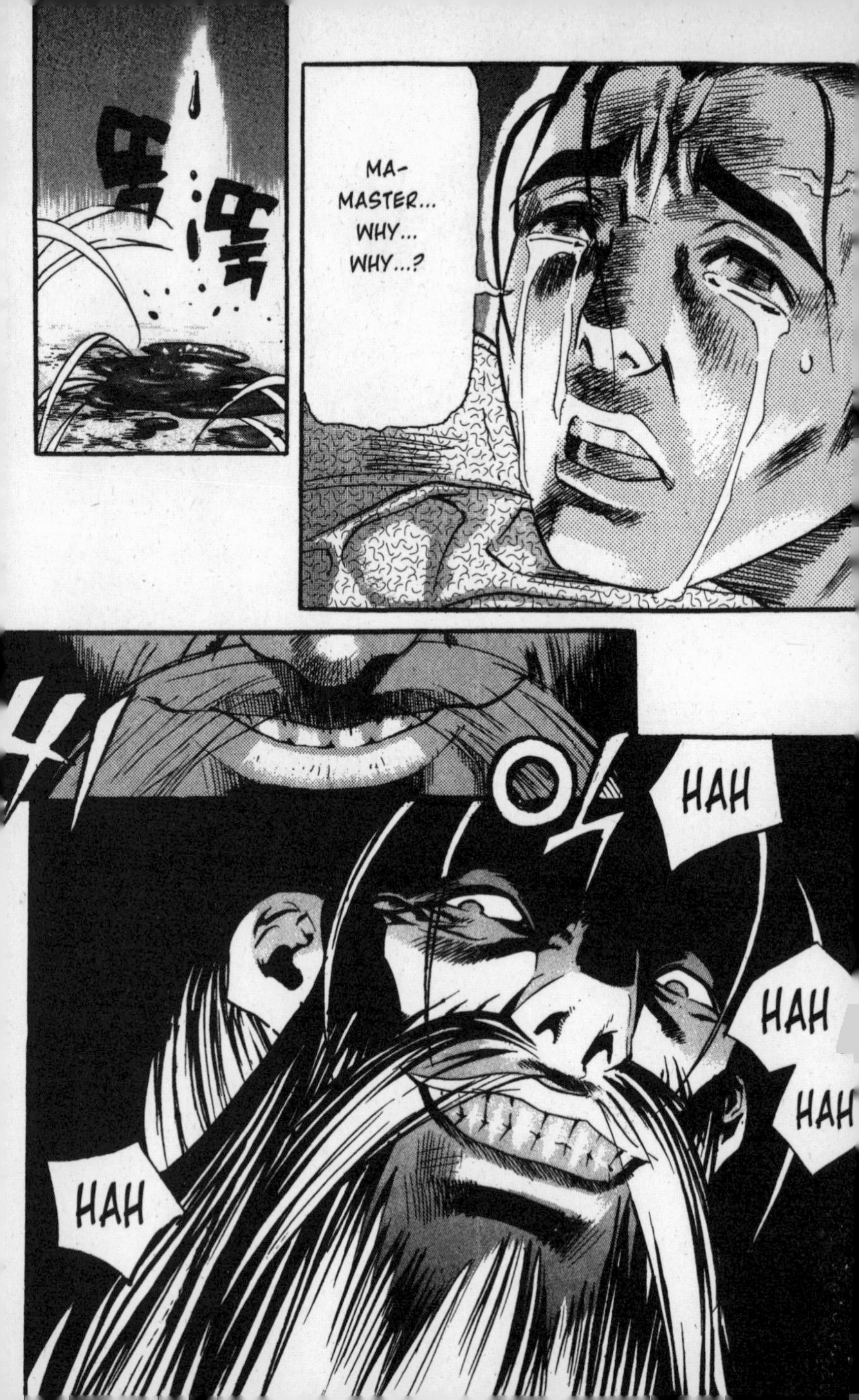
MA-
MASTER...
WHY...
WHY...?
HAH
HAH
HAH
HAH

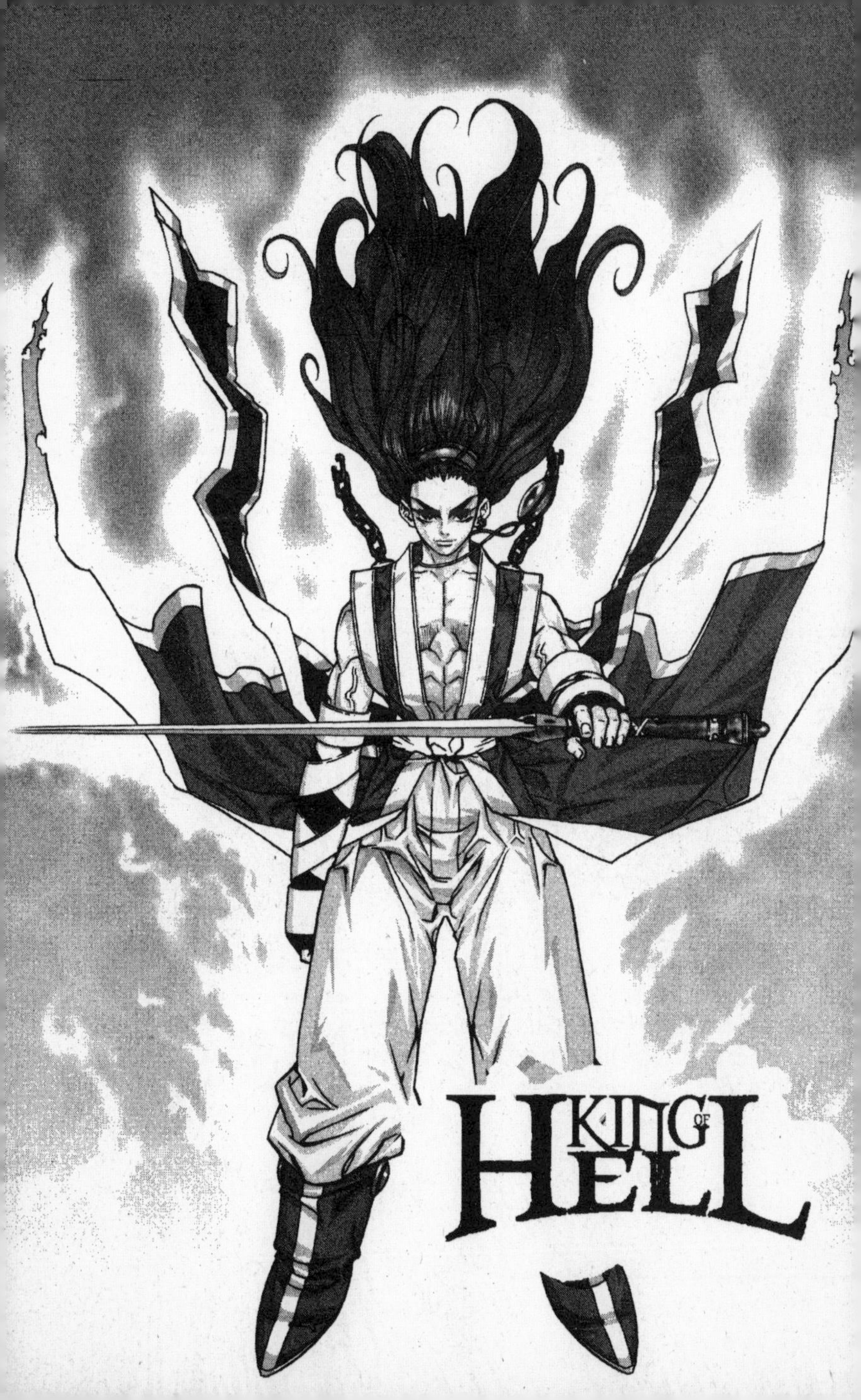
KING OF HELL

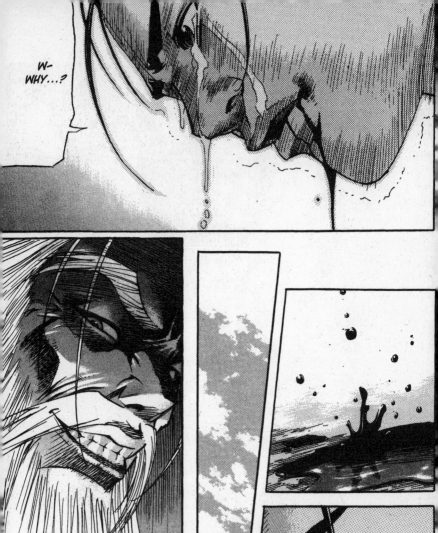

W-
WHY...?

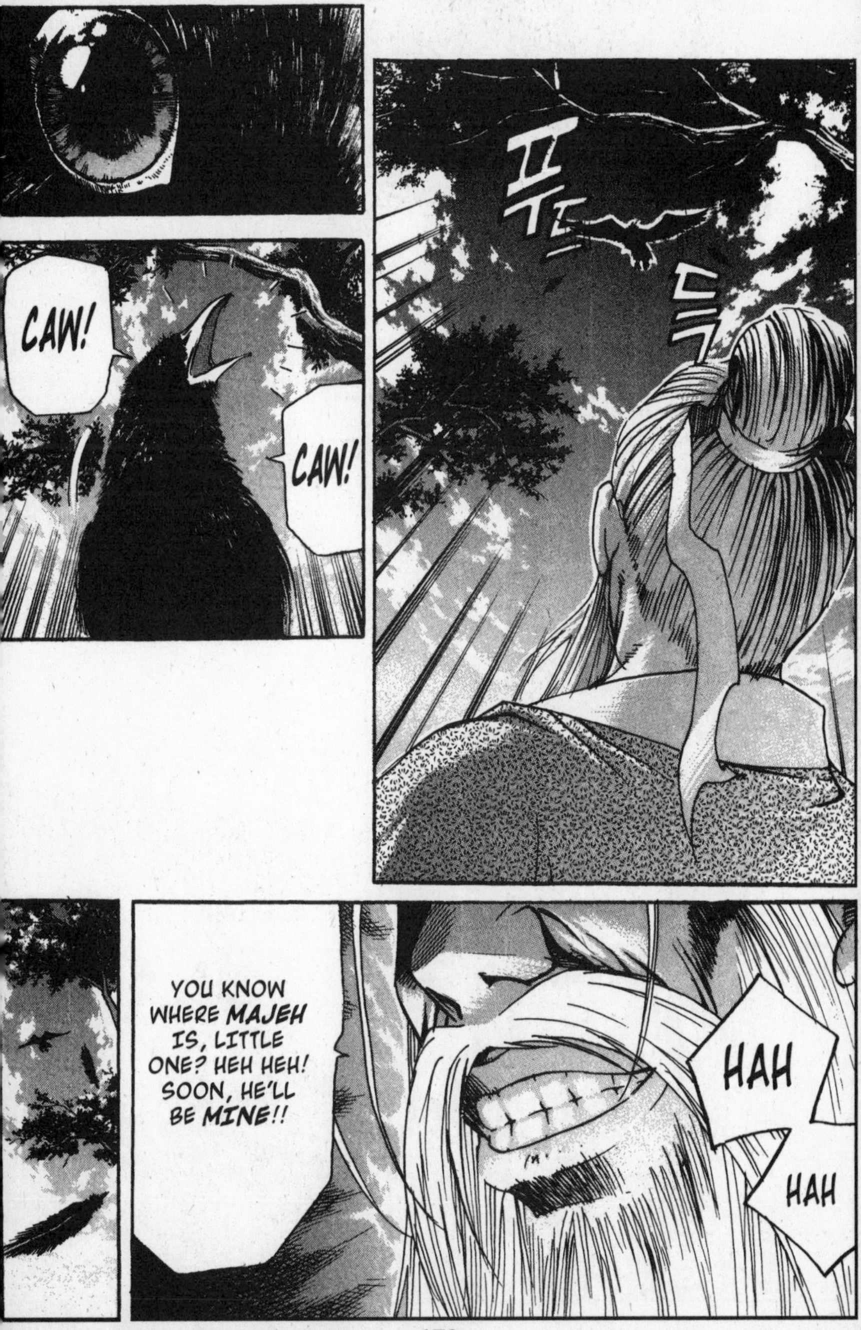

CAW!
CAW!
YOU KNOW WHERE **MAJEH** IS, LITTLE ONE? HEH HEH! SOON, HE'LL BE **MINE**!!
HAH
HAH

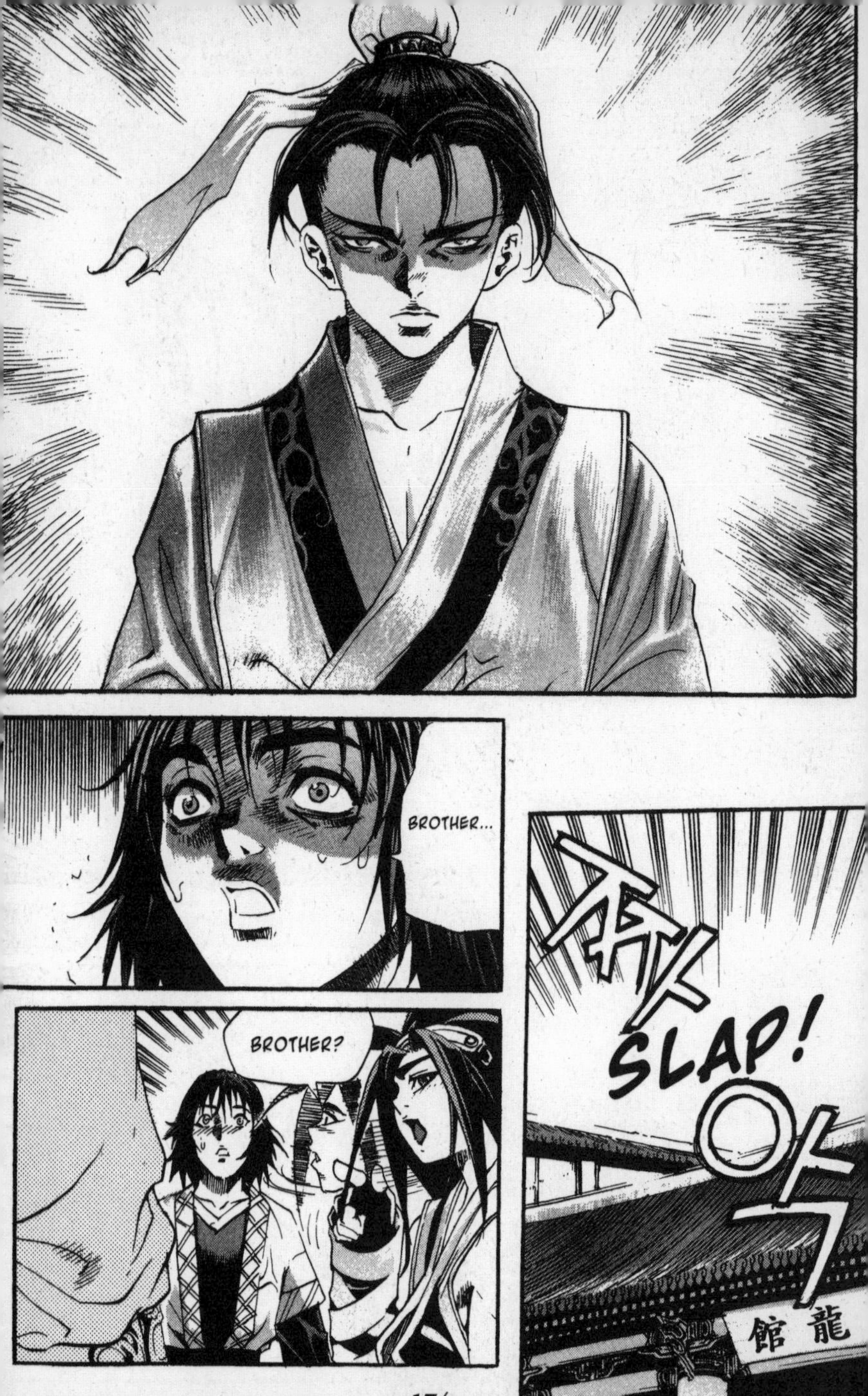
BROTHER...
BROTHER?
SLAP!
館 龍

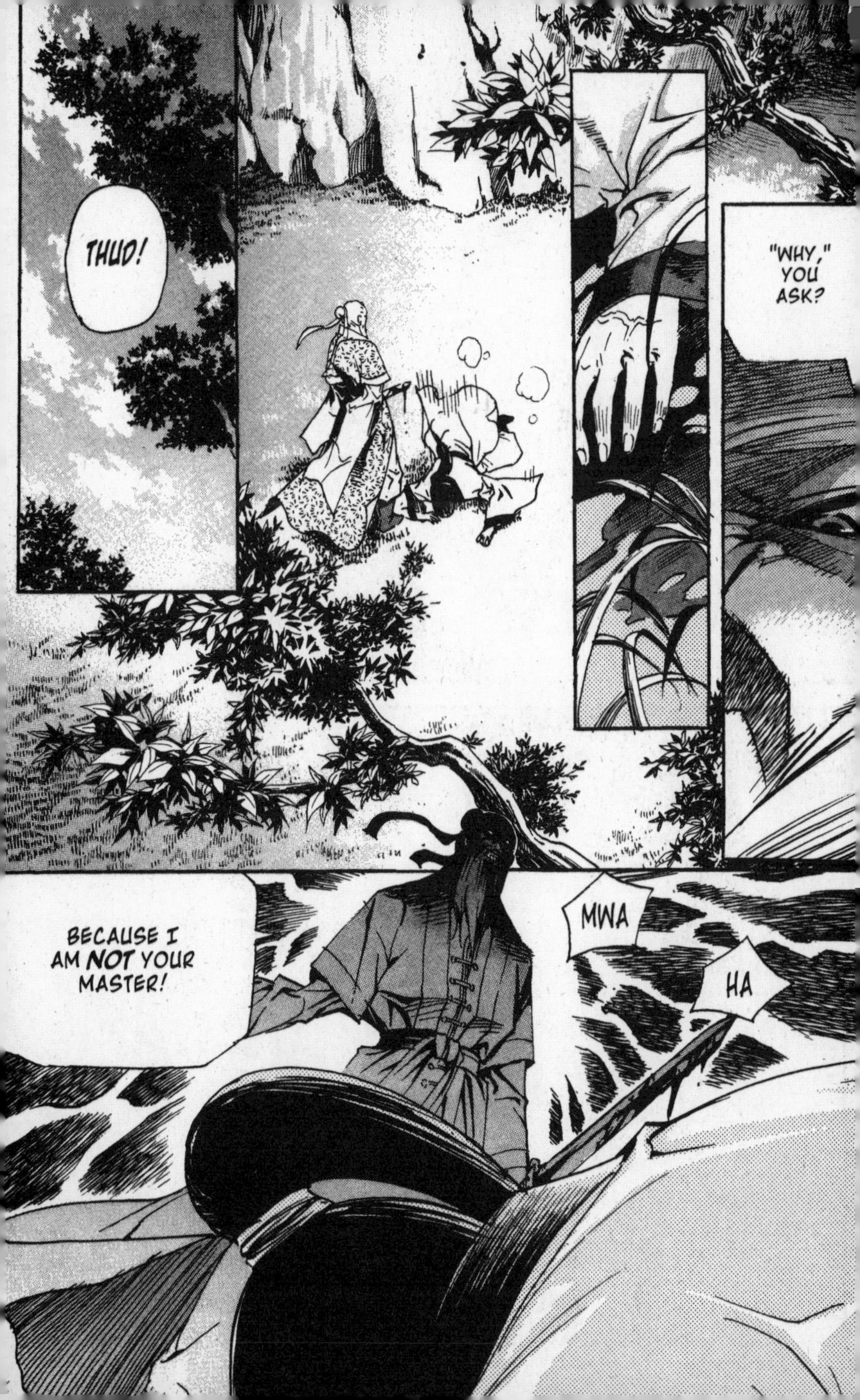
THUD!
"WHY," YOU ASK?
BECAUSE I AM **NOT** YOUR MASTER!
MWA
HA

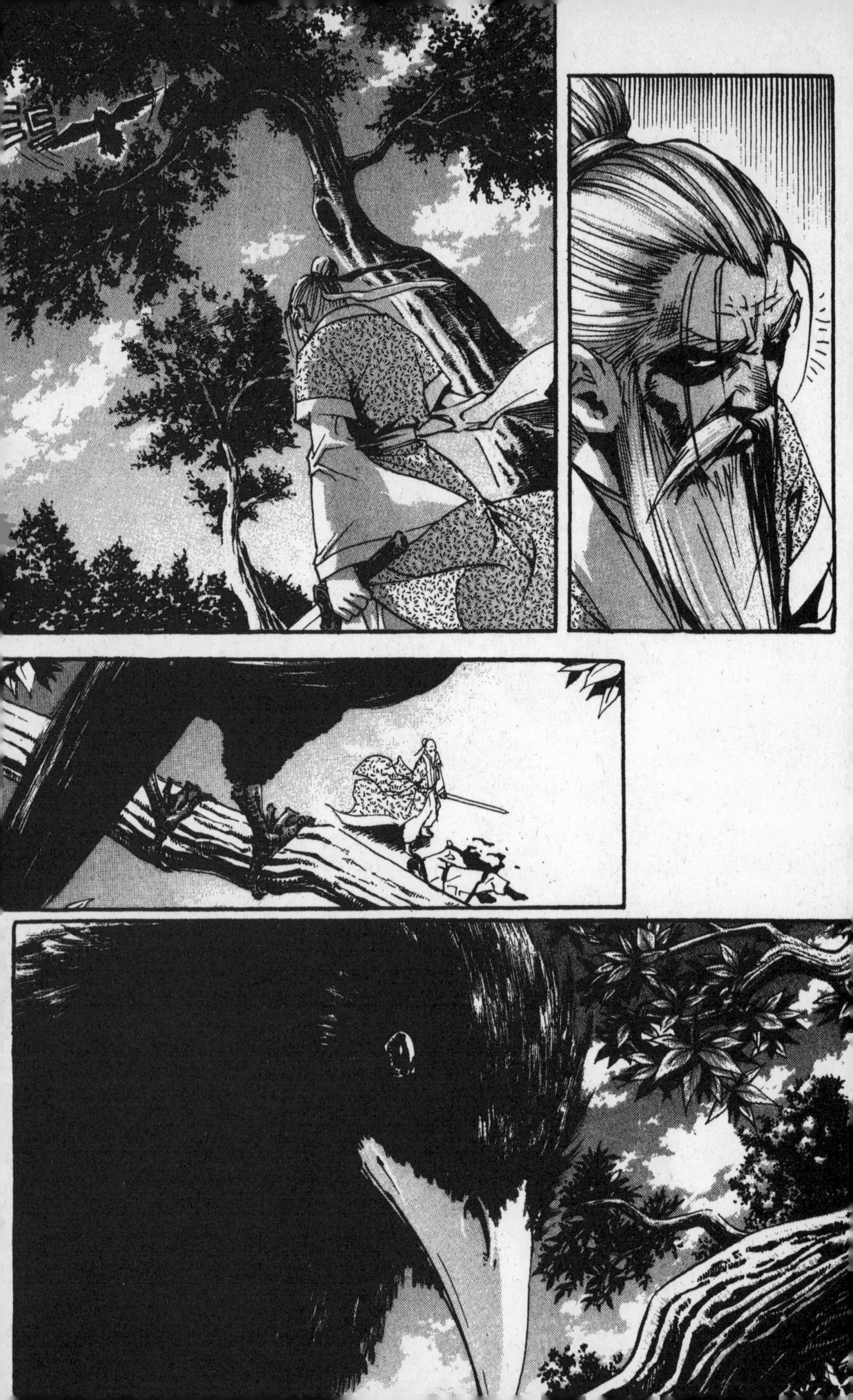

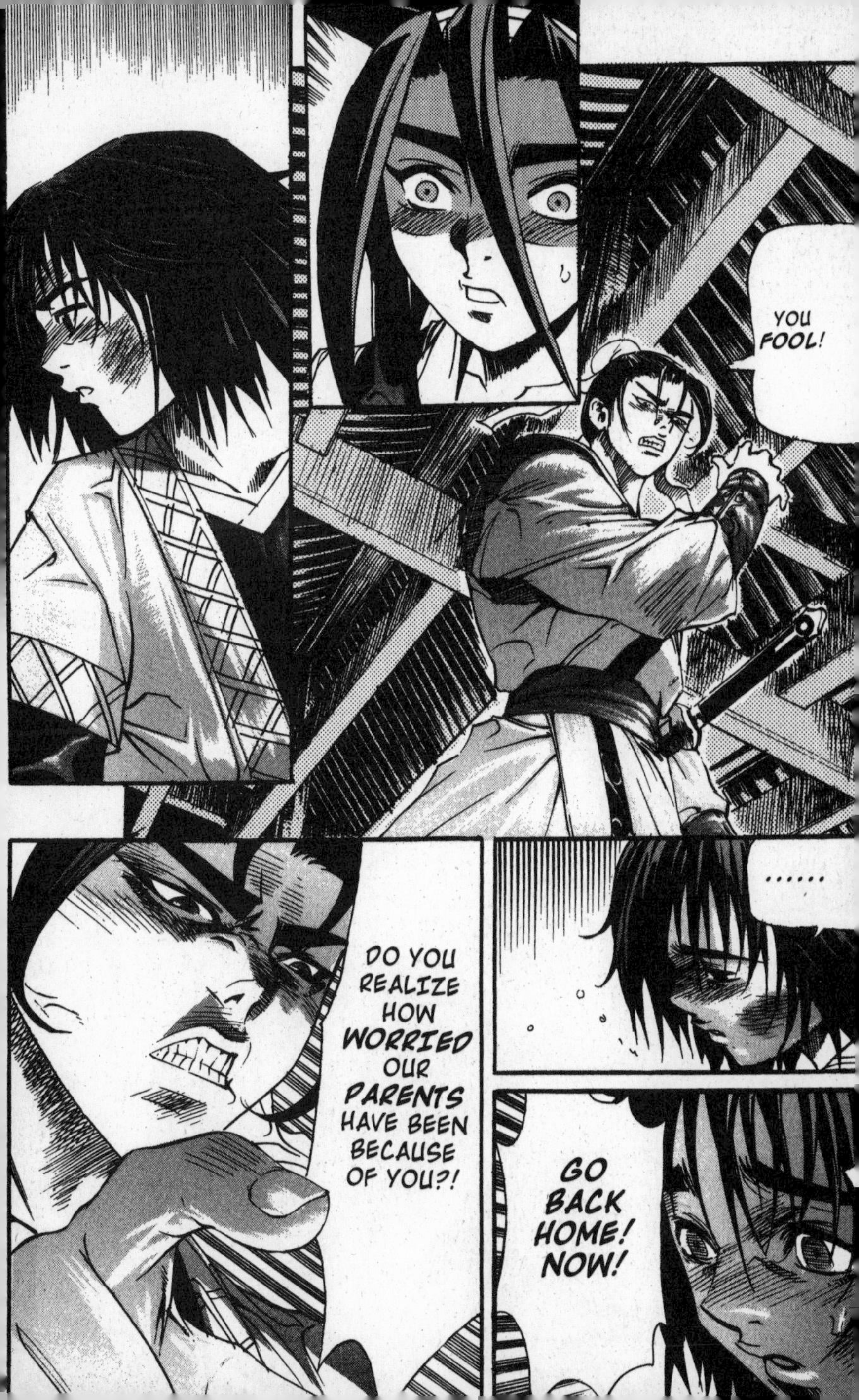
YOU FOOL!
DO YOU REALIZE HOW WORRIED OUR PARENTS HAVE BEEN BECAUSE OF YOU?!
......
GO BACK HOME! NOW!

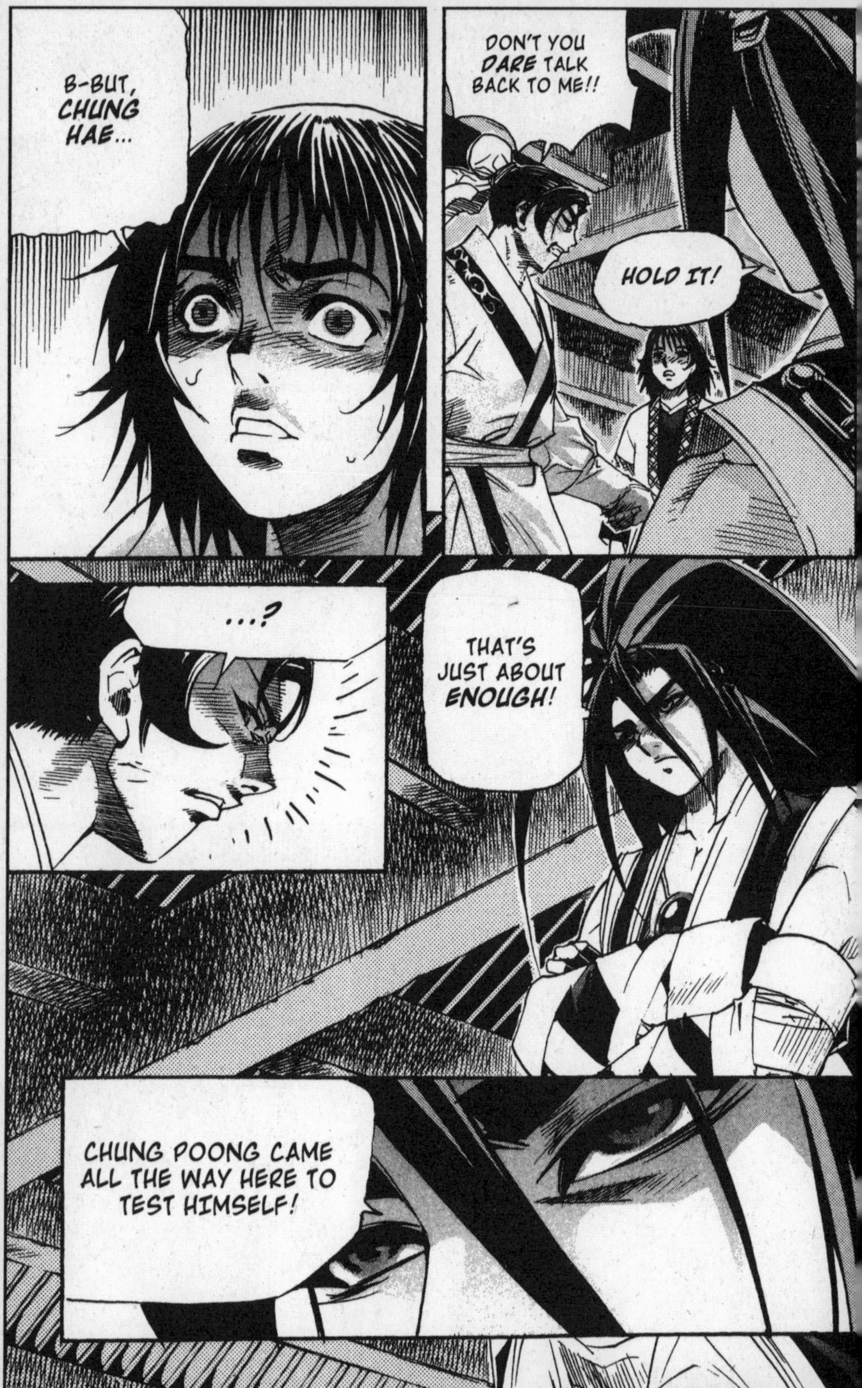
B-BUT, CHUNG HAE...
DON'T YOU DARE TALK BACK TO ME!!
HOLD IT!
...?
THAT'S JUST ABOUT ENOUGH!
CHUNG POONG CAME ALL THE WAY HERE TO TEST HIMSELF!

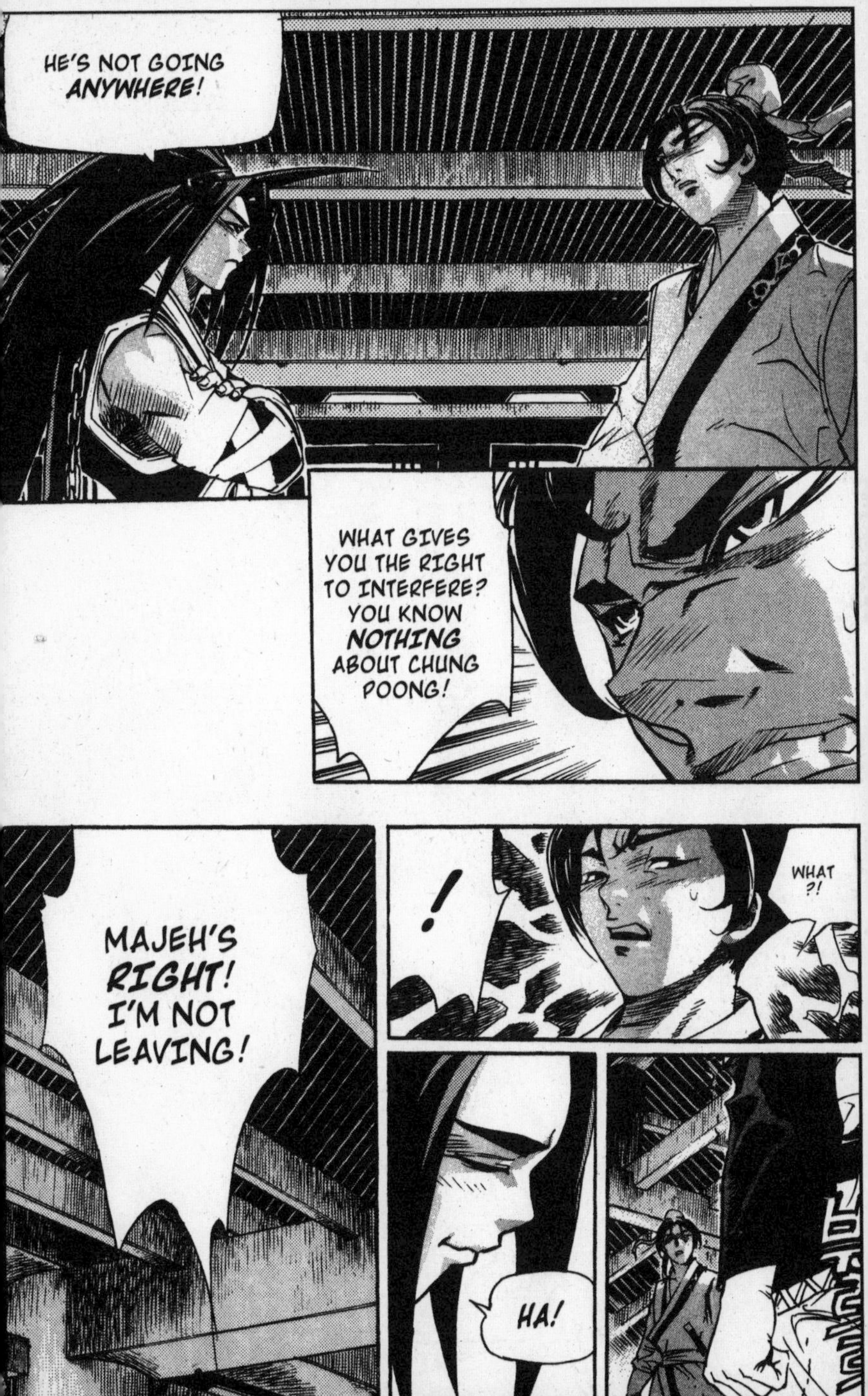

HE'S NOT GOING ANYWHERE!
WHAT GIVES YOU THE RIGHT TO INTERFERE? YOU KNOW NOTHING ABOUT CHUNG POONG!
MAJEH'S RIGHT! I'M NOT LEAVING!
!
WHAT?!
HA!

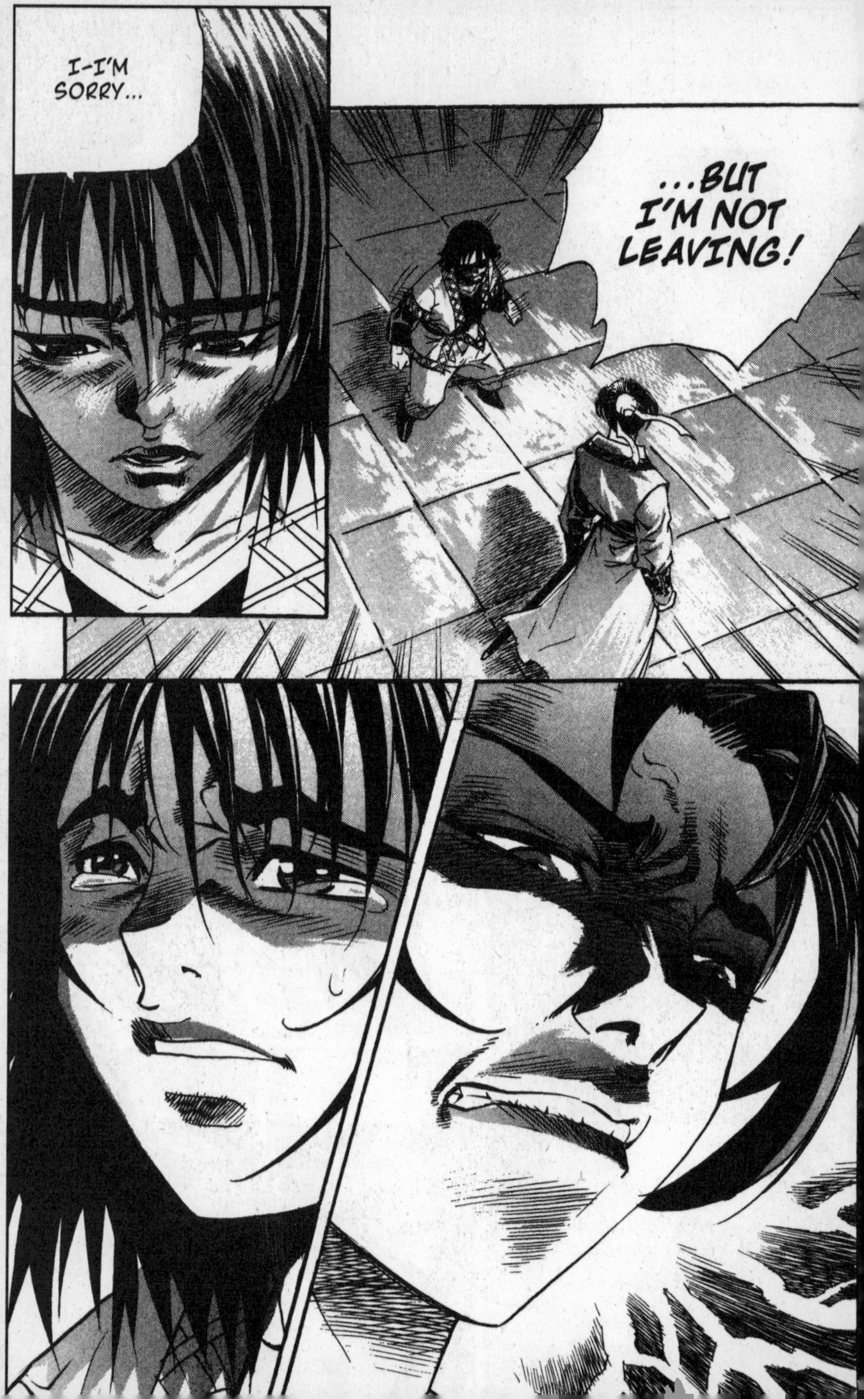
I-I'M SORRY...
...BUT I'M NOT LEAVING!

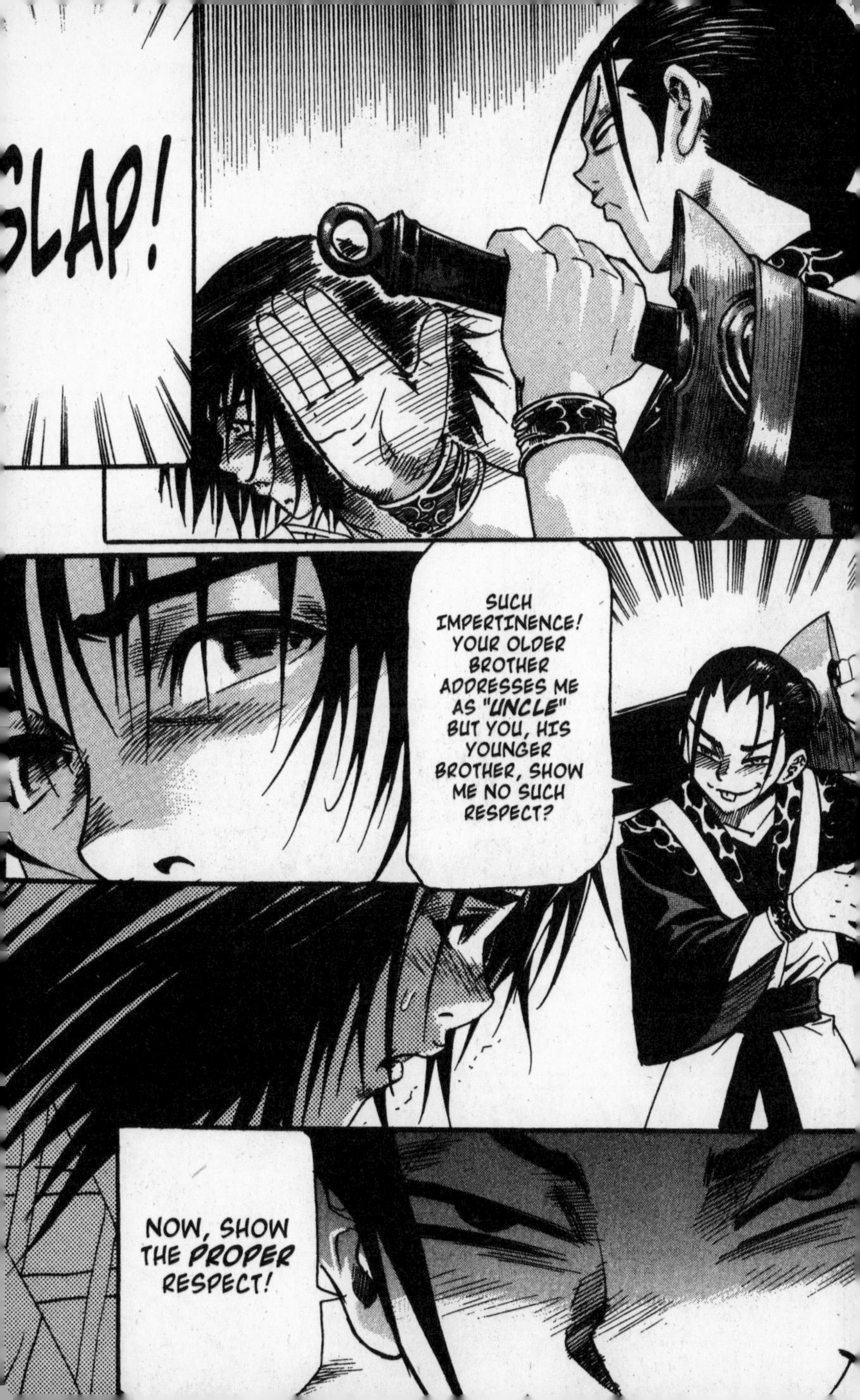
SLAP!
SUCH IMPERTINENCE! YOUR OLDER BROTHER ADDRESSES ME AS "UNCLE" BUT YOU, HIS YOUNGER BROTHER, SHOW ME NO SUCH RESPECT?
NOW, SHOW THE PROPER RESPECT!

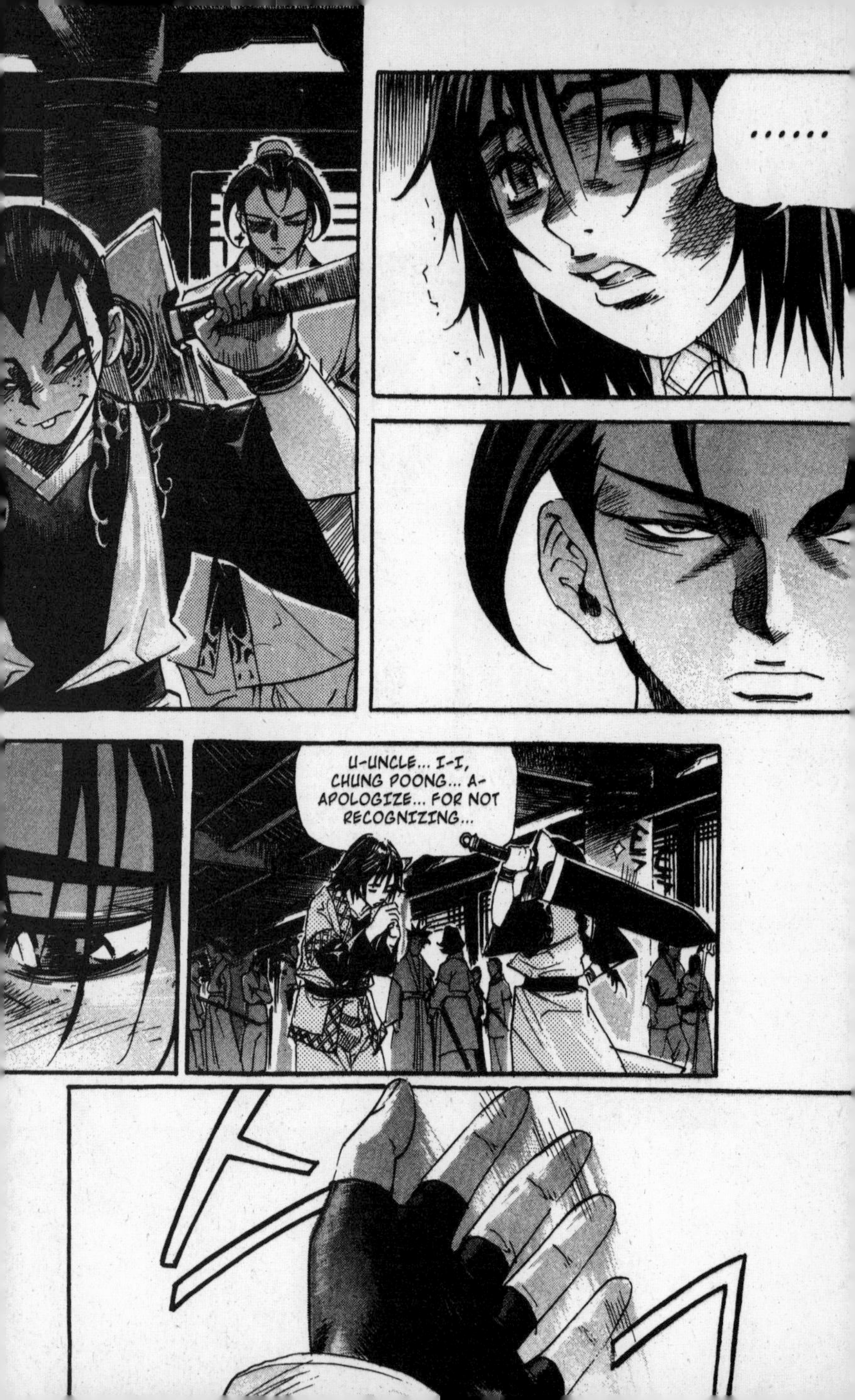
......
U-UNCLE... I-I, CHUNG POONG... A-APOLOGIZE... FOR NOT RECOGNIZING...

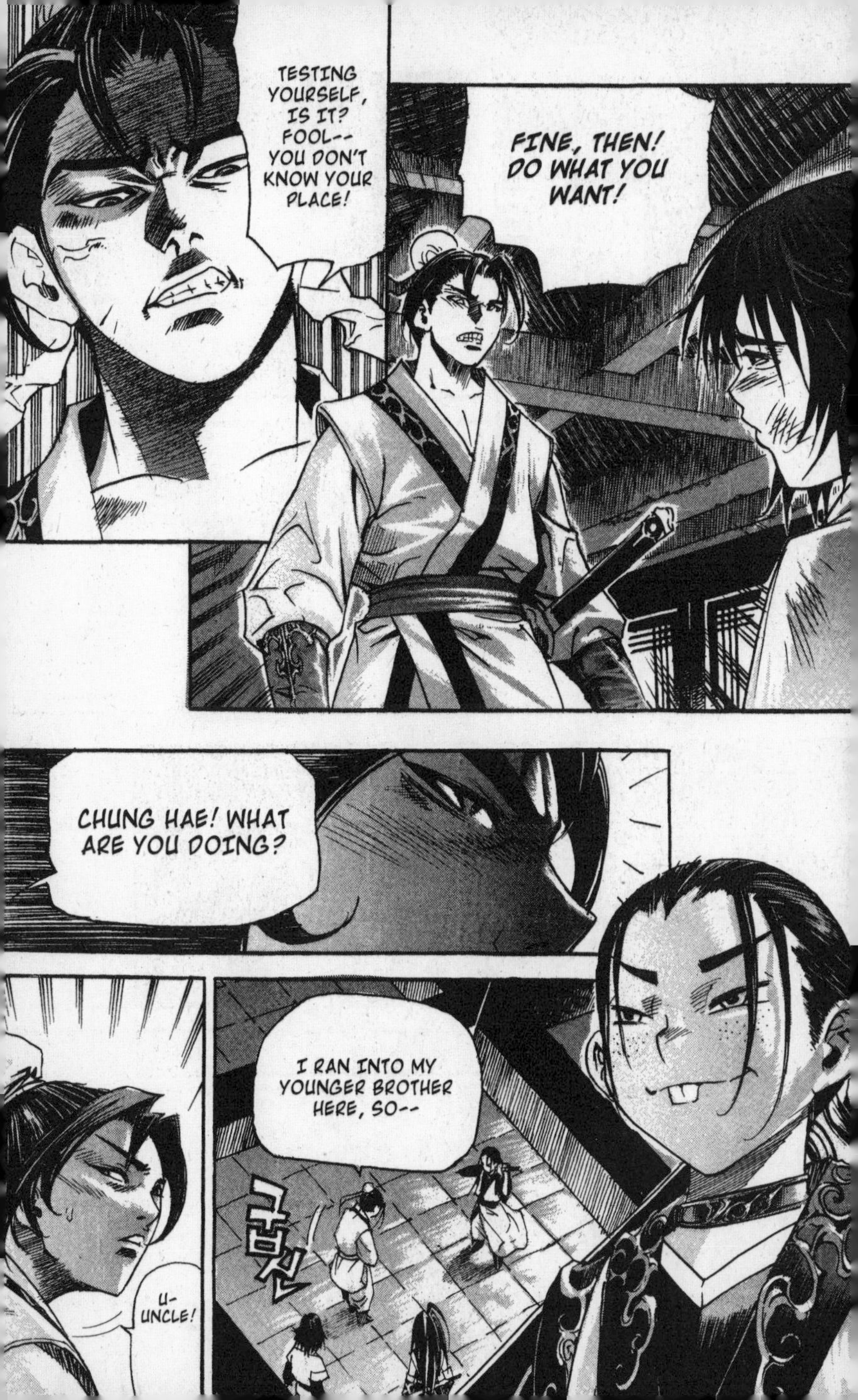
TESTING YOURSELF, IS IT? FOOL-- YOU DON'T KNOW YOUR PLACE!
FINE, THEN! DO WHAT YOU WANT!
CHUNG HAE! WHAT ARE YOU DOING?
U- UNCLE!
I RAN INTO MY YOUNGER BROTHER HERE, SO--

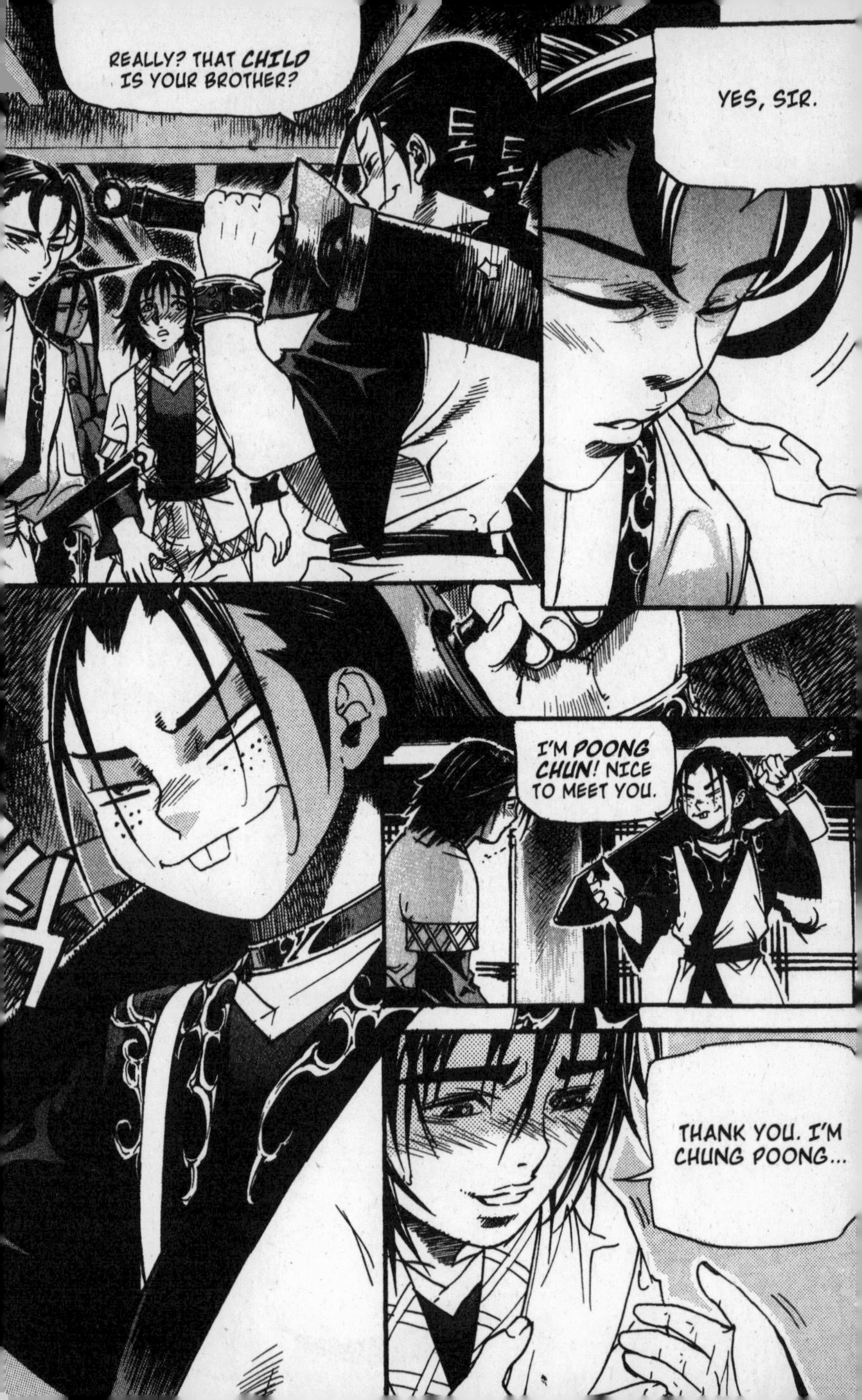
REALLY? THAT CHILD IS YOUR BROTHER?
YES, SIR.
I'M POONG CHUN! NICE TO MEET YOU.
THANK YOU. I'M CHUNG POONG...

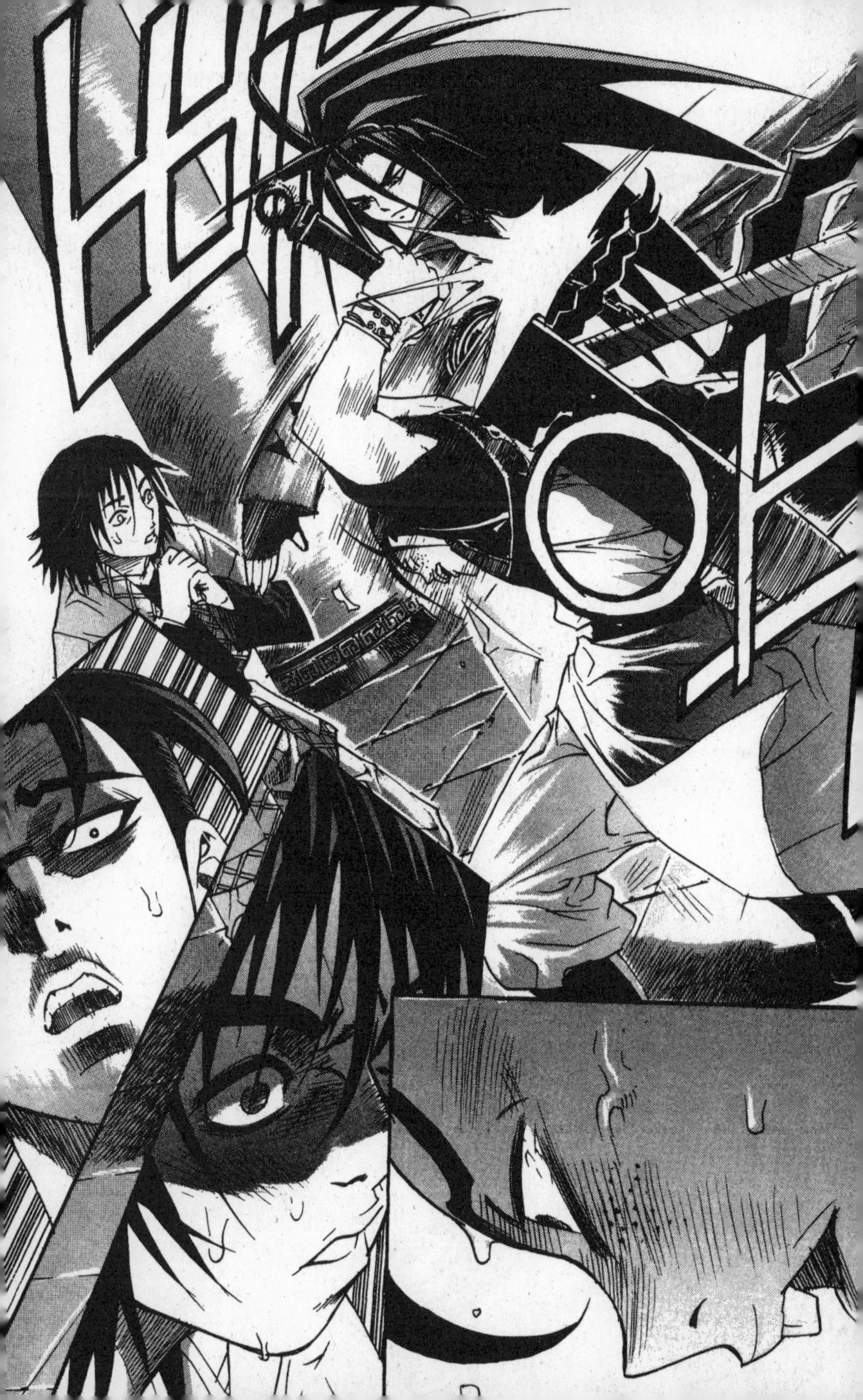

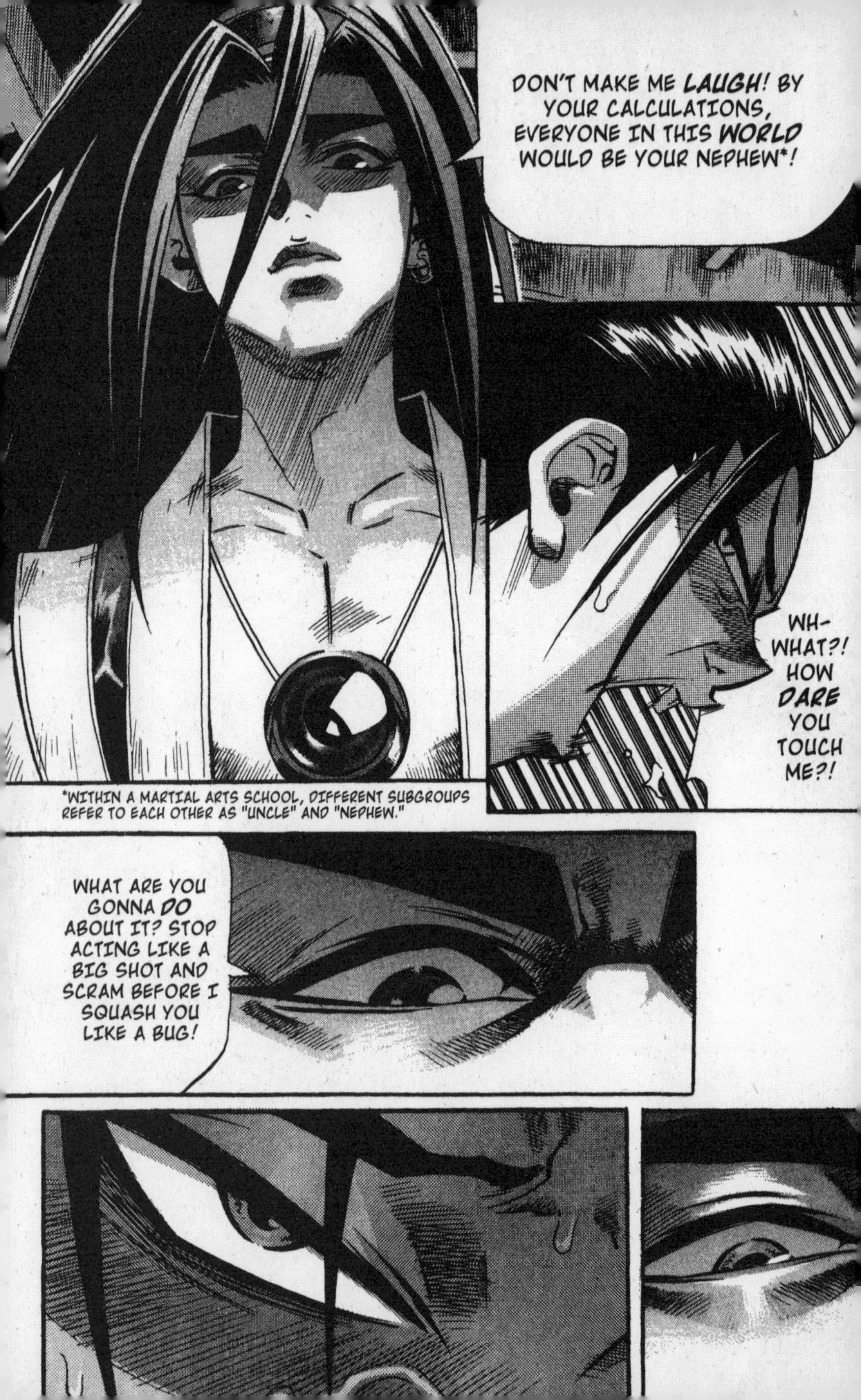
DON'T MAKE ME LAUGH! BY YOUR CALCULATIONS, EVERYONE IN THIS WORLD WOULD BE YOUR NEPHEW*!
WH-WHAT?! HOW DARE YOU TOUCH ME?!
*WITHIN A MARTIAL ARTS SCHOOL, DIFFERENT SUBGROUPS REFER TO EACH OTHER AS "UNCLE" AND "NEPHEW."
WHAT ARE YOU GONNA DO ABOUT IT? STOP ACTING LIKE A BIG SHOT AND SCRAM BEFORE I SQUASH YOU LIKE A BUG!

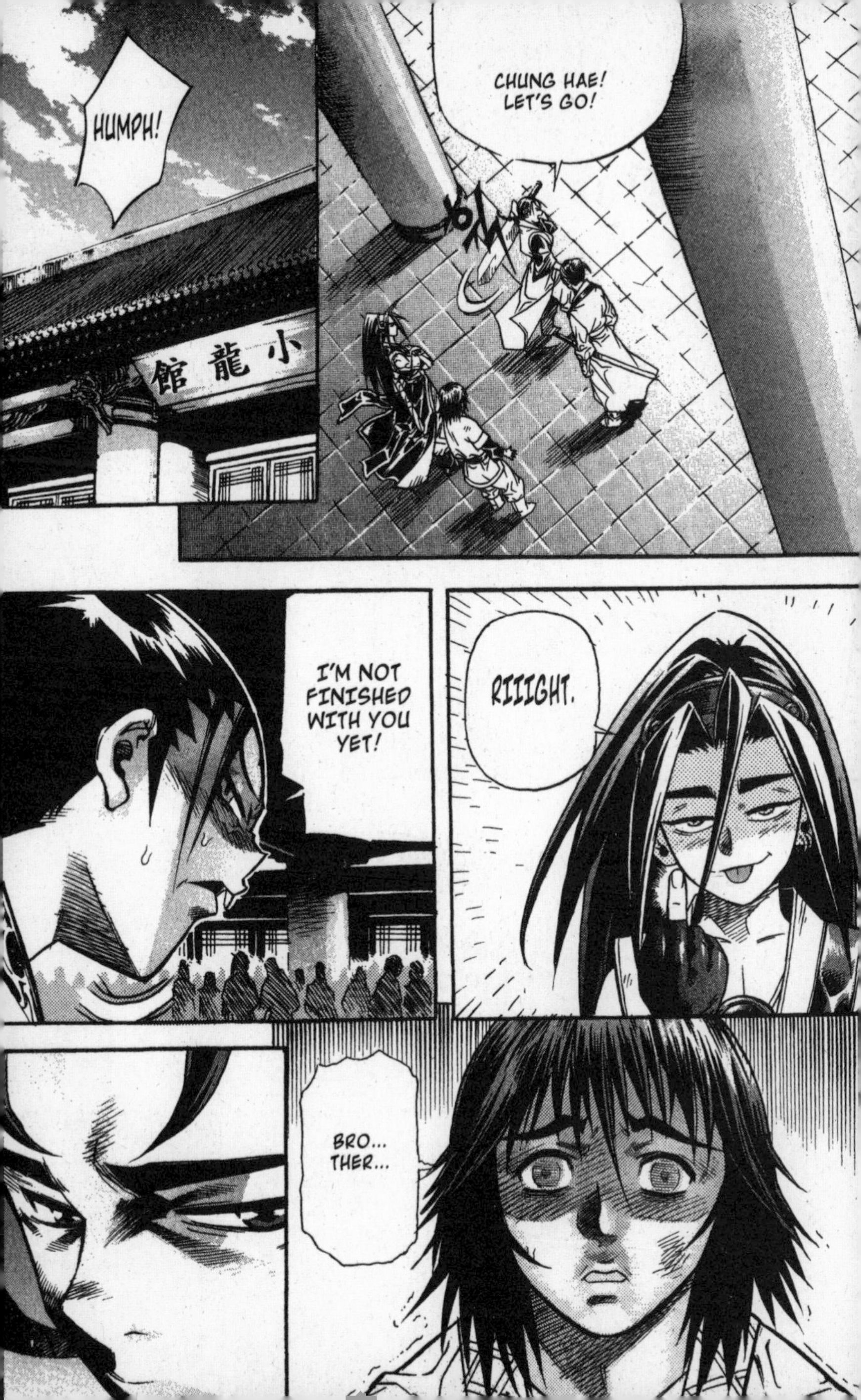
HUMPH!
CHUNG HAE! LET'S GO!
I'M NOT FINISHED WITH YOU YET!
RIIIGHT.
BRO... THER...

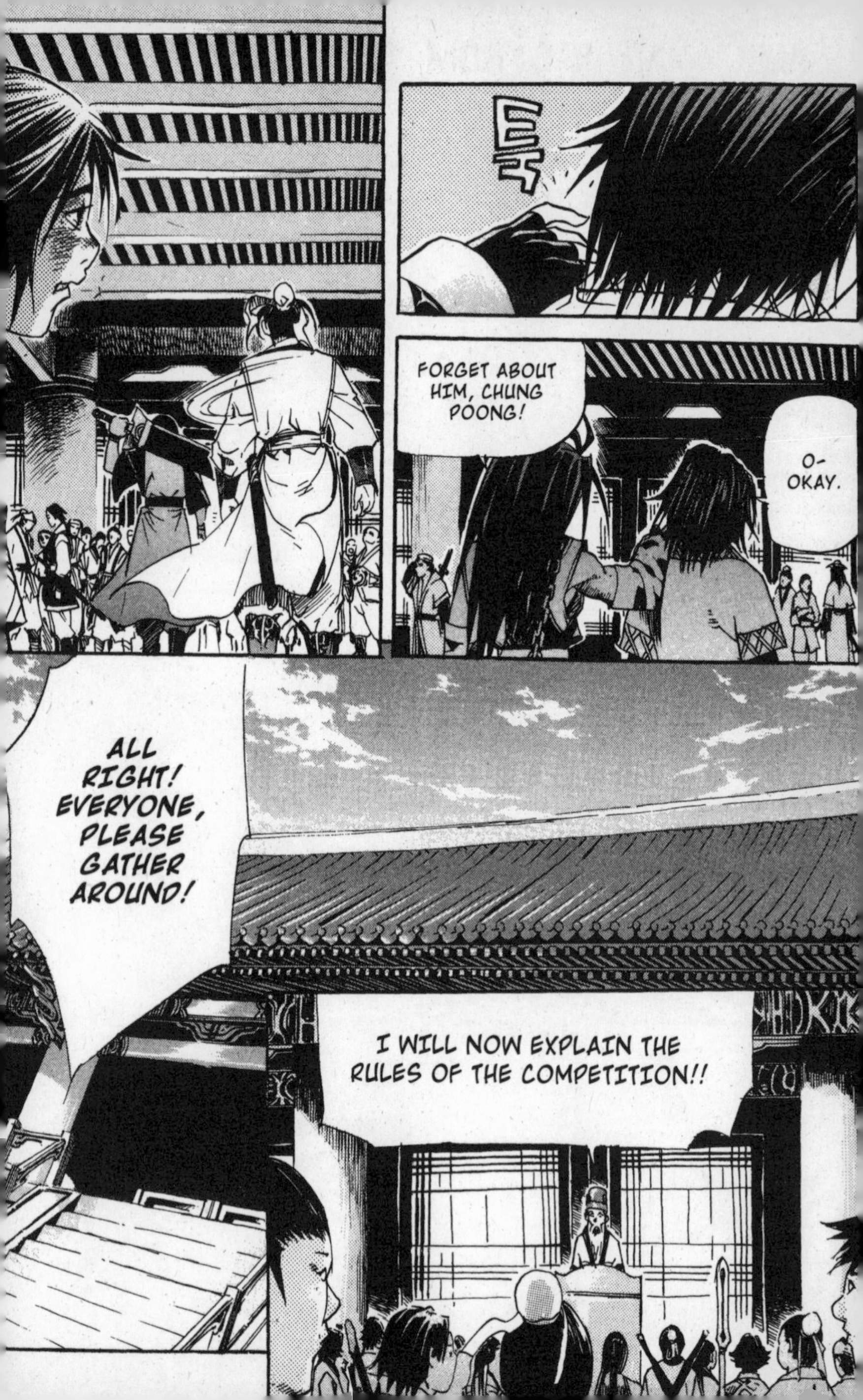
FORGET ABOUT HIM, CHUNG POONG!
O- OKAY.
ALL RIGHT! EVERYONE, PLEASE GATHER AROUND!
I WILL NOW EXPLAIN THE RULES OF THE COMPETITION!!

# ALSO AVAILABLE FROM 🐱 TOKYOPOP®

REALITY CHECK
REBIRTH
REBOUND
REMOTE June 2004
RISING STARS OF MANGA December 2003
SABER MARIONETTE J
SAILOR MOON
SAINT TAIL
SAIYUKI
SAMURAI DEEPER KYO
SAMURAI GIRL REAL BOUT HIGH SCHOOL
SCRYED
SGT. FROG March 2004
SHAOLIN SISTERS
SHIRAHIME-SYO: SNOW GODDESS TALES December 2004
SHUTTERBOX
SNOW DROP January 2004
SOKORA REFUGEES May 2004
SORCEROR HUNTERS
SUIKODEN May 2004
SUKI February 2004
THE CANDIDATE FOR GODDESS April 2004
THE DEMON ORORON April 2004
THE LEGEND OF CHUN HYANG
THE SKULL MAN
THE VISION OF ESCAFLOWNE
TOKYO MEW MEW
TREASURE CHESS March 2004
UNDER THE GLASS MOON
VAMPIRE GAME
WILD ACT
WISH
WORLD OF HARTZ
X-DAY
ZODIAC P.I.

## NOVELS

KARMA CLUB APRIL 2004
SAILOR MOON

## ART BOOKS

CARDCAPTOR SAKURA
MAGIC KNIGHT RAYEARTH
PEACH GIRL ART BOOK April 2004

## ANIME GUIDES

COWBOY BEBOP ANIME GUIDES
GUNDAM TECHNICAL MANUALS
SAILOR MOON SCOUT GUIDES

## CINE-MANGA™

CARDCAPTORS
FAIRLY ODD PARENTS MARCH 2004
FINDING NEMO
G.I. JOE SPY TROOPS
JACKIE CHAN ADVENTURES
KIM POSSIBLE
LIZZIE MCGUIRE
POWER RANGERS: NINJA STORM
SPONGEBOB SQUAREPANTS
SPY KIDS
SPY KIDS 3-D March 2004
THE ADVENTURES OF JIMMY NEUTRON: BOY GENIUS
TRANSFORMERS: ARMADA
TRANSFORMERS: ENERGON May 2004

## TOKYOPOP KIDS

STRAY SHEEP

# For more
# information visit
# www.TOKYOPOP.com

10103

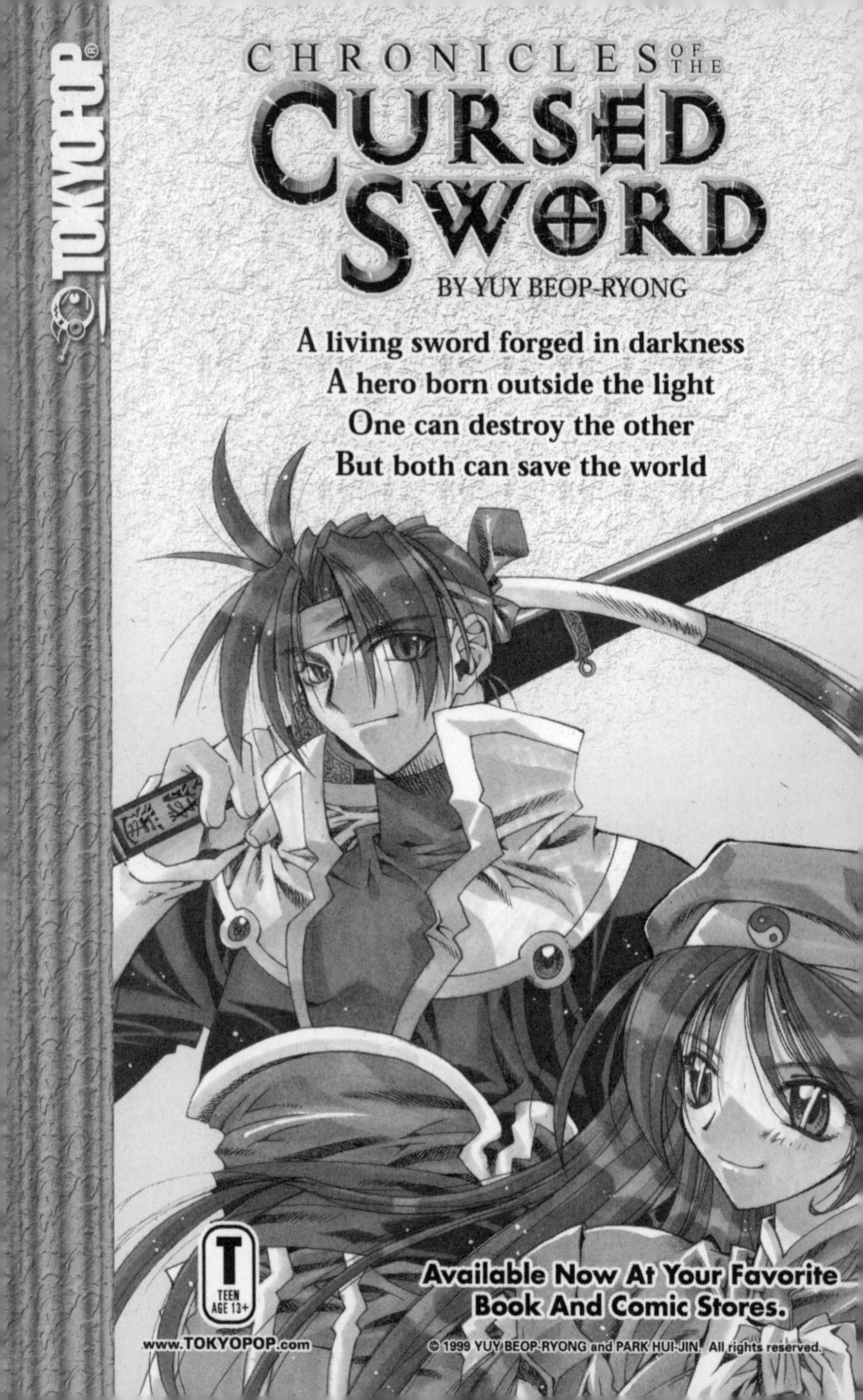
TOKYOPOP®
CHRONICLES OF THE
CURSED SWORD
BY YUY BEOP-RYONG
A living sword forged in darkness
A hero born outside the light
One can destroy the other
But both can save the world
T
TEEN
AGE 13+
Available Now At Your Favorite
Book And Comic Stores.
www.TOKYOPOP.com
© 1999 YUY BEOP-RYONG and PARK HUI-JIN. All rights reserved.

## IN THE NEXT VOLUME OF

# KING OF HELL

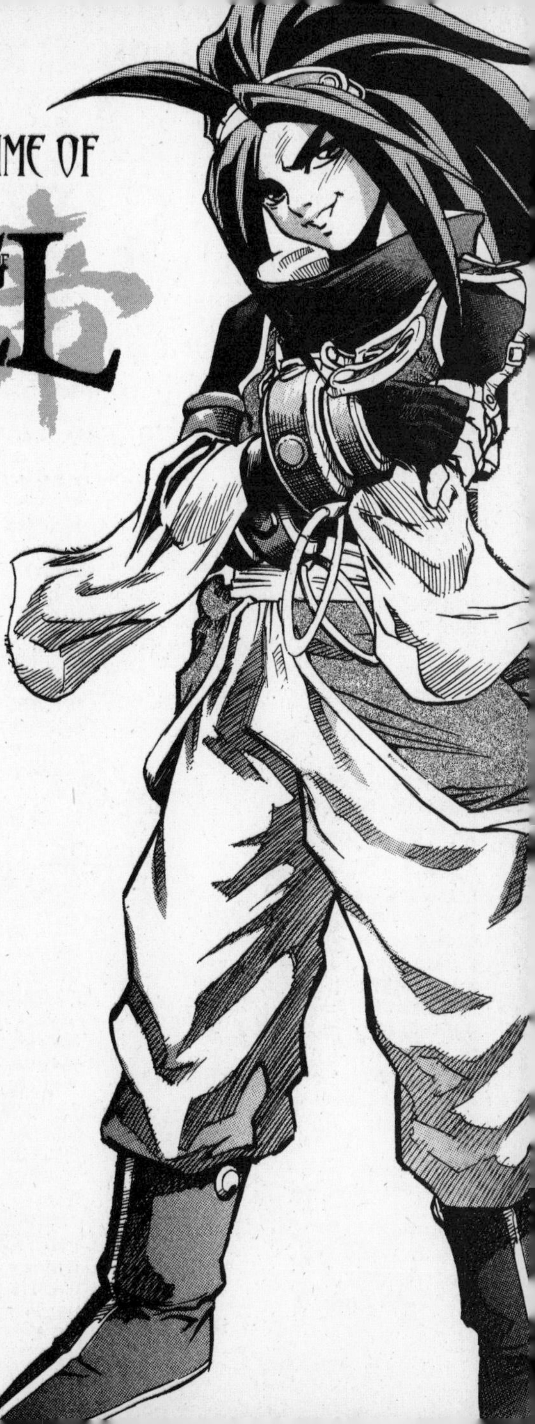

At last, the long-awaited Nakyang Martial Arts Tournament begins! Majeh's been itching to let loose, and heaven help his opponents. Who's first? The disciplined Dohak? The maniacal Mad Dog? Or maybe even Majeh's companion, the cowardly Chung-Poong? It all depends on who's on the White Team and who's on the Black Team. It's a battle royal between "good" and "evil"...and just wait 'til you see which side Majeh's on!

## MANGA

.HACK//LEGEND OF THE TWILIGHT
@LARGE
A.I. LOVE YOU February 2004
AI YORI AOSHI January 2004
ANGELIC LAYER
BABY BIRTH
BATTLE ROYALE
BATTLE VIXENS April 2004
BIRTH May 2004
BRAIN POWERED
BRIGADOON
B'TX  January 2004
CARDCAPTOR SAKURA
CARDCAPTOR SAKURA: MASTER OF THE CLOW
CARDCAPTOR SAKURA: BOXED SET COLLECTION 1
CARDCAPTOR SAKURA: BOXED SET COLLECTION 2
    March 2004
CHOBITS
CHRONICLES OF THE CURSED SWORD
CLAMP SCHOOL DETECTIVES
CLOVER
COMIC PARTY  June 2004
CONFIDENTIAL CONFESSIONS
CORRECTOR YUI
COWBOY BEBOP: BOXED SET THE COMPLETE
    COLLECTION
CRESCENT MOON May 2004
CREST OF THE STARS  June 2004
CYBORG 009
DEMON DIARY
DIGIMON
DIGIMON SERIES 3 April 2004
DIGIMON ZERO TWO  February 2004
DNANGEL  April 2004
DOLL May 2004
DRAGON HUNTER
DRAGON KNIGHTS
DUKLYON: CLAMP SCHOOL DEFENDERS
DV June 2004
ERICA SAKURAZAWA
FAERIES' LANDING January 2004
FAKE
FLCL
FORBIDDEN DANCE
FRUITS BASKET February 2004
G GUNDAM
GATEKEEPERS
GETBACKERS February 2004
GHOST!  March 2004
GIRL GOT GAME January 2004
GRAVITATION
GTO

GUNDAM WING
GUNDAM WING: BATTLEFIELD OF PACIFISTS
GUNDAM WING: ENDLESS WALTZ
GUNDAM WING: THE LAST OUTPOST
HAPPY MANIA
HARLEM BEAT
I.N.V.U.
INITIAL D
ISLAND
JING: KING OF BANDITS
JULINE
JUROR 13 March 2004
KARE KANO
KILL ME, KISS ME February 2004
KINDAICHI CASE FILES, THE
KING OF HELL
KODOCHA: SANA'S STAGE
LAMENT OF THE LAMB May 2004
LES BIJOUX February 2004
LIZZIE MCGUIRE
LOVE HINA
LUPIN III
LUPIN III SERIES 2
MAGIC KNIGHT RAYEARTH I
MAGIC KNIGHT RAYEARTH II February 2004
MAHOROMATIC: AUTOMATIC MAIDEN May 2004
MAN OF MANY FACES
MARMALADE BOY
MARS
METEOR METHUSELA June 2004
METROID June 2004
MINK April 2004
MIRACLE GIRLS
MIYUKI-CHAN IN WONDERLAND
MODEL May 2004
NELLY MUSIC MANGA  April 2004
ONE April 2004
PARADISE KISS
PARASYTE
PEACH GIRL
PEACH GIRL CHANGE OF HEART
PEACH GIRL RELAUNCH BOX SET
PET SHOP OF HORRORS
PITA-TEN January 2004
PLANET LADDER February 2004
PLANETES
PRIEST
PRINCESS AI April 2004
PSYCHIC ACADEMY March 2004
RAGNAROK
RAGNAROK: BOXED SET COLLECTION 1
RAVE MASTER
RAVE MASTER: BOXED SET March 2004

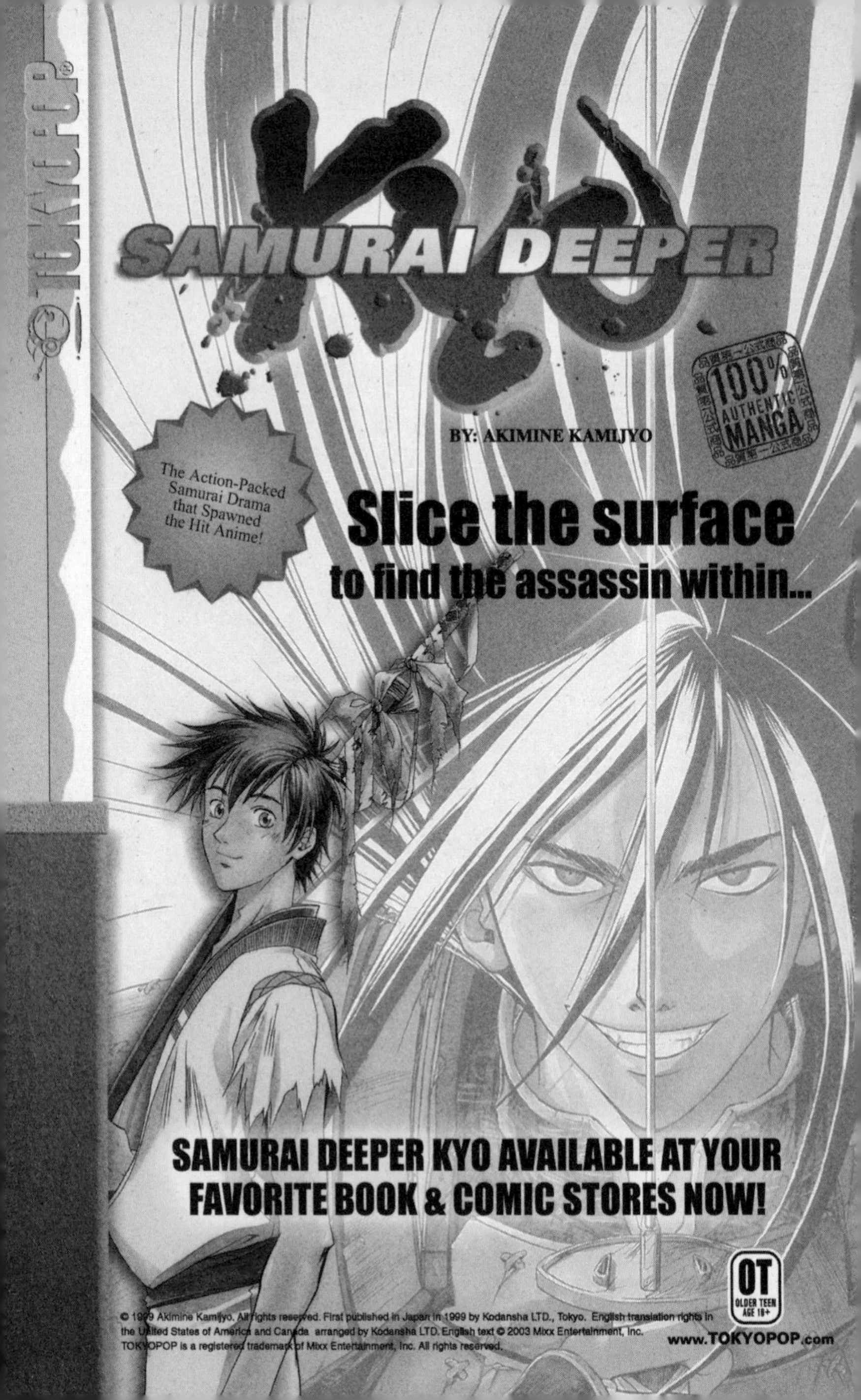